Sympathy and the State in the Romantic Era

Routledge Studies in Romanticism

1. Keats's Boyish Imagination
Richard Marggraf Turley

2. Leigh Hunt
Life, Poetics, Politics
Edited by Nicholas Roe

3. Leigh Hunt and the London Literary Scene
A Reception History of his Major Works, 1805-1828
Michael Eberle-Sinatra

4. Tracing Women's Romanticism
Gender, History and Transcendence
Kari E. Lokke

5. Metaphysical Hazlitt
Bicentenary Essays
Uttara Natarajan, Tom Paulin and Duncan Wu

6. Romantic Genius and the Literary Magazine
Biography, Celebrity, Politics
David Higgins

7. Romantic Representations of British India
Edited by Michael Franklin

8. Sympathy and the State in the Romantic Era
Systems, State Finance, and the Shadows of Futurity
Robert Mitchell

Sympathy and the State in the Romantic Era

Systems, State Finance, and the Shadows of Futurity

Robert Mitchell

Routledge
Taylor & Francis Group
New York London

Routledge
Taylor & Francis Group
270 Madison Avenue
New York, NY 10016

Routledge
Taylor & Francis Group
2 Park Square
Milton Park, Abingdon
Oxon OX14 4RN

Routledge is an imprint of Taylor & Francis Group, an Informa business

Printed in the United States of America on acid-free paper
10 9 8 7 6 5 4 3 2 1

International Standard Book Number-10: 0-415-77142-0 (Hardcover)
International Standard Book Number-13: 978-0-415-77142-9 (Hardcover)

Library of Congress Cataloging-in-Publication Data

Mitchell, Robert, 1969-
Sympathy and the state in the romantic era : systems, state finance, and the shadows of futurity / Robert Mitchell.
p. cm. -- (Routledge studies in romanticism ; 8)
Includes bibliographical references and index.
ISBN 978-0-415-77142-9 (alk. paper)
1. Sympathy in literature. 2. English literature--18th century--History and criticism. 3. English literature--19th century--History and criticism. 4. Financial crises in literature. 5. Finance, Public--Great Britain--History--1688-1815. 6. System theory in literature. 7. Capitalism and literature--Great Britain--History. 8. Literature and morals. 9. Romanticism--Great Britain. I. Title.

PR448.S95M57 2007
820.9'353--dc22 2006033856

Visit the Taylor & Francis Web site at
http://www.taylorandfrancis.com

and the Routledge Web site at
http://www.routledge.com

Contents

Acknowledgments

This project first began to take shape in Seattle in the late 1990s, a period in which the Pacific Northwest, like other regions such as Silicon Valley, was in the midst of the now infamous dot.com "bubble." Like many who elected not to vie for a job at Microsoft or any of the literally hundreds of start-up companies that popped up everywhere in Seattle and its environs, I watched the progress of the bubble with a mixture of fascination, suspicion, and envy. And I, no doubt like many others, felt some sense of relief and self-justification as the bubble broke, and economist after economist rushed forward to expose the practices of the purported "new economy" as, by and large, extraordinarily speculative, ungrounded, and short-sighted.

Yet there is a certain danger that this consensus about the financial recklessness of the dot.com era will obscure the extent to which this period also encouraged a completely *open* sense of the future on the part of many of those involved. Those who were living away from the West Coast hubs of the dot.com bubble may be familiar only with the big players that survived the crash (e.g., Amazon.com, eBay, Classmates.com) as well as some of the more infamous "losers" (e.g., Kozmo.com, Pets.com), but in fact, hundreds, if not thousands, of ephemeral companies emerged and then disappeared in the late 1990s. As economists never tire of pointing out, many of these were based on business plans that were decidedly unbusinesslike—I recall, for example, a business that intended to "parasite" worldwide tourism networks in order to provide low-income students with opportunities for study abroad—but, perhaps surprisingly, many of these extraordinarily speculative business plans received funding for short periods. Economists and critics have focused on the exploitative and short-term logic of such funding: venture capitalists provided start-up money only because they intended to "get out" within a few years by passing the bill on to less wary investors. However, rather than emphasizing the hypocrisy of investors, I want to stress the fervency of those who worked hard, even if unsuccessfully, to realize those projects. Many of the people who worked at these companies shared the belief that the present was no longer constrained by the past; that everything could be different. For some, perhaps, this commitment depended on a conscious or unconscious wager that hard work in the present could be parlayed into stock option wealth later, but it seemed to me that most were excited primarily by their consciousness of time as suddenly *open*, and undetermined by the past. This book is, at least in part, an effort to understand the potentials of that speculative openness by returning to the first century to witness this romance with finance and collective projects.

* * *

Every book requires a small armada of friends and colleagues willing to read and reread sections, chapters (and, in some cases, even the whole manuscript), and I thank those tireless comrades here. I am indebted to Raimonda Modiano, Mikkel Borch-Jacobsen, Gary Handwerk, John Toews, and Laurie Sears for their generous and helpful reading of a very early version of this project, and to Shannon Callies, who was an invaluable source of knowledge and inspiration about the role of finance in the dot.com world of the 1990s. I am grateful to Matt Cohen, George Erving, Sean Metzger, Inga Pollmann, Phillip Thurtle, and Priscilla Wald, who were willing to read multiple chapters multiple times. My thanks to the members of the NASSR listserv who responded to my various enquires, and to David Collings, Nora Crook, Tim Fulford, Nicholas Halmi, Jeanne Moskal, and E. Roy Weintraub for their help with several specific claims that I make in the book (though I am of course solely responsible for any errors). I thank the Arts and Sciences Research Council of Duke University for a grant that supported some of the research for chapter 1. I would also like to express my gratitude to John Miles for his help with proofing, and to the staffs at the British Library, Duke University's Perkins Library, the University of North Carolina-Chapel Hill's Davis library, and the University of Washington's Suzzallo Library for their invaluable help.

Abbreviations

BPW Rousseau, J.-J. (1988) *The Basic Political Writings*, trans. Cress, D.A., Indianapolis: Hackett.

CAS Smith, A. (1987) *The Correspondence of Adam Smith*, ed. Mossner, E.C. and Ross, I.S., in *The Glasgow Edition of the Works and Correspondence of Adam Smith*, Indianapolis: Liberty Fund.

Emile Rousseau, J.-J. (1979) *Emile, or On Education*, trans. Bloom, A., New York: Basic Books.

EPS Smith, A. (1982) *Essays on Philosophical Subjects*, ed. Wightman, W.P.D. and Bryce, J.C., in *The Glasgow Edition of the Works and Correspondence of Adam Smith*, Indianapolis: Liberty Fund.

Essay Rousseau, J.J. (1998) *Essay on the Origin of Languages and Writings Related to Music*, trans. Scott, J.T., Hanover, NH: University Press of New England.

L Rousseau, J.J. (1968) *Politics and the Arts; Letters to M. D'Alembert on the Theater*, trans. Bloom, A. Ithaca: Cornell University Press.

LJ(B) Smith, A. (1982) *Lectures on Jurisprudence*, ed. Meek, R.L. *et al.*, in *The Glasgow Edition of the Works and Correspondence of Adam Smith*, Indianapolis: Liberty Fund.

LPBS Shelley, P.B. (1914) *The Letters of Percy Bysshe Shelley*, 2 vols, ed. Ingpen, R., London: G. Bell and Sons.

LPWC Cowper, W. (1979–86) *The Letters and Prose Writings of William Cowper*, 5 vols, ed. King, J. and Ryskamp, C., Oxford: Clarendon Press.

LRBL Smith, A. (1985) *Lectures in Rhetoric and Belles Lettres*, ed. Bryce, J.C., in *The Glasgow Edition of the Works and Correspondence of Adam Smith,* Indianapolis: Liberty Fund.

LWDW Wordsworth, W. and D. (1967) *The Letters of William and Dorothy Wordsworth*, vol. 1: *The Early Years, 1787–1805*, 2nd ed., ed. de Selincourt, E., Oxford: Clarendon Press.

OCR Rousseau, J.J. (1959–95) *Œuvres completes*, 5 vols, ed. Gagnebin, B. and Raymond, R., Paris: Gallimard.

PH (1806–18) *The Parliamentary History of England, From the Earliest Period to the Year 1803*, 36 vols, London: T.C. Hansard.

PrW Wordsworth, W. (1974) *The Prose Works of William Wordsworth*, 3 vols, ed. Owen, W.J.B. and Smyser, J.W., Oxford: Clarendon Press.

SP Shelley, P.B. (1988) *Shelley's Prose, or, The Trumpet of a Prophecy*, ed. Clark, D.L., New York: New Amsterdam Books.

SPP Shelley, P.B. (1977) *Shelley's Poetry and Prose*, ed. Reiman, D.H. and Powers, S.B., London: W.W. Norton & Co.

T Hume, D. (1978) *A Treatise of Human Nature*, ed. Nidditch, P.H., Oxford: Clarendon Press.

TMS Smith, A. (1984) *The Theory of Moral Sentiments*, ed. Raphael, D.D. and Macfie, A.L., in *The Glasgow Edition of the Works and Correspondence of Adam Smith*, Indianapolis: Liberty Fund. Citations to this text are referenced as part-section-chapter-paragraph (e.g., *TMS* 3.ii.1.3).

WEB Burke, W. (1869) *The Works of the Right Honorable Edmund Burke*, 3rd ed., 12 vols, Boston: Little, Brown.

WN Smith, A. (1981) *An Inquiry Into the Nature and Causes of the Wealth of Nations*, 2 vols, ed. Campbell, R.H. and Skinner, A.S., in *The Glasgow Edition of the Works and Correspondence of Adam Smith*, Indianapolis: Liberty Fund. Citations to this text are referenced as volume-page (e.g., *WN* 1.341).

WSPP Wordsworth, W. (1965) *Selected Poems and Prefaces*, ed. Stillinger, J., Boston: Houghton Mifflin.

A note on periodicals: In citing from eighteenth- and nineteenth-century periodicals, I have employed the following conventions. When citing from daily or weekly periodicals such as *The London Journal*, *The Times*, and *The Examiner*, I indicate the issue, month, year, and day in the body of the text, except in those cases in which a daily or weekly periodical is available in a standard contemporary scholarly edition, such as Donald F. Bond's five-volume edition of *The Spectator*, in which case citations are indicated parenthetically. When citing from monthly periodicals such as the *Monthly Magazine and British Register* and the *Edinburgh Review*, I provide the publication month and year in the body of the text, and parenthetically indicate either issue or volume number, followed by page number.

Introduction

Ferments arise, imprison'd factions roar,
Represt ambition struggles round her shore;
Till, overwrought, the general system feels
Its motion stop, or frenzy fire the wheels. (Goldsmith 1793: 12)

I. SYMPATHY AND STATE FINANCE IN THE ROMANTIC ERA

In the August 22, 1818 issue of the antigovernment newspaper *The Political Register*, political journalist and government gadfly William Cobbett presented his readers with a rather unusual solution for what he saw as the problem of British ministerial despotism. What if, he asked, counterfeiters were to print millions of pounds worth of Bank of England banknotes, but rather than secretly trying to pass these off as real money, "they were generously *to throw their money by night, about the streets*" and stuff handfuls of the bills into letters? The next morning the nation would find itself awash in money, and anyone with pockets would fancy him- or herself a millionaire, at least for a moment. But in relatively short order, the system of paper money would collapse: "All money transactions would be at a stand. No buying, no selling." Flooding the streets with counterfeit bills would enable the imagination to grasp paper money *as* a social system, rather than a natural fact of life, and as people imagined to themselves the effects of such a massive increase in currency, money would cease to function as the invisible medium of exchange as its contingency was exposed—for "who, from that day forth, would ever *take a Bank Note*?" Cobbett acknowledged that the collapse of this social system would cause extreme hardship for those whose wealth depended upon financial speculation: "[t]hree hundred thousand families of Fundholders would be pennyless in an hour, and starving in a week." But Cobbett, who had railed against British paper money for almost a decade, argued that exposing the contingency of paper money would lead to a cascade of therapeutic destruction, as social system after social system collapsed: the fall of the system of paper money would in turn destroy the "borough system," as well as the system of British state finance that depended upon the Bank of England and the national debt. A massive campaign of forgery, Cobbett contended, would shatter these linked systems of government corruption, since nothing could "save the system from the effects of such a blow…a blow a million times surer than that of a thousand daggers all striking at once."

Many of Cobbett's contemporaries were horrified by his proposal, and at least one wrote a pamphlet in response, suggesting that even if Cobbett intended his "solution" to be understood satirically, simply to describe such a plan was to invite readers to put into action its "fatal tendency." His anonymous critic suggested that such a proposal could only have been imagined by a compassionless brute who wrote not from sympathy with the nation's poor, as Cobbett claimed, but rather out of resentment and spleen (Anon 1818: 7). Though twenty-first century readers may find the fury and horror evident in this response a bit excessive, Cobbett's proposal still has the power to fascinate precisely because it is so recognizably modern: one can update his plan simply by substituting computer hackers for Cobbett's counterfeiters; electronic bank accounts for the streets and post of early nineteenth-century London; and a fully internationalized system of finance, credit, and debts for the more British-centric financial system against which Cobbett railed. What is modern about Cobbett's proposal is not precisely his interest in paper money and national debts, nor even the connections he establishes between the instruments of state finance and collective imaginings: since the "Financial Revolution" of the early eighteenth century, scores of British and French authors had sought to understand the new financial systems of paper money and national debts upon which their governments had come to depend, as well as the role of belief and imaginings in these systems. Rather, what is modern about Cobbett's critique is his *systemic* understanding of the connections among state finance, imagination, and society. Cobbett's plan presents British society as a system—or more precisely, a series of interlocking social systems—that are maintained at least in part by the imagination, and he suggests that one can either discipline or crash "the System" as a whole simply by asking people to imagine the destruction of one particular system. It is his emphasis on these connections between collective imaginings and social systems—as well as his attempt to discipline these collective imaginings by making readers comprehend "the System"—that makes Cobbett's critique of state finance resonate with much more contemporary critiques and analyses of the "irrational exuberance," "millennial dreams," and "collective folly" and of the so-called New Economy of the 1990s, that modern, globalized conjugation of finance, production, and labor that increasingly has come to be described as a system dependent upon "feedback mechanism[s]" that produce "herd behavior that can spread through millions or even billions of people" (Shiller 2005: xiii), and in which credit mechanisms are employed to extract more and more work from laborers even as small investors are "systematically fleeced" (Henwood 2003: 194).[1]

Yet if Cobbett's satiric attack on early nineteenth-century state finance seems cast in a particularly modern mold, he was by no means the only author in that period that we now think of as the "Romantic era" to understand relationships among systems, state finance, and collective imaginative folly in this way. Authors that we now more commonly associate with late Enlightenment political theory, such as Thomas Paine, or Romantic imaginative literature, such as Samuel Taylor Coleridge, also wrote extensively on paper money and the national debt (Paine 1793 and 1796; Coleridge 1969–2002: vols. 4 and 6); novelist, essayist, and poet Thomas Love Peacock wrote a series of *Paper Money Lyrics* in 1825 (Peacock 1924–34, vol. 7: 95–146); and Anna Laetitia Barbauld criticized Britain's "baseless wealth" that "dissolves in air" (Barbauld 1812: 5) while Lord Byron satirically suggested in *Don Juan* that British financiers, rather than politicians, held "the balance of the world" in their hands (Byron 1986: 744). Even Percy Bysshe Shelley—that purportedly most ethereal of Romantic era poets (a "beautiful and ineffectual angel," as Matthew Arnold described him)—wrote extensively on paper money, the national debt, and systems of credit. Shelley, in fact, seems to have been inspired by Cobbett's counterfeiting proposal, for a few months after writing that he found Cobbett's "design to overthrow banknotes by forgery...very comic" (*LPBS,* vol. 2: 694), Shelley began a long prose text, entitled *A Philosophical View of Reform*, in which he traced the roots of contemporary political conflict in Britain back to the late seventeenth century, and specifically to the foundation of the Bank of England and the national debt. Shelley's account of the fraud and deceptions perpetrated by Britain's systems of paper money and national debt echoed elements of Cobbett's critique, but the poet's attempt to theorize the collective psychology that made such systems possible was far more innovative. Though Shelley concluded that financiers and politicians had come to determine collective "Opinion" by appropriating what he called "fertilizing streams of sympathy," he also believed that poets could counter the division in Opinion engendered by the systems of paper money and public credit by producing a countervailing "uniform enthusiasm." Describing poetry as "an intense and impassioned power of communicating intense and impassioned impressions respecting man and nature," he contended that poets served as "the mirrors of gigantic shadows which futurity cast upon the present," and as a result they could enable modes of speculation freed from finance and capable of maintaining an open relationship to the future (*SP* 240). Poetry, Shelley argued, produced the conditions for a libratory collective enthusiasm by "expanding" the imagination, producing "an identification of ourselves with the beautiful which exists in thought, action, or person, not our own" (*SP* 282–83), thereby enabling a new relationship to time and collective agency.

The obsession with state finance for Romantic era authors such as Cobbett and Shelley—and the more occasional engagement with this topic on the part of authors from Barbauld to Byron—was spurred by a collective recognition that the relationship between speculation and the state had reached a new phase, introducing into social relations what the early nineteenth-century journalist and political economist Francis Horner described as a "new principle of action, the effect of which cannot be clearly discerned" (Horner 1802: 196). Though state finance had been important to the British state since the early eighteenth century, it seemed to many Romantic era authors—and, subsequently, to many twentieth century historians—to have undergone a qualitative shift in the late eighteenth and early nineteenth century, deepening and intensifying its role in the lives of British citizens. The most significant political event of the Romantic era, the French Revolution, was from the start understood as an experiment in state finance, an interpretation exemplified by Edmund Burke's description of the new French republic as led by the "most desperate adventurers in philosophy and finance" (*WEB*, vol. 3: 545). Yet after war broke out between France and Britain, the British found themselves turning toward equally speculative mechanisms for obtaining money to fund their war with their republican foes. The results of Britain's own adventures in finance during the Romantic era were remarkable and long-lasting. A run on British banks in 1797 resulted in the Bank Restriction Act, which had the effect of substituting the "paper pound" for gold and silver currency from 1797 to 1821, while the national debt expanded from an already enormous £22 million in 1792 to the sum of £123 million by 1815 (Arrighi 1994: 160, citing Jenks 1927 and Ingham 1984: 106).[2] Yet, seemingly paradoxically, these crises in currency, banking, and national debt had the effect of normalizing all of these institutions. While a mid-eighteenth-century author such as David Hume could still entertain the possibility of a British state freed of its national debt, by the time that Shelley wrote *A Philosophical View of Reform* in 1819, it had become clear that the end of the national debt would mean the end of the British state as it was then constituted. In what one can only describe as a literal example of the classic Romantic trope of transcendence by way of failure, the financial crises of the Romantic era served as the foundation for Britain's unprecedented economic and industrial expansion in the later nineteenth century. Even as Britain, for much of the Romantic era, seemed ready to plunge into what Charles James Fox called in 1797 the "gulph of bankruptcy" (*PH,* vol. 32:1537), its apparent loss of financial foundation paved the way for its subsequent commercial triumphs. The transformation of the British pound into paper money, for example, effectively tied many foreign merchants to the future of British commercial success, since their paper credit was valid only so long as the Bank of England persisted and the British government remained in power (Harries 1811; Neal 1990a: 190, 215, 217), while the massive increase in British governmental expenditure, combined with the effects of Napoleon's

Continental Blockade, forced British capital (and foreign capital tied up in Britain) into industries such as iron works that subsequently provided the foundation for Britain's "industrial revolution" (Arrighi 1994: 160).

This book is an exploration of the efforts of a number of canonical eighteenth- and early nineteenth-century authors to understand this "new principle of action" introduced by state finance, and I focus particularly on a "Romantic" mode of analysis of the relationships among state finance, social systems, literature, and affective relationships between subjects. Shelley's approach to state finance highlights the central terms of this Romantic approach. For all of the authors that I consider here—a list that includes David Hume, Adam Smith, Jean-Jacques Rousseau, Ann Yearsley, William Wordsworth, and P.B. Shelley—state finance could not be fully comprehended through the categories of political economy, but required instead, or in addition, a more fundamental analysis of the capacities of the imagination to create social systems by linking sympathy to particular modes of "time consciousness." In this sense, I argue, eighteenth- and early nineteenth-century crises of state finance enabled Romantic theories of imagination, sympathy, and identification by providing occasions for the discernment of, and theories about, social systems.[3] It was no coincidence, I suggest, that theories of sympathy and identification emerged around periods of financial crisis (1720s, early 1750s, late 1780s, final years of the 1790s, and 1815–1821), for it was precisely during periods of financial panic that state finance became visible *as* a "system" that connected people to one another through affective bonds of belief, "Opinion," and desire. During these periods of crisis, the system of state finance appeared both totalizing and contingent: totalizing in the sense that the other systems of society seemed to depend upon it; contingent in the sense that the system of state finance appeared on the verge of collapse. Romantic theories of sympathy and identification emerged as responses to these perceptions of the contingency of the system of state finance, for these theories were attempts to understand the foundations and operations of social systems in ways that would explain, but also contain, the disruptive effects of finance. In ways that I describe at more length later in this introduction, such a claim has significant implications not only for our understanding of the relationship between Romantic era literary form and "the economy," but also for our understanding of key terms, such as "identification" and "imagined communities," by means of which literary critics have sought to understand the ideological dimensions of creative literature from this and other periods. My reading also contributes to our understanding of the transformation of the term "system" in the Romantic era, a period in which—as Clifford Siskin has noted—the primary sense of the term shifted from a description of a genre to a description of the totality of the social (Siskin 2001: 202).

My effort to illuminate this Romantic approach to state finance—that is, an approach that understands state finance in terms of imagination, systems, sympathy, and time consciousness—is also an attempt to romanticize the topic of state finance. As André Orléan has noted, the effects of finance in our own contemporary moment are not limited to the economy, but also "transform our manner of *conceiving* of life in common" [la vie en commun], and this was true in the Romantic era as well (Orléan 1999: 14; my translation and emphasis). For the authors that I consider here, debates about finance in the Romantic era did not concern solely the arcanae of credit, debt, taxation, and expenditure which often dominated such discussion, but were in addition understood as debates about the nature of social bonding and the ways in which the affective ties between people enabled collective "projects" (that is, collective action oriented toward the future). The authors that are the subject of this study recognized that state finance was a system designed to consolidate the labor of the past into "projects" that oriented the present toward events that would only arrive in the future. For most of the eighteenth and early nineteenth century, the primary project supported by British state finance was war with France, and the future event to which such activity was oriented was simply the continued commercial success of the British state, but as Shelley recognized, the labor represented by the national debt could be employed for other purposes, such as making "every peasant's cottage, surrounded with its garden, a little paradise of comfort" (*SP* 249). I am suggesting, then, that just as we have begun to see Romantic era debates about "enthusiasm" as theologically inflected debates about proper and improper social ties (Mee 2003), we should see debates about state finance as economically inflected versions of a similar concern (a task that perhaps becomes easiest at the point of intersection between the discourses of enthusiasm and state finance: namely, investment "enthusiasms" and "panics").

II. THE SYSTEM OF STATE FINANCE AND THE METHODOLOGIES OF LITERARY CRITICISM

Before outlining the specific contents of the six chapters of this book, I want to make a few comments about my methodology and its relationship to earlier critical work on literature and finance. My account of the importance of state finance for eighteenth- and nineteenth-century discussions of sympathy and social systems owes much to a significant bibliography of literary criticism that traces links between finance and literature (with the latter term understood broadly to include novels, poetry, drama, and philosophy). Scholars of the eighteenth century have been especially attentive to the importance of Britain's financial revolution for our understanding of literature, and I am indebted to a series of now-classic book-length studies that includes Colin Nicholson's reading of Augustan poems, such as Alexander Pope's *Dunciad*, as "capital satires" motivated by the fluctuations associated with state finance and public credit (Nicholson 1994); Sandra Sherman's suggestion that an "epistemological malaise" inspired by early eighteenth-century fluctuations of public credit encouraged the development of a "new kind of narrativity" apparent in both credit instruments, such as stocks and annuities, and new modes of fiction, such as Daniel Defoe's novels (Sherman 1996: 5); James Thompson's description of the ways in which eighteenth-century political economy and novels developed parallel and linked methods of imaginative "modeling" (Thompson 1996: 28); and Deidre Shauna Lynch's and Catherine Gallagher's accounts of the function of literary "characters" in training eighteenth- and nineteenth-century British readers to negotiate an increasingly commercial and speculative world (Lynch 1998; Gallagher 1994).[4] I have also drawn on several less field-specific discussions of the relationship between literature and finance, such as Patrick Brantlinger's account of "counterdiscourses," ranging from Augustan to postmodern satire, that seek to expose the "'misrecognition' at work under the aegis of public credit and national identity formation" (Brantlinger 1996: 4).[5] While British Romantic literary criticism has not yet produced a book-length discussion of relationships between national finance and literature, I have found helpful a number of more local studies that focus on links between finance and late eighteenth- and early nineteenth-century literary production.[6]

As my description of these earlier studies suggests, literary critics have tended to link eighteenth- and nineteenth-century finance to literature in two different ways. On the one hand, critics have highlighted ways in which eighteenth- and nineteenth-century literature alleviated anxieties produced by Britain's financial revolution. Sherman, for example, describes Defoe's novels as responses to an "epistemological malaise" (Sherman 1996: 5), while Lynch reads different understandings of character as ways of "assuaging anxieties" produced by Britain's new consumer and credit culture (Lynch 1998: 127). On the other hand, literary critics have also described eighteenth- and nineteenth-century literature and philosophy as "technologies" that trained readers to develop the subjective capacities, proclivities, and feelings necessary for the "new economy." Gallagher, for example, argues that the development of readerly capacities for "investing" in fictional characters was "one among many modes of facilitating property exchange and investment in the [eighteenth century], of creating the speculative, commercial and sentimental subject" (Gallagher 1994: 194), while, more recently, Ian Baucom has contended that subjective capacities of "abstraction" necessary for eighteenth-century financial practices did not depend solely upon new monetary technologies, such as bills of exchange, but also required "discursive forms—the novel central among them—that accompanied and enabled the rise of this finance capitalism" (Baucom 2005: 71). These two approaches to the relationship between literature and finance are not, of course, disjunctive, and for many of these critics, new literary forms and structures—the capital satire, the novel, the "full" character, and so on—are implicitly positioned as inventive responses to subjective anxiety produced by the increasing importance of speculation and finance.

While these subject-centered approaches provocatively illuminate ways in which literature helps to construct a social habitus, they arguably have been less successful in theorizing the precise nature of the linkage between finance and literature. Early accounts of eighteenth-century finance and literature often relied on a "New Historicist" premise of an homogenous cultural field within which metaphors, tropes, and modes of perception that originated in one discourse could migrate into—or, as Nicholson puts it, "infiltrate"—another (Nicholson 1994: xii). From this perspective, the topic of finance is relevant to literary criticism precisely because eighteenth-century financial discourse and literary production were involved in a process of reciprocal influence. In Sherman's account, for example, psychological expectations that structured early eighteenth-century financial practice came to guide readers' expectations about the new literary form of the novel, while at the same time expectations developed in novel-reading came to structure financial practice. Yet however helpful this premise of a unified cultural field may be for locating homologies between different areas of culture, and explaining the movement of structures from one discourse to another, such an approach nevertheless tends toward a structuralism that undercuts the importance of either finance or literature as intrinsically important subdiscourses. While metaphors, tropes, and modes of perception originating in finance may infiltrate literary discourse (and vice versa), if such slippage characterizes every other cultural discourse—law, politics, medicine, etc.—then finance and literature begin to seem like arbitrary points of departure and analysis.[7]

More recent accounts of relationships between finance and literature grounded in a psychoanalytically oriented Marxist literary criticism have been more attentive to the importance of discursive differentiation and phenomenological discontinuities between different areas of culture, attempting to account not simply for the "infiltration" of one discourse by another, but also for the processes that ensured that discourses such as finance and literature came to seem absolutely separate. However, in their effort to establish what Fredric Jameson calls "ontological priorities" (Jameson 1993: 187)—by, for example, situating "class interests" as the unity on the basis of which finance and literature come to appear as separate and distinct discourses—proponents of this second approach often find themselves turning to psychoanalytically inflected theories of subjectivity that threaten to return to the problematic premise of a homogenous social or cultural field.[8] Thompson, for example, makes a compelling case that though eighteenth-century political economy and novels appeared to eighteenth-century readers (as well as to ourselves) to be entirely separate discourses—the former constituting the "very science of value," the latter focusing on "subjectivity, a realm and a topic far removed from [economic] value" (Thompson 1996: 185)—in fact, these "two stories" "go hand in hand"; they are "dialectically related," "the presence of one" calling "on the palpable absence of the other" (Thompson 1996: 3). Thompson's description is valuable precisely because it captures *both* the fact of differentiation—political economy developed genres, systems of distribution, and readerships different from those of the novel—*and* the fact that such differentiation was the result of *one* process. Yet in his attempt to account for the unity of this process, Thompson turns to the notion of a "cultural imaginary" (Thompson 1996: 7), that threatens to return to precisely the premise of homogeneity from which his approach is otherwise such an important departure. Moreover, such an approach would be especially problematic if—as in the case of the present study—theories of the collective imagination and identification are themselves the subject of investigation.[9]

My approach, by contrast, seeks to account for structural similarities between different social systems while also emphasizing the importance of differentiation. I thus avoid attributing structural similarities between finance and literature to the "influence" of one on the other, and I account for differentiation without making recourse to claims about the "imaginary" nature of social relations (since such a premise is precisely the subject of my study). The methodology that I employ to accomplish these two goals is grounded in three terms that will reappear throughout the book: "financial capitalism," "system," and "affect." The first two terms bear on my approach to the relationships between different discursive fields—for example, state finance and sentimental moral philosophy—in the Romantic era. In order to account for both the autonomy of different discursive fields and their simultaneous dependence upon one another, I draw on Giovanni Arrighi's recent work on financial capitalism, on the one hand, and systems theory, particularly that of Niklas Luhmann, on the other. Luhmann's work provides us with a way of understanding the autonomy of modern social systems, while Arrighi's (when considered in the light of Luhmann) allows us to understand why the emergence of new social systems was particularly indebted to crises in state finance. In addition, I suggest, Luhmann's approach provides a methodological approach to the question of intersubjectivity that is able to *describe* Romantic era claims about sympathy and identification without implicitly depending upon the premises of those same theories.

Financial Capitalism

While Marxist historical and literary criticism traditionally either ignored finance completely or relegated it to a "parasitic" role on the more primary means of production, recent Marxist criticism has shown a marked interest in the dynamics of speculation.[10] One of the most impressive of these new accounts is Giovanni Arrighi's *The Long Twentieth Century: Money, Power, and the Origins of Our Times*. Drawing on Fernand Braudel's analysis of the development of capitalism in Europe between the thirteenth and seventeenth centuries, Arrighi argues that capitalism has developed into a world system through a series of "systemic cycles of accumulation" (Arrighi 1994: xi). The key feature of these cycles is that they are characterized by an

> alternation of epochs of material expansion...with phases of financial rebirth and expansion. In phases of material expansion money capital "sets in motion" an increasing mass of commodities (including commoditized labor-power and gifts of nature); and in phases of financial expansion an increasing mass of money capital "sets itself free" from the commodity form, and accumulation proceeds through financial deals. (Arrighi 1994: 6)

Arrighi suggests that the history of capitalism has been the history of four different cycles, which he calls the Genoese cycle (fifteenth to early sixteenth centuries), the Dutch cycle (late sixteenth to eighteenth century), the British cycle (mid-eighteenth century to early twentieth century) and the U.S. cycle (late nineteenth century to present) (Arrighi 1994: 6). For my purposes here, what I wish to stress is Arrighi's claim that transformations of finance *precede* (as well as conclude) restructurings of the material base; that is, "financial expansions have always been the initial and concluding moments of systemic cycles" (Arrighi 1994: 126). The logic that necessitates this is not hard to understand: since the fifteenth century, changes in the economic "base" have required sophisticated financial structures adequate to fund those changes. It is difficult, in this context, to make a hard and fast distinction between the economic base and financial superstructure of capitalism, for the importance of finance ensures that transformations of the former will depend upon *beliefs*—for example, beliefs about the risks of investing large sums of money in maritime endeavors, or a national bank—that are intrinsic to finance itself. Transformations of material relations of production are only possible, in other words, when blocks of investors become convinced that money should be expended on a given transformation of the "base."

In addition to troubling the distinction between economic base and financial superstructure, Arrighi also undercuts the notion that "the economy" can serve as the reference point for all cultural phenomena. Arrighi claims that modern societies are driven by two linked, but nevertheless relatively autonomous, logics: on the one hand, a "territorialist" logic of power, for which "control over territory and population is the objective, and control over mobile capital the means, of state- and war-making," and a "capitalist logic" of power, for which "control over mobile capital is the objective, and control over territory and population the means" (Arrighi 1994: 34). Neither the political logic of territory nor the economic logic of capital can be reduced to, or understood as simply reflections of, the other, though

Arrighi contends that the two systems are bound together "dialectically" (Arrighi 1994: 36). While the notion of a dialectical connection between the systems of territory and capital usefully emphasizes Arrighi's claim that capitalism becomes globally more extensive and structurally more intensive in each of its four phases, the relative autonomy that he grants to the logics of territory and capital suggest that they function more like structurally coupled subsystems than moments in a dialectic.

While Arrighi provides a compelling framework for understanding the historical development of state finance, his account must be supplemented in order to understand the relationship between state finance and the systems of *cultural* production—for example, poetry and sentimental moral philosophy—that are the focus of the present study. Arrighi does not ignore cultural production entirely, but his brief discussions are problematic, for he suggests that artistic products are essentially simply tactical devices employed within the political logic of territory. Arrighi contends that during historical periods in which the avenues for the investment of finance capital became limited or extremely risky, surplus capital was often diverted to cultural products, as witnessed by the Italian Renaissance of the fifteenth century and the Dutch Golden Age in the seventeenth century. However, since such "investment" could not in fact provide any real return of capital, Arrighi concludes that "conspicuous consumption of cultural products" must have served to *legitimate* ruling elites, since "[p]rimacy in art and learning was as good a means as any other to win legitimacy" (Arrighi 1994: 96). Such an understanding of art begs a number of key questions, not least the role of the otherwise unexplored category of "legitimacy" in Arrighi's general theory. Moreover, such a theory of cultural production seems best suited for modes of art that admit of public display, such as architecture, sculpture, painting, and patron-supported literature, and is far less able to account for the development of the market-oriented literature that increasingly dominated the eighteenth and nineteenth centuries. Systems of cultural production, in other words, are a blind spot in Arrighi's account of the historical development of finance, for his schematic attempt to understand art as a political tactic opens up more questions than it answers. In order to understand the relationship between finance and literature, we need to consider more closely the concept of system.

Social Systems

Like a number of other recent critics, I have found "systems theory"—particularly, though not exclusively, that of Niklas Luhmann—to be a productive approach for understanding the relationships among finance, politics, and cultural production.[11] While Luhmann, a sociologist, was primarily interested in developing a theoretical account of contemporary society, he also sought to distinguish the social systems of modernity from those that preceded it. He argued that in the seventeenth and eighteenth centuries, most western European countries were characterized by a movement from stratified to functionally differentiated social systems. By "stratified social systems," Luhmann has in mind societies that do not explicitly differentiate between different social functions such as "religion," "economy," and "politics," but instead ensure that all social communications and actions have meaning for all of these different areas. A stratified social system, such as that which characterized most parts of Europe in the Middle Ages, maintains order and perpetuates itself by maintaining a rigid caste hierarchy between different levels of society (for example, nobles vs. commoners). In a functionally differentiated society, by contrast, "functional systems for politics, the economy, science, law, education, religion, family, etc. have become relatively autonomous and now mutually furnish environments for one another" (Luhmann 1982: xii).

While these claims about the emergence of functional differentiation in the eighteenth century are similar in tenor to, and supported by, recent work on the rise of disciplines in the late eighteenth and early nineteenth centuries, Luhmann's theory of systems provides a more compelling way of approaching transformations in social structure, for it explains both the autonomy *and* interdependency of eighteenth- and nineteenth-century systems.[12] For Luhmann, the dynamics of a social system cannot be understood by referring it to its "context" or to an economic "base." Rather, systems must be understood as linked to an "environment," a term that denotes not something that surrounds the system, but rather everything that the system cannot process within its own terms. A system *produces* its corresponding environment, for "systems define their own boundaries," by "differentiat[ing] themselves and thereby constitut[ing] the environment as whatever lies outside the boundary" (Luhmann 1989: 6). The environment is "always more complex than the system itself," and as a result, a system cannot map its environment into itself, but rather establishes a code for dealing with the environment, which it uses to create and circulate communications within the system (Luhmann 1995: 25). For example, the modern system of economy communicates to itself through the code "payment/no payment," and anything that cannot be parsed into these terms cannot become the subject of communication within the system. The rise of functional differentiation in the eighteenth century thus meant the rise of a number of different autonomous subsystems—"politics, the economy, science, law, education, religion, family," for example—each of which established its own codes for dealing with its environment.

The fact of functional differentiation was legible to eighteenth-century British commentators and in fact many attempted to understand this development through concepts of "system." Eighteenth-century authors, as Luhmann notes, responded to functional differentiation in the "form of social theories that registered the peculiarities of each of society's most important functional domains," developing "theories that focused respectively on politics, on the economy, on science, and on education," for example (Luhmann 1982: xi). Miranda Burgess, Clifford Siskin, David Simpson, and others have documented the extent to which eighteenth-century authors employed concepts of "system" to describe these developments, noting that hundreds if not thousands of texts on "systems" of natural philosophy, moral philosophy, rhetoric, marine insurance, naval warfare, and other topics were written during this century (Burgess 2000; Siskin 1998b: 9–31 and 2001; Simpson 1993; see also Mitchell 2006).

One can distinguish between several different senses of the term "system" as it was used in the eighteenth and nineteenth centuries. Thus, system could denote (1) a *genre* of writing that was committed to the production of knowledge by means of deduction from sound principles: for example, John Stirling's *A System of Rhetoric* (1733) or Thomas Rutherford's *A System of Natural Philosophy* (1748). It could also refer to (2) a moralizing recognition of the nature of reality, as when Lord Shaftesbury suggested in *Characteristics of Men, Manners, Opinions, Times* (1711) that moral development was encouraged by understanding the natural world as a series of interlinked systems: for example, every individual animal was a system, but these systems were parts of larger systems (the species), which were parts of the system of living things, which was a part of the "systems of a globe or earth," and so on (Cooper 1999: 169). Such a perspective, Shaftesbury suggested, prepared one for the fact that "in the several orders of terrestrial forms a resignation is required, a sacrifice and mutual yielding of natures one to another" (245). In addition, Romantic era authors used the term system to refer to (3) an institution or series of institutions organized to achieve a particular result, often with the help, or implicit support, of the state; it was this sense of the term that underwrote, for example, both Edmund Burke's glowing descriptions of the British "political system" and much more critical charges by antislavery poets against the "system of slavery." Finally, by the early nineteenth century, system could refer not just to a discrete set of institutions, but also to (4) the totality of social institutions, or what Clifford Siskin calls "The System" (Siskin 1998b: 9). This sense of the term—prefigured in Burke's fear that the "French system" was serving as "the bank of deposit and the bank of circulation of all the pernicious principles that are forming in every state" (*WEB*, vol. 5: 344)—denoted an invisible totality that connected institutions in such a way as to determine all possibilities of individual and collective choice.[13]

Luhmann's sense of system is closest to the third of these meanings. Just as Luhmann emphasizes that a system can deal with its environment only by means of a filtering code, many Romantic era commentators stressed the extent to which a particular system limited itself to communications of a certain sort, though this observation was often inflected through moral judgments in a way that is absent in Luhmann's account. For Burke, for example, the virtue of the British "political system" was precisely that it attended *only* to political communications (in contrast, he claimed, to the French system, which sought to encompass all other social systems), while for Ann Yearsley, the slave trade constituted what she called a "destructive system" precisely because it parsed events solely through the code of profit and loss (Yearsley 1788: 26). Romantic era commentators interested in this third sense of system also emphasized, like Luhmann, both the material institutions and the logic of communication that allowed systems to reproduce, or perpetuate, themselves. Social systems, if they are to persist, depend upon bodies and material artifacts, but they must coordinate those into structures that facilitate continuing "communications," whether those take the form of payments, statements, judgments, or whatever other form communication takes in the particular system. The system of the slave trade, for example, depended upon the movement of ships and bodies, but as I note in chapter 3, it also depended upon investment instruments that located value in the future; this deferral of value had the effect of creating a continuing chain of investment communications. As this example suggests, systems, for Luhmann, perpetuate themselves through internal structures, both material and representational, that demand ever more "communication."

It is also this third sense of the term that best allows us to understand the development of the system of state finance in the early eighteenth century. Following the Glorious Revolution, the English government publicly solicited plans for different means of raising money (in large part to wage war against France), and it adopted several of these proposals in the 1690s. As economic historians have pointed out, these early efforts at state finance were problematic, for many of the loans obtained by the state from wealthy financiers were negotiated on terms of interest that threatened to beggar the state in the long run (Dickson 1967: 39–89). However, within two decades, British politicians and financiers had established the elements by means of which the system of British state finance would operate for the rest of the century. In schematic form, this system consisted of an oscillation between two different kinds of loans: during war years, the British government solicited short-term loans (or "unfunded debt") from both British and foreign financiers at relatively high interest rates; in periods of peace, attempts were made to retire these short term loans by means of "funded debt," which depended primarily upon so-called indirect taxes on commodities and services (rather than income or property). Before the passage of a bill authorizing a loan, the rate of interest was determined by legislators working in conjunction with London financiers, and then calls for subscription to the loans were publicized in print. For most of the century, the Bank of England handled the actual monetary transactions. While a relatively small number of financiers contributed the majority of the money for these loans—investors numbered no more than tens of thousands in a national population of millions—the effects of state finance were understood to affect far more than the fortunes of these individuals, as state finance was represented as a powerful force that acted on private finance, rates of currency exchange, and trade and commerce more generally.[14]

At the same time, however, British state finance functioned smoothly only if it was perceived *as* autonomous; that is, as independent of particular ministries, political decisions, or wars. As Michael D. Bordo and Eugene N. White note, the reforms in state finance that followed the South Sea Bubble of 1720 served to assure investors "that public finances would be divorced from narrow political and private interests, improving over the longer term the credibility of government's fiscal and debt management policies" (Bordo and White 1990: 5–6). For reasons I note below, state finance was a system in perpetual crisis—in part because the tendency of the French government to default on its loans provided an example of the possible collapse of the system of state finance—but it nevertheless functioned as an autonomous system for most of the eighteenth and early nineteenth centuries.

To call state finance an "autonomous" system does not mean that it had no relationships with other systems. As historians and literary critics have demonstrated, the autonomy of state finance was possible only as the consequence of the simultaneous emergence of other autonomous systems. Where earlier historical work on British state finance often focused exclusively on the development of state finance as a coherent system, treating events such as wars or partisan politics as simply "stimulus" for its development (Jenks 1927: 16), or locating its origin in the *lack* of other systems, such as the absence of an effective bureaucratic organization for collecting taxes at the end of the seventeenth century (Dickson 1967: 10), more recent work has demonstrated that the rise of the system of state finance depended upon the development of other functionally separate systems, such as military victualling networks and a system of tax collection that became increasingly efficient over the course of the eighteenth century. These other systems were necessary for the development of the system of state finance, for the British government could continue to raise money only if it could inspire "belief among its creditors that it had the capacity and determination to meet its payments" through a newly efficient system of tax collection, and it could use the money it raised only by developing coherent systems of troop supply (Brewer 1989: 88). In a different register, literary critics have stressed the connections between the autonomous systems of state finance and literature. Ingrassia, for example, argues that the system of finance and the novel were linked in the early eighteenth century, for financial investment required the use of narratives and novel-reading required imaginative "investment" (Ingrassia 1998: 7), while Thompson outlines a constitutive, yet disjunctive, relation between the systems of political economy and the novel, arguing that the two are "[i]nverses of one another": "political economy and the novel map, respectively, a zone of finance and a zone of affect, or money and feeling" (Thompson 1996: 3, 23). For Arrighi, Brewer, Ingrassia, and Thompson, in other words, state finance functioned as an autonomous system only because it was bound to a series of other functional systems.

Luhmann's concept of functional differentiation provides a fruitful way of understanding how state finance can function both as the autonomous system described by Jenks and Dickson and as part of a series of linked functional systems, as described by Arrighi and Brewer, and by literary critics such as Ingrassia and Thompson. "Autonomy," for Luhmann, does not imply the absence of relationships with other social systems; rather, functional differentiation means that social systems become increasingly linked to one another. To draw again upon the example of the subsystem "economy," Luhmann notes that "[i]n the general context of social differentiation the economy obviously remains dependent upon politics continuing to function, upon peace being assured, upon law being maintained, and upon decisions being made that are binding" (Luhmann 1982: 212). As a result,

> [d]ifferentiation from the rest of society makes possible, not self-sufficiency or independence, but rather a high degree of autonomy or self-regulation in the [system of] the economy. Especially with the help of the mechanism of money the economy builds its own values, its own goals, norms, criteria of rationality, and directions of abstraction, by means of which the behavioral choices in its domain are oriented. (Luhmann 1982: 200)

Precisely because a subsystem such as economy can treat politics, the family, law, and so on as part of its environment, it can develop increasingly complex and sophisticated techniques of self-communication (including the creation of specialized economic "subsubsystems," which treat other aspects of economy as part of their environment). Luhmann acknowledges that one system—economy, for example—may come to have "functional primacy," but this does not mean that it therefore "influences" the other systems; his concept of system is designed to emphasize that a system interacts with its environment solely within its own terms. This conception of social differentiation thus represents a more useful and precise redescription of Ingrassia's suggestion that "[d]iscrete financial and literary practices operate as connected parts of a relationally configured culture" (Ingrassia 1998: 7). Functional differentiation also represents a more subtle way of dealing with relationships between systems than that employed by Thompson, who argues, following Fredric Jameson, that the rise of the separate systems of "political economy" and "the novel" in the eighteenth century was produced by a contradiction between the *experience* of most Britons (which was thoroughly "domestic") and the *truth* of that experience (that it depended upon globalized trade relations) (Thompson 1996: 10). The concept of functional differentiation allows us to acknowledge the increasing importance of the system of economy, without at the same time suggesting that, through a network of invisible tentacles, it secretly controlled or influenced all other emerging systems.[15]

Luhmann's theory of systems also allows us to deal in a more precise way with the *temporality* of the system of state finance. The importance of "time consciousness" for state finance was first emphasized by intellectual historian J.G.A. Pocock, who argued that early eighteenth-century British structures of state speculation created an investing citizen who "does not even live in the present, except as constituted by his fantasies concerning a future"—that is, the future of financial returns (Pocock 1985: 112). Pocock's description of the system of state finance as one that privileges the future is compelling, and it has provided the template for most literary analyses of eighteenth-century finance. At the same time, though, by employing an essentially commonsense understanding of time, Pocock's approach risks missing what is most fundamental about the relationship between systems and temporality. As I note in chapter 5, there is in fact something a bit arbitrary about Pocock's decision to privilege the future in his account of state finance, since one could just as easily say, and with equal accuracy, that the financial revolution created an investing citizen who lives in the *past*, insofar as the "promissory" nature of national debts and paper money are tied to the fantasy of an irrevocable past promise (that is, the past promise of legislators to repay financiers through earmarked taxes). Rather than constituting a true paradox, however, the fact that we can understand early eighteenth-century investors as "living in" either the past or the future simply highlights our need for a more capacious approach to understanding the time of systems. As Luhmann notes, systems create their own temporalities by establishing rhythms of communications, and to the extent that no individual lives in one system, but rather stands at the intersection of multiple systems, one is forced to adjudicate between multiple temporal horizons (and since the time of one system is not necessarily that of another, crises can occur precisely because systems are "out of step" with one another).[16] Luhmann's system theory is itself indebted to phenomenological approaches to time, and I draw on both phenomenology, as well as Gilles Deleuze's postphenomenological analyses of time consciousness, to discuss the temporality of state finance and its connection to theories of the imagination and sympathy. As I hope to demonstrate in the chapters that follow, the advantage of this perspective is that it allows us to recognize that theories of the intersubjective imagination, sympathy, and identification developed in the long Romantic era were almost invariably attempts to create new systems of social relations by enabling new modes of temporal consciousness. Chapter 2, for example, describes Rousseau's attempt to oppose what he saw as a problematic "speculative" system of affective exchange by proposing a mode of "energetic" identification that functioned as an antisystem, *preventing* communication between individuals (while at the same time enabling individuals to aid others in need of help), while chapter 3 outlines the efforts of antislavery poets to create a system of poetry, founded on sympathy, that would oppose the "destructive system" of the slave trade, as poet Ann Yearsley described it.

As I note above, the emergence of eighteenth- and early nineteenth-century theories of imagination, sympathy, and identification corresponded to crises in the system of state finance. This is not surprising, for a "crisis" is a period during which a system begins to appear incapable of regulating itself, and communications both within and outside the system focus insistently on its nature and viability. It is during these periods, in other words, that the system becomes visible *as* a system, and the limits of the system—that is, its inability to process its environment by means of anything other than its own code—become phenomenologically available. Following the linkage that Glyn Daly establishes between Luhmann and the work of "post-marxists" such as Claude Lefort, Ernesto Laclau, Chantal Mouffe, and Jacques Rancière, we can say that these are moments when "the political" as such—that is, "that which shows the contingent nature of all structuring principles"—becomes visible (Daly 2004: 3). It is thus not surprising, then, that during these crises, new systems are proposed. While it might thus be possible to say that the potential collapse of one system enables the emergence of other systems, one cannot understand this relationship as one of "influence."

Yet state finance and sympathy nevertheless have a special affinity with one another, for early eighteenth-century commentators attempted to understand both of these topics through concepts of imagination. As Luhmann notes, "parallel structures, say, in legal theory, in the theory of power, or in the theory of knowledge," should not be understood as the result of the influence of a "central" system on other systems, but rather a consequence of the fact that

> the reflexive structure [of each system] suggests similar questions—e.g. questions concerning the limits of repeating the application of a process to itself; or the question of the identity of the process which, however much administrative processes must be anticipated in their application upon itself, still has to remain the same. (Luhmann 1982: 209)

As Luhmann notes, symbols of autonomy often operate as signifiers of new systems, and the imagination served precisely this function for early eighteenth-century commentators, who used this figure to begin to theorize state finance *as* a system.[17] By attributing the fluctuations of stock prices to the fickle nature of the faculty of the imagination (as well as to the caprice of figures such as "Lady Credit"), early eighteenth-century commentators such as Daniel Defoe signaled their awareness of a new system, as well as their difficulty in understanding this system within the terms of existing discourses. Roughly two decades later, Scottish moral philosophers such as

Hume and Smith returned to the concept of imagination in their attempts to describe the system of affective relations that they believed served as the foundation of both sociality and commerce. Because the imagination served as the inaugural figure for these two discourses, both were oriented toward similar questions, such as the possibilities and dangers inherent in the recursive logic of social relations purportedly mediated by this faculty. While systems of state finance and sentimental moral philosophy developed in different directions during the course of the eighteenth and early nineteenth centuries, the analogies between their leading questions made it possible for each system to perceive the other as a potentially significant part of its environment, especially during periods of "crisis."

While Luhmann's approach allows us to understand how social systems can be both autonomous *and* linked without appealing either to "influence" or an ultimate ground, one must return to Arrighi to understand why *finance*, specifically, has played such an important role in the process of functional differentiation since the eighteenth century. While Luhmann acknowledged that the subsystem of economy had become increasingly important by the eighteenth century, he has difficulty in explaining the nature of its primacy. He contends that the subsystem of economy came to have "functional primacy," which meant that it "guides social development and delineates for other subsystems their domains of possibilities," but within his account, it is not entirely how or why this should be the case (Luhmann 1982: 225). However, Arrighi's emphasis on the function of *crisis* in finance capitalism provides a way to understand the functional primacy of the economy—or, more specifically, the functional primacy of the financial subsystem of economy. For Arrighi, finance capital historically has extended its global and intensive reach precisely by *creating* conflicts between the systems of capital and territory, as such conflicts encourage investors continually to move their money from one investment to another (and, in a longer time frame, from one financial center to another). Financial capital functions, in other words, by constantly threatening to break down, and this endemic state of crisis encourages the continued creation of new subsystems designed to "manage" these crises.[18] However, as I have noted, these periods of crisis were also moments in which social systems became phenomenologically available—it is not when systems function well, but rather when they do not that they become visible *as* systems—and, as a consequence, moments in which the potential for radically different forms of social systems became palpable.

Affect

Arrighi's emphasis on the importance of perceptions of crisis brings me to my final theoretical category, affect. Insofar as *Sympathy and the State in the Romantic Era* is focused on understanding the emergence of *theories* of sympathy and identification, I have generally avoided making claims about how or if people "actually" identified or sympathized with one another. I have shied away from such claims in part to avoid the vicious circularity that would attend an attempt to explain the emergence of eighteenth-century theories of identification as a consequence of individuals "identifying with" (for example) class ideals, as well as to resist the Whiggish historicism that tends to locate the truth of eighteenth-century claims about sympathy and identification in more recent psychoanalytic concepts of identification. In addition, my emphasis on social systems does not depend upon claims about subjectivity or intersubjectivity, but rather describes the operation of systems of communication (some of which may produce communication by making claims about the nature of intersubjectivity).

Nevertheless, I am interested in something that lies at the borders of subjective experience—namely, the experience of the *limits* of systems—and it is in connection with this phenomenon that I use the term "affect." As in the case of Kevis Goodman's recent study of Romantic georgic poetry, I use affect to denote experiences of dissonance, interference, and static; that is, experiences that cannot be easily communicated within the terms of existing systems (Goodman 2004: 4, 7). However, where Goodman's concept of affect derives from Raymond Williams's attempts to clarify his notion of "structures of feeling" (Goodman 2004: 5–8), my understanding of affect owes more to Gilbert Simondon's and Gilles Deleuze's accounts of this term. For both Simondon and Deleuze, affect refers not to an experience with a determinate content (as is the case for "feelings," "emotions," or "sentiments"), but rather to experiences of intensity that seem to demand the invention of new systems of communication.[19] In addition, where Goodman's study focuses on signs of affect—those "uneasy silence[s]"—within one poetic tradition, the georgic (Goodman 2004: 7), *Sympathy and the State in the Romantic Era* focuses on those moments in Romantic era theory when sympathy and identification suddenly ceased to be understood as the transmission of sentiment between subjects, and were instead understood as signs of intensity which enabled the emergence of something new. I thus locate affect as a determining element in Rousseau's theory of an "energetic" mode of identification that exceeds imagination and representation; in Hume's description of affects that precede, and produce, a sense of self; in Yearsley's attempt to produce "powerful compassion" by means of virtual images; in Wordsworth's emphasis on the productive powers of the social parasite; and in Shelley's suggestion that identification explodes (rather than founds) personal identity. These are all privileged moments in my analysis, but not because I believe that they reveal the truth of sympathy or identification. Rather, they are important because they try to describe alternatives to the premise that ordered behavior (whether in the subject or the socius) always emerges from systems of unity, unification, and representation. I seek instead to understand how forms of ordered collective behavior could emerge from what Hobbes called "irregular systems": that is, systems that have no organizing center (Hobbes 1966, vol. 3: 210–11,

222). If affect exceeds the limitations of systems, it does so not because it "returns" to some sort of uncoded feeling or emotion, but rather because it signifies a speculative experience of temporality that is more complex than the temporalities of current systems allow. Affect should not be understood as feeling "before" its inscription in social systems, but rather as an experience of the virtual dimension of social systems. Systems may create their own time by linking communications with one another, but this takes the form of linear time (one communication after another). Affect, by contrast, is an experience of temporal simultaneity: the past, present, and future are suddenly experienced as coexisting. As Brian Massumi writes, affect is thus a "lived paradox where what are normally opposites exist, coalesce, and connect; where what cannot be experienced cannot but be felt" (Massumi 2002: 30). This experience of temporal simultaneity, while difficult if not impossible to communicate within a system, enables new systems to emerge precisely because it situates the present as the source of the future (rather than positioning the present as simply the link between the past and the future).

The speculative temporality of affect is thus fundamentally opposed to the speculative temporality of finance. While—as Pocock has noted—state finance may require imaginative projection into the future, it nevertheless demands that this projection be grounded in what is understood to be an irrevocable past (namely, the past promise by legislators to repay financiers). Within systems of state finance, the present is not understood primarily as the active *origin* of the future, but rather as the medium by which the past continues to exert its weight on the future. Affect, by contrast, is an experience of a mode of temporality that is much more fundamental than that of financial speculation. Where finance projects itself into the future by tying itself to the past, affect follows the path of what Shelley called "philosophic necessity" (*SP* 157), which makes the present— rather than the past—the "active source of future events."

III. OVERVIEW OF THE BOOK

The five substantive chapters that follow this introduction are ordered chronologically, each focusing on a different crisis of state finance, and each emphasizing a different aspect of the relationship among state finance, theories of intersubjectivity, and literary form. Chapter 1 begins with that event and period in which both Cobbett and Shelley located the origin of modern British finance, the financial revolution of the late seventeenth and early eighteenth centuries. Focusing on the key crisis of this period—the South Sea Company stock panic of 1720–21—I argue that the concept of the imagination was fundamentally transformed within the periodical and pamphlet literature that sought to describe, as well as control, this stock "bubble." While previous commentators have noted the importance of the term "imagination" to early eighteenth-century financial discourse, my claim focuses instead on morphology, as I argue that the very notion of a collective imagination—that is, an understanding of society as a collection of subjects bound to one another in "imagined communities" (to appropriate Benedict Anderson's felicitous phrase)—first emerged in financial discourse, as commentators sought in imagination a term that would enable them to describe finance *as* a system.[20] In the latter half of this first chapter, I argue that such an understanding of the imagination was the foundation of subsequent theories of sympathy developed in Scottish moral philosophy, a claim that I support with a discussion of David Hume's theory of sympathy in the *Treatise of Human Nature*, as I read his discussion of intersubjectivity in that text as an attempt to extend this "collective" understanding of imagination beyond financial discourse and into a more general theory of the formation of social systems.

The second chapter focuses on the relationship between state finance and the efforts of sentimental moral philosophers Jean-Jacques Rousseau and Adam Smith to understand the tendency of the collective imagination to produce rivalry and violence. Eighteenth- and nineteenth-century critics of national debts never tired of reminding their readers that modern British and French state finance first emerged as a means to fund war. For some commentators, this suggested that the "imaginary" social relationships that enabled modern finance were intrinsically linked to domestic and international violence. The connection between war and state finance was stressed again in both the period leading up to, and during, the Seven Years' War (1756–63), and this chapter explores Rousseau's and Smith's different responses to this perceived link between government speculation and violence. While Smith and Rousseau agreed that the speculative capacities of the imagination enabled *all* social relations, Smith sought to contain the projective capacities of this faculty by tying sympathy to the past and the dead, while Rousseau sought to escape social systems entirely by theorizing a nonsubjective, nonrepresentational mode of identification. As I note in the coda to this chapter, recent psychoanalytically inflected attempts to describe the violence of nationalism in terms of "imaginary" and "symbolic" identification find themselves running up against the same aporiae that troubled Rousseau's and Smith's accounts of imagined communities.

Where chapter 2 considered Smith's and Rousseau's efforts to *limit* the violent potential of imagined communities by containing their speculative tendencies, chapter 3 discusses authors who considered precisely the opposite problem—namely, how sympathy and imagined community could be sparked in cases where it appeared to be lacking—by focusing on the efforts of poets in the 1770s and 1780s to create an aesthetically coherent system of antislavery poetry. While the "system of slavery" was of course not equivalent to the system of state finance, proslavery advocates stressed the linkage between the two systems, suggesting, for example, that "abolition [of the slave trade] would be the ruin of the trade of the country," for without commerce in slaves, it "would be impossible to collect money to diminish the national debt" (Newnham, cited in Clarkson 1808, vol. 2: 99). Opponents of slavery sought to counter these claims by imagining other systems of commerce and social relations, and this chapter examines the legacy of Smith's and Hume's differing understandings of sympathy in the antislavery verse of a number of poets. I argue that while poets such as Hannah More, William Cowper, and Samuel Jackson Pratt developed a representational theory of sympathy that sought to generate sympathy by representing the real sufferings of slaves, an author such as Ann Yearsley developed an approach that borrowed more from Hume, wagering that sympathy was most effectively activated through readers' imaginative production of "virtual" images located in the future. These two strategies implied two different models of political readership: where the representational strategy implied a subject whose sympathy (and by extension, political engagements) was grounded in affects that originated outside itself in the sufferings of others, Yearsley presumed a self-legislating subject, for whom political engagement emerged on the basis of speculative and self-validating imaginative activity.

While the French Revolution dampened enthusiasm for the antislavery cause for much of the next decade, interest in speculative poetic images resurfaced a few years later in the canonically Romantic poetry of William Wordsworth, as the young poet sought to articulate a theory and practice of "images of tranquility" in a series of poems composed in 1797–98. I follow previous criticism in emphasizing the dominance of financial terminology and metaphors in Wordsworth's verse from this period, but rather than focusing on the poet's struggles with debt and questions of vocation and profession, I instead emphasize the spectacular crisis of public credit and state finance that occurred just as Wordsworth was writing poems such as *The Ruined Cottage*, "The Pedlar," "The Old Cumberland Beggar," and his contributions to *Lyrical Ballads*. In the early months of 1797—the same months in which Wordsworth's own financial problems became most pressing—a French invasion panic led to a run on British banks, which nearly depleted the specie holdings of the Bank of England. Parliament stabilized the situation through the Bank Restriction Act, which established paper money as the sole national currency, but the Act produced an angry debate—waged in Parliament, periodicals, and pamphlets—between Pitt's supporters and the opposition on the nature of money, state finance, and debt. I suggest that both Wordsworth and British legislators found themselves grappling with the same basic question: how could a system of wealth be grounded in potentially irremediable debt? Both Wordsworth and the British government also located a potential solution to their problems by valorizing what Michel Serres calls "parasitic" social relations: that is, human interactions "organized with one-way relations," in which only one party benefits (Serres 1982: 5). However, rather than reading Wordsworth's emphasis on speculative parasitism as a sign of his "bad faith," I suggest instead that his attempt to create a speculative "image of tranquillity" holds important resources for literary critics in their own efforts to parasite the past by drawing off from a system its virtual potentials.

The fifth chapter also considers the relationship between state finance, sympathy, and poetic images by exploring the extent to which Shelley's reflections on the national debt and paper money helped him to develop a poetics grounded in what we might call "speculative time consciousness." Focusing on prose texts such as "Essay on the Punishment of Death," *A Philosophical View of Reform*, and *A Defence of Poetry*, and late verse such as *The Mask of Anarchy* and the poems of the *Prometheus Unbound* volume, I argue that Shelley understood institutions of state finance as grounded in a "savage" mode of impoverished time consciousness that tended to confirm the causal power of the past in every economic transaction. In order to encourage in his readers the development of their capacity for a much more expansive and speculative mode of time consciousness, Shelley developed a series of "imageless images" designed to counter the belief that individuals were indebted to the past. These images, by facilitating what Shelley called "identification with the beautiful," were intended to allow the reader to *act* in the present on the basis of his or her access to an undetermined future.

I conclude with a brief discussion of the ways in which the Romantic approach to state finance that I outline in this book allows us to reconceptualize our own contemporary cultures of speculation, while at the same time expanding our understanding of Romantic era theories of intersubjectivity. Though the Romantic era has often been understood as the period in which the "self-authenticating" or "autonomous" subject came fully into its own, recent literary criticism has outlined the extent to which authors in the Romantic era also theorized *inter*-subjectivity by emphasizing forces such as sympathy, identification, and love that bound subjects to one another in local, national, and transnational imaginary communities (see e.g. Pinch 1996; Henderson 1996; Vermeule 2000). I follow the lead of these earlier critics by stressing the importance of theories of intersubjectivity for Romantic era authors, but my focus on state finance highlights the extent to which accounts of sympathy and identification were attempts to understand social relations *as* social systems that were dominated by the logic of recursivity and speculation. I am also hopeful that these chapters will allow us to distinguish the *variety* of Romantic era theories of sympathy and identification. Such a task is especially important in the case of concepts of identification, for though earlier critics have traced and historicized the fortunes of concepts of sympathy in the eighteenth and nineteenth centuries, the history of "identification" in this period has been curiously neglected. No doubt this can be attributed in large part to the fact that historical discussions of identification have focused almost exclusively on its elaboration within psychoanalytic theory (e.g., Meissner 1970 and 1971; Wollheim 1974; Florence 1978; Borch-Jacobsen 1988; Fuss 1995). Perhaps this disinterest can also be attributed in part to a sense, apparently shared by many literary critics and intellectual historians, that critics should use psychoanalytic conceptions of identification to decode the seemingly less precise attempts by eighteenth-century authors to understand intersubjectivity.[21] Yet such disinterest in the history of identification in the Romantic era is nevertheless surprising, for while eighteenth- and nineteenth-century theories of sympathy were in some sense simply repackagings of an old term, "identification"—in the psychological sense of "identifying oneself with"—was a brand new term, first coined in the mid-eighteenth century by Jean-Jacques Rousseau (Force 1997). I thus hope that my discussion of different Romantic era theories of identification—ranging from Rousseau's theory of "energetic identification," to Wordsworth's claim that poets identify while readers sympathize, to Shelley's understanding of identification as a mode of self-alienation—contributes to the historicization of this term.

1 Finance and the exchange of passions

The origins of the collective imagination

> [T]his surprising Fall of the Reputation of Stocks is not *by* Management, but for *want* of Management. Believe me, Sir, there are no French Agents or Popish Plots in the matter, but 'tis for want of Agents, and for want of *Plot*; these Men are confounded and amazed by the Surprise of their own Affairs. (*The London Journal*, September/ October 1, 1720)

"[I]t is by the imagination only," Adam Smith wrote in *The Theory of Moral Sentiments* (1759), that we ever have access to the emotions and affects of the other, for it is only by means of this faculty that "we place ourselves in his situation, we conceive ourselves enduring all the same torments, we enter as it were into his body, and become in some measure the same person with him" (*TMS* 1.i.1.2). Though couched in the idiom of mid-eighteenth-century Scottish sentimental moral philosophy, Smith's claim nevertheless has a recognizably modern flavor. We can discern in it the paradigm of more recent suggestions that, for example, nationalism operates by establishing an "imagined community" among members of a polity; that humanitarianism in the age of mass media depends upon the refinement of our abilities to bring home imaginatively the sufferings of others; and that gender identity depends on a series of imaginative acts, in which we continuously "identify" with valorized images of subjectivity while at the same time "disidentifying" with terrifying subjective possibilities.[1] Smith's understanding of the importance of the imagination in establishing social relations—an understanding that he shared with contemporaries such as David Hume and Jean-Jacques Rousseau—has to come to seem so obvious that it takes on the form of common sense itself. For how could I ever have access to the feelings of others—or, more generally, access to the other at all—if not through something like that process of imaginative, representational identification that Smith outlines?

Yet if such a claim about the imaginative foundations of society has come to seem obvious, it was, for all that, a decidedly emergent form of common sense when Smith first articulated his position. If Smith had proposed even a generation earlier that imagination and sympathy mediated most, if not all, social interactions, such a claim would have met with surprise and incredulity. Before the eighteenth century, concepts of the imagination were almost invariably used to explain quasi-corporeal processes internal to the individual, rather than interactions that occurred *between* subjects, and though seventeenth-century authors had sometimes cited this "faculty" to explain aberrant forms of sociality, such as religious enthusiasm, the imagination was understood as too unpredictable, too liable to usurp the role of reason, for it to serve as the necessary ground of all social relations. The claims made by Smith and his contemporaries thus represented a fundamentally new commonsense understanding of imagination, one that firmly linked its effects to the operation of even normal social relations.[2]

It is admittedly not entirely clear what significance we ought to attribute to this relatively rapid emergence, in the eighteenth century, of a new common sense concerning the imagination and its relationship to social relations. Perhaps its emergence in the eighteenth century was simply something of an historical anomaly—a vague, anachronistic intimation of a principle that would only later come to have real theoretical utility after being tempered and sharpened by Marxist and psychoanalytic theory? Or perhaps we should take a stronger approach, and understand these claims about the imagination as ideologically necessary; as intrinsic components of a capitalist system that was effecting fundamental social transformations—transformations of labor relationships, epistemological approaches to the world, and emotional relationships with others—in ways that would eventually propel a middle class to power? While the latter approach would of course also have to account for the ideological role of subsequent post-Marxist and psychoanalytic theories of imagination, it at any rate would have the virtue of explaining how and why Smith and his fellow sentimental moral philosophers were able to establish a new mode of common sense through their theories.

This chapter in fact seeks to chart a path between these two perspectives—the perspectives of anomaly and necessity, respectively—by approaching eighteenth-century claims about society and imagination in a way that accounts for both their anomalous and their systematic aspects. More precisely, I focus on the emergence of a kind of system that was able to transform conceptual anomalies into systemic necessities. And, as it turns out, it is precisely Smith's emphasis on the speculative nature of imagination—its capacity to project the self beyond its borders—that provides the clue that will allow us to understand the nature of this system. For if we look more closely at the real origins of the notion of a "collective imagination," we shall find that it first emerged in that most speculative of early eighteenth-century discussions: the discourse on state finance that helped to create early eighteenth-century French and British investing cultures. By attributing the rise and fall of public credit and the vagaries of commercial exchange to the imagination, early eighteenth-century authors shifted the term from its traditional role as an explanatory term for processes within an individual—that is, as a quasi-corporeal faculty that mediated between animal spirits and intellect—to a principle that explained affective relationships *between* individuals. It was this latter, protosociological sense of the term that served as the foundation for Hume's, Smith's, and Rousseau's subsequent theories of sympathy and identification. The moral philosophy of these authors responded to the systems of state finance developed in early eighteenth-century Britain and France both by appropriating the concept of the collective imagination from financial discourse, and by seeking to resolve the conflicts and factions purportedly engendered by state finance by creating a new system of discourse (sentimental moral philosophy) that treated actual financial phenomena as part of its environment, rather than as an element within its system.

This chapter has five parts. I begin by outlining the extent to which seventeenth-century discussions of the imagination relied upon a classical hierarchical schema of the faculties of the soul that discouraged interest in the intersubjective dimensions of the imagination. I then outline the socialization of the faculty of imagination in early eighteenth-century financial discourse. In the third part, I explain how such conceptual innovation was possible by focusing on the interplay between the primary genre (satire) and the primary media (print journalism and occasional pamphlets) within which these new concepts appeared, arguing that the distributed authorial nature of early eighteenth-century journalism and occasional pamphlets, in combination with the quick turnover and large volume of these media, established a context that encouraged conceptual "mutation." Moreover, insofar as these periodical communications were themselves central to the operation of state finance, there was also a selective pressure for concepts capable of explaining the rapid transfer of representations between individuals, and the traditional association of concepts of the imagination with processes of amplification and feedback provided precisely such a term. The fourth part focuses more narrowly on one of the earliest explicitly philosophical discussions of the collective imagination, David Hume's theory of sympathy, as developed in *A Treatise of Human Nature* (1739–40). While Hume's insistence on both faction and virtual property as the keys to the dynamics of the imagination emphasized the linkage of his theory of sympathy to early eighteenth century financial discourse, his *Treatise* was also intended to provide a philosophical system for understanding social systems: that is, it was intended to serve as an instance of a literary form that could both describe, as well as intervene in, the dynamics of all social systems. I conclude this chapter with a critical discussion of the extent to which our contemporary category of "ideology" allows us to understand the social and cultural functions of theories of sympathy and identification in the eighteenth century.

I. IMAGINATION, THE HIERARCHY OF FACULTIES, AND CLOSED SOCIAL SYSTEMS

Just as for classical and early modern philosophy, the imagination played an important role in seventeenth-century theological and philosophical discourse. In England, anatomists and physicians such as Robert Burton and Thomas Willis postulated about the anatomical location of the faculty of imagination; natural philosophers such as Francis Bacon and Thomas Hobbes speculated on the power of the imagination over matter (often in order to critique earlier—and what they saw as the more extravagant—claims made by alchemists such as Paracelsus); and theologians such as Henry More and Meric Casaubon theorized about the role of imagination in producing religious fanaticism. In France, René Descartes questioned whether imagination was necessary for thought, that defining attribute of the subject, and Descartes's pupil Nicholas Malebranche further pursued Bacon's earlier speculations about the power of imagination over matter and bodies.

Yet even as more and more seventeenth-century authors took interest in the powers of the imagination, the continued persistence of an Aristotelian paradigm for understanding the faculties of the soul meant that such discussion almost invariably focused on the role of imagination within the subject, rather than between subjects. Two basic principles governed the Aristotelian understanding of the imagination. First, the imagination held the middle place within a hierarchy of faculties that led upward from sensation to reason. Second, *all* thought required the help of imagination, for thinking itself required the support of images (*phantasmata*), and thus, the mediation of the imagination. When imagination kept its proper place in this hierarchy, it facilitated perception, thought, and movement by mediating between sensation and reason; when imagination usurped the governing role of reason, hallucinations and madness resulted. Seventeenth-century authors rarely questioned these principles, preferring instead to describe more specifically the anatomical specificities of the hierarchy of faculties.[3] In *The Anatomy of Melancholy* (1621–51), for example, Burton, localized the imagination within the "middle ventricle" of the "fore part" of the brain, where it received influxes of animal spirits (Burton 2001, vol. 1: 154), while Thomas Willis argued in *Two Discourses Concerning the Soul of Brutes* (1683) that the imagination was "planted in the middle part of the Brain," where it could "receiv[e] the Sensible Species [of external objects, which were at] first only impressed on the Organs of Sense, and from thence by a most quick Irradiation of the spirits delivered inwards" (Willis 1971: 38).[4] Burton explained that hallucinations resulted when imagination usurped the "governing" role of reason by "keeping the species of objects" and overly "amplifying them" (Burton 2001, vol. 1: 160, 253); individuals with particularly "powerful and strong" imaginations were at greatest risk of such internal revolt, the consequence of which might be a state of melancholia, or—a more positive possibility—a capacity for artistry (Burton 2001, vol. 1: 159).

The overwhelming emphasis of this neo-Aristotelian schema on the role of imagination in mediating between faculties within an individual discouraged interest in the ways in which this imagination might mediate *between* subjects. Seventeenth-century authors did not deny that imagination might under some circumstances link two separate individuals, but such instances were invariably presented as isolated and anomalous. The purported power of the mother's imagination to mark her unborn child is one particularly well-discussed example of such an exception. As Dennis Todd notes, "[b]ecause of its corporealizing power, the imagination was generally believed to have some degree of control over material things" (Todd 1995: 59), and while under normal circumstances, this capacity was restricted to the translation of reason's commands into bodily action, under extreme circumstances the imagination might also affect nearby bodies. The capacity of the imagination to control external matter explained how a fetus could be marked if the mother was exposed to mental shocks or inordinately desired some object: being surprised by a rabbit might produce a rabbit-shaped birthmark on the fetus, while craving strawberries could produce a strawberry-shaped birthmark. Bacon and Malebranche postulated that the power of the imagination over foreign bodies might even extend to small groups. In *The Advancement of Learning* (1605), for example, Bacon defined fascination as "the power and act of imagination, intensive upon other bodies than the body of the imaginant," and he was willing to grant that in some cases the imagination might facilitate a "contagion that passeth from body to body." However, he contended that adherents of "the school of Paracelsus, and the disciples of pretended Natural Magic" had greatly overestimated the capacities of such imaginative influence, and in any case, these were anomalous and unusual instances (Bacon 1825–34, vol. 2: 172).[5] In *The Search for Truth*, Malebranche outlined a slightly more extended field of action for the effect of one imagination on another, suggesting that both madmen and "great people" possessed strong imaginations that could exert influence over others (Malebranche 1997: 87–196). However, he too presented these instances as problematic exceptions to the normal workings of the imagination.

In England, religious theorists employed this same schema to explain the fervency—the "enthusiasm"—of Protestant dissenting groups. In the wake of the proliferation of Protestant groups such as the Diggers, Levellers, and Fifth Monarchy men, "enthusiasm" became an important element of "the Protestant attempt to subdue its [own] more extreme expressions" (Klein 1994: 160).[6] Lawrence Klein notes that where a century earlier religious opposition was represented as a matter of heresy, in the seventeenth century many authors "transferred religious arguments from issues of doctrine to estimations of social personality" (Klein 1994: 162), and the imagination played an important role in this psychosociological approach to the question of the origin of extreme Protestant dissent. In *Enthusiasmus Triumphatus* (1656, 1662), for example, Henry More argued that religious "*Enthusiasme* is nothing else but a misconceit of being *inspired*," a self-deception that he attributed to a "Temper" that "disposes a man to listen to the Magisterial Dictates of an over-bearing *Phansy*, more than to the calm and cautious insinuation of free *Reason*" (More 1966: 1). Yet if, from the side of the individual, enthusiasm was the result of "the enormous strength of *Imagination*" which allows the soul to "sin[k] into Phantasmes (More 1966: 1, 4), *groups* of enthusiasts could form if the self-deceived messiah and his followers all had the same "melancholic" temperament, which allowed their imaginations to become disordered in the same way (More 1966: 22). While this explanation begged the question of how exactly similarly tempered people affected one another, it nonetheless extended the power of imagination to groups, rather than focusing discussion on its power over isolated individuals. Moreover, as Meric Casaubon noted in *A Treatise Concerning Enthusiasm* (1655), in such cases the opposition between "real" and "imaginary" causes was of limited utility in explaining the mechanics of enthusiasm, for enthusiasm's origin in a disordered imagination (rather than authentic inspiration) did not make its effects any less real. The impression of being inspired, Casaubon argues, was a "real, though but imaginary, apprehension of it in the parties, upon some ground of nature; a reall [sic], not barely pretended, counterfeit, and simulatory, for politick ends" (Casaubon 1970: 4).

II. IMAGINATION, SOCIAL SYSTEMS, AND INTERSUBJECTIVITY IN EARLY EIGHTEENTH-CENTURY FINANCIAL DISCOURSE

While these seventeenth-century accounts of fetal development, fascination, madmen, and enthusiasm represent intriguing accounts of the power of one individual's imagination over others, their significance lies precisely in their exceptional character. For seventeenth-century theorists, the social systems enabled by the imagination were all small and "closed": the proto-social system of mother and fetus could not be expanded beyond these two individuals, and the social systems of madmen and enthusiasts were small and hermetic; one was either mad or not, an enthusiast or not, and "rational" claims from the environment of the sane or nonbelievers were held to have no meaning or force within these small groups. Normal social relations were mediated by reason, not by imagination, and the gulf between this perspective, on the one hand, and the notion of a "collective imagination" that bound *all* the members of entire polity to one another, on the other, was vast and unbridgeable. The concept of the collective imagination simply made no sense and had no theoretical utility if one sought to understand social relations primarily in terms of an individual's responses to the demands of God and reason.

In order for the concept of a collective imagination to become thinkable, social relations had to be conceived as a "system" that established its own, autonomous, principles of action, and these principles had to be understood as mediated by the imagination. Such an approach to social relations was certainly possible within philosophical discourse, and Thomas Hobbes's attempt to link the imaginative dynamics of the passions to his distinction between irregular and regular social systems represents the most well-known example of such an endeavor. "System" is arguably one of the central concepts of Hobbes's philosophy, discussed at length in *Leviathan* (in the chapter entitled "Of Systems Subject Political and Private"), but it is also a notion implicit throughout his philosophy. Within the terms of Hobbes's materialist philosophy, social systems were dominated by the dynamics of imaginative activity, for, as Hobbes argued in *Human Nature*, all "conception is imagination and proceedeth from *sense*" (Hobbes 1966, vol. 4: 61). In *Leviathan*, he tied each of the passions that motivates social actions to imaginative activity: "glory" is "the passion which proceedeth from the imagination or conception of our *own power*, above the power of him that contendeth with us"; pity results from "*imagination* or *fiction* of *future* calamity to *ourselves*, proceeding from the sense of *another* man's calamity," while its contrary, "*hardness of heart*," "proceed[s] either from *slowness* of imagination, or some extreme great *opinion* of their own *exemption* of the like calamity, or from hatred of all, or most men" (Hobbes 1966, vol. 3: 40, 44, 45). Thus, in contrast to earlier authors such Bacon and Malebranche, who positioned imagination as a tool that might, in some circumstances, be employed to manipulate others, Hobbes positioned imagination as the faculty that first made possible intersubjectivity by binding individuals to one another by means of affects such as glory and pride.

However, the traditional commitment of natural philosophy to a fully rational subject ensured a philosophy such as Hobbes's a less than welcoming reception.[7] Far more promising was a genre such as satire, which provided authors with opportunities to take the small closed systems of madmen and enthusiasts as a paradigm for social relations as a whole.[8] The Third Earl of Shaftesbury's gently satirical "Letter Concerning Enthusiasm" (1708) provides an example of this approach. Like his theological predecessors, Shaftesbury argued that enthusiasm was the result of an imagination that had become "inflamed," and that it was propagated among "a multitude seized with the same spirit" (Cooper 1999: 9, 10, 23).[9] Yet Shaftesbury contended that enthusiasm was not an anomaly, limited to a small number of groups and individuals, but was in fact inherent in most, if not all, social phenomena. Its ubiquity did not render it unproblematic, but it did mean that dangerous passions engendered by enthusiasm could be countered only by enthusiasms of good passions (Cooper 1999: 11). Such a perspective oriented attention away from physiological explanations of the imagination and toward an analysis of the social processes by means of which representations were circulated between people. The imagination, Shaftesbury suggested, should not be understood solely as a physiological faculty that participated in perception, but also as the point where collectively generated representations ("Opinion") take hold of the individual. In a passage in *Characteristics of Men, Manners, Opinions, Times* (1711), Shaftesbury compared the function of the imagination to a "mint," suggesting that in order to combat bad enthusiasms, one must

> contend with Fancy and Opinion and search the mint and foundry of imagination. For here the appetites and desires are fabricated. Hence they derive their privilege and currency. If I can stop the mischief here and prevent false coinage, I am safe. (Cooper 1999: 143)

Since one cannot avoid the contagions of fancy and opinion that imagination engenders, the solution lies instead in a discipline of the imagination: one prevents "false coinage" by "minting"—or, more accurately, stamping—only those collectively generated representations that are deemed good.[10]

As the economic metaphor at the heart of Shaftesbury's description of the imagination hints, this satirical understanding of society as a system ruled by the dynamics of the imagination could be applied to the apparent paradox that seemed to many commentators to define the "Financial Revolution" that had occurred in late seventeenth- and early eighteenth-century England/Britain. As I noted in the introduction to this book, the financial revolution depended upon three developments that collectively allowed state finance to become a system of economic "communication," in Luhmann's sense of the term (that is, a system that enabled loans to circulate between investors). First, the government had to be willing to earmark future taxes to pay the interest (and eventually principal) on loans made to the state by private individuals; without such security, private loans to the state were extremely risky for investors, since both English and French monarchs had proven themselves willing to break otherwise unsecured promises about interest rates on loans in the past. Second, the receipts for these loans had to become negotiable in both the domestic and foreign markets: that is, investors had to be able to sell these loans to third parties in exchange for immediate cash (Neal 1990a: 5–7; Dickson 1967: 50). Finally, the government had to support a series of different investment mechanisms, which would allow investors to choose between investment options. When England went to war with France in 1689, all three of these developments coincided. Though the English government initially attempted to finance the costs of its conflict with France by means of short-term loans, legislators quickly realized that a protracted engagement would make this avenue economically unviable, and in 1692 the House of

Commons requested "Proposals for raising a Sum of Money towards the carrying on the War against France upon a Fund of perpetual Interest." The result was a number of suggestions, including several plans that were adopted, such as the proposal for a Bank of England (and the corresponding national debt), a "Million Dollar Bank," and state lotteries (Dickson 1967: 50). While each of these institutions arguably constituted its own subsystem of "the new economy"—lottery tickets, for example, were negotiated and redeemed in a different manner than annuities—it was precisely their autonomy from one another that enabled them to constitute collectively a system by means of which private loans to the state began to circulate in a public arena (Dickson 1967: 76–79).[11] Yet this financial revolution thus presented early eighteenth-century commentators with a seeming paradox, for state finance apparently produced systemic unity precisely through differentiation; its emergence as a system, that is, depended upon the creation of multiple subsystems.

Late seventeenth- and early eighteenth-century commentators turned to concepts of the imagination in order to understand this paradoxical link between systemic unity and differentiation. The use of the term "imagination" to describe system dynamics was especially evident in debates about "public credit," that broad term employed to denote both various paper monetary instruments, including bills of exchange, banknotes, and stock certificates, as well as the "Publick Faith" that supported these instruments. Though many of these institutions were intended to be, and were explicitly understood as, nation-building institutions, designed to bind investors both financially and emotionally to the post-Restoration government, the rise and fall of stock prices—trajectories that were easily monitored through publications such as John Freke's *Price of All Stocks* and John Castaing, Jr.'s *Course of the Exchange*, as well as the stock listings included in most early eighteenth-century newspapers—highlighted the extent to which these paper instruments were part of a system that operated beyond state control, responsive only to collective "Opinion" or "Fancy." Journalists such as Daniel Defoe used the term "imagination" to stress the autonomy of the new system of public credit. In the late 1690s, Charles Davenant had provided the schema for this argument, asserting that the imaginary nature of credit placed it outside direct government control: "[o]f all beings that have existence only in y[e] minds of men, nothing is more ffantasticall, and Nice than Credit, Tis never to be forced, It hangs upon opinion, It depends upon our passions of hope and fear" (Davenant 1942: 75). A few years later, Defoe drew on this schema in his articles for *The Review*, noting in the June 14, 1709 issue that "Credit" was a "substantial Non-Entity," an "invisible Phantom" that could fall upon "a Man, or a Body of Men, or a Nation insensibly," but could not be reached by laws or Acts of Parliament (Defoe 1938, vol. 6, no. 31: 122). In the October 22, 1706 issue, Defoe had argued against some forms of credit, claiming that "[a]ll Credit built on the Foundation of Project…is a *Deceptio Visus* upon the Imagination, an *Ignis fatus* that draws People into Ditches and Dirt," and he recommended that investors move slowly (Defoe 1938, vol. 3, no. 126: 502–3). However, in the June 14, 1709 issue, he contended that the power of the imagination to bind together a polity was also the efficient cause of the nation's strengths, for it was by the imaginary bonds of Credit that "all our War and all our Trade is supported" (Defoe 1938, vol. 6, no. 31: 122). "Great is the Power of the Imagination!," Defoe wrote, echoing the same phrase used by Burton in the much earlier *Anatomy of Melancholy*, and he even mused satirically on the quasi-physiology of the collective imagination, describing its "infinite Branches, the secret Springs and Streams which maintain its Variety and Circulation, by which, as by Veins and Arteries, it conveys the quickning Spirits to all the remotest parts of that Politick Engine, the Constitution" (Defoe 1938, vol. 3, no. 126: 502–3; vol. 6, no. 32: 125). Yet where Burton focused on the role of imagination in the production of individual cases of melancholia, Defoe suggested that the puzzling phenomena associated with Credit could be understood only by recognizing the power of the imagination to regulate national collective behavior. Stock prices, he suggested, moved up and down within a system that seemed to respond only to itself, and thus could not be swayed by anything from its environment, such as political or moral considerations.

The social importance of understanding the dynamics of the system of public credit was emphasized by the collapse of the South Sea Company "bubble" in 1720. The South Sea Company had been founded in 1711 by the Harley ministry as part of a Tory attempt to reduce government debt, and interest in the Company's stock was fanned by long-standing perceptions of an "infinite" wealth to be found in South Sea trade, a perception encouraged by news of Woodes Rogers's extremely profitable 1711 trip to the coast of Mexico (Markley 1995: 152). Prices for South Sea stock remained relatively stable from the Company's inception until 1720, when the Company and the House of Commons agreed to issue more stock, again as a means of government debt reduction. Public interest in the stock was intense, and prices rose rapidly, eventually reaching a high point near the end of June 1720.[12] Investment was also encouraged by the apparently unlimited rise in the price of stock for the Compagnie des Indes (now often referred to as the Mississippi Company) in neighboring France. However, the South Sea Company bubble burst the next month, and many investors who had bought stock at inflated prices lost enormous sums of money, a problem that had been compounded by the willingness of the Company directors to extend credit for stock purchases.

Both the rapid increase of stock prices, and the subsequent crash, inspired an extensive periodical and pamphlet debate, in which concepts of the imagination loomed large. Some authors employed the now-traditional critique of imagination as the agent of unnatural trade. In a letter in the March 4, 1721 issue of the *Weekly Journal or Saturdays-Post*, for example, the author claimed that the English, in contrast to the French and Germans,

> are remarkable for a *solid Gravity*, which only *seems to think*, and yet *distinguishes nothing*; how could it else be that such Numbers of people should lay out *substantial Fortunes* for a Thing which has *no Being* but in *Imagination*?

However, the authors of the Whig *London Journal*, while equally convinced that the failures of the South Sea Company had to be explained in terms of the dynamics of the imagination, argued that it was not possible to distinguish imaginary from real forms of value. In the March 3,1720 issue, for example, "Cato" (Thomas Gordon) argued that phenomena such as the South Sea Bubble were a consequence of the fact that "we often take the Appearance of Things for Things themselves, and mistake our own Imagination for Realities, and our Delusions for Certainties and Truth." Yet, he continued, these imaginary causes led to real effects:

> Now, tho' all the Whimsies of this kind have no Foundation but in Opinion, yet they often produce as certain and regular events, as if the Causes were adequate in their own Nature to the Events. The Opinion of a Physician or a Medicine does often effect the Cure of a Patient, by giving to his Mind such Ease and Acquiescence as can alone produce health. The opinion of a General, or of a Cause, makes an Army fight with double Vigour....

Rather than simply despairing about the capacity of imagination to usurp its proper role (by turning Fancies and Opinion into realities), Gordon also sought to understand and explain the specific dynamics of the contagious flow of representations. Likening the role of the imagination in commerce to the interactions between doctors and patients and between generals and troops had the effect of normalizing, at least to a limited extent, a sociological understanding of the imagination.

The transition from a narrowly epistemological to a more broadly sociological version of the imagination is especially clear in the satirical text *Observations on the Spleen and Vapours*, by "Sir John Midriff, Kn[t] M.D.," published in the wake of the South Sea Bubble. Midriff described for his readers numerous patients who suffered from fits and delusions apparently caused by "the spleen" or "vapours." However, in every case, Midriff traced the origin of the symptoms back to his patients' obsession with their South Sea stock, and in nearly every case, suggested that their obsession with stock prices was both caused by, and had further troubled, the "disordered imagination" of each. Even the doctor himself was not immune from this collective hallucination, for Midriff explained that the obsessions of his patients "dwelt so on my own Imagination, that I began to think the Distemper infectious.... And just as I imagin'd, many of the Symptoms soon took hold of me" (Midriff 1721: 20). While the text was intended as a satire, Midriff provided an analysis that explained how representations could pass from one person to another: a representation first came to "dwell on" the imagination of an unaffected individual in a relatively innocuous way, but it then gave rise to a representation of imaginative infection ("I began to think the Distemper infectious"). In earlier seventeenth-century accounts, the imagination of one person affected another by a process of imprinting (for example, the mother imprinted a form onto the fetus), but in Midriff, this model of imprinting was replaced by a model of contagion. For Midriff, the imagination enabled an infectious flow of discrete representations within a linguistic (and presumably national) community, and there was no apparent limit to the field of its action (it was not limited to a subsection of people with similar temperaments, for example). By suggesting that the disordered imagination of each person was caused by the same thing—the rise and fall of South Sea stock prices—Midriff provided an explanation of the mechanism by which individual imaginations were bound to one another, thus forming a "collective imagination." Though Midriff's discussion of his patients' similarly disordered imaginations is reminiscent of More's earlier claims about small groups of enthusiasts, the concepts of imagination employed by these two authors were fundamentally different. More's claims about the "melancholic" temperament of enthusiasts were meant seriously and intended as relatively precise physiological descriptions. In Midriff's satirical text, by contrast, "the imagination" simply serves as a placeholder for those contagious affective dynamics able to link ever more people into larger and larger systems.

Earlier historical and literary work has tended to emphasize thematic continuities between older seventeenth-century understandings of the imagination and its employment in early eighteenth-century financial discourse, rather than focusing on the structural differences noted above. Pocock, for example, stressed that eighteenth-century commentators drew on the traditional understanding of the imagination as a faculty with "subversive, creative, and destructive power" (Pocock 1975: 456), while Nicholson and Ingrassia noted that discussions of the imagination in the context of the financial revolution drew on traditional associations of the faculty with "female inconstancy" (Nicholson 1994: 47; Ingrassia 1998: 7). These are entirely valid observations that no doubt capture the psychological motivations of early eighteenth-century commentators as they drew upon concepts of the imagination in order to explain what seemed to be an increasingly dynamic world. Yet if left unqualified, such observations obscure the striking divergence between seventeenth-century philosophical and theological discussions of the imagination and the employment of this term in eighteenth-century financial discourse. Even at their most intersubjective—as in, for example, theological commentary on enthusiasm—seventeenth-century theories of the imagination still severely limited the field of action for this faculty, describing its effects as confined to small sects of fanatics who shared similar "temperaments." Early eighteenth-century commentators, by contrast, suggested that the powers of the imagination embraced all of human society. Though such claims often were intended to be taken satirically, the premise of much of Augustan satire—that it could effect a disciplining of imaginatively generated fears and hopes—itself reinforced the suggestion that social relations really were controlled by the dynamics of the imagination.[13]

III. PERIODICALS, COMMUNICATION, AND CONCEPTUAL MUTATION

The distinction between seventeenth-century philosophical discussions of the imagination and the collective imagination that emerged in financial discourse is a qualitative, not a quantitative, difference: one cannot arrive at the conception of a collective imagination by imagining more and more members as belonging to "enthusiastic" groups; rather, one must fundamentally reconceive the very nature of social relations. Yet given the long tenure of the Aristotelian schema for understanding the role and powers of the imagination, how can we account for the fact that conceptions of this faculty changed so quickly in the early eighteenth century—and in financial discourse, of all places? The fact that the financial revolution spurred (and depended upon) the creation of numerous linked social systems was a necessary—but not a sufficient—condition for the transformation of concepts of the imagination; in addition, this sort of change depended upon a "medium" capable of encouraging conceptual transformations.

Journalism and occasional literature—the venues within which state finance was most frequently discussed—provided precisely such a medium within which concepts of the imagination could be transformed quickly. The capacity of early eighteenth-century journalism to promote such conceptual transformation was a function of the twofold way in which it provided readers with information. In an obvious way, pamphlets and newspapers provided information—in the sense of discrete facts—about particular aspects of state finance: for example, narrative accounts of relevant legislative measures; prices and availability of particular securities, stocks, and lottery tickets; payment schedules for stocks and securities; and so on. However, journalism also established the informational *context* for state finance: that is, it established the field of possibilities from which individuals made choices.[14] Early eighteenth-century newspapers and pamphlets provided such a context in part because they served as the primary medium within which opinions about state finance had to be communicated. As Terry Mulcaire has noted, journalistic analyses of the effects and causes of the new financial order were not intended to be neutral reflections on institutions understood to lie beyond the discursive reach of newspapers or the pamphlets and books they advertised; rather, these writings were the means by which authors sought to influence those same institutions (Mulcaire 1999). Equally important, early eighteenth-century newspapers and pamphlets provided an informational context by establishing the temporality within which financial opinions had to be formed and decisions made. As Niklas Luhmann notes, one of the key characteristics of contemporary "mass media" is its acceleration of communication:

> Mass communication is not communication in the usual sense, intended to change opinions or influence action. It may do this or it may not, but its real impact on society involves time: as soon as information or opinions are published, common knowledge has to be taken for granted, and actions have to be based on imputed knowledge, whether opinions are really changed or not. (Luhmann 1982: 248)

Despite the differences between eighteenth-century journalism and contemporary mass media, Luhmann's emphasis on the temporal dimension of communication helps us to understand the importance of the acceleration of printed communications. As Jeremy Black notes, early eighteenth-century journalism offered "a predictable sequence of communication for which the only real counterpart was the weekly sermon" (Black 2001: 9), and the wealth of information and opinions about finance that appeared weekly, semiweekly or even daily in these early eighteenth-century newspapers and occasional pamphlets became part of the "common knowledge [that] ha[d] to be taken for granted" by all investors. The publication of stock and security prices on a weekly or daily basis also mediated between the "long" temporality of state finance instruments such as 99- year annuities and the more experiential temporalities of daily life, making it possible for long-term debt instruments to take on pressing urgency in the present as the price of exchange of these instruments fluctuated.

The informational context established by early eighteenth-century newspapers and pamphlets—a context characterized by an accelerated cycle of communications—provided an environment that favored conceptual mutation. The capacity of periodical literature to serve as an environment for conceptual mutation was in part a function of the dispersed and heterogeneous nature of its authorship; rather than embodying the voice of a single author, early eighteenth-century journalism often depended for its content upon editors and readers responding to one another (Black 2001: 11). The daily or weekly publication cycle of newspapers, combined with the fact that editors needed to fill four pages in each issue with communications that would appear new to readers, meant that numerous explanations for financial phenomena could appear in very quick order, without any felt need for coordinating such opinions into logical consistency. At the same time, as I noted above, these voluminous communications about finance were intended not only to locate for readers important facts about state finance, but also to produce consequences: that is, periodical authors represented "facts" about state finance in order to *produce* a desired future for Britain. Such a context demanded nearly constant innovation, as authors responded to changes in stock prices and dynamics, and the speedy publication cycle meant that early eighteenth-century periodical literature allowed for far more rapid mutations of concepts of imagination than was possible in, say, philosophical discourse, which relied on the much lengthier and less frequently published form of the monograph.

If the informational context of early eighteenth-century periodical literature explains how concepts of the imagination could quickly mutate, it also explains why discussions of finance would "select for" claims about the imaginative origins of both investing behavior and social systems. The imagination was by no means the only concept with which commentators sought to explain the dynamics of finance, for the rise and fall of stock prices was also attributed to "plots," supernatural influence, and the inevitable cyclicity of history. Yet concepts of imagination had an especial affinity for finance. Early eighteenth-century finance depended upon print journalism for its very operation, with the result, as both Nicholson and Mulcaire have stressed, that every journalistic communication "about" finance was at the same time a communication that itself altered the dynamics of finance. The traditional associations of the imagination with terms such as "amplification," "inflammation," and "contagion"—that is, with process that we would now describe as instances of self-reflexivity and feedback—meant that concepts of the imagination were especially well-suited both to explain, as well as to perpetuate, the self-reflexivity intrinsic to the dynamics of finance. From this perspective, the specific aspects of each theory of the imagination that appeared in early eighteenth-century periodicals were less important than the fact of their regular recurrence, for such a recurrence promoted the belief that one explained social dynamics by means of the imagination. If, as Benedict Anderson has noted, journalism enables "imagined communities," in the case of the early eighteenth century, periodicals performed this function not simply because they allowed readers to imagine other citizens performing the same "ceremony" of newspaper reading (Anderson 1991: 35), but also—and arguably, more fundamentally—because such periodical literature served as a medium in which a conscious, theoretical understanding of society *as* an imagined community emerged.

By the collapse of the South Sea Bubble in 1720, then, "the imagination" had undergone a significant discursive transformation in both Britain and France. Early eighteenth-century economic commentators no doubt initially drew on a traditional, epistemological understanding of the imagination in order to stress the "inversions" and "enthusiasms" of the new financial order. However, by linking these purported inversions to state finance, the intersubjective possibilities of imagining became prominent. Commentators repeatedly stressed that understanding the operations of the new economy was equivalent to understanding the laws and principles that governed "opinion" and "belief," which was itself equivalent to understanding the laws and principles of imagination. As a result, when authors such as Davenant, Defoe, Gordon, and Midriff explained the nationalist sociology of finance as an effect of imagination, they were not so much applying an old understanding of this term to new social developments, but in fact creating a new theory, reconfiguring imagination as the agency that enabled the system of finance (and perhaps even trade) through its ability to communicate joy and fear, violence and peace through a national "body." This new understanding of the imagination did not displace the traditional epistemological and hierarchical understanding of this faculty—these latter continued to play important roles throughout the eighteenth century, especially in discussions of aesthetics—but in its passage through early eighteenth-century financial discourse, the imagination had acquired an intersubjective dimension. The imagination, in short, had entered early eighteenth-century economic discourse as an epistemological faculty and had been transformed into a protosociological principle of explanation.

Recognizing the emergent nature of this understanding of the imagination as sociological mechanism also expands our sense of the cultural functions that claims about the imagination performed for early eighteenth-century subjects. Historians and literary critics such as Pocock, Ingrassia, Thompson, and Sherman have highlighted one mode of cultural work, arguing that the imagination functioned as a rhetorical figure that allowed early eighteenth-century authors to displace anxiety. Pocock, for example, contends that the figure of the imagination allowed authors such as Defoe to register their uneasiness with capitalism, that apparently irrational "new force in human affairs" that created "new modes of war and prosperity" (Pocock 1975: 454), while literary critics such as Ingrassia and Sherman have argued that the gendering of imagination (through the figure of "Lady Credit," for example) was a means by which commentators consolidated insecurities about the new economy with more traditional suspicions about the place of women and sexuality in political and economic culture. Terry Mulcaire has outlined an alternative approach to the question of cultural work, suggesting that we read early eighteenth-century discussions of the dynamics of the imagination "not only as a cause of ideological anxiety but also as a crucial political and economic resource for an emerging liberal market economy" (Mulcaire 1999: 1030). Mulcaire claims that for post-Restoration readers, a figure such as Lady Credit not only expressed fears about living in a world devoid of "Intrinsick Value," but also was cited by Whig authors in order to encourage the *desire* upon which public credit depended. "To imagine the destruction of Credit," Mulcaire writes,

> is to make the threat of it into a new source for the multifarious pleasures of the polite imagination, and to stimulate and reaffirm the polite imagination in this way is to come to the support of the imaginary regime of Credit. (Mulcaire 1999: 1040)

Mulcaire's invocation of "the polite imagination" is problematic, for it seems to rely on the same theory of the collective imagination that I have described above, but we can redescribe his point by suggesting that a figure such as Lady Credit facilitated the self-communication of the system of state finance by encouraging investors to monitor and regulate their affective states.

Theories of the collective imagination functioned in a very similar manner in at least two respects. First, they managed a potential contradiction between the "theory" of state finance, on the one hand, and its reality, on the other. Whether or not they were in favor of national debts, state-chartered joint-stock companies, and government lotteries, most late seventeenth- and early eighteenth-century commentators agreed that these institutions of investment bound citizens to the state by tying an individual's fortunes to the political stability of the governing regime. Yet this nationalist understanding of state finance was troubled by the fact that foreign investors also invested in "national" companies, and it was vexed as well by the obvious linkage between the stock prices of the British South Sea and the French Mississippi Companies. In this context—even if arguably against the reality of investment patterns—theories of a *national* collective imagination helped to strengthen the notion that state finance and state stability were linked, for such a theory ensured that even a financial "crisis" in fact bound citizens to one another in the realm of imagination (even as such binding produced "factions" at the level of political and economic interests). The theory of a national collective imagination should not be understood precisely as an example of "false consciousness," but rather as an historically contingent way of marking the fact that French and British systems' state finance were separate, but at the same time structurally coupled.

In addition, the collective imagination served as a theoretical principle (rather than figure) that encouraged early eighteenth-century readers to develop at least two regimens, or practices, of the self. On the one hand, by establishing the constant possibility of imaginative "infection" from the *socius*, it encouraged regimens of individual prophylaxis (for example, Shaftesbury's commandment that individuals "search the mint and foundry of imagination" in order to "prevent false coinage"). Yet these same theories of the collective imagination made it clear that there could be no complete prophylaxis; or more precisely, truly effective prophylaxis depended upon a more refined ability to submit only to "good" contagions. Moreover, Gordon's and Midriff's analogies between the role of the imagination in public credit and the effects of the physician on a patient's health made it clear that there could be no formula that would provide clear guidance for making such distinctions; each individual would have to decided on a case by case basis. As a result, theories of the collective imagination encouraged individuals to refine their capacity to be affected (i.e., their "sensibility"). Theories of the collective imagination served as a focal point for orienting these regimens, enabling each reader to postulate a malleable point of affective connection between him- or herself and the national imagination.

IV. IMAGINATION AFTER THE SOUTH SEA COMPANY: DISCIPLINARITY, HUME, AND SYMPATHY

The South Sea Company Bubble brought to the fore a paradox that had vexed commentators on state finance during the first two decades of the eighteenth century. On the one hand, the institutions of state finance seemed to unify society both by linking its members through the psychology of investment and by coupling autonomous social systems to one another. Yet at the same time, the institutions of state finance seemed to fracture society by establishing a zero-sum logic in which the conflicts between "factions"—Whigs vs. Tories; Country vs. City; stock-jobbers vs. merchants and the landed aristocracy—became increasingly entrenched, bitter, and potentially violent. Moreover, precisely *because* state finance coupled together different social systems, the faction and violence it encouraged could be propagated throughout the entire social fabric. State finance, in other words, unified by differentiating, and the "unity" that was thereby created was not necessarily pacific in nature. While this paradox might be addressed in token fashion—as in, for example, the 1720 Act that sought to discourage future speculative bubbles by prohibiting the formation of private joint-stock companies (Ashton 1959: 121)—such "solutions" seemed to have little impact on the fundamental logic of differentiation upon which the system of state finance depended.

In the two decades leading up to the Bubble, concepts of the imagination played an important role in the efforts of commentators to understand and control this paradox, but in the wake of the Bubble's collapse, discourse about the relationship between finance and social systems itself became more differentiated. In the first few decades after the Bubble, three different discursive approaches to the question of faction emerged, discourses that we can abbreviate as "political economy," "conservative political philosophy," and "sentimental moral philosophy." This discursive differentiation was a consequence of what Clifford Siskin has described as the larger process of eighteenth-century "disciplinarity," in which autonomous discursive systems, or "disciplines," were established by means of distinction from other discursive systems, a process that Siskin describes as "proliferation through limitation" (Siskin 1998a: 48; see also Luhmann 1982, 1999; Poovey 1998: 144–263). While all three of these approaches were responses to the question of faction, each developed a different schema to address the perceived fracture of society into autonomous social systems, and concepts of the imagination continued to play an important role in the explanation of the dynamics of systems only within one of these discourses, that of sentimental moral philosophy.

The discourse of political economy that emerged in the mid-eighteenth century in both Britain and France was distinguished from seventeenth- and early eighteenth-century writing about commerce, wealth, and value both in terms of institutional structure and theoretical approach. Seventeenth-century authors wrote frequently on economic topics, and as I noted above, from the 1690s on, scores if not hundreds of authors debated the causes of commercial and financial behavior in books, pamphlets, and newspapers.[15] Yet rather than constituting a continuing *system* of communication about "economics," these earlier economic writings on topics such as wealth, commerce, taxation, and public credit were almost invariably oriented toward topical events and legislation. As Margaret Schabas notes, the system of communication that came to be called "political economy...did not form a domain in its own right until the mid-1750s," for it was not until that period that institutional mechanisms—such as "chairs and societies in political economy (notably in Sweden and Italy)" and "the establishment of periodicals on economics (especially in France)" (Schabas 2005: 10–11)—emerged that made possible a persisting system of communication about economic matters. Equally significant, political economists constituted their subject of communication precisely by excluding most of the moral or psychological considerations that had concerned their predecessors, developing abstractions, such as "the market" or "the economy," that enabled analyses focused more exclusively on flows of money and goods (Poovey 1998: 217).[16] James Thompson describes the development of this more "objective" approach to the causes and transformations of wealth by suggesting that, by the 1750s, "the language of monetary theory" had been transformed into a discourse "less subjective, less focused on the trust of the individual subject," and as a result, the production of wealth could be treated "more as an objective system separate and apart from human actors" (Thompson 1996: 83). Political economy, in other words, was able to envision the production of wealth as a system—and it was able to generate a system of communication about this system—by excluding the imagination from its considerations.[17] Rather than understanding imagination as the medium of the system of wealth, the discourse of political economy imagined money as this ground of possibility.[18]

A second mode of response to the systemic crises of early eighteenth-century state finance emerged in the work of "conservative" Tory commentators, who parsed these phenomena through the distinction power/nonpower. Critics such as Jonathan Swift and Henry St. John, Lord Bolingbroke, unconvinced that the imagination would ever give up the secrets of its operation, turned their attention instead to what they understood as the *political* causes of its unsettling, arguing that the Bubble (and the new financial order more generally) was the consequence of "plots," "conspiracies," and "factions."[19] Swift and Bolingbroke represented the financial revolution as a system designed to take money from the landed class and give it to a "monied interest," in part because it seduced the nobility into making foolish investments—in, for example, South Sea Company stock—but more fundamentally because it encouraged war with Spain and France. From the perspective of these conservative critics, Britain's wars were "paid for by the gentry's land taxes," while at the same time monied investors "collected yearly interest from the government and paid no taxes" (Kramnick 1968: 59; see also Dickson 1967: 15–35). The result of this scheme, Swift argued, was that "*Power*, which, according to the old Maxim, was used to follow *Land*, is now gone over to *Money*" (Swift 1955–68, vol. 3: 5). The financial revolution, Swift wrote in "A Letter from Dr. Swift to Mr. Pope," was no less than a "scheme of politicks," which "se[t] up a money'd Interest in opposition to the landed"; he contended that were "the possessors of the soil" allowed to judge "what is for the advantage of the kingdom," then "Funds of Credit and the South-Sea Projects would neither have been felt nor heard of" (Swift 1955–68, vol. 9: 32). Bolingbroke's periodical *The Craftsman* refined this conservative political approach to the question of state finance throughout the 1720s, '30s, and '40s, describing the effects of state finance as the result of plots and conspiracies.[20] Within this system of conservative political thought, the key distinction was between those who held power and those who did not. As a result, these commentators had relatively little use for a term such as "imagination," since it made little difference whether it was "imagination," "avarice," "passion," or another psychological mechanism that caused people to misrecognize the interests of the nation; rather, what was important was to locate and describe the different plots and conspiracies that stood behind the "schemes of politicks."[21]

While both political economists and conservative political propagandists turned away from the imagination in their attempts to understand the structures of the new economic order in the several decades after the South Sea Bubble, a third strategy—sentimental moral philosophy—embraced the imagination, employing this term to understand society as the meta-system that made possible the more limited systems described by political economy and conservative political philosophy. An early version of this approach was evident in the work of Scottish "moral sense" philosopher and "Real Whig" Francis Hutcheson. Writing in the late 1720s, Hutcheson expressed concern about the effects of faction in contemporary British society, but suggested that social divisions resulted from the dynamics of "systems," rather than from intentional plots or malice.[22] Contending that "[m]ankind are...insensibly link'd together, and make one great *System*, by an invisible *Union*," Hutcheson sought to understand faction as a consequence of the formation of "limited systems" (a term he drew from Shaftesbury), rather than the "schemes" and "plots" of Swift and Bolingbroke (Hutcheson 1729: 178). Hutcheson saw the emergence of limited systems as reversible events, and he argued against those who would "artfully raise and foment this Party Spirit; or cantonize [the populace as a whole] into several Sects for the Defence of very trifling Causes" (Hutcheson 1729: 209). While it was not entirely clear, in Hutcheson's account, what served as the *medium* that enabled both the grand system of society and the limited systems of factions, the imagination was charged with this role in the subsequent moral philosophies of authors such as David Hume, Adam Smith, and Jean-Jacques Rousseau. The concept of imagination allowed authors such as Hume, Smith, and Rousseau to understand society *as a system*, while "sympathy" (for Hume and Smith) or "identification" (for Rousseau) named the dynamic principle that kept this system in communication with itself. Sentimental moral philosophy, in short, sought to establish itself as the system that dealt with system of society.

Sympathy, system, and faction in Hume's *Treatise*

The theory of sympathy that Hume developed in his first publication, *A Treatise of Human Nature* (1739–40), exemplifies the relationship among imagination, sympathy, and the conception of society as a system. Hume was born in 1711 into "a good [i.e., prosperous] Family," but as a younger son, his "patrimony...was of course very slender," as Hume later noted in his autobiographical sketch "My Own Life" (1776) (Hume 1932, vol. 1: 1). Hume's father urged him to take up law, while Hume himself hoped to find a profession that would allow him to focus on reading and writing (Hume 1932, vol. 1: 1), but instead, at the age of twenty-three, he traveled to Bristol to become a merchant. He began by working as a clerk for Michael Miller, a West Indies sugar merchant who, as Ernest Campbell Mossner notes, was almost surely invested in the slave trade (Mossner 1980: 88). Miller and Hume apparently found one another grating, and after being fired by Miller, Hume traveled to France, where he turned to writing, and began to compose *A Treatise of Human Nature: Being an Attempt to Introduce the Experimental Method of Reasoning into Moral Subjects*, the first two volumes of which were published in London in 1739 (*T*). As his subtitle suggests, Hume understood the *Treatise* as an intervention in moral philosophy, and one of the central terms of the moral theory developed in the book was "sympathy."

Hume's understanding of sympathy bore little resemblance to its predecessors. Renaissance authors generally understood sympathy as a "principle of mobility" that assimilated distant objects with one another (Foucault 1973: 23), while late seventeenth- and early eighteenth-century authors, though often using the term in a much more psychological sense, nevertheless employed sympathy to denote an automatic, quasi-physical response to the sight of another's suffering. In *An Inquiry Concerning Virtue and Merit*, for example, Shaftesbury claimed that all our pleasures resulted at least in part from sympathy, but he left unexplained the mechanism of this psychological act (Cooper 1999: 204). As G. R. Morrow observes, earlier thinkers such as Shaftesbury, Hutcheson, and Butler were interested in "the 'other-regarding' impulses—including, of course, pity, compassion, sympathy," but "these thinkers merely accepted these characteristics as given, as gifts of an all-wise Creator of the universe who designed man for society (or otherwise, as the case might be)" (Morrow 1923: 62). For Hume, by contrast, sympathy was an intrinsically imaginative act. His theory of sympathy was designed to account for the "communication" of sentiments that occurred in a variety of social situations, and he contended that "[w]hatever other passions we may be actuated by; pride, ambition, avarice, curiosity, revenge or lust; the soul or animating principle of them all is sympathy" (*T* 363).

Hume's analysis of sympathy was part of his more general attempt to understand how social stability occurs even in the absence of epistemological certainty. Book 1 of the *Treatise* ("Of the Understanding") focused on problems of epistemology, and it was in this section of the text that Hume developed the skeptical conclusions for which he has become best known, such as his critique of the notions of causality and personal identity. Taken on its own, book 1 presents a picture of an isolated, uncertain, and intrinsically fallible subject. By contrast, books 2 and 3 ("Of the Passions" and "Of Morals") focus on the psychology of social relationships. Yet as Nicholas Phillipson has noted, the seemingly distinct projects of book 1 and books 2 and 3 were intrinsically related, for the skeptical conclusions of book 1 also showed that

> we are competent and happy when we are able to take our beliefs for granted and we do this when experience has convinced us of their utility and we are able to believe them out of habit.... [However, since it] was hard to live by habit in an unstable social world...perfect stability and perfect understanding were possible only in the most civilized societies in which men and women shared common ideas of morality, justice and political allegiance, and obeyed them out of habit. (Phillipson 1989: 48)

Books 2 and 3 thus analyzed the general principles of social psychology that enabled social relationships and dynamics in a world in which epistemological certainty was impossible. Hume was interested in precisely those "forces" of opinion and belief that were central to early eighteenth-century financial discourse, but he sought to create a *science* of their dynamics.

Such a science seemed necessary in part because of the apparent consensus that the financial revolution had led to, or at least encouraged, "faction." As I noted above, this charge was the centerpiece of the conservative criticism of Swift and Bolingbroke, who argued that modern methods of state finance had created a state in which the rule of opinion and belief created ever more divisive factions. While laws against "stock-jobbing" were passed in 1734, a new round of government borrowing in 1739, undertaken in order to fund war with Spain over the trading rights of the South Sea Company, emphasized the possible return of speculative bubbles. Even commentators sympathetic to the government had to acknowledge this link between state finance and faction: Prime Minister Robert Walpole, for example, defended his policy of state finance in a pamphlet published in the mid-1730s, but acknowledged that "this Age" had produced a "predominant Spirit of Faction" (Walpole 1735: 3).[23] Hume's interest in factions was thus not unusual, and—as Walpole's pamphlet suggests—many Britons in the 1730s and '40s saw factions as the direct result of the system of state finance.[24] Yet where commentators such as Swift and Bolingbroke sought to explain faction as the result of plots and conspiracies, Hume's *Treatise* turned to concepts of the imagination and sympathy as explanatory principles.

For Hume, the imagination was the medium upon which all social systems depended, and sympathy was one of the forces that encouraged the formation of more limited systems. Hume analyzed the dynamics of sympathy in the context of a discussion about the objects and relationships that produce impressions of "pride" and "humility" in an individual. Pride and humility, Hume suggested, could be occasioned by almost anything that is "either part of ourselves, or something nearly related to us," and such objects range from immaterial qualities such as "the good or bad qualities of our actions and manners," to physical objects such as "the beauty and deformity of our person, houses, equipage, or furniture" (*T* 285). The faculty of the imagination allowed us to "relate" these objects to ourselves, for "these relations are nothing else but qualities, by which the imagination is convey'd from one idea to another" (*T* 305).[25] Of all external things that can produce feelings of pride, "property" held pride of place, for it is the relation, Hume contended, "which is esteem'd the closest, and which of all others produces most commonly the passion of pride" (*T* 309).

Hume stressed that pride and humility were emotions that occurred only within a field of intersubjectivity, and he positioned sympathy as the agent that established this field. While the "original" causes of pride and humility are those things or qualities that are part of, or that we relate to, ourselves—personal qualities, property, and so on—these original causes "have little influence, when not seconded by the opinions and sentiments of others" (*T* 316), and sympathy is the mechanism that facilitates this "seconding." Hume described sympathy as a three-step process. First, I observe another person's expression of admiration (or disgust) as it is directed toward me, and thus form an idea of his or her internal emotion. Second, because this individual is similar to me (we are both Britons, or both people), the imagination makes use of this quality of resemblance to associate his or her identity with my identity—and thus, by further association, I associate his or her idea of admiration (or disgust) with myself. Finally, this idea is converted into an "impression," with the result that I now feel the pride in (or disdain for) myself that others feel for me. Hume contended that the field opened up by sympathy is effectively equivalent to that of society itself: "the great uniformity we may observe in the humours and turn of thinking of those of the same nature" is a result of sympathy, and its strength is such that even "men of the greatest judgment and understanding...find it very difficult to follow their own reasoning or inclination, in opposition to that of their friends and daily companions" (*T* 316).

Hume's introduction of sympathy in the context of a discussion of pride and humility emphasized the extent to which he understood the sharing of affects as a force that produced social distinctions. Where earlier eighteenth-century accounts often positioned sympathy as a force that allowed individuals to (in Shaftesbury's words) "shar[e] contentment and delight with others" (Cooper 1999: 204), Hume emphasized its role in the production of social differences. (Pride, for example, depends upon a sense of being above others, while humility is the feeling of being below others.) If sympathy allowed individuals to "take on" the sentiments of others, and pushed them to "associate" with one another irrespective of "any advantages they can ever propose to reap from their union," Hume provided no guarantee that such intersubjective closeness would produce harmony. On the contrary, Hume suggested that sympathy tends to make us very partial, aligning ourselves with some people against others (*T* 318–24).[26] Sympathy was, in short, an entirely generic mechanism, serving as the "animating principle" of all sorts of emotions, including "pride, ambition, avarice, curiosity, revenge or lust" (*T* 363). Sympathy was as capable of fragmenting as of unifying social systems, and Hume's emphasis on the link between pride and the sharing of sentiment seemed to gesture toward Thomas Hobbes's analysis of the role of "Glory" in producing the "Warre of all against all."[27]

Faction, justice, and the gift of affect

Yet if Hume did not in fact incline toward a Hobbesian solution to the problems of social faction, it was because he located within sympathy itself a kind of affective property exchange—the "gift" of sentiment—that was capable of providing a foundation for social order. Amelie Rorty and Adela Pinch have noted that one of the peculiarities of Hume's account of pride and humility is that it positioned these passions as the *source* of precisely that sense of self upon which they might seem to depend. Hume argued that while the "object of pride and humility" may be the "self," this "view" of the self is itself "actuated" by the passions of pride and humility (*T* 286, 277); consequently, as Pinch notes, "though pride is the passion that seems most to originate *from* a sense of personal identity...in fact for Hume the reverse is true: the passion of pride produces a sense of self" (Pinch 1996: 22; see also Rorty 1982).[28] "I" can become proud of my physical and mental possessions only to the extent that my sense of an "I" is actuated by the esteem (and contempt) of others. Nor is the importance of sympathy as the medium of the sense of self limited to pride and humility, for sympathy enables a sense of subjectivity in the case of most, if not all, passions. As Duncan Forbes notes, for Hume, "sympathy is a phase of our self-consciousness"; thus, given

> what Hume has to say about sympathy...it is difficult to see how an individual can ever become conscious of himself at all apart from society—sympathy, as expounded in the *Treatise*, being not a feeling belonging to the individual but a means of communication between men.(Forbes 1975: 105–6)[29]

"After the fact," of course, we will infer that the "I" must have been there all along, but Hume's point is that passions that depend upon sympathy always anticipate subjectivity. Sympathy opens me to a "gift" of passion from the other, and it is only following this affective donation that a sense of the "I"—as well as a sense of "the other"—can emerge. For Hume, sympathy is not to be understood as a process in which a self greedily appropriates the sentiments of others, but rather as a process in which a sense of self is *produced* by the movement—the donation—of sentiment from one person to another.

In describing Hume's theory of sympathy as grounded in the logic of the gift, I do not intend the latter term as shorthand for selfless acts of generosity, but rather as a form of transfer that creates social *systems* through structures of indebtedness.[30] As Marcel Mauss famously noted in *The Gift*, within "archaic societies," gifts entailed three forms of obligation: an obligation to give, an obligation to receive, and an obligation to return gifts (Mauss 1990: 13–14, 39–43). These obligations created social systems, for to be given a gift was already to be bound within a social system that determined one's identity, whether or not the recipient wanted or accepted the gift (to refuse the gift was also to establish an identity within the social system).[31] While Hume's descriptions of the sympathetic communication of affect from one person to another described "gifts" that differed in type from the material objects that were the subject of Mauss's account, there are nevertheless useful parallels between their descriptions. For both Mauss and for Hume, the gift can be experienced as a sort of possession by the other. Mauss used the Maori term *hau* to describe the way in which recipients of a gift believed that the spirit of the giver inhered in the gift itself, and in similar fashion, Hume described sympathy as a sort of possession by the other, suggesting that "[a] good-natur'd man finds himself in an instant of the same humour with his company," and a "cheerful countenance infuses a sensible complacency and serenity into my mind" (*T* 317). As these quotations highlight, Hume believed that to be "possessed" by the affect of the other had the potential to create enduring social bonds, just as Mauss saw the circulation of gifts as the basis for social stability, though both also stressed that the creation of social systems by no means precluded the possibility of rivalry and violence.[32] For Hume, many of our relations to others and the world are guided by unconscious habits, but our sense of *identity*—that is, the awareness of self in relationship with others—is produced by the imaginary, or virtual, gift of passion from one individual to another—and "sympathy" names that openness to the affective donations of others that stands at the origin of subjectivity.

A new tye: Sympathy, justice, and the founding convention

Hume relied on the gift-structure of sympathy in order to describe how isolated social systems became bound to another in ever more expansive unities, eventuating at last in that meta-social system, "society." For Hume, the existence of social systems was by no means to be taken for granted, or as a given. While it was certainly true that social systems provided remedies for the many "inconveniences" of the individual—such systems overcame the physical weakness, inadequate labor power, and exposure to "fortune and accidents" of isolated individuals (*T* 485)—these benefits were beside the point if individuals had no way to perceive that social systems could be the solution to their inconveniences. Hume insisted that society depended upon the "artificial" institution of a system of justice, by which he meant that justice and society initially emerged from a "founding convention," and both continued to depend upon a system of education for their maintenance. Hume insisted that one had to account for, rather than simply assume, the emergence of social systems from a collection of individuals. In his narrative of the emergence of society, Hume outlined a series of "phase shifts"—from isolated individuals to the "unit" of the family; from a series of family units to small social systems; from small social systems to the system of society—and in each case, the mechanism that enabled these phase shifts was the gift-structure of sympathy.[33]

In Hume's account, the family functions as the first social system that bridges the state of natural inconvenience and artificial society. His account initially seems to privilege the role of the "instincts" in the formation of the family, for he contended that the "natural appetite betwixt the sexes... unites them together, and preserves their union, till a new tye takes place in their concern for their common offspring" (*T* 486). However, while prospective parents may be drawn toward one another by implanted instincts, the family itself emerges only when the birth of the child provides an occasion for sympathy to transform a series of three people into a social system. Thus, the child serves the parents as the constant source of "donated" affect that binds them to their progeny as well as to one another, while Hume describes the child itself as almost pure affective opening to the parents: children's minds are "tender," and they are thus especially susceptible to the sympathetically driven forces of custom and habit (*T* 486). As Gilles Deleuze notes, for Hume, the family, "is explained by the sexual instinct and by sympathy—sympathy between parents, and sympathy of parents for their offspring" (Deleuze 1991: 39).[34]

Sympathy again provides the mechanism for the phase shift from the family to a more expansive form of social system, that of (limited) "society."

Deleuze notes that for Hume the family is not itself enough to guarantee the passage to society, for while "families are social units...the characteristic of these units is that they are not added to one another" (Deleuze 1991: 39). However, the social system of the family allows each member to become "sensible of the advantages, which they may reap from society, [and it also]...fashions them by degrees for it, by rubbing off those rough corners and untoward affections, which prevent their coalition" (*T* 486). More specifically, the family allows individuals the time and security to perceive that external *property* functions as the primary source of social conflict; that is, each individual is able to discern that the "principal disturbance in society arises from [external] goods...from their looseness and easy transition from one person to another" (*T* 489).[35] The family also provides a stable site from which individuals can enter into new social systems capable of quelling disputes over goods. The awareness of property as a cause of social tension inspires each individual to enter into a "convention...to bestow stability on the possession of these external goods," as each realizes that the passion of self-interest "is better satisfy'd by its restraint, than by its liberty" (*T* 489, 492).

While Hume stressed the extent to which the founding convention of this new social system depends upon self-interest and "confin'd generosity," his more general account of intersubjective relations ensures that the founding convention also depends upon sympathy. Hume insists that every emotional relationship to others is founded on sympathy: each pleasure that we take in the company of others, as well as more negative relationships—pride, ambition, and so on—are all "animat[ed]" by sympathy (*T* 363). It is by sympathy, in short, that we recognize one another *as* human beings; that is, as sentient beings with whom we can adopt conventions. Moreover, within Hume's account, it seems likely that the founding convention itself required the gift-structure of sympathy for its propagation, as the first individual to conclude that society would be beneficial effectively "sparked" the agreements of others. For Hume, sympathy is so fundamental to human nature that "no sooner any person approaches me, than he diffuses on me all his opinions, and draws along my judgment in a greater or lesser degree" (*T* 592), and it was precisely such a collective enthusiasm that would enable the formation of society around conventions.

Sympathy again plays a crucial role in Hume's account of the movement from limited societies to the metasystem of "society" itself. Hume suggested that while justice—and thus, society—was initially bound in its field of application to small groups, it was capable of being extended by means of sympathy. Thus, we can perceive as unjust actions against a people "so distant from us, as no way to affect our interest,"

> because we consider it as prejudicial to human society, and pernicious to every person that approaches the person guilty of it. We partake of their uneasiness by *sympathy*; and as every thing, which gives uneasiness in

> human actions, upon the general survey, is call'd Vice, and whatever produces satisfaction, in the same manner, is denominated Virtue; this is the reason why the sense of moral good and evil follow upon justice and injustice.... *Thus self-interest is the original motive to the* establishment *of justice; but a* sympathy *with public interest is the source of the* moral approbation, *which attends that virtue.* (*T* 499–500)

From the family of three to the system of society that encompasses the world, the donation of affect that sympathy enables continually provides a template for cooperation and consensus, without which there cannot be even a community of two.

Speculation, time consciousness, and sympathy

Hume's account of the founding convention seemed to provide a solution to the problems of ungrounded opinion and divisive faction outlined by authors such as Swift and Bolingbroke. For these latter authors, British social stability was threatened by a financial system that replaced a ruling elite grounded in ownership of land with self-interested merchants and financiers whose claims to power were based on an "imaginary" wealth that would only appear in the future (if ever). For these conservative critics, the financial revolution had displaced grounded social ties with speculative relations, and the only solution—if one was still possible—was to return to the foundation of land and nobility. Hume's account of the founding convention, by contrast, suggested that *society was speculative from the start*, for property, including property in land, emerged only as the consequence of collective "investment" in a future system. The founding convention worked (and continues to work) because each individual anticipates the future actions of his fellows: "the actions of each of us...are perform'd upon the supposition, that something is to be perform'd on the other part" (*T* 490). No matter how much the other may "express" his "resolution" to perform actions, this is still a collective bet on the future, and without such speculation, society could never begin. The "general sense of common interest" that underwrites the founding social convention is not generated out of past experience, but arrives from the future, and thus society could emerge only because each individual was able to jump beyond the past (the realm of experience) and into an imagined future. Hume's account thus suggests that late seventeenth-century financial instruments such as annuities and joint-stock companies should not be understood as displacing the purportedly true foundation of wealth in hereditary land; rather, they simply harnessed the speculative social essence in new forms. Such a conclusion did not thereby provide blanket justification for every speculative financial endeavor and instrument, and Hume by no means denied that Opinion could become unhinged as a consequence of speculative "bubbles." However, his analyses were designed to calm the fears that disturbed opinion precisely by revealing the foundation of society as stable *because* it was speculative. The foundation of society, Hume argued, was immanent to the social sphere itself, and as such, society could remain stable even in the absence of "landed" wealth.[36]

While Hume's account of the speculative origins of society tended to justify the promissory structure of eighteenth-century financial and commercial institutions, it also pointed toward an alternative mode of what we might call "futural time consciousness" that exceeded these limited commercial applications of speculation. As Hume made clear, the founding convention was only *partially* based on "experience," for while individuals had past experience of the conflicts to which external goods could lead, they had no experience of the future state that was to result from the convention itself. The founding convention thus required a collective speculative openness—a leap—toward a future that could not be legitimated by anything in the past. Hume stressed that the relationship to the future involved in the founding convention differed significantly from the "time consciousness" of a promise, for promises always depended upon *prior* "human conventions" (*T* 490). Promises, in other words, depend upon a "closed" form of expectation, for they assume the *continuity* of social relations from the present to the future, and simply specify a determinate content, or action that is to occur in the future. While the promise is thus able to create a "community" from a collection of self-interested individuals—"when each individual perceives the same sense of interest in all his fellows, he immediately performs his part of any contract," and thus, "[a]ll of them, by concert, enter into a scheme of actions, calculated for common benefit" (*T* 522)—promises were by the same token incapable of inaugurating fundamentally *new* forms of sociality, such as that which emerged from the founding convention. The founding convention depended on what we might call "open," or formal, anticipation: that is, an anticipation of a *new form* of social relations, with the specific content of those relations left unspecified.[37] Hume's account of the origin of society thus outlined two very different kinds of speculative social relations: on the one hand, those which were based on open anticipation, such as the founding convention; on the other, those which were based on closed expectation (that is, all social relations based on promises). The "promissory" instruments of the financial revolution, such as annuities and joint-stock certificates, clearly depended upon the latter, closed mode of speculative expectation, and while Hume's account of the promise no doubt legitimated these financial institutions, it is vital to recognize that Hume's account also established the theoretical possibility of another, much more fundamental and explosive mode of social speculation.

The womb of time and Hume's investments in literary form

While the imagination served Hume (and later Rousseau and Smith) as the key term of a system of moral philosophy that claimed to be capable of understanding society as a system of systems, such a vision of totality could not be translated easily into *effects* on particular subsystems, as Hume quickly discovered. Lacking any educational institutional affiliation, Hume was not able to create a system of students who could take up the project of the *Treatise*, and for decades after its publication, the *Treatise* was not so much rejected, but—even worse—simply ignored. Hume later described the book as having fallen "*dead-born from the press*" (Hume 1932, vol. 1: 1.); comparing his *Treatise* to a speculative financial enterprise, he wryly suggested that "[f]ondness for what I imagin'd new Discoveries made me overlook all common rules of Prudence; & having enjoy'd the usual Satisfaction of Projectors, 'tis but just that I should meet with their Disappointments" (Hume 1954: 5).

As a result of the *Treatise*'s failure to find a wide readership in the 1740s, Hume abandoned the genre of philosophical treatise, at least temporarily, in favor of the essay. He immediately returned to the issue of faction and party in this latter genre, but separated his reflections on political and economic topics from his discussions of sympathy and the family. In *Essays, Moral and Political* (1741, 1742, 1748), *Political Discourses* (1752), and *Essays and Treatises on Several Subjects* (1753), Hume sought (in Nicholas Phillipson's words) to "exercise his metaphysical discoveries about the manner in which man tries to make sense of the world, to analyze the way in which modern Britons tried to make sense of the political life of Walpolian Britain" (Phillipson 1989: 2). However, the new form in which he developed his reflections—the essay—suggested that he no longer believed that the instabilities inherent in a polity grounded in imaginative and sympathetic social relations were best resolved through the genre of systematic philosophy. As Hume noted in the first edition of *Essays, Moral and Political*, he had originally intended to follow the weekly publication format inaugurated by Addison and Steele and more recently employed by Bolingbroke, "thereby comprehend[ing] the designs of both the SPECTATORS and CRAFTSMEN" (Hume 1741: iii). While Hume opted for a different format—an essay collection rather than a periodical—his explicit goal was still to "repress, as far as possible" the destructive tendencies of "PARTY-RAGE," which encouraged individuals to "hate one Half [of one's fellow citizens], under Pretext of loving the Whole" (Hume 1741: iii, v, vi). Hume was still committed to the position that government and property were founded on "opinion" and property, and repeated that claim in the fifth of his *Essays, Moral and Political* ("Of the First Principles of Government"). He also remained interested in the psychological dynamics of families, discussing that topic in the next essay ("Of Love and Marriage"). However, the explicit links between government and family established in the *Treatise* were no longer obvious in the essay form. By 1752, Hume further distinguished his discussions of property from his moral philosophy by isolating his reflections on the former topic in *Political Discourses*, which focused almost entirely on economic topics (the essays in that collection include, for example, "Of Commerce," "Of Money," "Of Interest," "Of Public Credit").

This difference between Hume's *Treatise* and his subsequent essay collections was a function of his transformed understanding of the *function* of philosophy in a polity dominated by commerce and state finance. Where the *Treatise* was premised on the belief that social stability resulted from a citizen's ability to understand the systems that motivated human behavior, the form and content of the *Essays* suggested that such deep reaching analyses were not necessary; rather, citizens must be taught more local techniques for anticipating the future consequences of present actions. Hume stressed to his readers throughout his essays that they were living in a society in which the future was hard to predict, and there were very real limits to political and economic foresight. The goal of the essays was thus to encourage readers to develop different skills, each tied to a specific system of behavior, for locating those tendencies that reason could foresee—or, at any rate, could foresee as clearly "as she can do any thing, that lyes in the womb of time" (Hume 1752: 141). As a result, many of the essays—and especially those focused on economic topics—established much more specific addressees than the general "subject" assumed by the *Treatise*. In *Political Discourses*, for example, the chapter entitled "Of Taxes" sought to engender an "attentive, disinterested legislature," while the next chapter ("Of Public Credit") addressed both the legislature and individual citizens, since public credit was the result of the actions of both groups (Hume 1752: 118). As Thomas Pfau notes, Hume's essays both suggested the need for, and provided the content of, "the public institution of a master rhetorician offering his services of articulate therapy to a people repeatedly depicted as on the cusp of disintegration" (Pfau 1997: 294). Such a project aimed at strategies of prediction tied to specific social systems, rather than a "deep" knowledge of the system of society as a whole. As a result, "sympathy"—the theoretical center of the description of social relations in the *Treatise*—tended to disappear from Hume's essayistic writings. Though sympathy emerged again in the *Enquiry Concerning the Principles of Morals* (1751), in which Hume attempted to simplify and popularize the claims of the *Treatise*, it was displaced in the latter text from the central position it had held in his earlier philosophy, appearing simply as a synonym for "social feeling, benevolence, natural philanthropy, rather than the name of the process by which the social feeling has been constructed out of non-social or individual feeling" (L. A. Selby-Bigge in Hume 1975: xxvi).[38]

CONCLUSION: SYSTEMS, IDEOLOGY, AND TIME CONSCIOUSNESS

As I noted above, the theory of sympathy that Hume developed in his *Treatise* appropriated the concept of the collective imagination developed in early eighteenth-century financial discourse, positioning the speculative dynamics of this faculty as the foundation of sociality itself. By describing the imagination as the foundation of *all* social systems, Hume was able to account for the importance of the virtual dimensions of property in the production of factions, but at the same time he was also able to detach this sociological understanding of imagination from its imbrication in financial discourse. Thus, while Hume agreed with earlier commentators such as Midriff that the subject was the site of constant imaginative "panics" and "infections" from its fellows, the *Treatise* depicted this as the endemic condition of subjectivity, rather than a disorder that could be "cured." For Hume, the dynamics of finance were simply an instance of imaginative social relations, and as a result, topical debates about finance could be relegated to the environment of the system of moral philosophy developed in the *Treatise*, or isolated in the "economic" essays that Hume wrote in the 1750s.

In recent years, commentators have employed concepts of "ideology" as a way of recovering the linkages between Hume's moral philosophy, on the one hand, and his political and economic theory, on the other. The ideological dimension of Hume's theories has been interpreted from at least two very different perspectives. On the one hand, a series of studies grounded in an essentially liberalist perspective have called for the need to consider the political implications of such apparently apolitical texts as Hume's *Treatise*. Assuming an essentially bourgeois understanding of politics as a system in which competing interest groups negotiate demands and responsibilities, much of this literature has focused on the question of whether Hume is best understood as a "conservative" or a "liberal" (with the former term implying a belief that social faction was best contained by reliance on previously established beliefs, and the latter suggesting that we can and "need to improve our beliefs by deliberate resort to extensive experience and by engaging in profound reflection" (Stewart 1992: 8)).[39] On the other hand, critics working from a more Marxist perspective have argued that Hume's theories of imagination and sympathy helped to "naturalize" the shift from centralized, authoritarian structures of political control and economic exchange to decentralized, bourgeois governmental and commercial institutions. Terry Eagleton, for example, argues that developing eighteenth-century British, French, and German societies required modes of thought and feeling that would allow individuals to "individually authenticate" social laws and norms, rather than see those as external impositions, and he reads Hume's theory of sympathy as part of this project of the "aestheticization" of the "whole of social life" (Eagleton 1990: 27, 37), while Patrick Brantlinger reads Hume's writings as part of the reification of "the economy" as a system (purportedly) distinct from other systems of social life (Brantlinger 1996: 33–34, 92–100).[40]

While both liberal and Marxist modes of ideological analysis have contributed significantly to our understanding of Hume's texts and contexts, both approaches also incur two risks. To begin with, both neglect the extent to which theories of imagination and sympathy allowed eighteenth-century authors such as Hume to understand society as a *system*. Responding to the functional differentiation of early eighteenth-century British society, Hume employed the concept of imagination to frame and understand the formation of both "limited systems" (to use Shaftesbury's term) as well as the unity that joined all of these into the system of "society." If there is an ideological dimension to Hume's theories, then, it lies not in the ideological *reconciliation* that Hume's theories of imagination and sympathy purportedly provided, but rather in his attempt to *ground* all social systems in the more limited mode of "closed" imaginative projection. Contemporary critics of both the liberal and Marxist camps risk replicating precisely this same ideological move when they suggest that early eighteenth-century British finance *really did* bind individuals to one another and to the long-term stability of government through the mediation of imaginary relations, for such claims about the function of the imagination in finance unwittingly adopt an essentially Humean understanding of society as a system maintained in the imagination. As a result, far from contesting the ideological aspects of Hume's philosophy, these approaches risk confirming the notion that society springs from what Eagleton describes as "the instinctual economizing of the mind." (And from this perspective, the fact that recent literary criticism substitutes psychoanalytic conceptions of identification in place of Hume's term "sympathy" in order to describe the nature of social ties is of minimal importance compared to the shared understanding of society as an imaginary system.)

Yet if ideological approaches to Hume's theories of imagination and sympathy risk underestimating how deeply a Humean perspective informs current conceptions of society and ideology itself, these approaches also risk underestimating the extent to which Hume's texts *exceed* "ideological capture." As I noted above, Hume's *Treatise* distinguished between two modes of speculative imaginative dynamics: on the one hand, the open anticipation of the founding convention; on the other, the closed expectation of the promise. While the latter mode arguably described and justified the social conditions necessary for the operation of the institutions and instruments of the financial revolution, the former open mode could not be so easily aligned with the new economy. As Giovanni Arrighi notes, capitalism has developed since the fifteenth century precisely by shifting geographic centers in order to *avoid* open anticipation. The generation of capital always requires the calculation of risk, but such calculations depend upon precedent, and a feeling that the future will be continuous with the past; as a result, "risks" that are "not just high but incalculable" are "beyond the horizon of rational capitalist enterprise" (Arrighi 1994: 122). In Arrighi's historical account, capitalism has developed historically through crises of overaccumulation, in which a system centered on a specific geographic region (e.g., the Genoese system of the fifteenth century or the Dutch cycle of the seventeenth century) finds itself deadlocked, having created conditions under which capital builds up only at the cost of reducing the possibilities for low- or even medium-risk investment. In these moments, capital takes flight to another geographic center—for example, from the Netherlands to Britain—where investment seems more calculable, more "promising." Capitalism thus transforms itself, becoming geographically more extensive and structurally more intensive, precisely by avoiding the potentialities of open anticipation.

From this perspective, the virtue of Hume's account is precisely that it distinguishes between the closed future of the promise and the open future of founding convention. To insist on the promissory nature of Hume's "imagined community" is to stress system maintenance (the status quo) over system emergence, but Hume's text in fact provides a theoretical framework for understanding both the phenomenological mechanisms that enable social systems to perpetuate themselves and the phenomenological potentialities that enable new systems to emerge. To read the *Treatise* as a text oriented toward ideological closure is thus to privilege his analysis of what perpetuates a system over his analysis of what allows for the emergence of new systems, and to read the causality *of* systems back into the potentiality that enables new social formations.

2 The violence of system

Rousseau and Smith on identification and sympathy

> [R]etaliation seems to be the great law which is dictated to us by Nature. (*TMS* 2.ii.1.10)

> It is imagination which extends for us the measure of the possible, whether for good or bad, and which consequently excites and nourishes the desires by the hope of satisfying them. But the object which at first appeared to be at hand flees more quickly than it can be pursued. (*Emile* 81; *OCR* 4: 304)

In the wake of the spectacular collapse of the South Sea Bubble, and during a period in which state finance seemed to have stabilized (much to the disappointment of critics such as Bolingbroke), David Hume had returned to the question of "opinion" that had concerned earlier writers on state finance. As I noted in the last chapter, Hume, rather than blaming the imagination for producing problematic and divisive contagions of opinion, instead had argued that *all* social relations were enabled by this faculty. Yet if the system of society was in fact instituted in the imagination, what sort of epistemology was adequate to understand its dynamics? On this question, Hume had wavered. On the one hand, he outlined an epistemology that positioned individuals as "subjects" who represented the world to themselves, and who engaged the world *as* representation. On the other hand, he contended that the movement of affect from one individual to another *preceded* subjectivity, which suggested an alternative epistemology that posited more fundamental, and nonrepresentational, affective engagements with others. This alternative epistemology grounded society in the structure of the gift, and suggested that subjectivity, far from being a foundation, was instead a mode of consciousness initiated and enabled by donations of sentiment from others. While the fact of affective gifts "proved" the viability of community to the subject, such gifts also enabled factional violence by propagating contagions of anger and resentment.

Writing a decade after Hume, and in the context of escalating military and fiscal tensions between France and Britain, Jean-Jacques Rousseau and Adam Smith each sought to come to terms with the apparent conflict between these two different epistemologies proposed by Hume. I argue in this chapter that Rousseau pushed the conflict between these models of knowledge to its breaking point, for he contended that the imagination was a *fundamentally* speculative faculty that ensured that all social relations were essentially conflictual. For Rousseau, the violence of imagination's speculative dynamics could be avoided only by escaping social systems entirely, and the possibility of such an escape from sociality depended upon a more precise understanding of the nature of the affective link between subjects, which he called "identification." However, echoing Hume's ambivalent commitment to two competing epistemologies, Rousseau developed two theories of identification. One theory linked identification to imagination, representation, and system, while the other presented identification as a force that operated outside the faculty of imagination, prior to representation, and beyond the reach of social systems. Smith's version of sympathy, by contrast, published a few years after Rousseau's, grounded itself firmly and fully within imagination and representation, and Smith, like Hume, sought to understand sympathy as a form of indebtedness. However, where Hume had argued that personal identity was enabled by a sympathetic debt to actually existing others, Smith positioned a debt to the dead at the core of his moral philosophy. The different understandings of debt to which each of these authors turned suggested different relations of individuals to the state: like Hume, Rousseau sought to reduce the role of the state, while Smith argued that limited state violence was necessary in order to arrest the anarchic violence that sympathy could engender.

My emphasis in this chapter on state finance as an interpretive horizon for understanding the role of violence in Rousseau's theory of identification and Smith's theory of sympathy departs from earlier critical work on these two authors. Previous critics have been more inclined to focus on Rousseau's theory of pity than on his discussion of identification, and have tended to contextualize his texts against the background of Enlightenment aesthetic theory, seventeenth- and eighteenth-century moral and political philosophy, the critique of theatricality, or more general reflections on the metaphysics of transparency and writing.[1] Smith's theory of sympathy has been the subject of considerable critical attention, but historically oriented discussions have tended to focus on contexts such as the political concerns of the Scottish literati, debates about theatricality, the influence of French literature on British moral philosophy, and the rise of bourgeois ideology.[2] By focusing attention on the resonances between state finance and Rousseau's and Smith's theories of intersubjectivity, I highlight the ways in which these theories were attempts to understand how logics of speculation could enable both the unity of society *and* its division into what Shaftesbury and Hutcheson had called "limited systems." At the same time, the homologies that I locate between crises of public credit and Smith's and Rousseau's theories of intersubjectivity should be understood less as a matter of "influence" than as a consequence of the fact that both authors grounded their understandings of system in the "medium" of the imagination, and focused on the possibilities of recursive behavior within this field; as a result, both encountered the same paradoxes and tautologies that plagued the systems of French and British state finance.

I. HAPTOPRAXOLOGY: ROUSSEAU ON IMAGINATION, SPECULATION, AND IDENTIFICATION

Rousseau's career as a political and moral theorist was indebted to state finance in a very practical way, for he began to write on political economy, commerce, and the imagination while he was working in the household of the wealthy French financier Claude Dupin, who had served as secretary of the king's finances and had made a fortune in land speculation (Aucuy in Dupin 1913, vol. 1: viii–xvii). Rousseau met both Charles and his wife Louis-Marie-Madeleine (the wealthy daughter of another financier, Samuel Bernard) in Paris in 1742, and the aspiring writer almost immediately made a fool of himself by sending Mme Dupin a love letter, which she returned to him along with words of admonishment (*OC*, 1: 292; Cranston 1983: 164–65). Rousseau promptly apologized, and briefly served as tutor for the Dupins' son in 1742. A few years later, in 1745, he accepted a permanent position as secretary to the Dupin household, a job that he held until 1751 (Cranston 1983: 203–16). His duties were not well-defined, but involved helping members of the Dupin family with their various literary compositions: for example, he assisted Claude's son, Dupin de Francueil, in his attempt to write a book on chemistry, and advised Mme Dupin in her efforts to write a book of moral essays. In addition—and more relevant to the concerns of this chapter—Rousseau assisted Claude Dupin as the latter developed both a short "reflection" on, as well as a much more lengthy three-volume response to, the Baron de Montesquieu's *L'Esprit des Lois* (*The Spirit of the Laws*: 1748). While not credited with explicit co-authorship of either of Dupin's responses to Montesquieu, Rousseau was likely one of the "deux...amis" with whom Dupin claimed to have composed his three-volume *Observations sur un livre intitulé, De l'esprit des loix: divisées en trois parties* (*Observations on a book entitled The Spirit of the Laws, divided in three parts*; Dupin 1750–51, vol. 1: i).[3]

While Montesquieu was friendly with the Dupins, his critique of public credit, tax farming, and finance in *The Spirit of the Laws* almost guaranteed that the book would not be warmly received by Rousseau's employer. Montesquieu had satirized the social dynamics of public speculation in his *Lettres persanes* (1722), arguing there that the spectacular rise in price of Mississippi Company stock depended upon a collective hallucination grounded in the imagination (Montesquieu 1873: 124), and in *The Spirit of the Laws*, he continued his attack on the institutions of the new economy in a more systematic fashion. He returned to the example of the Mississippi

Company, but also extended his critique to paper money—arguing that, while acceptable in principle, paper money became problematic as soon as it ceased to bear a direct correspondence with specie—and the French practice of tax farming, arguing that tax farmers "impoverish [the state] in a thousand ways" (Montesquieu 1949: 218, 388, 375).[4]

Dupin's published responses to Montesquieu sought to justify these same institutions. The financier had already begun a defense of finance in *Oeconomiques*, published three years before *The Spirit of the Laws*. *Oeconomiques* developed a systematic understanding of commerce within which finance played a key and beneficial role: while willing to grant that agriculture, arts, and commerce were the three primary sources of the state's riches, Dupin contended that finance was necessary in order both to "simplify" commerce and to "accelerate" its movement (Dupin 1913, vol. 1: 54, 107; translation mine). As Dupin noted in his "Advertisement" to the book, this meant that

> finances are the sinews [nerfs] of war and the support of peace; that which moves all parts of the body politic; that which maintains the laws, justice, the dignity and the splendor of the state; it is the most solid bond which can unite the people.(Dupin 1913, vol. 1: iii; translation mine).

Dupin's enormous *Observations* continued this defense of finance and public credit, responding literally sentence by sentence to the sections of Montesquieu's *The Spirit of the Laws* devoted to commerce, finance, and taxes. Where Montesquieu argued against the establishment of public banks and joint-stock companies in absolute monarchies, Dupin contended that commerce and public credit were indispensable in every polity, insofar as they simplified "les opérations du Commerce" and thereby "accelerated" its movements, and he described at length different measures that would support public "confiance" (confidence) (Dupin 1750–51, vol. 3: 58–73).

While Dupin's description of finance as the necessary support of peace—and, when that failed, the vigorous sinew of war—was no doubt in large part a self-interested defense of his own source of wealth, we should also see both Montesquieu's critique, and Dupin's defense, of public credit as part of a larger debate, conducted in both France and Britain during the 1740s and '50s, about the link between government speculation and mimetic state violence. During the two decades following the twin disasters of the South Sea and Mississippi Companies, state finance seemed to have "normalized" in both France and Britain, in part because the bubbles had allowed each government to write down its total amount of debt, much to the frustration of the many investors who thereby lost sizeable sums of money (Marion 1927–31, vol 1: 90–112; Bordo and White 1990: 5–8; Dickson 1967: 122–76; Neal 1990a: 89–117). Yet if public credit in the 1740s and '50s seemed less volatile than in the first two decades of the eighteenth century, the total volume of money in public funds in both France and Britain had continued to grow, and mini-panics still occasionally occurred—in 1745, for example, the Bank of England was temporarily forced to stop specie payment for notes (Dickson 1967: 216, 225; de Bolla 1989: 124). Even more troubling, this increase in the volume of money involved in state finance seemed to be both a function of, as well as a contributing cause to, hostilities between France and Britain. War between France and Britain in 1744, for example, forced both countries to expand the size of their long term loans: between 1742 and 1748, Britain raised more than £20 million with public long term loans, while in France in 1748, the expenses of the recent war were estimated at 180 million livres (Dickson 1967: 216–19; Marion 1927–31: 170).

The precise causality between public debt and war was complicated and confusing, each seeming to function as cause of the other. On the one hand, increases in public debt seemed to be an *effect* of war, since the decision to engage in hostilities required each government to raise money. On the other hand, public debt seemed to be a *cause* of war, since legislators in both countries were convinced that military success over the other was the only way to step out from under the ever-increasing debt that each country found itself committed to pay. As the anonymous author of *The Necessity of Lowering Interest and Continuing Taxes* noted, "France is at present as much incumbered with Debts as we are, and the Nation which first eases itself of its Burthen will be enabled to give the Law to the other, and to the rest of Europe" (Anon. 1750: 9).[5] Commentators in both countries recognized that their ostensibly separate systems of state finance were in fact coupled together, creating a metasystem that committed both states to ever-escalating cycles of debt expansion and military violence. In this context, both Montesquieu's and Dupin's books should be understood as systematic attempts to understand—and thereby direct the course of—this metasystem, with Montesquieu's *The Spirit of the Laws* emphasizing the factionalism, violence, and "corruption" of the institutions of the new economy, while Dupin defended paper money, and positioned finance as a force of peace, a "solid bond which can unite the people."

This conflict between Montesquieu and Dupin served as the starting point for Rousseau's reflections on economy and finance, first begun in 1750 in his *Discours sur les arts et les sciences* (Discourse on the Arts and Sciences). While he had read Dupin's *Oeconomiques* and had probably helped the financier compose his critical *Réflexions* and *Observations* on *The Spirit of the Laws*, Rousseau's own position was much closer to Montesquieu's. Even before he left the employ of the Dupins in 1751, Rousseau lamented in his first *Discourse* that contemporary statesmen "speak only of commerce and money" (*BPW* 12; *OCR*, vol. 3: 19), while in his 1755 article on "political economy" for Diderot's and D'Alembert's *Encyclopédie*, he contended that though "[p]ublic funds must necessarily pass through the hands of the leaders," the government became corrupt when it relied too much on taxes and national debt, for the escalation of the latter was a sign of "an increase of useless desires." "A government has reached its final degree of corruption," Rousseau contended, "when the only thing left of its sinews [nerf] is money" (*BPW* 128, 130, 129; *OCR*, vol. 3: 264, 267, 266). Rousseau's ambivalence toward state finance later turned to outright enmity, and in his *Project de Constitution pour la Corse* (*Constitutional Project for Corsica*, 1765), he argued that state finance was not the "nerve of public power [le nerf de la force publique]," as Dupin had contended, but rather the "fat of the body politic" (Rousseau 1953: 316–17, translation modified; *OCR*, vol. 3: 525–61).[6]

While his critique of state finance echoed Montesquieu's earlier charges against this institution, Rousseau traced the dynamics of commerce and finance back to the imagination in a far more penetrating way than had the author of *The Spirit of the Laws*. Like Montesquieu and Dupin, Rousseau was interested in developing a systemic understanding of the "laws" that determined finance specifically, and commerce more generally, but Rousseau took seriously Montesquieu's suggestion in the *Persian Letters* that the imagination was the key to the dynamics of the system of finance. In the *Discours sur l'origine et les fondements de l'inégalité parmi les hommes* (*Discourse on the Origin and Foundation of Inequality Among Men*, 1754), for example, Rousseau argued that commerce had its origins in the confusions of people and goods that imaginative comparisons engendered. Rousseau depicted a natural state of isolated individuals who initially remained relatively uninterested in their fellow humans. Trouble began, however, when each person eventually began to feel pride (orgueil) about his or her mental superiority over animals and eventually extended this paradigm to their fellows (BPW 61; OCR, vol. 3: 166). This comparative passion served as the precondition for social relationships and the development of the first forms of property (BPW 64; OCR, vol. 3: 170). The imagination was responsible for these dynamics of social valuation because it was fundamentally a faculty of speculation; as Rousseau wrote in Emile, the imagination was the faculty that

> extends for us the measure of the possible, whether for good or bad, and which consequently excites and nourishes the desires by the hope of satisfying them. But the object which at first appeared to be at hand flees more quickly than it can be pursued. (*Emile* 81; *OCR*, vol. 4: 304)[7]

Imagination produced a perpetually restless, acquisitive subject, one that was constantly propelled from one possession to the next (*Emile* 447; *OCR*, vol. 4: 821). Individuals in the state of nature were isolated from their fellows precisely because they lacked imaginative capacities, while an individual in society obsessively compared him- or herself imaginatively to others (*BPW* 56; *OCR*, vol. 3: 158). If the reliance of eighteenth-century governments on taxes and national debt depended upon "an increase of useless desires," as Rousseau contended in his article on political economy, this was simply another instance of the same speculative tendencies of the imagination that had created "social man" in the first place. Like Hume, Rousseau's discussion of the role of imagination in contemporary financial and commercial phenomena led him to position this faculty as the foundation of sociality itself.

Representation and energetic identification

Yet Rousseau's harsh criticisms of commerce left him with a dilemma, for in criticizing the speculative aspects of contemporary finance and commerce, he was attacking precisely that speculative capacity that, by his own account, made society itself possible. Was it then possible, in Rousseau's system, to have any relation to the other that would not depend upon the mimetic and rivalrous dynamics of the imagination? In attempting to resolve this question, Rousseau followed Hume's lead by developing a more thorough analysis of the imaginative "act" by means of which individuals participated in the affects and sentiments of others. However, rather than appropriating an older term, such as sympathy, Rousseau coined a new concept—"identification"—in order to explain the imaginative dynamics of social relations. He also developed two different accounts of the field of application of identification, outlining in *Essai sur l'origines des langues* (*Essay on the Origins of Languages*) an epistemology that implied that *every* relation to the other was mediated by representation and imagination, while in his *Discourse on Inequality*, he created an alternative to epistemology—a "haptopraxology"—that left open the possibility of relations to others that bypassed the imagination.

Rousseau's *Essay on the Origins of Languages* was probably composed in 1754, at the same time that he was writing the *Discourse on Inequality*.[8] In the *Essay*, the concept of identification emerged in the context of a discussion of pity that was designed to highlight differences between "natural" and "civilized" humans. Rousseau argued that

> Social affections develop in us only as a function of our knowledge. Pity, although natural to the heart of man, would remain eternally inactive without the imagination that puts it into play. How do we let ourselves be moved to pity? By transporting ourselves outside of ourselves; by identifying ourselves with the suffering being. We suffer only as much as we judge he suffers; it is not in ourselves, it is in him that we suffer. Consider how much this transport presupposes acquired knowledge! How could I imagine evils of which I have no idea? How would I suffer in seeing someone else suffer if I do not even know that he is suffering, if I do not know what he and I have in common? He who has never reflected cannot be clement, or just, or pitying.... (*Essay* 306; *OCR*, vol. 5: 395)

Rousseau suggested in this passage that the imagination enables—"activates"—pity by creating an identification of "ourselves...with the suffering being." Identification, for its part, requires a kind of "knowledge" that can only be provided by the imagination. This imaginative knowledge is fundamentally dependent not on content—for example, the specific details of someone's situation—but rather on formal capacities such as projection (imagining evils that are not currently experienced) and reflexive judgments (we judge *that* the other suffers). The imagination thus named for Rousseau the capacity of a self-representing subject to link itself to a virtual sphere, within which it could be gripped by a number of topological deformations, such as "movement" outside of itself and "transport" toward the other. Identification named the most extreme deformation of this virtual intersubjective topology, when the self-representing subject let itself be caught up by—and even virtually became—the other. Rousseau contended that identification was impossible without the imagination, for this latter faculty enabled the system of virtual relations that constituted intersubjectivity itself. Imagination, in short, was the precondition of identification, but also the precondition for all social relations (of which pity was simply one example).

Rousseau's more general argument in the *Essay* was designed to convince his readers that pity—as well as its two preconditions: the intersubjective imagination and identification—had a history, and that all three were tied to the development of social systems. Just as Freud would later argue in his *Three Essays on Sexuality* that pity develops late in the history of the child (Freud 1953–74, vol. 7: 193), Rousseau contended that pity, imagination, and identification emerged only after humans had left the "natural" state for the state of civilization.[9] For Rousseau, humans may have interacted with one another in the natural state, but such interactions did not take the form of systems of social relations. Social systems depended upon the imagination, for this faculty was the necessary medium of properly social communication; in its absence, neither social relations in general nor the specific act of identification in particular was possible.

Yet if imagination was the necessary ground of intersubjectivity—it was only through imagination that one perceived the other *as* other—it was also for Rousseau an intrinsically speculative "faculty." The imagination, as Rousseau wrote in *Emile*, created social relations by orienting individuals toward "the possible, whether for good or bad," and it "excited" and "nourished" desires. Because he believed that the imagination was an inherently speculative faculty, Rousseau held out little hope that one could "regulate" it in the manner suggested by earlier authors such as Shaftesbury and Midriff. The problem for Rousseau was not *particular* modalities of imaginative activity; rather, it was imaginative activity itself. If all social relations were imaginary in their essence, could one ever engage others without encouraging economy and speculation? Was a nonimaginative relationship with others possible?

In the *Essay*, identification denoted the impossibility of thinking relationships with the other outside of imagination and subjectivity, but Rousseau's *Discourse on the Origin of Inequality* signaled an attempt to think the possibility of nonimaginative and nonsubjective relations with others. The theoretical difficulty of such a task is evidenced by the well-known discrepancy between the accounts of pity and identification in the *Essay* and the *Discourse*. In both texts, identification was introduced in the context of a discussion of pity, with the former term denoting the efficient cause of the latter.[10] However, where the *Essay* presented identification as a fundamentally imaginative phenomenon that occurred *after* humans left the state of nature, the *Discourse* reversed the relationship, presenting identification and the passions it facilitated as occurring *prior* to the subjective development of a virtual imaginative space.

Rousseau's attempt to divorce identification from imagination in the *Discourse* was a function of his desire to position pity as an intrinsic component of human psychology, rather than, as in the *Essay*, a passion that emerged historically. Thus, in the *Discourse*, Rousseau argued for two fundamental principles of human nature: self-preservation (*amour de soi*) and pity (*la pitié*).[11] As in the *Essay*, identification in the *Discourse* was positioned as the precondition of pity, as Rousseau argued that the commiseration inspired by pity "will be all the more energetic [*énergique*] as the witnessing animal identifies itself more intimately with the suffering animal" (*BPW* 54; *OCR*, vol. 3: 155). However, because the *Discourse* described pity as an *innate* principle in humans (rather than a capacity that emerged later in history), both pity and its mechanism, identification, were at their strongest in the state of nature: "it is evident that this identification must have been infinitely closer [*infiniment plus étroite*] in the state of nature than in the state of reasoning" (*BPW* 54; *OCR*, vol. 3: 155–56). Since Rousseau continued to maintain that the development of imaginative capacities occurred after the fall from the state of nature, neither pity nor identification could be grounded in the imagination in the *Discourse*. The conclusions of the *Discourse*, in short, seemed to contradict the position outlined in the *Essay*: in the *Discourse*, identification and pity did not require imagination and reflection, while in the *Essay*, both imagination and self-reflection were intrinsic to these processes.

While previous commentary on the discrepancy between these two accounts has tended to read the *Essay* as either in contradiction with, or as a "deconstruction" of, the purportedly theoretically less sophisticated account of identification in the *Discourse*, I suggest that in fact Rousseau has two theories of identification, which are tied to two different models of perception.[12] In the *Essay*, Rousseau outlined a theory of representational identification, which required the support of imagination and self-representation. In the *Discourse*, by contrast, he sought to develop an alternative theory of "energetic identification" that took place as a corporeal reflex, beneath self-consciousness and prior to imagination. As a result, the discrepancy between the *Essay* and the *Discourse* is less a conflict about the truth of identification than a conflict between two different models of perception. Where the *Essay* privileged an epistemology that was inseparable from the theory of the intersubjective imagination, the *Discourse* pointed toward a quasi-epistemology—what I call a "haptopraxology"—that theorized modes of perception that took place below reflection and judgment.

In Rousseau's first model of perception, outlined in the *Essay*, all perceptions of others required "recognition." This was equivalent to the claim that these perceptions operate within the space of self-representation: that is, to perceive that another creature suffers is to *recognize* that the other suffers. However, as Rousseau made clear in the *Essay*, such recognition required a subjective economy by means of which the subject imaginatively spread himself over several "places": the subject simultaneously represented to himself the figure of the other, the figure of himself, and the connecting link between these two figures. Rousseau argued that such representation was inherently imaginative, for only by means of the retentive and discriminative capacities of the imagination could the subject make comparisons between past conditions-of-self and the present condition-of-the-other that enabled perceptual recognitions of suffering.[13] In this model, perceiving others in general (and suffering others in particular) depended upon representation and imagination. However, because Rousseau understood imagination as a fundamentally speculative faculty, perceptual recognition of others would always lead to an economy of *social* recognition; that is, a social system in which individuals circulated judgments about one another.

In the *Discourse*, Rousseau developed an alternative model of perception. Rousseau argued in the *Discourse* that imagination was *not* a necessary support for either the temporal extension of consciousness (memory) or judgment. Both of these activities, Rousseau argued, took place prior to the development of imaginative capacities; natural man, for example, perceived, felt, and had ideas, but did not imagine: "[h]is imagination depicts [*peint*] nothing to him" (*BPW* 46; *OCR*, vol. 3: 144). In the *Discourse*, in other words, Rousseau claimed that the ability to perceive—that is, to have ideas of external objects—was not equivalent to self-representation, and thus did not require imagination.Perception was dependent upon sensations, but sensations *as such* were different from sensations *as* signs or images. Rousseau was clear on this point even in the *Essay*, in which he lamented that we fail to make a necessary distinction between signs and sensations: "we attribute both too much and too little dominion to sensations; we do not see that often they affect us not only as sensations but as signs or images" (*Essay* 319; *OCR*, vol. 5: 412). While sensations as signs or images "manifest" something to consciousness by means of representation and imagination, sensations as such do not manifest themselves to consciousness. Rousseau's point was not that sensations were immediately "present to self" in a way that signs and images are not, for natural man was no more aware of sensations than of signs of images. His point was rather that sensations operated outside the realm of phenomenal manifestation, and instead indexed a capacity for affectivity that was prior to, and served as the ground of, representation itself.

Within the theory of perception of the *Discourse*, one can perceive the other without recognizing him. Thus, while imagination may be the necessary condition of a system of intersubjective relationships, this faculty was not required for the perception of others. Rousseau would no doubt have agreed with Adam Smith's claim that since "our senses will never inform us" of what another person feels, "it is by the imagination only that we can form any conception of what are his sensations" (*TMS* 1.i.1.2), but Rousseau's point was that natural man perceives others without representing those others to himself, and without recognizing those others *as* other.[14] This distinction between perception and recognition itself pointed to the possibility of a response to the other that would not be tied to a system of intersubjective exchange, but would rather emerge from an "energetic" mode of identification that did not require imagination, representation, or subjectivity. Energetic identification was not linked to the visual register, but was rather triggered by the cry (*le cri*). "Man's first language," Rousseau wrote,

> the most universal, the most energetic [*énergique*], and the only language he needed before it was necessary to persuade men assembled together, is the cry of nature.... [t]his cry was elicited only by a kind of instinct in pressing circumstances, to beg for help in great dangers. (*BPW* 49; *OCR*, vol. 3: 148)

As Derrida has noted, the cry is not equivalent to the voice for Rousseau. The voice is a mode of signification, and thus requires imagination, representation, and a system of intersubjective relationships; the cry, by contrast, is a *force* that triggered in natural man a corporeal reflex of energetic identification.[15] Energetic identification, in turn, impelled natural man to action, a response that required neither that natural man "feel" the other's affect, nor that he recognize the other as other. The becoming-one of "energetic identification" was not to be understood as an *imaginative* union between two entities, but instead designated for Rousseau a union of praxis. In the *Discourse*, Rousseau described the effect of energetic identification as the bonding of living beings into a cooperative unity; it is "what carries us without reflection to the aid [*secours*] of those we see suffering" (*BPW* 55; *OCR*, vol. 3: 156).[16] This union of praxis occurred outside of representation, imagination, and morality—and thus outside of all social systems—and it required only the perception of the other. Energetic identification occurred outside of subjectivity, and as such, did not involve a subjective "spreading" toward the other, but rather a differential of attraction between two bodies such that one moved toward the other.

What the *Discourse* outlined, then, was not so much an epistemology as an "haptopraxology"; that is, a theory of the ways in which affects of force and "touch" (*haptos*) were tied to action (*praxis*). Within such a haptopraxology, perceptions did not have to be posed by a subject before itself, but rather augmented the body's capacity to act in certain ways. For Rousseau, "nature" stood as the guarantor of such praxis. The true agent of energetic identification was not "the subject" or even the individual, for energetic identification required something greater than subjectivity or individuality itself to direct the attention of the individual to the other. When Rousseau wrote that "the witnessing animal identifies...with the suffering animal" (*BPW* 54; *OCR*, vol. 3: 155), the "subject" of this reflexive verb is not, properly speaking, the individual animal, but nature itself. Energetic identification named nature's unification with itself through the medium of individuals. Energetic identification, in short, was a work of nature: nature as *vis mediatrix naturae*, directing the attention of the individual before the individual became a "subject."[17] Since the subject can never pose energetic identifications before itself, they appear inscrutable and "inhuman," alien visitations that occur before, beyond, or outside the subject.

Rousseau's descriptions of the link between the cry and energetic identification had precedents in earlier French and British moral philosophy, but Rousseau did not make this mode of identification the foundation of sociality, as earlier critics might have been inclined to do. In *Réflexions critiques sur la poésie et sur la peinture* (*Critical Reflections on Poetry and Painting*, 1719), for example, Abbé Du Bos had argued that nature hinders egoism (*amour-propre*) by implanting an instinctual openness to the forceful affects of others; nature has ensured, Du Bos wrote, that "the emotions [*l'agitation*] of everyone who comes near us would have a powerful sway over us." For Du Bos too, the result of such a "sway" was aid: "The cries of a man to whom we are attached only by humanity make us fly to his aid with an automatic movement which precedes all deliberation" (Du Bos 1740, vol. 1: 38–39; translation from Marshall 1988: 17–18). As David Marshall has noted, Du Bos understood this instinctual sentiment as "the primary foundation of society," but in Rousseau's account, nature's cries and the force of its sway do not appear as the guarantee of society (Marshall 1988: 18). Instead, nature employs energetic identifications to propel individuals toward one other in the absence of social systems, such as the state that Rousseau described in the *Essay*, in which each individual is "isolated in the midst of mankind."[18] Rousseau understood energetic identification as an *a*social force, for this mode of affective identity did not enable communications or "exchanges" between subjects, but rather undid relationships between individuals as soon as aid had been granted. Rather than creating enduring social systems that bound subjects to one another, energetic identification called into being evanescent systems of bodies.

"Imagination" was for Rousseau the faculty that replaced these evanescent systems of bodies with enduring social systems. Imagination accomplished this by instituting the temporality of speculation, for which the possible always determined the nature and value of the actual. Identification did not disappear within the calculable time and space inaugurated by the imagination, but because it was no longer directed by nature, it fell under the sway of egoism (*amour propre*) and subjectivity. Identification still coordinated the activities of people, but it no longer accomplished this along natural, asocial articulations. Instead, individuals became joined along trajectories determined by the intersubjective forces of "public esteem" and "opinion," and one identified with the other only to the extent that one could *represent* that other to oneself.

Presence, narration, and intensity

Previous commentators have read the conflict between energetic and representational identification as a consequence of Rousseau's metaphysical commitment to presence. I suggest, however, that the theoretical tension between these two modes of identification was a result of Rousseau's attempt to distinguish between energetic and representational identification along a temporal, rather than simply conceptual, axis.[19] That is, instead of opting for an *analytic* distinction between representational and energetic identification, Rousseau tended to make this distinction by means of narrative. "In the beginning," Rousseau suggested, energetic identification held sway, but following the birth of imagination, only representational identification was possible. The problem with such a narrative, as Jacques Derrida notes, is that within the terms of Rousseau's philosophy, the "fall" from energetic to representational identification could not be triggered by anything outside of imagination, but instead had to be initiated by imagination itself. For Rousseau, as Derrida writes, "[i]magination alone has the power of *giving birth to itself*...it receives nothing that is alien or anterior to it," which implies that the imagination, as well as everything that Rousseau found problematic about representational identification, such as its reliance on signs and subjectivity, must have been there all along, at least "virtually" (Derrida 1976: 186). As Derrida notes, it is not possible to *narrate* the transition from energetic to representational identification without inscribing the latter in the former; as a result, energetic identification is located within a series of impossible transitions: from nature to culture, from animality to humanity, and from amorality to the system of morality. Rousseau's attempt to narrate a fall from energetic and representational identification meant that the former appears to be simply a wishful inversion of the latter, rather than a theoretically viable mode of affective engagement.

Yet as I noted above, Rousseau's distinction between energetic and representational identification was *not* primarily a distinction between "presence" and "absence," nor was it intrinsically bound to the temporal narrative Rousseau developed. Energetic identification must be thought of in terms of *force* and *intensity*, rather than representation. It disorganizes the subjective relationship to the body, in the sense that, under the sway of energetic identification, individuals temporarily cease to be solicitous of their own bodies and become part of a larger living unity that includes both the sufferer and those who aid the sufferer. Like what Gilles Deleuze calls "sensation," energetic identification "acquires a body through the organism," and it "takes on an excessive and spasmodic appearance"; it is "immediately conveyed in the flesh through the nervous or vital emotion" (Deleuze 2003: 40). Like Brian Massumi's description of affect as "a prepersonal intensity corresponding to the passage from one experiential state of the body to another and implying an augmentation or diminution in that body's capacity to act," energetic identification is oriented toward "praxis" and movement, though neither of these terms can be understood as directed by a subject (Massumi in Deleuze and Guattari 1987: xiv).

And in fact, even if Rousseau generally sought to distinguish between energetic and representational identification along an historical axis, at other points he hinted that they were better understood as *analytically* distinct, even if in fact entangled with one another. In the *Discourse*, for example, he suggested that energetic identification occurred even in contemporary society in certain situations, such as marketplace brawls. When the implicit violence of market economy erupted into actual fistfights, "the rabble [*le canaille*], the women of the marketplace...separate the combatants and prevent decent people from killing one another" (*BPW* 55; *OCR*, vol. 3: 156). The *canaille* and the women of the marketplace do not treat the riot or brawl as a spectacle (which would encourage representational identification, allowing them to maintain a subjective distance from the combatants), but instead they become "involved" at a practical, rather than an imaginative level. In addition, in his *Discourse on Political Economy*, written a year after his *Discourse*, Rousseau imagined the possibility of a polity in which energetic and representational identification would be reconciled. "If, for example," Rousseau wrote, citizens

> are trained early enough never to consider their own persons except in terms of being related to the body of the state, and not to perceive their own existence except as part of the state's existence, they will eventually come to identify themselves in some way with this larger whole [s'identifier en quelque sorte avec ce plus grand tout]....(*BPW* 125; *OCR*, vol. 3: 259)

Neither of these examples is unproblematic: in the first, for example, "the rabble" and women of the marketplace have the potential for energetic identification only because Rousseau believes that they are more "primitive" than others, while the submission to the state demanded by identification, as he described it in his *Discourse on Political Economy*, seems frighteningly totalitarian. Yet at the same time, both examples highlight his willingness to concede that energetic identification should not be understood simply as a capacity lost in the mists of the past, but rather as an immanent potential that persists underneath subjectivity, always able to surge forth and disrupt social systems. The fact of this potential by no means mitigated Rousseau's distrust of sociality, for he remained convinced that social systems depended upon the speculative powers of the imagination. Unlike earlier eighteenth-century commentators, Rousseau was dismissive of the idea that the speculative powers of this faculty could be "regulated," for, he suggested, every attempt to regulate the imagination from within its own sphere simply perpetuated its rule; only a form of communication that was not a communication could escape the system. This paradox could not be understood within an epistemology that itself relied upon the premise of the intersubjective imagination, but instead required an haptopraxology capable of thinking affects that emerged from elsewhere than representation.

Literary form and systems of communication

The *Discourse* served as an occasion for Rousseau to develop his antisystem theory, and, fittingly the publication of the text was oriented toward the destruction of social systems of communication. As Dena Goodman notes, the *Discourse* was a contribution to, but at the same time an attempt to undermine, the "republic of letters" encouraged by authors such as D'Alembert and Diderot (Goodman 1994).[20] While the republic of letters was a well-established notion by the mid-eighteenth century, generally understood as a distributed community of publishing authors bound to one another by principles of "reciprocity, cosmopolitanism, status based on merit, and fidelity to truth" (Goodman 1994: 23), the mid-eighteenth-century version of the republic of letters developed by Diderot and D'Alembert linked those general principles to specific anthropological claims. For both Diderot and D'Alembert, "communication of ideas was the basis of human society," and for D'Alembert, communication of ideas depended upon "the recognition by individuals of the similarity between themselves and other human beings." Such recognition enabled a form of "commerce" of ideas between authors and readers, motivated by the authors' desire for esteem and reputation among their readers (Goodman 1994: 26, 27). Diderot and D'Alembert sought to instantiate this understanding of the republic of letters in part by means of their multivolume *Encyclopédie*, which solicited articles from authors, and bound readers and authors together through the mechanism of literary subscription, which Diderot described as an "excellent method" recently arrived from England ("Souscription" in Diderot and D'Alembert 1969, vol. 3: 590).

Rousseau initially participated in this endeavor by contributing articles to the *Encyclopédie*, but an exchange of published essays with D'Alembert revealed the extent of Rousseau's antagonism toward the anthropological principles upon which this republic of letters was based. This literary exchange began with Rousseau's prize-winning *Discourse on the Arts and Sciences*, in which he suggested that the progress of the sciences and arts upon which the republic of letters depended was inimical to human virtue and happiness. D'Alembert responded three years later with his "Essai sur le société des gens de lettres et des grands, sur la réputation, sur les mécènes, sur les récompenses littéraires" ("Essay on the Society of Men of Letters and Aristocracy, Reputation, Patronage, and Literary Rewards," 1753), in which he argued that however barbarous elements of French society might be, a virtuous republic of letters could be developed within it. Rousseau responded with his *Discourse on Inequality*, in which he questioned not only the virtue of the republic of letters, but also "the naturalness of the sociability on which the history of civilization, and thus the Republic of Letters, was based" (Goodman 1994: 39). D'Alembert's response took the form of an *Encyclopédie* article on "Geneva" (1757), which addressed Rousseau's attacks on the theatricality of social relations by arguing that theater was not in fact the enemy of virtue. Rousseau answered with his *Letter to M. D'Alembert on the Theater* (1758), a thorough criticism of all forms of theatricality that, as Goodman notes, signaled "Rousseau's philosophical break with the Enlightenment Republic of Letters" and the beginning of his attempt to "create his own myth of the solitary seeker of truth, the lone man of virtue in a corrupt world" (Goodman 1994: 39).

While each of Rousseau's contributions to this debate constituted a further communication in Diderot's and D'Alembert's republic of letters, each of his texts also sought to *end* communication by drawing attention to the paradoxes and tautologies of the system of the republic of letters itself. Rather than accepting the form of the system of the republic of letters and producing knowledge within it, Rousseau focused attention on form itself by destabilizing terms such as "civilization," "virtue," "opinion," and "commerce," by which the system sought to validate itself. Thus, while Rousseau argued against social systems *in* the *Discourse*, by means *of* the *Discourse* itself he sought to end a social system—the republic of letters—by creating a communication that would end the possibility of communication itself.

II. THE GENERAL DISPOSITION TO EXCHANGE: SMITH ON SYMPATHY AND DEBT

Across the Channel and at about the same time that Rousseau was struggling with ways of moving beyond the constraints of social systems, Adam Smith was also reflecting on the recursive nature of imaginative social dynamics, and the relationship of those dynamics to both intersubjectivity and exchange. Smith had read Rousseau's *Discourse*, citing it in a letter he wrote to the *Edinburgh Review* (*EPS* 250–6), and like Rousseau, Smith was committed to describing the ways in which what he called "sympathy" could lead to violence and conflict. However, where Rousseau looked beyond representation and imagination for solutions to rivalrous and mimetic social relationships, Smith remained committed to the primacy of subjective representation, and sought instead to contain the disruptive potential of sympathy by locating the subject between a form of debt to the dead, on the one hand, and the power of the state, on the other.

Smith was, along with Hume, a member of the Scottish literati that hoped to modernize Scotland through commerce and "politeness." When Scotland became part of Britain through the Act of Union in 1707, the former was agriculturally backward and riven by internal factions.[21] By the 1720s, when both Hume and Smith were attending university at Edinburgh, a small but focused literati had begun the project of making Scotland into a "civilized" country. While this group wanted to stress the historical roots of Scotland's kingdom, they were equally committed to the belief "that preserving liberty and independence" was first and foremost a matter of "constitutional reform and encouraging trade and commerce" (Phillipson 1989: 7).[22] They were also committed to a culture of "politeness," and in Edinburgh,

> taverns, coffee-houses and salons had begun to generate a sophisticated club culture which was designed to show how learning and letters could generate politeness, eradicate religious and political faction and perform the patriotic task of civilizing the country and strengthening its "independence."(Phillipson 1989: 7; see also Eagleton 1990: 42–43; Klein 1994 and 1995)

For this literati, the key question of modernization was how trade could be encouraged while at the same time factions—and especially those apparently enabled by modern forms of public credit—were discouraged, since, as Adam Smith wrote to Sir William Petty on February 21, 1759, while perhaps "a little faction now and then gives spirit to the nation the continuance of it obstructs all public business" (*CAS* 28).

Given this social context, it was thus perhaps not surprising that Smith, like Hume, began his career with reflections on morality. *The Theory of Moral Sentiments* (1759) was Adam Smith's first book-length endeavor, published after he had been the chair of Moral Philosophy at the University of Glasgow for seven years. Smith began the thinking that resulted in *The Theory of Moral Sentiments* sometime in early 1752, when he had been asked to deliver lectures on natural jurisprudence, politics, and logic to replace an ailing Thomas Craigie (Raphael and Macfie in *TMS* 1–2). While Smith was probably expected to regurgitate the moral theory developed by his own mentor, Francis Hutcheson, who had been professor of Moral Philosophy at Glasgow from 1730 to 1746, he instead developed in his lectures and later in *The Theory of Moral Sentiments* a system of moral philosophy that diverged significantly from Hutcheson's "moral sense" philosophy.

Like Hume's moral philosophy, Smith's theory of morality was grounded in a theory of sympathy. However, the theoretical centrality of sympathy for Smith's moral theory was more evident than in the case of Hume: where Hume's *Treatise* turned to sympathy in the context of an analysis of pride and humility, Smith's *Theory* began with an extensive discussion and definition of this term.[23] Like Hume, Smith stressed that sympathy was not equivalent to pity or commiseration, but instead denoted "our fellow-feeling with any passion whatsoever" (*TMS* 1.i.1.5). He was also in agreement with Hume in situating the imagination as the causal mechanism of sympathy, for Smith suggested that when we perceive an individual expressing an emotion of any sort, we imaginatively duplicate in ourselves both the emotion, and the situation that engendered it. So, for example, when we see someone else suffering,

> [b]y the imagination we place ourselves in his situation, we conceive ourselves enduring all the same torments, we enter as it were into his body, and become in some measure the same person with him.... His agonies, when they are thus brought home to ourselves, when we have thus adopted them and made them our own, begin at last to affect us, and we then tremble and shudder at the thought of what he feels. (*TMS* 1.i.1.2)

For Smith, as for Hume, sympathy mediated virtually every social relation, and understanding the dynamics of the social field required that one understand the laws and limits of sympathy.

However, as a number of commentators have noted, Smith's theory of sympathy was far more reliant than Hume's on a model of imagination as "theater." Where Hume tended to focus on the transmission of sentiment, for Smith sympathy always involved a sort of virtual, or representational, theater, in which the spectator placed himself in the *situation* of the other (rather than simply appropriating the sentiment of the other). "Sympathy," Smith wrote, "does not arise so much from the view of the passion, as from the situation which excites it" (1.i.1.10). Sympathy thus denoted for Smith our capacity to transport ourselves, imaginatively, from the position of spectator to actor, and then back to the position of spectator, for "the emotions of the by-stander always correspond to what, by bringing the case home to himself, he imagines should be the sentiments of the sufferer" (*TMS* 1.i.1.4). As Jonas Barish notes, Smith "puts the condition of spectatordom at the heart of the moral experience" (Barish 1981: 24); David Marshall seconds this claim, arguing that for Smith, the language of theater is not "mere convention, tradition, or figure of speech," but rather an attempt to "address the theatrical character of the way people face each other in the world" (Marshall 1986: 169).

As a consequence of his understanding of sympathy as a theatrical, interpretative act, Smith found himself stressing, to a far greater extent than Hume, the potential lack of correspondence between the sentiments of the sympathetic "spectator" and the "actor" that was the subject of sympathy. He noted, for example, that

> [w]e sometimes feel for another, a passion of which he himself seems to be altogether incapable; because, when we put ourselves in his case, that passion arises in our breast from the imagination, though it does not in his from the reality. (*TMS* 1.i.1.10)

We might call this "simulacrum sympathy," for while our own passion may seem to be an imitation, or copy, of the other's passion, it is in fact a "copy" that has no original. Smith provided a number of examples of simulacrum sympathy, noting that "[w]e blush for the impudence and rudeness of another, though he himself appears to have no sense of the impropriety of his own behaviour" (*TMS* 1.i.1.10); we feel anguish at the sight of a madman, though "the poor wretch, who is in [the state of madness], laughs and sings perhaps, and is altogether insensible to his own misery"; and the mother feels pangs of anguish when her child cries, though the "infant... feels only the uneasiness of the present instant, which can never be great" (*TMS* 1.i.1.10–12). "We even sympathize with the dead," imagining their privations and our own inability to help them, for they are "shut out from life and conversation... [and] laid in the cold grave, a prey to corruption and the reptiles of the earth." Yet, he noted, this sympathy with the dead was based on an illusion, since the "happiness of the dead... most assuredly, is affected by none of these circumstances" (*TMS* 1.i.1.13). Nevertheless, it was precisely this illusory sympathy with the dead, Smith suggested, which allowed us to generate an idea of death itself, for our "idea of that dreary and endless melancholy of death" arose from this simulacrum of the sentiments of the dead.

Sympathy, the dead, and the gold standard

While many critics have read Smith's discussion of sympathy with the dead as a curious aside, or as simply one of several examples of our capacity to take on sympathetically affects that others do not actually feel, his claims about the relationship between death and sympathy are in fact central to the logic of *The Theory of Moral Sentiments*. It is puzzling that this passage has received, in general, such cursory treatment, for its importance is highlighted both by its prominent position in the text (the last paragraph of the first chapter), as well as by Smith's claim that the dread of death that sympathy with the dead enables is "one of the most important principles in human nature" which "while it afflicts and mortifies the individual, guards and protects the society" (*TMS* 1.i.1.13).

Esther Schor is among the few critics who have recognized the importance of Smith's discussion of the dead, for she notes that Smith positions this "originary act of sympathy for the dead as the motivation for all subsequent occasions of sympathy" (Schor 1994: 5). Schor contends that within Smith's *Theory*, the notion of an "unpayable debt" serves as the link between our inaugural sympathies for the dead and our subsequent sympathies with the living. Noting that Smith describes our sympathy with the dead in economic terms (the dead exact a "tribute...of fellow-feeling"), Schor argues that Smith also positions this sympathy with the dead as a potential double bind. On the one hand, the closer we seem to come to forgetting about the dead (and thus ending our indebtedness to them), the more our sympathy seems "doubly due"; on the other hand, the more sympathy we give to the dead, the more we are aware that in fact "our sympathy can afford them no consolation [which] seems to be an addition to their calamity" (*TMS* 1.i.1.13). Schor implies that Smith resolves this potential double-bind by suggesting that the unpayable nature of our debt to the dead, rather than draining us of our capacity for sympathy, instead creates a sympathetic "surplus" that can be discharged among the living. Smith's account of the role of the dead in enabling sympathy with the living thus captures the seeming paradox—described more recently by economist Geoffrey Ingham—that the creation of currency depends upon relationships of debt (Ingham 2004). In Smith's account, however, because this emotional "currency" cannot be paid back to the dead—as would be the case with state-issued money, for example, which is paid back in taxes—it must be expended on living others (see Figure 2.1). For Smith, Schor argues,

> [t]he mourner at the grave is merely one point in a network of emotional exchanges which constitutes the moral circulation of a society. The dead, because they cannot be remediated—because they both evoke and warrant our feelings of "dreary and endless melancholy"—provide the gold standard for the endlessly circulating currency of sympathy which constitutes a normative morality. For Smith, the moral authority of the dead, not of a transcendental God nor of the individual human body, "guarantees" the social circulation of sympathy, pity, compassion, approbation, and censure by which the living regulate their actions.(Schor 1994: 37)

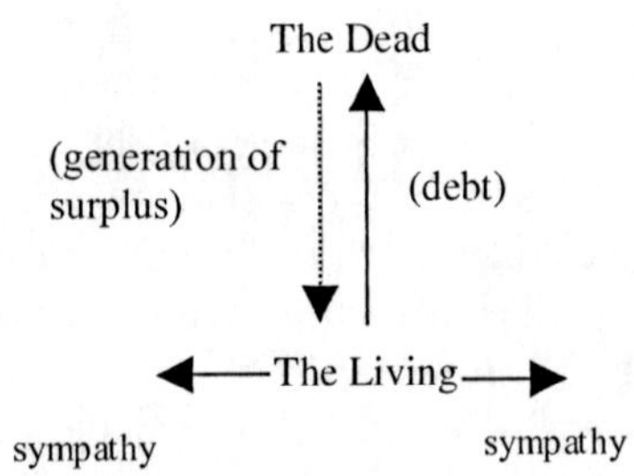

Figure 2.1 The emergence of emotional currency by means of debt.

As Schor's analysis highlights, Smith's opening claim about the dead is fundamental to his vision of the "exchange" of sympathies between living spectators and actors, as well as the more general production of social order.

Schor insists that her description of the dead as the "gold standard" of sympathetic exchange among the living in Smith's account is not simply a clever metaphor, but rather highlights the resonance within Smith's theory of sympathy of "the crisis of public confidence caused by the proliferation of paper money" in the eighteenth century (Schor 1994: 37). Thus, just as Smith suggested in *The Theory of Moral Sentiments* that "sympathy transmutes the dead into a vital moral resource" (Schor 1994: 37), he would later argue in the *Wealth of Nations*—begun in the early 1760s, though not published until 1776 (*CAS* 104 note 2)—that "paper money has the power to 'convert this dead stock [of gold and silver currency] into active and productive stock'" (embedded quote from *WN* 1: 341).[24] And just as Smith argued in the *Wealth of Nations* that public confidence in paper money required the continued circulation of coins, so that people can always see small amounts of "real" money in circulation, *The Theory of Moral Sentiments* suggests the importance of the textual circulation of the "local dead":

> Smith's admonition to keep small coins in circulation suggests the importance, at once, of a national dead and a local dead; of the circulation of texts of unspecified grief circulating among the graveyard poems of Blair, Hervey, Young, and Warton; and of the simultaneous transmission of sympathies through literature and the accessibility of the dead to citizens of small literary means. (Schor 1994: 39)

Smith's solutions to problems of disorder in the spheres of sympathy and money were homologous, in short, because each attempted to resolve the apparent paradoxes of forms of recursivity that had their origins in the imagination.

Where Schor links Smith's analyses of sympathy and money by appealing to a "crisis of confidence" that seems primarily epistemological in nature, my earlier discussion of the Seven Years' War emphasizes the much more immediate stakes of such a crisis, for the buildup to the war, and the war itself, seemed to point toward perpetually escalating cycles of both violence and debt. Between the start and end of this war with France, the national debt in Britain nearly doubled from £72,289,000 to £139,516,800. As de Bolla notes, perhaps even more significant than this increase in the national debt was the fact that the difference between "the total specie circulating in the economy and the total debt" became increasingly evident, as the volume of debt expanded far beyond the volume of available specie (De Bolla 1989: 108, 111). Though the Seven Years' War was fought in the hopes of ridding Britain of its debt—to free it from the economic claims of the past—it instead seemed to auger the possibility of a "infinite debt"; that is, a debt that could never be paid off (De Bolla 1989: 111).

If, as De Bolla argues, by the end of the Seven Years' War, "opinion had evolved, or perhaps been pushed, into an acceptance of a permanent discrepancy between the total circulating specie and the debt" (De Bolla 1989: 111), this was only possible to the extent that the claims of the dead could be understood as the source of current value, rather than simply a drain upon the living. It is from the perspective of this topical crisis that we can understand the significance of Smith's homologous solutions to the crises of sympathy and public credit: in each case, he resolved crisis by positioning the claims of the dead as a form of currency that could be deployed in the present.[25]

Resentment, the dread of death and social order

Though Schor's account captures the connections between Smith's moral and economic philosophies and his belief that indebtedness was fundamental to both spheres, it is also important to recognize that Smith was not convinced that sympathy could, on its own, maintain social order. Even in his opening discussion of our sympathy with the dead, Smith suggested that the maintenance of social order required a mode of *constitutive* violence by suggesting that the "dread of death" which sympathy produces "guards and protects the society" (*TMS* 1.i.1.13). Society, for Smith, depends not simply on the sympathetic excess that is produced by our relationship with the dead, but also upon our fear of death, and he suggested that the latter depended upon our sense of an "external" power capable of destroying us. In what follows, I outline the connection Smith established between the originary tribute demanded by the dead, on the one hand, and the role of the state in managing the fear of death through structures of resentment and executions, on the other.

While *The Theory of Moral Sentiments* is in many ways a conduct book that explained to its readers how individual virtue may be obtained through the proper exercise of sympathy, it is also a sociological account of the formation of groups. Thus, in addition to Smith's explanations of sympathy as the origin of our various moral judgments of approbation and disapprobation, it includes numerous descriptions of the ways in which groups form around acts of reward and punishment. Smith was interested in a wide variety of group phenomena, ranging from the aesthetic responses of theater spectators (*TMS* 2.i.5.3) to the admiration of the rich by the poor (and by extension, the origin of class divisions) (*TMS* 1.iii.2.3), to more violent forms of group behavior, such as patriotism and soldierly self-sacrifice (*TMS* 6.ii.2.2) and revenge cycles (*TMS* 2.ii.1.7).

Smith suggested that all of these group phenomena could be traced back to the tendency of sympathy to produce groups by creating a "concord" of sentiment among a series of individuals. Smith frequently focused on cases of social concord that exemplified either an increase of collective pleasure or a decrease of collective suffering, and scholars have tended to highlight these examples. The pleasure of seeing others feel as we do, Smith claimed, is the highest of all pleasures—"nothing pleases us more than to observe in other men a fellow-feeling with all the emotions of our own breast" (*TMS* 1.i.2.1)—and as a result we often unconsciously moderate our emotional state to allow for a sympathetic concord. In the case of someone who loses a son, for example, the suffering individual "longs for that relief which nothing can afford him but the entire concord of the affections of the spectators with his own," yet he unconsciously recognizes that this concord can be achieved only if he "lower[s] his passion to that pitch, in which the spectators are capable of going along with him" (*TMS* 1.i.3.7). The sufferer is able to do this by sympathizing with those indifferent spectators around him, for

> [a]s their sympathy makes them look at it [i.e., his situation], in some measure, with his eyes, so his sympathy makes him look at it, in some measure, with theirs, especially when in their presence and acting under their observation: and as the reflected passion, which he thus conceives, is much weaker than the original one, it necessarily abates the violence of what he felt before he came into their presence....(*TMS* 1.i.4.8)

The *desire* for sympathetic concord in fact allows the sufferer to suffer less, and thus produces this concord itself. This example highlights the fact that, for Smith, one of the primary positive social effects of sympathy is the moderation of emotional differences between members of a group, such that a unity of sentiment is achieved, and it suggests that sympathy overcomes the isolation of individuals, binding groups together through shared happiness, and turning outcasts—for example, the lone sufferer—into one of the group.

Yet however much sympathy might facilitate this sort of unification of society, its tendency to produce emotional "concord" harbors a more problematic possibility. If one supposes, for example, that the man from the example above "lost" his son not to disease, but to civil strife or war, then, in this situation, the sufferer may find himself positioned between two antagonistic groups, one of which is responsible for his suffering. Within Smith's model, what sort of unity would sympathy generate in this circumstance, and toward what "end" would this unification tend? It is by no means clear that the occasion of the man's suffering would serve to bind together these two groups through a shared increase in pleasure or a collective decrease in suffering, for one of these groups was itself responsible for the suffering in the first place.

Smith took up these sorts of questions in a section entitled "Of MERIT and DISMERIT; or, the Objects of REWARD and PUNISHMENT," which presents a very different representation of the "final cause" of sympathy, one focused around the concepts of resentment and revenge. In this section, Smith outlined the ways in which sympathy enables us to judge others as deserving of reward (merit) or punishment (demerit). At the basis of our judgments of merit and demerit are the sentiments of gratitude and resentment: we judge someone meritorious when we feel grateful to that person, and conversely we judge someone as demeritorious when we feel resentful toward that individual. Smith acknowledged that much of our gratitude and resentment is grounded in self-interest; for example, I feel grateful when someone directly benefits me. Yet our gratitude and resentment also can be extended sympathetically to our companions. So, for example, "[w]hen we see one man assisted, protected, relieved by another, our sympathy with the joy of the person who receives the benefit serves only to animate our fellow-feeling with his gratitude towards him who bestows it" (*TMS* 2.i.2.5). In similar fashion, sympathy focuses emotions such as anger and abhorrence toward the parties responsible for producing a companion's suffering in the first place, for "as we sympathize with the sorrows of our fellow-creature whenever we see his distress, so we likewise enter into his abhorrence and aversion for whatever has given occasion to it" (*TMS* 2.i.2.5).

More significantly, however, these sympathetically generated sentiments of gratitude and resentment also encourage us to *act* like our companion or friend. We help those toward whom we feel gratitude, and we even harm those toward whom we feel sympathetic resentment (*TMS* 2.i.2.5). In an especially vivid example, Smith cited sympathetic resentment as the cause of revenge, asking his readers to imagine a situation in which "we see one man oppressed and injured by another." In this situation, Smith argued, "[w]e are rejoiced to see him attack his adversary in his turn, and are eager and ready to assist him whenever he exerts himself for defence, or even for vengeance within a certain degree." And should this object of our sympathy be slain—that is, "[i]f the injured should perish in the quarrel"—we are literally possessed by his spirit of resentment, for

> we not only sympathize with the real resentment of his friends and relations, but with the imaginary resentment which in fancy we lend to the dead...as we put ourselves in his situation, as we enter, as it were, into his body, and in our imaginations, in some measure, animate anew the deformed and mangled carcass of the slain, when we bring home in this manner his case to our own bosoms.... We feel that resentment which we imagine he ought to feel, and which he would feel, if in his cold and lifeless body there remained any consciousness of what passes on earth. (*TMS* 2.i.2.5)

Revenge and blood feuds, then, are the result of an imaginary possession of the living by the dead, as the spirits of the living are forced by sympathy to play out the antagonistic desires of the departed.

Smith's focus on the violence inherent in resentment, in combination with his suggestion that we tend to restrict our sympathetic gratitude and resentment to our local party of companions, highlighted the possibility that sympathy often worked *against* widespread social unity precisely by creating factions within society.[26] While the friends of the "injured" party will certainly be motivated by resentment to take revenge on the perceived aggressor, what is then to prevent the friends of the aggressor from protecting or avenging their own companion? The introduction of acts of violence within the social field threatens to transform sympathy into a disruptive force that binds together one set of individuals only at the expense of any widespread social bonding. Smith acknowledged this, noting that

> [t]he moment that injury begins, the moment that mutual resentment and animosity take place, all the bands of [society] are broke asunder, and the different members of which it consisted are, as it were, dissipated and scattered abroad by the violence and opposition of their discordant affections. (2.ii.3.3)

It is vital to note that disruption and dissipation are not autonomous forces working counter to sympathy, but rather are facilitated *by* sympathy itself. Sympathy, in other words, disrupts society as much as it binds it together.

Smith attempted to resolve this problem by suggesting that sympathy facilitates our ability to distinguish proper from improper cases of gratitude and resentment. He argued that the ripplelike expansion of the sentiments of gratitude and resentment from our own person to the circle of our companions *should* indicate to us that these sentiments are most proper when they become universal, that is, when our sympathetic gratitude or resentment is with no particular person or party, but rather with the "impartial spectator," that simulacrum that represents all people. Thus, Smith claimed, the sentiments of gratitude and resentment

> seem proper and approved of, when the heart of every impartial spectator entirely sympathizes with them, when every indifferent by-stander entirely enters into, and goes along with them.
>
> He, therefore, appears to deserve reward, who, to some person or persons, is the natural object of a gratitude which every human heart is disposed to beat time to, and thereby applaud: and he, on the other hand, appears to deserve punishment, who in the same manner is to some person or persons the natural object of a resentment which the breast of every reasonable man is ready to adopt and sympathize with. (*TMS* 2.i.2.3)

Moreover, while we may initially sympathize with the resentment of an injured party, should we subsequently come to judge that individual's resentment as excessive, our support will wither. Thus, Smith wrote,

> this too violent resentment, instead of carrying us along with it, becomes itself the object of our resentment and indignation. We enter into the opposite resentment of the person who is the object of this unjust emotion, and who is in danger of suffering from it. (*TMS* 2.i.5.8)

Here, Smith seemed to hold out the possibility that sympathy is able to correct its own excesses by directing our attention away from improper and toward proper opportunities for sympathizing. He called this orientation toward proper objects of resentment *justice*—a force, he contended, that was vital to the maintenance of society, for without it, society "break[s] asunder" the moment that resentment enters the social field (*TMS* 2.ii.3.3; see also *TMS* 2.ii.1.1-5). The final cause of justice—the reason that Nature has "implanted in the human breast" the sense of justice—is thus the preservation of society.[27]

Yet precisely because the sense of justice is so vital to social order, society does not depend only on its spontaneous emergence within each individual, but also enforces it through "force." Justice, Smith wrote, "is not left to the freedom of our wills, [and] may [thus] be extorted by force" (*TMS* 2.ii.1.5). The power capable of occupying such a position is the state, and its capacity to "extor[t] by force" the observance of justice depends upon both the threat and the use of violence, including the execution of individuals. The civil magistrate, Smith contended, has the power of "preserving the public peace by restraining injustice," and to disobey the commands of the "sovereign" is "not only blamable but punishable" (*TMS* 2.ii.1.8). While the perfect state, for Smith, is one in which everyone would be capable of sympathizing with the impartial spectator immediately—thus rendering external institutions of sovereignty unnecessary—because individuals in fact tend to restrict their sympathies to their companions, the state becomes the necessary support of justice.

It is important to recognize, however, that the power of the state depends upon the same channels of sympathy as resentment. With or without the support of the state, the sense of justice operates by turning our gaze toward the possibility of our own harm or death. When we contemplate the commission of an unjust act, we instantly become aware of the possibility that others will revenge themselves upon us. Justice, operating through the fear of death, "overawe[s] [potential aggressors] into a respect for [the] innocence [of potential victims]"; without this, aggressors "would, like wild beasts, be at all times ready to fly upon [victims]" (*TMS* 2.ii.3.4). While justice thus achieves its ends by appealing to our self-interest—our fear of being attacked in turn—this subjective economy of fear and interest is itself dependent upon sympathy. We are able to conclude that others will resent—and thus attack—us only because we are able first to sympathize with these others. Even more fundamentally, our fear of death—that backdrop against which our moral choices unfold—is possible only on the basis of sympathy, since, for Smith, even our own death does not really "belong" to us, but is donated to us by our initial sympathy with the dead. Justice may require a self-interested fear of death for its operation, but this fear of death itself requires both an anterior sympathy with the dead and a current sympathy with the situations of others. Thus the state, in enforcing sentiments of justice through punishment, does not operate beyond sympathy, but rather forces the sympathetic flow of sentiments in a particular direction.

In an unexpected way, Smith's emphasis on the role of the state in maintaining social harmony through violence and the fear of death aligned his position with that sketched out by Hobbes, despite Smith's lengthy critique of the author of *Leviathan* in the final part of *The Theory of Moral Sentiments* (*TMS* 7.iii.2.1ff). Smith objected to Hobbes's claim that all human actions were motivated by self-interest, and he took pains to highlight the fact that sympathy "cannot, in any sense, be regarded as a selfish principle" (*TMS* 7.iii.1.4). Yet while sympathy itself may not be a selfish principle—it is, for Smith, simply the psychological mechanism that enables an imaginary transposition of positions—it can certainly serve to facilitate self-interested thoughts and actions. Smith's objection to Hobbes thus obscures the fact that both believe that society can be maintained only through the fear of death operating in conjunction with a sovereign power. Smith differed from Hobbes on this point only in his attempt to specify precisely the psychological mechanism that enabled this fear, pinpointing sympathy as the efficient cause of fear.

Smith's Hobbesianism is exemplified by his discussion of state-sponsored executions, for the latter, as they are described in the *Theory*, dramatize the halt of resentment.[28] Smith argued—arguably against the realities of eighteenth-century executions—that "[w]hen an inhuman murderer is brought to the scaffold, though we have some compassion for his misery, we can have no sort of fellow-feeling with his resentment" (*TMS* 2.i.3.2).[29] Smith contended that even the "violator of the laws of justice" will begin to detest himself, since "[b]y sympathizing with the hatred and abhorrence which other men must entertain for him, he becomes in some measure the object of his own hatred and abhorrence" (*TMS* 2.ii.2.3). Executions thus resolve the threat of ever-expanding resentment by allowing individuals a state-sponsored opportunity to draw the lessons that they *should* have drawn from simply observing the ripplelike spread of sympathy in other cases, the lesson that resentment is only proper when it is "universal," which in this case means applied by the state. Sympathy, for Smith, ensured justice and therefore the preservation of society, but it did so only by revealing the threat of a Hobbesian state of all against all, while at same time allowing us to recognize state-sponsored violence as the solution to this possible destruction of the *socius*.[30]

Genre, system, and *The Theory of Moral Sentiments*

The questions of violence and faction that subtended Smith's account of sympathy in *The Theory of Moral Sentiments* did not prevent the book from finding an audience eager for this sort of moral philosophy. Shortly after the book's publication, Hume wrote Smith that "the Public seemed disposed to applaud [Smith's book] extremely" (Hume, cited in *TMS* 25), and the *Theory* received positive reviews in the May 1759 *Critical Review*, the July 1759 *Monthly Review*, the 1759 *Annual Register* and (in France) the October 1760 *Journal encyclopédique* (TMS: 28–29; Ross 180–94), with reviewers praising the book for its "elegant" style and its religious probity (*TMS* 27–29). A French translation of the *Theory* appeared in 1764, and even after the publication of the *Wealth of Nations* (1776), Smith remained far better known in France as a moral philosopher than as a political economist (*TMS* 30; Chisick 2004: 246). In Britain, the *Theory* went through five subsequent editions, the last published shortly before Smith's death in 1790 (Raphael and Macfie in *TMS*: 28–29)

The fact that Smith's reflections on sympathy were so much better received than Hume's account as outlined in the latter's *Treatise* was due to several factors. Smith's institutional affiliation with the University of Glasgow had allowed him opportunities to test his approach to moral philosophy for several years before publishing *The Theory of Moral Sentiments*. As Francis Hutcheson had discovered when he earlier held the same chair in Moral Philosophy, popular teachers were also often able to engender informal networks of former students willing to promote and defend their mentors' books (Sher 1990: 94-99), and Smith likely benefited from such support as well. In addition, as John Dwyer notes, the success of Smith's *Theory* was facilitated by the consonance of its claims with a larger Scottish discourse that linked sentimentality with classical and Stoic interpretations of virtue (Dwyer 1993).

Yet the success of Smith's version of sentimental moral philosophy was arguably in largest part a function of his willingness to dispense with the extensive epistemological reflections with which Hume had begun his book. While *The Theory of Moral Sentiments* was written in the genre of system—and while, as I have argued elsewhere, it contained one of the most deep-reaching eighteenth-century accounts of the relationships between the genre of system and social systems (Mitchell 2006)—Smith began his account of moral sentiments *in media res*. Rather than beginning with philosophical proofs, in the style of Hume's *Treatise*, Smith began with numerous concrete examples of sympathy taken from daily life, a decision that appealed to Smith's reviewers. The author of the July 1759 review in the *Monthly Review* praised Smith's "agreeable manner of illustrating his argument, by the frequent appeals he makes to fact and experience" (*TMS* 27), while Edmund Burke, in his article for the 1759 *Annual Register* applauded the "numerous and happy" illustrations contained in the text

(Burke, cited in *TMS* 28). The wealth of illustrations in the *Theory* followed a recipe that Francis Hutcheson had already established as successful in his lectures at the University of Glasgow (Sher 1990: 95) but it also, and more significantly, made it possible for readers to link Smith's claims to a variety of genres, such as novels, poems, and sermons (Dwyer 1993).

Smith, in short, had created a system of moral philosophy able to propagate itself by accommodating ever more examples of its central claims. Where Hume had sought, through his *Treatise*, to regulate social systems by means of systematic reflection on sympathy, Smith opted for a form of regulation that denied the appearance of systematicity. Rather than sharpening his readers' skills at systematic thought, the *Theory* encouraged a perpetually mobile attentiveness to the ways in which sympathy ordered particular situations.

CODA: AFFFECTIVE, IMAGINARY, AND SYMBOLIC IDENTIFICATION

Rousseau and Smith developed their theories of imaginative identification in a period of escalating conflict between Britain and France, as a mimetic rivalry focused around attracting investors led to actual war between the countries in 1756. Given this phenomenological background, it is not surprising that the violent potential of both recursive and speculative social processes dominated each of their accounts of the dynamics of social systems. For Rousseau and Smith, exchange and reciprocity led as easily to the formation of antagonistic minisystems as to a global unity. For Rousseau, exchange and reciprocity produced closed imaginative social systems; that is, systems that could not be reformed precisely because they tended to seal off their own speculative logic from the possibility of any influence from the "outside." For Smith too, the fact that humans were dominated by a "general disposition to exchange" (as he later described it in the *Wealth of Nations*) led to problems when it came to sentiments, and the possibility of escalating and uncontrollable violence haunts *The Theory of Moral Sentiments*. Rousseau sought to resolve the problems to which exchange led by formulating an "haptopraxology" capable of theorizing an affective "outside" of representation, while Smith, adopting an epistemology fully committed to representation, hoped that conflict could be stemmed by suspending the subject of imagination between a form of possession by the dead, on one side, and the terrifying power of the state, on the other.

If Smith's account of sympathy and imagined communities seems particularly modern, it is because poststructuralist social theory—particularly in its psychoanalytically inspired versions—almost invariably shares with Smith the belief that social relations are entirely contained within the sphere of representation. It is not difficult to locate within Smith's account of intersubjectivity the elements and structure of more recent Lacanian-

Marxist accounts of sociality: just as Smith sees subjectivity as grounded in a constitutive debt to the dead, tending toward imaginative rivalry, and stabilized by the state's capacities to "symbolically" resolve rivalry by drawing upon our "dread of death," contemporary theorists such as Slavoj Žižek see social systems as dependent upon "symbolic" identification and the constitutive terrors and pleasures of "the Real" to forestall the violence produced by imaginary identification (see e.g., Žižek 1989 and 1993). Žižek's emphasis on the importance of the Real echoes Smith's insistence on the constitutive role of the dead. Žižek insists that while ideologies such as nationalism may be grounded in forms of belief that have "a reflexive structure proper to…intersubjective space"—that is, ideology, like public credit, persists "only insofar as subjects believe in its existence" (Žižek 1993: 202, 201)—one cannot fully account for the unity of imaginary communities in terms of "identifications." Imaginary identifications may initiate, and symbolic identifications may resolve, mimetic rivalry and violence, but in addition there must be an affective surplus—what Žižek calls variously *jouissance*, the Thing, or the Real—that "animates" these "ideological practices" (Žižek 1993: 202). It is this affective surplus that, within Žižek's account, transforms the *logical possibility* of being in common into the "plenitude and vivacity" of community, and it is also that which (echoing Smith) transforms the constitutive negativity at the heart of the subject into the *dread* of death. These similarities between Smith and contemporary social theory need not be understood as the result of Smith's "influence" on contemporary theory, but rather indicate a convergence that is the result of a shared understanding of the subject as the locus of mimetic and recursive imaginative relations.

Yet if contemporary poststructuralist psychoanalytic cultural criticism seems to echo key elements of Smith's account of group psychology, it also finds itself consistently troubled by the same aporae that motivated Rousseau's account of "energetic" identification. In attempting to account for the *source* of the affective surplus that Žižek suggests is central to an adequate theory of ideology and social systems, psychoanalytic thought has continually found itself appealing to an untheorized mode of "affective" identification that precedes, and founds, representational identification. As Mikkel Borch-Jacobsen has noted, though identification was for Freud "*the* fundamental concept, the *Grundbegriff*, of psychoanalysis," Freud also remained caught between "two different theories of identification, at least one of which is radically incompatible…with psychoanalysis" (Borch-Jacobsen 1988: 176).[31] Freud most frequently positioned identification as a process that occurred *within* representation; that is, as an operation by means of which the ego binds itself to its representations of others.[32] In the case of the Oedipal drama, for example, to say that the young boy identifies with his father is to say that the boy's ego transforms itself by molding itself around its representations of the father, who serves as a model (*Vorbild*) (Freud 1953–74, vol. 18: 106). However, at other crucial moments Freud described identification as a process that occurred *prior* to representation and prior to the formation of ego—as when, for example, he described in *The Ego and the Id* a "direct and immediate" form of identification of the infant boy with his father which took place "earlier than any object-cathexis" (that is, prior to the formation of the ego and its capacity for representations) (Freud 1953–74, vol. 19: 31). This latter mode of "primary" identification could not be a process that happened *to* the ego, but instead described a mode of affective donation that *founds* the ego itself.

Nor did Freud limit this primary mode of identification to the prehistory of the subject, for his analysis of panic in *Group Psychology and the Analysis of the Ego* hinted that the radical openness of primary identification was always under the surface, ready to irrupt again in adult life in cases of group panic. *Group Psychology* was intended to prove that groups were bound together by both vertical and horizontal lines of identification, for Freud contended that each member of a group identified with the group leader, taking him or her as "ego ideal," while at the same time, members of the group also identified with one another. Yet Freud *also* claimed that in cases of panic—that is, periods during which the bonds of identification between members of a group are dissolved—fear can be "increased to enormous proportions through induction (contagion)" (Freud 1953–74, vol. 18: 96). Within Freud's account, "contagion" cannot be simply a synonym for identification, since panic depends on precisely the dissolution of the bonds of identification that constituted the group, but must rather denote a social "tie" that operates below, or beyond, both identification or object-cathexis.[33] In short, in both of these cases—the primary identification that founds the ego, and the affective "contagion" that is enabled when group identifications disappear—Freud found himself appealing to a mode of identification that psychoanalysis was unable to think in its own terms. Nor has such an appeal been limited to Freud: Jacques Lacan, for example, argued in "Au-delà du 'Principe de réalité" ("Beyond the Reality Principle") that a form of "affective identification" must precede representational identification (Lacan 1966: 73–92), while, more recently, cultural critics such as Teresa Brennan have proposed that subjectivity begins with a "gift" of affect from mother to child (Brennan 1992). Yet as Žižek (correctly) insists, psychoanalysis can have nothing to do with any sort of "primary" or "affective" identification, since such a mode of "communication"—a mode in which "*communication does not take place between subjects, but directly between affects*"—undercuts the very framework of psychoanalysis itself (Žižek 1993: 218).

If this dilemma of psychoanalysis recalls Rousseau's struggles to distinguish between representational and energetic identification, it is because contemporary critics invested in psychoanalysis are struggling with this same Rousseauvian problematic: *how* to think that force that exceeds, but at the same time inaugurates and makes possible, systems of subjectivity? Insofar as some of the most exciting work on the relationships between eighteenth- and nineteenth-century finance and literature has relied on psychoanalytic principles, particularly in its Žižekian formulation, there is little doubt that psychoanalytically inflected cultural criticism has much to offer this area of research.[34] Yet it also seems fair to say that contemporary cultural critics invested in this approach have generally sought to minimize the epistemological tensions that traverse their understanding of subjectivity by following Smith's path, focusing on the psychological operations that *maintain* social systems, rather than those that operate in tenuous moments of destabilization. Neither Smith's account in *The Theory of Moral Sentiments* nor contemporary psychoanalytic social theory covers over completely the forms of affect that operate beyond or below representation, but hints of its antisystemic potentialities appear only at the ragged edges of their accounts, such as in Smith's description of the role of the dead in the emergence of social systems, in Freud's account of the origin and dissolutions of "groups" (whether the small group of the family or larger social systems), and in Žižek's emphasis on the affective surplus that is necessary for every system of ideology. Yet I suggest that in order to understand more fully the *emergence* of new systems, cultural critics must look beyond "the subject" and "representation," and aim at something more like Rousseau's "haptopraxology." While Rousseau's effort to theorize an energetic mode of identification was no doubt hindered by his desire to restrict it to an inaccessible origin of history, his approach nevertheless highlights the importance of understanding affects not as a form of psychic energy that must be bound, but rather as the enabling condition of systems themselves.

3 Antislavery poetry and the speculative subject

> For it is remarkable in human nature, that though we always sympathize with our relations, and with those under our eye, the distress of persons remote and unknown affects us very little. (Kames 1767: 17)

> What, then, can oratorical imagery effect? Well, it is able in many ways to infuse vehemence and passion into spoken words, while more particularly when it is combined with the argumentative passages it not only persuades the hearer but actually makes him its slave. (Longinus 1987: 89)

In the last chapter, I considered Rousseau's and Smith's efforts to limit the violent potential of sympathy, its tendency to produce autonomous systems and self-perpetuating factions. In this chapter, I am interested in authors who considered nearly the opposite problem, namely, the question of how sympathy could be sparked in cases where it appeared to be lacking. I focus on the British antislavery movement of the 1770s and '80s, and especially on the role of antislavery poetry in this effort.[1] For many eighteenth-century critics of slavery, the continued existence of the slave trade demonstrated the power of system: British merchants and politicians, they suggested, had created what a contemporary observer described as a closed "system of slavery" that disabled benevolence by systematically occluding occasions for sympathy (Nickolls 1788: 4). While some critics argued that the dehumanizing effects of the slave trade could be negated by abolishing this particular form of commerce, others wondered whether perhaps the cancer had already spread to the more general system of British commerce itself. This virtual unity of the slave trade system and British commerce as a whole was stressed by both critics and slave merchant advocates. The latter emphasized the extent to which British state finance and public credit had come to depend upon the properties, income, and taxes of slave traders and plantation owners, and advocates used these facts to attempt to convince their listeners that financial destruction would be visited upon Britain should it seek to regulate or abolish the slave trade. For critics such as Ann Yearsley, however, these claims simply confirmed that British commerce had itself become a "destructive system" that had to be reformed in its entirety (Yearsley 1788: 26).

I focus here on the efforts of antislavery poets to create a system of poetry that would enable new forms of imaginative and sympathetic social relations capable of resisting, and perhaps even reforming, the destructive system of the slave trade. Yet the development of such a literary system was a particularly difficult task, for antislavery poets found themselves beholden to a number of seemingly incompatible demands. First, to the extent that antislavery poetry aspired both to direct political action and poetic excellence, it was not at all clear to what criteria these poems should be beholden. Should such verse follow the path of political "eloquence" and simply arrange facts about the slave trade in a way that moved readers to action, or was it instead to be assessed by what eighteenth-century rhetorical treatises described as poetry's "licence" to produce readerly transport by deviating from the truth? Most antislavery poets chose the former route—agreeing with Hannah More that, in the case of slavery and the slave trade, "Art wou'd weave her gayest flow'rs in vain" (More 1788: 4; ll. 51-54)—and sought instead to produce transport by soliciting their readers' sympathy for suffering slaves. Yet here as well, antislavery poets found themselves in a difficult position, for, as Julie Ellison notes, eighteenth-century theories of sympathy provided little encouragement to antislavery advocates. Smith had argued against "whining and melancholy moralists, who are perpetually reproaching us with our happiness, while so many of our brethren are in misery" (*TMS* 3.3.9), and Scottish moral philosophers consistently had argued that sympathy neither could, nor should, be extended much beyond one's own limited circle (Ellison 1999: 10–12). Yet because antislavery advocates sought to accomplish precisely such an extension of sympathy to distant others, thereby creating systems of sympathetic relations even in cases in which such bonds did not seem to "naturally" arise, they were under pressure to explain how, or why, *poetry* was able to exceed the laws of natural sympathy.

For many poets, these competing and contradictory demands made it difficult, if not impossible, to imagine a viable system of antislavery poetry, and I consider in this chapter the example of William Cowper, who, only a year after initially finding the abolition of the slave trade a topic quite amenable to "poetical management," concluded that, in fact, to write verse on this topic produced a "degradation of poetry" (*LPWC*, vol. 3: 103, 178). For other poets, however, these contradictory requirements demanded the invention of new conceptions of sympathy and new understandings of the effects of poetry. As an example of this latter strategy, I focus on Ann Yearsley's "A Poem on the Inhumanity of the Slave-Trade" (1788), which positioned verse as a literary form that was particularly able to extend the purportedly "natural" limits of sympathy.[2] For Yearsley, poetic language produced sympathy not primarily as a consequence of its referential capacity (that is, its ability to represent the actual sufferings of victims to those in political and economic power), but rather on account of its ability to model virtual social relations (that is, present potential social relations that had no true referent in the reader's past or present). For Yearsley, sympathy resulted from the imagination's speculative activity—its ability to figure virtual social relationships—rather than its purported capacity to "transmit" sentiments from the victims of the slave trade to readers.

In addition to emphasizing the vexed position of a "system" of late eighteenth-century British antislavery poetry, it is my hope that this chapter will also contribute to the ongoing discussion of the relationship between the system of antislavery advocacy and the development of the system of British capitalism in the late eighteenth century. The British antislavery movement is a fascinating case study of the limits of system autonomy: on the one hand, the movement developed as a planned and well-organized system of communication, publication, and legislative pressure; on the other hand, it was designed to intervene directly in the operations of another system (the specific "system of slavery" for some; the system of British commerce as a whole, for others). Since the publication of Eric Williams's *Capitalism and Slavery* in 1944, the nature of the antislavery movement's intervention has been hotly contested. Williams suggested that abolitionism, whatever its moral impetus, "intervened" by facilitating Britain's move away from an increasingly costly slave labor system to a much more efficient capitalist wage-labor system, and for both Williams and critics who have followed his lead, antislavery literature is thus best understood as a sort of ideological cover for the transformation of capitalism itself (Williams 1994).[3] More recently, historians such as Thomas Haskell have sought to reverse this argument, suggesting that the system of capitalism enabled the emergence of an autonomous system of moral thought—of which the antislavery movement was one component—by providing people with what Haskell calls "recipes" for understanding how one's own actions could have significant effects in distant places. At stake in this debate is the interpretation of homology: if both the system of antislavery advocacy and the late eighteenth-century British system of commerce valorized the same kinds of "recipes" for thinking about the effect of one's actions on distant others, do those homologies prove system linkage or simply "resonance" between systems? I argue that by focusing on the role of the virtual in Yearsley's poetry, we can understand both how antislavery poetry could encourage a capitalist habitus yet at the same time constitute an autonomous system with potentialities that exceeded its use-value for capitalism.

I. LITERARY FORM AND THE QUESTION OF A SYSTEM OF ANTISLAVERY POETRY

British antislavery poetry arguably extends back at least to the start of the eighteenth century, but the volume of verse directed against the slave trade increased dramatically in the 1770s and 1780s.[4] This discursive explosion was spurred in part by James Ramsay's and Thomas Clarkson's graphic prose exposés of slave-trade conditions (Ramsay 1784; Clarkson 1788), which in turn encouraged the formation of antislavery societies in the late 1780s, such as the Society for Effecting the Abolition of the Slave Trade, founded in 1787. The Society proved especially capable of establishing extensive systems of correspondence and literary distribution: within months of its formation, the Society had distributed hundreds of copies of circular letters describing its activities, isolated influential individuals to whom copies of the Society's publications were sent, organized petitions, and started to back legislative attempts to limit or abolish the slave trade and slavery; in the early 1790s, the Society also helped to organize boycotts of products produced by slaves, such as sugar and rum.[5] The system of literary distribution was especially impressive: by 1788, the Society had published roughly 25,000 copies of antislavery reports and 50,000 copies of antislavery pamphlets and books (Clarkson 1808, vol. 1: 571). As a result of these organizational efforts, antislavery poets had access to a large and developed publication and distribution network, and (as Wylie Sypher notes) British antislavery literature of the 1770s, '80s, and '90s can be understood as the "earliest instance of modern propaganda" (Sypher 1969: 1).[6]

Antislavery verse of the 1780s was thus assured of a relatively large readership, but at the same time its specific role in this campaign was not entirely clear. Like antislavery prose accounts and political speeches, antislavery poetry aspired to speech that had, in the language of eighteenth-century rhetorical and aesthetic theory, "power": that is, which truly moved listeners or readers into action. Yet the explicitly political goals of antislavery verse meant that it was not prima facie obvious whether this kind of poetry instantiated its own specific mode of power (which could be distinguished from that instantiated in prose accounts or political speeches on antislavery topics) or whether instead it was simply a dressed-up version of these more explicitly political modes of speech. As Savir Kaul has noted, a great deal of eighteenth-century poetry remained explicitly political even as the novel and drama retreated from such concerns, but the genre of antislavery verse was oriented toward more specific concrete legislative actions—the passage of specific bills, for example—in ways that other "political" poems, such as Pope's *Windsor Forest* or Goldsmith's *The Deserted Village*, clearly were not (Kaul 2000: 10–17). This then begged the question: given their explicit and specific political goals, were antislavery poets actually developing a new system of *poetry*, thus lending the cultural authority of verse to the political cause of antislavery, or were they instead producing works of propaganda that simply mimicked the form of poetry?

Dominant eighteenth-century rhetorical and aesthetic theory made this a difficult question for antislavery poets and reviewers to answer, for "powerful" poetry—that is, poetry that transported and moved readers—was generally associated with "fancy" and the fabulous, while antislavery poets found themselves wanting to insist that their verse remained loyal to "historical fact." Poetry and political oratory were often treated together in the large number of treatises on aesthetics and rhetoric produced during the eighteenth century, and while both verse and legislative oration were understood to produce a "transport" of the reader, these two forms of speech were frequently contrasted with respect to their relationship to "truth."[7] Powerful political speech (often simply called "eloquence") was understood to hew closely to truth (though it often employed figurative language); elevated poetic language, by contrast, found its essence in tropes and figures (though it still had to remain in the realm of the probable). Longinus's *Peri Hupsous* (*On the Sublime*), translated into English in 1712 (and again in 1724 and 1739), provided the basic schema of this distinction, for Longinus argued that images "which are found in the poets contain...a tendency to exaggeration in the way of the fabulous and...they transcend in every way the credible, but in oratorical imagery the best feature is always its reality and truth" (Longinus 1987: 89). This claim was echoed by many authors of treatises devoted in whole or part to rhetoric. Adam Smith informed his students that while it was the business of oratory to "relate facts," poetry aimed at "amusement and intertainment [sic]," and as a result, poets were granted "Poeticall licence" to deviate from facts and truth (*RLBL* 177, 188).[8] Hugh Blair, in his *Lectures on Rhetoric and Belles Lettres* (1783), argued that while "[t]he Historian, the Orator, the Philosopher address themselves, for the most part, primarily to the understanding" for "their direct aim is to inform, to persuade, or to instruct," "the primary aim of a Poet," by contrast, "is to please, and to move; and, therefore, it is to the Imagination, and the Passion, that he speaks" (Blair 1965, vol. 2: 312). In *The Philosophy of the Passions* (1771), James Usher distinguished between "orators" and "poets," arguing that while both employed "the force of figurative language" to move the affections of their listeners, the former did so in the cause of "persuad[ing people of] truth," while poetry often labored to create "fictions" (Usher 1772: 166, 169–70).

These theoretical alternatives put antislavery poets in an awkward position. To the extent that antislavery verse was designed to constitute a powerful communication within the system of politics, poets could adopt the premises of political oratory, which suggested that power resulted from the eloquent arrangement of facts. Adopting the mantle of political oratory would also allow these poets to counter the charges of proslavery advocates (and occasionally reviewers of antislavery poems), who claimed that antislavery activists exaggerated the sufferings of slaves.[9] Yet to the extent that their poetry was to be antislavery *verse*, its power, according to these aesthetic theories, should be the result of its transcendence of fact. In the June 1788 issue of *The European Magazine, and London Review*, an anonymous reviewer of slave trade poems captured this tension, noting that, in general, "[t]he subject [of the slave trade], while it has *truth* for its outlines, is highly susceptible of that *fictitious* colouring in which the 'Muse of HORROR' delights," a description that did not provide much encouragement for the belief that truth and the Muse could cooperate in this endeavor (vol. 13: 424).

Rather than resolving this problem of the discursive system to which antislavery poetry belonged—was it simply versified political speech or a valid species of poetry?—many poets and reviewers opted to stress the referential over the fictional aspects of their verse, arguing that poetic language could produce powerful speech through versified (but accurate) representations of misery. In the February 1788 *Monthly Review*, the anonymous reviewer of William Roscoe's *The Wrongs of Africa; A Poem, Part the First* (1787) isolated the basic premises of this approach, arguing that

> Fiction is sometimes said to be the soul of poetry. There are subjects, however, in which fancy can scarcely pass beyond nature;—in which, consequently, the poet's office is rather to describe than to invent. The wrongs of Africa afford us a subject of this kind. So numerous and horrid are the miseries created by that cruel species of commerce, the *slave trade*, that the poet, in order to produce the strongest impression on the imagination and feelings of his readers, has only to follow the track of the historian, and clothe plain facts in the dress of simple and easy verse. (vol. 78: 137)

Hannah More echoed these sentiments in *Slavery, A Poem* (1788), suggesting that in antislavery verse

> ...Art wou'd weave her gayest flow'rs in vain,
> For Truth the bright invention wou'd disdain.
> For no fictitious ills these numbers flow,
> But living anguish and substantial woe;
> (More 1788: 4. ll. 51–54)

In Book 2 of *Humanity, or The Rights of Nature* (1788), Samuel Jackson Pratt made a similar claim, arguing that his representations of the sufferings of slaves were based in fact ("history") rather than fancy:

> Ah! think not, WHITE, the Muse from fancy brings
> Those woes, for Hist'ry sanctions what she sings,
> Her bloody Annals still does Truth unfold,
> Stain'd with the victims of soul-spotting gold.
> (Pratt 1788: 82)[10]

Antislavery verse, according to these critics and poets, was not poetry by virtue of its power to produce fictions, but rather by its capacity to refer to real states of affairs; it was sanctioned not by invention but by "Hist'ry."

Yet privileging the truth-telling over the fictional aspects of antislavery inevitably brought into question its status as verse, a problem recognized by both poets and critics. Captain John Marjoribanks, for example, wondered in *Slavery, An Essay in Verse* (1792) whether his "plain unvarnished narration of mere melancholy matter of fact," "unembellished by fancy or fiction," should even be called a "poem," and he defended his use of verse as merely tactical, for while "the more intelligent part of the world, would prefer good sense and plain prose...yet there may be no inconsiderable number of others, of a more romantic turn, who could not easily be prevailed upon to peruse a pamphlet, but would seize with avidity on any thing in the form of a poem" (Majoribanks 1792: 3, 5–6).[11] Antislavery poets could depend upon the prestige of poetry, Majoribanks suggested, to drive readers to antislavery verse, even if the poems were substandard. This suggestion was echoed by the Reverend J. Jamieson, who, in the Advertisement to *The Sorrows of Slavery, a Poem* (1789), contended that poetic form was useful only to the extent that the representation of "simple historical facts in the language of poetry...might attract the attention of some who would not otherwise give themselves the trouble of looking into the subject" (Jamieson 1789: unnumbered page). However, as an anonymous contributor to the November 1788 *Monthly Review* noted, this strategy was potentially self-defeating in the long run, for the proliferation of poor quality poems would initiate a decline in the status of poetry itself:

> In the manufacturing of verse, there was never perhaps a greater number employed than at present; but few indeed give evidence of writing under the genuine inspiration of the Muses. Hence poetry has been sinking into disrepute. The quantity of rhyming trash which in our time has issued from the press, has not only disgusted the critic, but so generally disappointed the poetical reader, as greatly to diminish the demand for publications under the name of *poems*. (vol. 79: 429)

This reviewer isolated the contradiction at the center of these ambivalent defenses of antislavery poetry: it was impossible to draw upon the prestige of verse without affecting the system of poetry itself, since every verse publication became part—and therefore contributed to the overall prestige—of the system of poetry itself. Since flooding the market with substandard poems would destroy the demand for poetry, Marjoribanks's and Jamieson's attempts to expand the audience for antislavery sentiments by means of mediocre verse would undercut its own foundation.

Not all poets were convinced that the topic of antislavery necessarily produced bad poetry, yet even for those authors who argued that their verse could remain true to both "history" and poetry, the traditional opposition between rhetorical eloquence and poetic fiction seemed to deprive antislavery verse of its claim to "power." This worry was evident in the terms of impotence that dominated self-reflexive descriptions of poetry in antislavery verse: More worried that her "art...weave[s] her gayest flow'rs in vain," while Anna Laetitia Barbauld's narrator bemoaned the fact that "[t]he Preacher, Poet, Senator in vain/ Has rattled in her sight the Negro's chain" (Barbauld 1791: 5). For other poets, this fear of powerlessness was manifested as doubt about whether their words could adequately describe the horrors of slavery. The narrator of Gratia Willson's "To the generous ASSERTORS of LIBERTY for the oppressed AFRICANS," described the forced separation of a mother and child, and wondered "What words can speak the anguish of each heart,/ ...What pow'r of language painting the parting pangs"? (Wilson 1788: 267–68). In recognition of these inherent difficulties of the genre of antislavery poetry, poets often longed for the power of other generic forms. In the Preface to *The Dying Negro* (1773), Thomas Day imagined "the scenes I would present to my countrymen, could I boast an eloquence like" that of Jean-Jacques Rousseau's (Day and Bicknell 1773: vi); in *Slavery, A Poem*, Hannah More suggested that perhaps the moment for poetry to speak powerfully on the slave trade had passed, and the narrator wished for the "[s]trange pow'r" of Thomas Southerne's much earlier play *Oroonoko, or The Royal Slave* (1696), but then sadly admitted that "not to me, sweet Bard, thy pow'rs belong" (More 1788: 4; l. 49); while Barbauld, in her *Epistle*, suggested that perhaps "The Muse" was "too soon awaked" (Barbauld 1791: 5).

II. THE SUPPLEMENTS OF FORM: SYMPATHY, MOTHERHOOD, EMPIRE

In order to resolve this tension between the referential and inventive aspects of antislavery verse, authors made recourse to a series of "supplements" designed to link truth-telling to rhetorical power, thus enabling a valid system of antislavery poetry. In place of the transport that poetry was to provide through its inventiveness, antislavery poets offered the supplemental transport of sympathy: by faithfully describing slaves' sufferings, authors sought to move their readers to the affective place of these oppressed individuals. Such an act of powerful rhetorical transport, if achieved, would serve as the motive force that propelled the audience of antislavery poetry into practical action on behalf of slaves. Unfortunately, however, dominant eighteenth-century theories of sympathy provided little encouragement for the hope that practical fellow-feeling could be inspired simply by faithfully representing the sufferings of strangers and distant others; rather, the analyses of sympathy by authors such as Hutcheson, Hume, Smith, and Kames suggested that sympathy would be engendered only if readers *already* thought of slaves as part of their "home." In order to resolve this problem, antislavery poets had to supplement the supplement of sympathy, employing images of motherhood and empire as ways of linking the plight of slaves with readers' self-interest and sense of "home."

The meeting point for sympathy and the "plain facts," "Hist'ry," and "Truth" that antislavery verse sought to capture was the "living anguish and substantial woe" of the slave body in pain. Portraits of suffering bodies abounded in antislavery verse, as poets described the horrors of the Middle Passage and plantation slavery, or focused on figures such as the slave "Quasi" or romantic couples separated by slavery.[12] Some authors took what one can only describe as sadistic pleasure in depicting a body reduced to pure suffering. In *Humanity*, for example, Pratt demanded that his readers

Behold that axe the quivering limb assails,
Behold that body weltering in its wails!
Ah! hear that Bludgeon fall, that lash resound,
Ah! see those wretches writhing on the ground!
(Pratt 1788: 83)[13]

The premise for such representation, often articulated in the poems themselves, was a theory of practical sympathy, which proposed that representations of suffering would spark similar feelings in readers, which in turn would lead readers to alleviate their own suffering by relieving that of the slaves. Pratt's opening appeal to "Humanity" in his antislavery poem provides a concise description of this theory of practical sympathy:

Oft as our neighbour sinks in sudden grief,
Thou wak'st as sudden to afford relief.
Oft as the stranger's bosom heaves with sighs,
The soft responses in our bosoms rise: (Pratt 1788: 3)

Pratt's "Humanity"—structurally identical to what Hume and Smith had called "sympathy"—operated as a force of systemic connection, employing grief and sighs to link even strangers together in a system of affective resonance and practical response. Such an account suggested that sympathy provided antislavery verse not only with a supplement of "transport" almost identical to that which good poetry was supposed to enable from within itself, but in addition, employed this transport as a way of widening the reader's social system to include even far distant suffering strangers.[14]

Yet Scottish theories of sympathy provided little support for this hope that sympathy might expand the reader's social system of "neighbors." Authors such as Hutcheson, Hume, and Smith had consistently argued that representations of distant suffering, no matter how accurate or detailed, would fail to elicit anything but passing interest on the part of readers precisely because the efficacy of sympathy depended upon the exclusion of many people from the reader's social system.[15] Francis Hutcheson had established the paradigm for this claim in the third edition of *An Inquiry into the Original of Our Ideas of Beauty and Virtue* (1729), suggesting that the force of sympathy was analogous to that of gravity, in the sense that both gravity and sympathy "perhaps exten[d] to all Bodys in the Universe," but both also "increas[e] as the Distance is diminish'd, and [are] strongest when Bodys come to touch each other." This natural restriction of sympathy was absolutely necessary, Hutcheson argued, for "a general Attraction, equal in all Distances, would by the Contrariety of such multitudes of equal Forces, put an end to all Regularity of Motion, and perhaps stop it altogether" (Hutcheson 1729: 222). Hume presented a more complicated picture, suggesting in *A Treatise of Human Nature* that sympathy might very well encourage us to help a stranger. If, for example,

> I saw a person perfectly unknown to me, who, while asleep in the fields, was in danger of being trod under foot by horses, I shou'd immediately run to his assistance; and in this I shou'd be actuated by the same principle of sympathy, which makes me concern'd for the present sorrows of a stranger. (*T* 385)

However, Hume's stranger had to be physically present for sympathy to develop—sympathy is elicted only for those strangers "who [are] present with us" (*T* 384)—and he too insisted that sympathy diminished to the extent that we believed ourselves unrelated to another person (*T* 323).[16] In *The Theory of Moral Sentiments*, Smith argued that while the impartial spectator might hinder us from actively pursuing ends that we knew harmed others, little, if any, sympathetic pain would result from the misfortunes of geographically and causally distant sufferers. Smith suggested, for example, that "a man of humanity in Europe" might feel momentary sorrow upon hearing that "the great empire of China, with all its myriads of inhabitants, was suddenly swallowed up by an earthquake," but such feelings would quickly pass (*TMS* 3.3.4). He defended this claim with a logic of globality similar to that outlined by Hutcheson, arguing that even if our sympathetic attachments were spread out equally across the globe, we would always find more happy than unhappy people, and as a result, distant sufferings would fail to interest us. Lord Kames provided an even more intriguing variation on this theme, suggesting that the logic of the market often had to supplement natural sympathy: "contracts and promises are not confined to commercial dealings: they also serve to make benevolence a duty, independent of any pecuniary interest." "Pactions and agreements" are necessary "to extend the duty of benevolence," Kames contended, precisely because "it is remarkable in human nature, that though we always sympathize with our relations, and with those under our eye, the distress of persons remote and unknown affects us very little" (Kames 1767: 16, 26). Where Pratt suggested that sympathy *established* new social systems, eighteenth-century theorists of sympathy consistently argued the opposite, describing sympathy as a force that operated only within existing social systems. As a result, while antislavery poets often relied implicitly on

Scottish Enlightenment accounts of sympathy to provide their verse with a supplement of affective transport, such theories in fact tended to undercut these poets' hopes that accurate representation of slaves' sufferings would result in praxis on the part of British readers.

In order to provide the supplement of sympathy with any purchase, then, antislavery poets first had to demonstrate to readers that distant suffering slaves were in fact part of a reader's system of self-interests. For a number of authors, the system of the family—and especially the category of motherhood—provided the necessary link between readers and slaves. More, for example, suggested in *Slavery; A Poem* that the "deepest, deadliest" fault of the slave trade was that it tore babies from mothers:

> Whene'er to Afric's shores I turn my eyes,
> Horrors of deepest, deadliest guilt arise;
> I see, by more than Fancy's mirror shown,
> The burning village and the blazing town:
> See the dire victim torn from social life,
> The shrieking babe, the agonizing wife!
> She, wretch forlorn, is dragg'd by hostile hands,
> To distant tyrants sold, in distant lands!
> (More 1788: 7–8; ll. 95–102)

The result of this separation, More claimed, was the loss of any beneficent continuity and tradition between generations, for "[t]ransmitted miseries and successive chains" are "[t]he sole sad heritage her child obtains!" (More 1788: 8; ll. 103–4). That feelings of "deepest, deadliest guilt" arise in More's (apparently female) narrator as a result of *this* particular scene is a function of an implicit sense of community among women: to live guilt-free as a mother requires that all mothers be able to pass on more than simply miseries and chains to their children.[17]

Where the supplement of motherhood might establish a community between female readers and suffering slaves, a more inclusive supplemental strategy depended upon a description of the ways in which abolition of the slave trade would facilitate Britain's colonial and imperial endeavors. As Christopher L. Brown notes, this strategy was in part forced upon abolitionists by the traditional association between empire and slavery, which ensured that "to the many with an investment in the colonial economy or concerned with Britain's standing among European rivals, an empire without slavery was simply unthinkable," and as a result, "imagining an end to slavery required an alternative concept of empire" (Brown 1999: 273, 293).[18] The virtues of a reformed empire were described in a number of antislavery poems as well as more general poems that contained antislavery themes. Cowper had developed such a strategy in his earlier (though not exclusively antislavery) poem *The Task*, suggesting in the first book of that work that the slave trade had degraded the British themselves, forcing them into bestial behavior in which they hunted after Africans as though the black skin of these latter made them "lawful prey" (Cowper 1980–95, vol. 2: 140; l. 15). Yet, Cowper suggested, the legislative decision to exclude slavery from Britain itself was "noble, and bespeaks a nation proud/And jealous of the blessing" (Cowper 1980–95, vol. 2: 140; ll. 43–44). Britain need only extend the abolition of slavery and it at the same time would extend and ennoble its empire:

> Spread it [the abolition of slavery] then,
> And let it circulate though ev'ry vein
> Of all your Empire, that where Britain's power
> Is felt, mankind may feel her mercy too.
> (Cowper 1980–95, vol. 2: 140; ll. 44–47)

In *Slavery; A Poem*, More echoed this representation of freedom as a "blessing" that had been granted to Britain under the condition that it "spread" this gift. She asked her readers,

> Shall Britain, where the soul of Freedom reigns,
> Forge chains for others she herself disdains?
> Forbid it, Heaven! O let the nations know
> The liberty she loves she will bestow;
> Not to herself the glorious gift confin'd,
> She spreads the blessing wide as humankind;
> (More 1788: 18; ll. 251–56)

Other authors focused more specifically on the commercial benefits to Britain of abolition.[19] In *A Poem on the African Slave Trade* (1792), Mary Birkett consoled the legislator who despaired that an end to slavery might mean the abandonment of "the wealth abundant which in Afric lies" with the knowledge that these riches could be regained. Britain had only to

> ...search her [i.e., Africa's] fertile land,
> Let the mind rays of commerce there expand;
> Her plains abound in ore, in fruits her soil,
> And the rich plain scarce needs the ploughman's toil;
> Thy vessels crown'd with olive branches send,
> And make each injur'd African thy friend;
> So tides of wealth by peace and justice got,
> Oh, philanthropic heart! will be thy lot.
> (Birkett 1792: 12–13)

Birkett's conclusion, that nationalist commerce ("tides of wealth") and morality (the "philanthropic heart") could be unified through the abolition of slavery was exemplary of antislavery rhetorical strategies that connected abolition with national commercial interests.[20]

The supplements of sympathy, motherhood, and empire in antislavery poetry highlighted the problems poets encountered in establishing an autonomous system of antislavery poetry. Sympathy with slaves could provide "transport," but such sympathy became possible only to the extent that readers already saw slaves as part of a nexus of self-interest, for, as Scottish moral philosophers had consistently stressed, sufferings perceived as distant elicited momentary interest, and did not begin to demand a practical response until they became sufficiently close. Responding to this logic, antislavery authors suggested that modes of self-interest based on the institutions of the family or empire were the preconditions of the "closeness" necessary for sympathy, suggesting that until readers saw their own interests in motherhood or empire served, they would not be truly moved by the real sufferings of slaves across the Atlantic.

III. ANTISLAVERY VERSE, THE POWERS OF THE FUTURE, AND STATE FINANCE

The difficulties that antislavery poets encountered in establishing their verse as a valid species of poetry were in large part a function of its peculiar relationship to the future. Antislavery poetry was in one sense occasional verse, a response to a particular institution (slavery or the slave trade in general), or, more frequently, specific events (antislave trade or slavery legislative bills). Yet unlike commemorative occasional verse, which was intended to produce pleasure or feelings of virtue in the present by referring back to an event lodged in the past, antislavery verse provided pleasure and feelings of virtue in the present by means of an *anticipation* concerning a future event. This future event (the end of the slave trade or slavery) was not one for which each reader could take complete individual responsibility—it was not, in other words, an action that readers could *promise* to fulfill—nor was it an event that was certain to happen; it was rather a future event of uncertain actualization. The fact that pleasure in the present could be provoked by the anticipation of an uncertain event-to-come presented a potential dilemma: what guaranteed that readers would not postpone the *actual* event so that they could continue to produce pleasure and virtue from its anticipation? What, in other words, bound present pleasure to a commitment to ensure that the anticipated event really occurred?

For antislavery poets committed to a referential model, it was "self-interest" that provided the requisite tie. Self-interest, in other words, guaranteed that readers would not perpetually defer the end of the slave trade or slavery in order to produce a continuous stream of pleasure simply from the anticipation of this event, for if slavery and the slave trade destroyed the familial or national self, then readers *had* to support antislavery measures or else risk destroying the very subject that took pleasure in the present from reading these poems. To take present pleasure in these poems was to invest in the future of the self.

Yet to supplement representation with self-interest carried its own risks, for it inadvertently conceded a common ground to proslavery proponents, who sought to "bring home" the *benefits* of slavery for the British family. Where "sympathy" functioned as the medium by means of which anti-slavery poets linked the sufferings of slaves to self- or national interest, proslavery advocates deployed images of state finance as the medium that tied virtuous domesticity *to* slavery. Supporters of the slave trade reminded their auditors and readers that Britain, in the wake of the costly Seven Years' War and American Revolution, still had an enormous national debt, and the slave trade was one of the few ways Britons could finance its cost. One advocate contended that "whatever losses might arise from [the regulation or outlawing of the slave trade, it] should not fall on a particular class of individuals, but be national also," and Britons would have to turn to financiers in order to "rais[e] a fund of at least 60 to 70 millions sterling" (*PH,* vol. 28: 95). The slave trade, another advocate contended, "could not be called a private business; it was a public business" (*PH,* vol. 28: 314), especially since plantation owners in the West Indies claimed to owe at least £20 million to Britain (*PH,* vol. 29: 260). British state finance and slavery had been tied to one another almost from the beginning of the Financial Revolution, for, as P.G.M. Dickson notes, the popularity of South Sea Company stock prior to the 1720 Bubble was owing to the fact that even when the Company's claims to fortified ports in America were rendered unviable, the British government was able to negotiate with Spain for the Company to receive a thirty-year right to the "*Asiento de Negros*, the contract to supply New Spain with African slaves" (Dickson 1967: 67). Moreover, as Ian Baucom notes, by the 1770s slaves themselves had become a form of finance instrument, "treated not only as a type of commodity but as a type of interest-bearing money" (Baucom 2005: 61).[21]

Advocates for the slave trade were able to draw on these facts to suggest that the slave trade *had already colonized the future*: the extinction of the slave trade was equivalent to the extinction of the future of British commerce. Aldermann Newnham, for example, contended that "abolition [of the slave trade] would be the ruin of the trade of the country," for without the trade, it "would be impossible to collect money to diminish the national debt." As a result "[e]very man in the kingdom would feel the abolition come home to him" (Newnham, cited in Clarkson 1808, vol. 2: 99). The fact of state finance, these slave trade advocates suggested, ensured that the existence of both the British family and the British empire depended upon the slave trade.[22] If, as Brown notes, "an empire without slavery was simply unthinkable," then this was especially true in a period of massive state debt (Brown 1999: 273). In such a context, to argue that the end of the slave trade or slavery promised the best future for either self- or national-interest was a tenuous strategy with which to counter the advocates of the system of slavery.

IV. THE FAILURE OF SYSTEM: THE CASE OF COWPER'S ANTISLAVERY VERSE

William Cowper's well-known and troubled engagement with the antislavery cause provides an exemplary case study of the tensions that were inherent in this mode of poetry. As Cowper noted in a 1788 letter to his friend John Newton, the slave trade had long been a topic of obsession for him —"[i]t is a subject on which I can ruminate 'till I feel myself lost in mazes of speculation never to be unravell'd" (*LPWC*, vol. 3: 106)—and he had already included several sections critical of the slave trade in his long poems *Charity* (1782) and *The Task* (1785). However, Cowper quickly discovered that establishing antislavery poetry as its own species of poetry was a difficult task—and one, he finally concluded, that was doomed to failure.

By the late 1780s, Cowper's prestige, as well as his earlier attacks on slavery and the slave trade in sections of long poems such as *Charity* and *The Task*, positioned him as the ideal candidate for the production of verse specifically designed to help with the antislavery cause. In late 1787 and 1788, antislavery advocates solicited Cowper's help, and during the winter and spring of 1788, he wrote four poems on this topic: "The Negro's Complaint," "The Morning Dream," "Sweet Meat has Sour Sauce, or the Slave Trader in the Dumps," and "Pity for Poor Africans." Cowper allowed the first two poems to be published and set to music, the former to the tune of the anti-Walpole ballad "Hosier's Ghost" and the latter to "Tweedside."[23] "The Negro's Complaint" offered readers the opportunity to sympathize with the righteous indignation of a slave "forced from home and all its pleasures," while "The Morning Dream" presented a vision of Liberty freeing Britain from the institution of slavery.

Yet after publishing these two poems, Cowper's belief in the efficacy of such verse changed drastically over the course of the next few months. In mid-February, he was still optimistic about the possibility of effective antislavery verse, writing to his cousin Lady Hesketh that the abolition of the slave trade was "a theme so susceptible of poetical management" (*LPWC*, vol. 3: 103). By late March, though, he had become much less sanguine about the role poetry could play in the movement, noting that he could "not perfectly discern, at present, the probable utility of what I have done, for it seems an affair in which the good pleasure of King Mob is not likely to be much consulted; but at least it can do no harm" (*LPWC*, vol. 3: 131). By early June, however, he had not only begun to doubt the efficacy of such verse, but was beginning to conclude that poetry itself was damaged by its engagement with such a topic, writing to John Newton that

> [t]he more I have consider'd it [the slave trade and slavery] the more I have convinced myself that it is not a promising theme for verse. General censure on the iniquity of the practise will avail nothing, the world has been overwhelm'd with such remarks already, and to particularize all the horrors of it were an employment for the poet and his readers of which they would necessarily soon grow weary. (*LPWC*, vol. 3: 172)

Cowper's sense of an unbridgeable gulf between poetry and events that involved "such meanness in the design and such cruelty in the execution that I both hate and despise the whole operation" was confirmed again in mid-June, when he wrote to Walter Bagot that he "fe[lt] it a degradation of poetry to employ her in the description of it [abolition of the slave trade]" (*LPWC*, vol. 3: 178).

Cowper's disillusionment with antislavery poetry was dependent upon two factors. First, Cowper concluded that antislavery poetry could "exhaust" its readers. Repeated, direct representation of suffering, Cowper suggested, had an effect (and affect) opposite that desired by the poet, for such depictions threatened to overwhelm its readers' sympathies.[24] Second, as his comments about "King Mob" suggest, Cowper understood his poems to exert their pressure and influence in public, but not legislative spaces, a belief that was certainly encouraged by the distribution of Cowper's verse through the medium of song. While verse might exert its power on the system of people who made up "King Mob," Cowper could see no necessary link between that system and the legislative system that passed and repealed laws. Parliament, he suggested in another letter written in the midst of his reflections on antislavery verse, was ruled by eloquence. While such elevated language might produce effects that were equivalent to mob violence, Cowper was nevertheless certain that the mob and the legislature constituted two different and separate systems.[25] Unfortunately, eloquence was a mode of communication restricted to the legislative system, and it was politically efficacious in ways that poetry directed to the mob could never be.

Cowper's limited conception of political poetry as a vector of propagating affect within the "mob" perhaps explains his dissatisfaction with his poem "Sweet Meat has Sour Sauce." While critics often have seen "Sweet Meat" as one of his better and more interesting antislavery poems, Cowper himself described it as "ludicrous," and suppressed its publication. Unlike Cowper's other antislavery verse, which seemed to assume that readers would automatically sympathize with representations of suffering, "Sweet Meat" relies on a different strategy, encouraging its readers to reflect on the limits and proper objects of sympathy. The narrator of the poem, a slave trader, explicitly demands the reader's pity and financial help, bemoaning the fact that, if a bill limiting slavery passes, he will no longer be able to practice the "art" of "prepar[ing]/ A pretty black cargo of African ware" with tools such as chains, the "cat with nine tails," and "screws for the thumbs"

(Cowper 1980–95, vol. 3: 15; ll. 34, 26–27, 12, 18). The mere thought of this loss, the slave trader exclaims, threatens to "break [his] compassionate heart" (l. 36)—and, the narrator seems to assume, the reader's as well. The narrator even provides the reader with a model for sympathetic engagement within his story, describing "how it enters my soul like an awl;/This pity, which some people self-pity call,/ Is sure the most heart-piercing pity of all" (Cowper 1980–95, vol. 3: 15; ll. 38–40). By invoking the word "pity," the narrator demands of his readers that they "domesticate" his despair in their own souls (as well as act on that feeling; two lines later, he asks the reader to "Come buy off my stock"). Yet by including the suggestion that this is simply "self-pity," Cowper forces readers to recognize the irony of the slave trader's claim, for if it is true that "self-pity.../Is sure the most heart-piercing pity of all," why then should the reader feel for anyone but him- or herself? The title of the poem makes clear that the reader is supposed to recognize the irony of this appeal for sympathy—and thus, by extension, the irony and insincerity of real slave traders' calls for sympathy for their potential economic losses—for "sweet meat" comes to have "sour sauce" when readers recognize where their sympathetic attachments should lie. In "Sweet Meat," then, poetic language does not "transmit" sentiment, but instead encourages the reader's reflexive interrogation of sympathy. Such a poetics bore an ambivalent relationship to popular poetry, which, Cowper had argued, exerted its effects in the system of the mob. Since the mob was presumably unable to master the reflexivity and irony of a poem such as "Sweet Meat," Cowper concluded that "Sweet Meat" was a "ridiculous" poem, since its ironic and self-reflexive use of language deprived it of its intended audience.[26]

While some of Cowper's concerns about the proper audience for antislavery verse could be addressed at the level of distribution, the basic problems he located with respect to the form of antislavery itself were not so easily resolved.[27] If antislavery poetry was to establish itself as a valid form of poetry, poets could not simply rely on established theories of sympathy, motherhood, and empire, but instead they would have to reformulate fundamentally these theories.

V. YEARSLEY: THE CRAFTY MERCHANT AND THE DESTRUCTIVE SYSTEM

It was precisely such a reformulation that is at the center of Ann Yearsley's *A Poem on the Inhumanity of the Slave Trade*. As in the case of the verse discussed above, Yearsley's poem employed a number of different antislavery topoi, linking sentimental tableaux to discussions of the effects of slavery on motherhood and empire. However, *A Poem on the Inhumanity of the Slave Trade* also developed a new conception of the mechanism of sympathetic engagement, as well as the means by which sympathy facilitated political actions. To a limited extent, Yearsley extended the reflexive understanding of sympathy developed in Cowper's "Sweet Meat," for her poem sought to encourage sympathy for slaves precisely by reflecting on the *limits* of sympathy with slavers. This reflexive understanding of sympathy enabled Yearsley to theorize the political authority of verse by situating sympathy as an *effect* of poetic language; rather than simply understanding verse as a means of describing an existing situation, Yearsley positioned poetic language as capable of initiating the reader's capacity for imaginative productivity by producing a "strong" future that was not bound to the present either by ties of self-interest or by the links of "probable" causality.

Yearsley's poetic engagement with the topic of commerce was encouraged by the circumstances surrounding her emergence as a poet, for Yearsley's background was represented by both herself and others as lower-class (she was, until the age of 30, a milkwoman near Bristol).[28] She thus required "discovery" by a middle- or upper-class sponsor, a form of support initially provided by Hannah More, from whose home Yearsley had obtained slops for her pigs. Upon reading some of Yearsley's verse, More decided to "be the means of promoting [Yearsley's] prosperity" (More, cited in Wu 1997: 151), and More's patronage included helping Yearsley to publish and promote a volume of poetry (*Poems, on Several Occasions*, 1785). However, this relationship did not last happily or long, for More wished to control the money made from the sales of *Poems*, claiming to friends that Yearsley was incapable of doing so herself. Yearsley, on the other hand, interpreted this request as a desire to keep her in economic dependency. The two split in 1786, and engaged in public sniping against one another for several years thereafter. Perhaps as a result of her economic background and experiences with More, Yearsley seemed especially attuned to the interrelationships between economics, emotion, and the politics of poetic representation, and in *A Poem on the Inhumanity of the Slave Trade*, she highlighted many of these connections in the context of slavery (a poem that itself may have been an attempt to outdo her former patron's *Slavery, a Poem*, published three months earlier).

A Poem on the Inhumanity of the Slave Trade is structured around the narrative of "Indian Luco" and his bride Incilanda. The poem begins with an appeal to all those citizens of Bristol "who feel for human woe" (l. 31), and then summons those readers to the sight of Luco, a "dingy youth...sullen in chains" (l. 52). Luco's story is a relatively standard antislavery narrative. The reader is introduced to Luco as he is being transported in chains from his native land (left unspecified) to the New World. The reader is then returned to Luco's native land, where both his mother and Incilanda search for him, unaware that he has been transported away as a slave. Later in the poem, Luco's fate on a sugar plantation in the New World is described: though a solid worker, he is whipped, but suffers in silence. Eventually, his physical pain and emotional sorrow over the loss of his family is too much, and he attempts suicide, but is prevented from doing so by sailors on a barge. The plantation owners, in order to make a lesson of Luco for the other slaves, burn him alive.

Previous commentators have tended to focus their attention on this narrative component of the poem. Mary Waldron summarizes Yearsley's poem as "a dramatic blank-verse narrative in which a young couple are separated by the cruel and brutal Christian traders," and Wylie Sypher's reading focuses solely on the story of Luco and Incilanda (Waldron 1996: 169; Sypher 1969: 198–99). Other critics also have described Yearsley's poem as primarily "affective" in nature, often positioning Hannah More's *Slavery* as its "rational" foil. Moira Ferguson, for example, argues that where a poet like More employed abstract and sedate images of slaves, Yearsley "eschews unnamed, unvoiced abstractions and represents insurgency in the person of Luco, an oppressed individual with agency, a colonized other, acting as Yearsley acted against More" (Ferguson 1992: 171). Alan Richardson also suggests that the "essayistic, propositional approach" of Hannah More's *Slavery* can be usefully contrasted with "Yearsley's greater reliance on pathetic narratives and vignettes" (Richardson 1997: 77).[29]

I suggest, however, that while the story of Luco and Incilanda is certainly an important element of *A Poem on the Inhumanity of the Slave Trade*, Yearsley does not treat its capacity to evoke emotion as a given, but instead makes the power of its narrative dependent upon a series of images of sympathy that she intersperses throughout the poem. The concluding stanzas of the poem highlight Yearsley's general goal: rather than simply invoking a preexistent emotional capacity for sympathy, she sought to reconstitute the contours of the reader's self-interest, commanding "social love" to

> ...touch the soul of man;
> Subdue him; make a fellow-creature's woe
> His own by heartfelt sympathy, whilst wealth
> Is made subservient to his soft disease. (ll. 420–23)

Yearsley's invocation of "social love" (and its attendant movements of sympathy and the selflessness) suggests that one cannot simply expect such processes to occur automatically; rather, they are facilitated, or encouraged, by the power of language. Yearsley had already prepared the reader for such a claim at the start of the poem, contending in the second stanza that she will "dare the strain/Of Heav'n-born Liberty till Nature moves/ Obedient to her voice" (ll.14–16). Nature, like social love, is not something that can be depended on to produce moral responses of its own accord; rather, the poet must use her strain (in the sense of poetic voice) to strain against (in the sense of effort) what appear to be natural borders.

Yearsley suggested that the forces working against the poet were those of custom and law, which take on the appearance of inevitability and "naturalness." The narrator contends that we consciously "feel enslaved" by these institutions, but nevertheless we "move in [their] direction" (ll.

20–21). Custom, for example, allows sinners to fill a church "with mouthing, vap'rous sighs and tears,/Which, like the guileful crocodile's, oft fall,/ Nor fall but at the cost of human bliss" (ll. 26–28). The question posed by *A Poem on the Inhumanity of the Slave Trade* is thus the following: how can poetic language be employed in such a way that custom and law can be countered? Can poetry force human nature into a moral response in which the interest of the other becomes the interest of the self? This would then allow the reader to transcend a false emotional economy in which tears fall only "at the cost of human bliss."

Yearsley's solution depended upon facilitating the productive and reflexive powers of the imagination. This solution is suggested in the brief prefatory dedication of the poem, addressed to "the Right Hon. And Right Revd. Frederick, Earl of Bristol, Bishop of Derry, Etc., Etc." Following the split between More and Yearsley, Frederick Augustus Hervey had become Yearsley's new patron, and in an earlier poem ("Effusion; To the Right Honourable The Earl of Bristol") she had described him as the "best support" of her "pow'rs" (Yearsley 1787: 168). In *A Poem*, Yearsley writes to her sponsor that her intention in this poem "is not to cause that anguish in your bosom which powerless compassion ever gives; yet my vanity is flattered when I but *fancy* that your Lordship feels as I do" (unnumbered page). This dense sentence contains two claims about the capacities of representation, both of which are figured along an axis of "power." First, Yearsley established an implicit distinction between powerful (that is, active) and powerless compassion; the latter was tied to a specific form of anguish, while the former was presumably not. Also implicit in this distinction is the suggestion that the Earl—and all of us who read over the shoulder of the Earl—can engage this poem correctly only by learning how to adopt a stance of powerful compassion. Yet what would it mean to read in such a manner? The next clause in the sentence proposes an answer and model, for Yearsley suggests that, at least with respect to her feeling of personal power (vanity), her own imaginative representation of the Earl of Bristol's response to her poem takes precedence over any actual response that he might have. In other words, whether or not the Earl *actually* feels as Yearsley imagines him to is beside the point; in an inversion of her economic relationship with the Earl, Yearsley founds her sense of power upon *her* imaginative representation of him. The implicit moral of this story (which will be repeated in the poem) is that active, practical compassion comes about as a result of an imaginative production that works against the grain of real economic relationships.

This moral is taken up consistently throughout the poem. So, for example, Yearsley suggested that the supposed cultural inarticulacy of Africans was a function not of an innate lack of creativity, but rather of the extent to which the institution of slavery prevented Africans from externalizing and actualizing the contents of their productive imaginations. She described the slave Luco's soul as "lost/In dear internal imag'ry," suggesting that

Luco does not lack a rich store of mental contents, but rather is temporarily unable to find a path that would mediate between internal imagery and external reality (ll. 56–57). Later in the poem, Luco is again presented in the process of contemplation, and again his imaginative activity is prevented from externalizing itself in practical action:

> ...pausing faintly, Luco stood,
> Leaning upon his hoe, while mem'ry brought,
> In piteous imag'ry, his aged father,
> His poor fond mother, and his faithful maid.
> The mental group in wildest motion set
> Fruitless imagination. (ll. 244–49)

Luco's imaginative "fruitlessness" is mirrored by his silent resistance to the institution of slavery itself, for his pause makes explicit the fact that his loss of imaginative outlet comes as a consequence of his forced cultivation of the soil.

While the productivity of Luco's imagination was hindered by a social system that was effectively beyond his control, Yearsley did not let her readers off the hook so easily, and immediately after introducing Luco, she commanded her readers to produce an image that would reveal the power of imagination to create new systems. She conjured up the image of a Christian slave merchant who, against calls for abolition, mounts a plea couched in the language of domesticity: "I know the crafty merchant will oppose/The plea of nature to my strain, and urge/His toils are for his children" (ll. 75–77). Yearsley countered this plea with a "challenge," demanding her reader to "Behold that Christian!," and she then asked her imaginary interlocutor to

> ...Bring on
> Thy daughter to this market, bring thy wife,
> Thine aged mother (though of little worth),
> With all the ruddy boys! Sell them, thou wretch,
> And swell the price of Luco! (ll. 83–87)

Yearsley demanded that the "crafty merchant" imagine his own family as part of the economic system, an imperative that is underlined by the parenthetical suggestion that the mother, because of her age, would be of "little worth." Anticipating the startled reaction of her auditor, Yearsley turned this horror back upon itself, asking:

> ...Why that start?
> Why gaze as thou wouldst fright me from my challenge
> With look of anguish? Is it *nature* strains
> Thine heart-strings at the image? (ll. 87–90)

Yearsley's narrator contends that such anguish is nothing short of hypocrisy, for "Justice" would hold the actions of slave traders against any feelings of familial preference on the part of horrified readers.

The *cause* of the "anguish" that Yearsley's narrator imagines her readers feeling is not so simple to locate as might first appear to be the case, for whatever horror results from this image depends upon a complicated and sophisticated interplay of the real and the virtual. Yearsley's scenario did not present her readers with an image of real suffering (for example, an actual slave or even the idealized "Luco" who is to stand in for such slaves), nor did she ask her readers to imagine selling their own children. Rather, Yearsley asked her readers to imagine a slave merchant who is himself devoid of sympathy, and who sells his entire family (that is, both the generations of parent and child). Yearsley thus focuses attention on a simulacrum, or virtual image, for while there were certainly slave owners who sold the children they conceived with slave women, and while advocates of the slave trade sometimes hinted that *African* slave traders placed no familial limits on the objects of slavery, there were presumably no *Christian* traders who sold their own parents.[30] Such a figure of the Christian family-seller exists *only* in the imagination.

Why should readers find such a figure horrifying? While it is tempting to conclude that Yearsley grounded this feeling of readerly anguish in "natural" feelings of familial love, the details that Yearsley provided do not support such a conclusion. Readers are not asked to imagine the sale of *one* child or parent, but of all the children, the wife, and even the reproductive origin of the merchant himself, his mother. Yearsley is asking the reader to imagine a world in which all familial attachments have been relegated to the "environment" of the economic system, and if such an image produces horror, it does so not by multiplying the shock of destroyed familial ties, but rather by revealing the logical impossibility of such a system. It is impossible, in other words, that such a system could extend beyond one generation: by selling his children, the merchant has deprived himself of anyone to whom he could pass on his property, and by selling his wife, he deprives himself of the possibility of creating a new lineage. He may still possess the Name of the Father (he sells only his mother, apparently), but this lineage necessarily ends with him. Yearsley's image is thus reminiscent of the vignettes employed by Immanuel Kant in *Groundwork for a Metaphysics of Morals* to prove the *moral* impossibility of actions such as lying and suicide; this vignette, in other words, deconstructs the slave trade by extrapolating its foundational logic to the point that it reveals its tendency to deprive itself of its own conditions of possibility (Kant 1981: 14–15, 36–37). The horror of this image, then, is produced by its revelation of absolute nothingness, the passage to the abyss, rather than being motivated by feeling that purportedly comes upon us "naturally" when we see an example of an ill-treated child or parent. Yearsley had little faith that "Nature," on its own, would produce the proper response to the suffering of slaves (else why would the trade exist in the first place?), and suggested that a sympathetic moral response was instead enabled by an imaginary negation of the phenomenal world.[31]

Yearsley's image of the crafty merchant suggested that the inner logic that pitted family and capital against one another could be captured—at least at that historical moment—only in an imaginative act in which the reader imagined a *system* of crafty merchants. To "see the crafty merchant" was to make visible the limits of the system that enabled such actions, and to produce for oneself proof of the disjunction between family and capital, sympathy and self-interest. Active, practical sympathy for Luco became possible only when the reader first imagined a system devoid of sympathy. The virtual extinction of sympathy was the condition of its real instantiation.

Yearsely's interest in the anomalous figure of the crafty merchant thus set her verse against the tendency toward the "typical" shared by both antislavery verse and the financiers of the slave trade itself. As Ian Baucom has noted, the slave trade depended on the existence of maritime insurance, which indemnified financiers against losses, and insurance was itself

> a business that could only operate once its actuarial science had invented the 'typical' (typical risk, typical life expectancy, typical value of a given commodity) and subordinated to the greater, because more abstract, truth of the typical all the vagaries and waywardnesses of the particular. (Baucom 2005: 39–40)

Baucom argues that this same drive toward the typical at play in insurance also emerged in a number of eighteenth- and early nineteenth-century literary endeavors, such as the rise of the historical novel and modern historical writing. All of these endeavors were attempts "to situate an individual work, object, or event within the determining historical circumstances of its age, to discover in the individual, not what is exceptional *to* but what is typical *of* a given historical moment" (Baucom 2005: 40). This same tendency was also evident in antislavery verse, which often based its moral appeal on the premise that the sufferings it depicted were, however unpleasant and extreme from the British reader's perspective, in fact typical of slave life. Yet where Yearsley's figure of Luco arguably followed that "typicalizing" strategy, her figure of the crafty merchant did not; he is anomalous, exceptional, out of place. Rather than relying on the typicalizing strategy that served as the foundation of the system against which she was writing, Yearsley employed the image of the crafty merchant to suggest that the truth of the present could not be located (at least solely) in the typical, but rather required a passage through a figure of the future that had no referential support. She was not *predicting* that such a system would come to pass; rather, her image is virtual in the sense that Brian Massumi has described: that is, the realm where the "past and future brush shoulders with no mediating present"; the virtual is "a liminal realm of emergence, where half-actualized actions and expressions arise like waves on a sea to which most no sooner return" (Massumi 2002: 31).[32] The power of Yearsley's image of the crafty merchant, in other words, does not depend upon its "true" representation of present reality or even the probable future; rather, it produces power precisely because this one "bad" future is necessarily tied to a multitude of other, potentially more positive, "half-actualized actions and expressions." The virtual reveals both the contingency of the present system and the possibility of something new.

Yearsley's critique of the "system" of capital was not lost on her reviewers. Moira Ferguson has claimed that "[t]he press read Yearsley's poem without nuance, refusing to internalize or address her multiple significations" (Ferguson 1992: 172). However, the reviewer of Yearsley's poem in the *Monthly Review* of March 1788 *did* seem aware that Yearsley's critique extended to the system of commerce as a whole, even if the author of the review sought to defuse that critique by castigating it as a fault of Yearsley's too-highly pitched emotion. "[I]n the heat of invective," the reviewer wrote, "she mingles too many curses and execrations with her arguments," and cited Yearsely's lines "—Curses fall/On the destructive system that shall need/Such base supports!" as an example of Yearsley's "scolding" (vol. 78: 246).[33] The reviewer's charge of emotionalism and shrewish scolding acknowledged, but attempted to bracket within gendered terms, Yearsley's social critique. What was elided by this critique was the power of Yearsley's image of the "crafty merchant," for rather than using poetic language to describe a real referent that would demonstrate the truth of slavery, Yearsley's "strain" was designed to produce sympathy by forcing her readers to imagine its future extinction in a system of absolute self-interest.

It is not entirely clear whether *A Poem on the Inhumanity of the Slave Trade* offered a commercial alternative to the system of "av'rice." Philip Gould suggests that the poem's narrator attempts "to distinguish between commerce and 'Av'rice'," and argues that the narrator's rhetorical question—"Shall the sons/Of Commerce shiv'ring stand, if not employ'd" in slaving (ll. 365–66)—demands a negative answer, suggesting that the sons of Commerce *can* find employment beyond the slave trade (Gould 2003: 52). This would certainly be consistent with Yearsley's earlier reflections on commerce. In "Clifton Hill; Written in January 1785," for example, the poem's narrator "hails" the "useful channel!," from which "Commerce spreads her wings,/From either pole her various treasure brings," and the narrator explicitly connected commerce to a happy family ("Wafted by thee [commerce], the mariner long stray'd,/Clasps the fond parent, and the sighing maid") (ll.182–85). Yet in *A Poem on the Inhumanity of the Slave Trade*, the possibilities for pacific commerce are left implicit; rather than tying her virtual image to a specific prognosis for the future of commerce, Yearsley leaves the production of powerful compassion to the virtual itself.

CONCLUSION: FINANCE, ANTICIPATION, AND THE VIRTUAL

Yearsley's *A Poem on the Inhumanity of the Slave Trade* was in some respects typical of late eighteenth-century British antislavery verse, in the sense that it employed a standard set of abolitionist devices, such as attempts to incur sympathy by asking the reader to imagine the sufferings imposed by slavery, descriptions of the destruction of the home and family, and ruminations on the consequences of the slave trade for the British empire. Yearsley's verse thus engaged some of the risks I noted above, such as the dilemma that direct appeals to readerly sympathy might quickly exhaust the emotional resources of both auditors and poets, or the danger that linking depictions of the "real facts" of the slave trade to appeals to the reader's self-interest would inadvertently grant proslavery advocates the grounds upon which they could make a case *for* slavery. Yet even as it employed stock elements of antislavery poetry, Yearsley's verse avoided these two dilemmas by interrogating the virtual dimensions of domesticity and self-interest. Rather than seeking to spark sympathy by asking the reader to imagine a scene that purportedly had some real referent, such as Pratt's command to "Behold that body weltering in its wails!," Yearsley asked the reader to create virtual images that did not require validation by "real facts." Rather than employing description in the service of representation, Yearsley's descriptions of fractured homes and the future of commerce were designed to encourage the representational functions of the subject to return to their ground, namely, *the production* of images. In contrast to the reading subject implicit in many antislavery poems—that is, a subject whose sympathy originated in, and was legislated by, sentiments that came from its "outside"—Yearsley's reading subject was (to use Peter de Bolla's felicitous phrase) "self-legislating," for its sympathetic affect emerged from its own imaginative activity, rather than being determined by external events (De Bolla 1989: 27–102).

Yearsley's emphasis on the virtual dimension of sympathy and the self-legislation of the imagination provides a productive entry point into a long-standing debate about the relationship between antislavery poetry and the development of capitalism. At the heart of this debate is the status of homology between two apparently different systems: on the one hand, the well-organized system of late eighteenth-century British antislavery advocacy (of which antislavery poetry was an element); on the other, the much broader "system" of British capitalism. The slave trade was central to both of these systems, and antislavery advocacy was intended to intervene directly in the British economic system by destroying the legitimacy of a specific form of trade and finance (the slave trade). Yet the antislavery movement itself often relied upon, and even seemed to promote, habits of perception and structures of circulation intrinsic to the capitalist *habitus*, such as the tendency to operationalize abstract, "typical" cases of suffering (a tactic that paralleled the rise of "the typical" in insurance theory); the valorization of "consumer choice" and free market ideology as means and justification for ending slavery; a "moral investment" approach to the pleasures of reading antislavery literature, which tied the affect of the reading experience to future events such as the end of the slave trade or slavery; and a reliance on both the commodity form and "fashion."[34] There was thus both a temporal and a structural correspondence between the antislavery movement and the system of commerce that it opposed. The question, then, is how to understand the homologies between the strategies of the antislavery movement and the larger, more distributed "system" of capitalism: do these homologies reveal that the antislavery movement was inscribed within the system of capitalism, or do they simply indicate points of resonance between two autonomous systems?

Recent debate about the relationships of autonomy or dependency between the systems of antislavery advocacy and capitalism has its origins in Eric Williams's classic *Capitalism and Slavery*. Williams suggested that the "autonomy" of the system of antislavery advocacy was in fact illusory, for however pure the intentions of antislavery advocates, their movement had the effect of morally justifying the movement away from an increasingly inefficient system of slave labor and toward a wage-labor system. While some critics have disputed Williams's chronology, arguing that the system of slavery was still profitable during the period that antislavery efforts began in earnest (1770s and '80s), more recent advocates of the Williams' thesis have noted that strict chronology is not necessarily the point; if the antislavery movement, "like Smith's political economy, reflected the needs and values of the emerging capitalist order," then it could just as easily have functioned proleptically, providing in advance a moral justification for an "emergent" economic order (Davis 1975: 350). For supporters of the Williams' thesis, the homologies between the systems of antislavery and capitalism prove that antislavery advocacy was an element within the developing logic of capitalism, serving as a sort of feedback loop by means of which capitalism could anticipate and justify new forms of labor.

Against such readings, critics of the Williams' thesis have argued that correspondences between the logic of late eighteenth-century capitalism and the system of antislavery advocacy do not prove that the latter was an element of the former. One of the most sophisticated of these responses is that of historian Thomas Haskell, who seeks to reveal "connections" and linkages" between antislavery advocacy and the system of capitalism while at the time avoiding the reduction of "humane values and acts to epiphenomena" (Haskell 1998: 237). Haskell's ingenious solution consists of arguing that antislavery advocacy was able to constitute an autonomous moral system *precisely because of* its connections to "the market." Haskell notes that eighteenth-century merchants had to develop increasingly sophisticated "recipes" for thinking about the relationship of business at home to actions and events that were far distant, both temporally and geographically. He suggests that "new habits of causal attribution" developed in the sphere of business in turn enabled more sophisticated and efficacious moral action by "expanding the range of causal perception and inspir[ing] people's confidence in their power to intervene in the course of events" (Haskell 1998: 260, 269). Haskell thus grants that the ability of slave trade opponents to perceive their efforts as efficacious required patterns of thinking developed in "the market," but he rejects the contention that the origin of antislavery morality in the market thereby inscribed these efforts within capitalism. Haskell ends up with an essentially liberalist solution to the problem of system autonomy, implying the "the market" and "morality" are reciprocally linked systems, with the former lending recipes to morality while the latter apparently "moralizes" capital.[35]

While Haskell provides a compelling and nuanced account of the multiple ways in which systems can function autonomously and yet still remain linked, his emphasis on causal prediction as the "link" that frees the moral system of antislavery from capitalism highlights some of the limits of his approach. Haskell's account implies that antislavery literature produced practical sympathy because readers, already "trained" to look for causal relations between distant events and their own behavior, were convinced by antislavery literature that they were causally involved in the production of "typical" cases of suffering (as these were depicted in prose and poetry). Yet even as Haskell's account seems to explain why readers of antislavery literature might come to feel dreadfully guilty, it does not explain how or why readers would feel capable of changing the *system* in which they now recognized their complicity. Haskell argues that readers could come to feel "responsible for" the evils of slavery only if they could perceive how their own actions causally contributed to the sufferings of slaves, yet he conflates the perception of individual responsibility with the "inspiration" and "confidence" that one has the power to "intervene in the course of events." To understand how my individual actions contribute to the suffering of another is not equivalent to understanding how my individual action could change the system (a distinction elided by Haskell's more ambiguous phrase "to intervene in the course of events"). The problem, in other words, is that the market "recipes" that Haskell positions as the basis of moral reasoning assume an already constituted system for their efficacy, while antislavery efforts were oriented toward an unknown system-yet-to-come. If, by the 1770s, one could employ causal reasoning to invest (or not invest) *money* in a slave trade venture, this was because the system as a whole remained stable and made the possibility of receiving a return calculable. Yet recipes of causal prediction would be of little value when dealing with such an unprecedented event as the destruction of the "system of slavery." Haskell's account, in short, explains the genesis of what Yearsley called "that anguish in [one's] bosom which powerless compassion ever gives," but does not explain why or how readers of antislavery literature in general, and verse in particular, would feel *empowering* sympathy.

If readers did in fact feel empowered—and not simply irremediably guilty—when reading these poems, it could only be because this verse, prior to articulating causal links of responsibility, first enabled an intuition of the *in*calcuable and unprecedented: that is, that things could be otherwise. Yeasley's partial refusal of realistic reference focuses our attention on this moment of antislavery poetry, highlighting a mode of readerly "anticipation" that was virtual, rather than causally predictive. Yearsley's image of the crafty merchant suggested that, underneath the lines of sympathy that flow out from the subject along paths of real relations and causal linkage, one encounters the *ground* of sympathy, which is tied to neither realistic reference nor the anticipations of causal prediction. The ground of sympathy *is* speculative, but not in the mode of the "recipes" of commerce or finance; the ground of sympathy deals not in possibilities and probabilities, but with potential, and the emergence of the new. Rather than seeking to validate their images with an appeal to "the typical," Yearsley exploited the potential of the virtual, where, as Brian Massumi puts it, "what cannot be experienced cannot but be felt" (Massumi 2002: 30).

4 Systems and the parasite
Wordsworth and the financial crisis of 1797

> Polybius adds, that *parasite* was...an honourable name among the ancient Gauls, and was given to their poets; but of late it has been made a term of reproach, and used for a flatterer and mean dependent. ("Parasite" in Chambers 1788)

> The parasite invents something new. Since he does not eat like everyone else, he builds a new logic. He crosses the exchange, makes it into a diagonal. (Serres 1982: 35)

In the last chapter, I noted that Ann Yearsley's speculative poetic images presented solutions to two formal problems that had vexed earlier attempts to create a system of verse that both encouraged "good" poetry and undercut the "destructive system" of the slave trade. By focusing on speculative future events that *might* be produced by the slave trade, Yearsley's images—unlike those of many of her fellow poets—could not be contested by the appeals of proslavery advocates to the "real facts" of this system. In addition, by positioning sympathy as a consequence of the reader's discovery of his or her own powers of imaginative production, rather than as an automatic response to representative tableaux of slaves' sufferings, Yearsley's images were designed to invigorate, rather than exhaust, her readers' emotional resources. Yet as it turned out, the potential of Yearsley's innovations was undercut by a structural change in the system of antislavery communication itself. In the 1770s and 1780s, antislavery poetry had been able to take advantage of the system of printing, distribution, and readership created by antislavery advocates. However, this reliance on a wider system of communication proved to be a detriment in the 1790s, for in the immediate wake of the French Revolution, antislavery advocates muted their activities, fearing that their cause would be injured if it was linked with French radicalism. While antislavery verse was not destroyed by this tactic, the relative dearth of antislavery poems between 1790 and 1807 effectively undercut any emergent trends from the late 1780s.[1]

Yet even as Yearsley's speculative poetic images were trapped within a deliberately stalled system of antislavery verse, a strikingly similar form of poetic practice came to dominate William Wordsworth's first "mature" poems. In the mid- to late 1790s, the young poet moved away from relatively traditional locodescriptive verse and generic representations of sufferers and toward a more self-reflexive mode of poetry, one which, in a poem such as *The Ruined Cottage*, isolated "images of tranquillity" that allowed readers to interrogate their own responses to scenes of affect and suffering.[2] Like Yearsley's speculative images, Wordsworth's images of tranquility produced readerly sympathy not by "secur[ing] some determinate knowledge," but rather by" "invigorat[ing] and sharpen[ing] and refin[ing]' the process of judgment" (Pfau 1997: 119). While Wordsworth's images were not, like Yearsley's, designed to intervene in the specific social system of slavery, they did seek to establish an alternative to the economic system more generally; in place of the real currency and speculative practices of the economy proper, Wordsworth's images were to provide a spiritual form of "wealth" and "interest." And even as Yearsley's practice of speculative poetic imagery faded within antislavery verse, Wordsworth's speculative images moved to the center of what Francis Jeffrey called, in an October 1802 volume of the *Edinburgh Review*, the "new system" of British Romantic poetry (vol. 1: 66).

Why was Wordsworth's practice of speculative poetic imagery able to establish itself within an emergent system of British Romantic poetry even as Yearsley's very similar images faded from view? This is, no doubt, a thorny question, and one has to look in part to the reliance of antislavery poetics upon a communication system established and largely controlled by antislavery advocates. Yet this chapter explores another reason, one that bears on the more general question of how systems of literary communication come into being. Though Wordsworth may have drawn upon the devices of earlier poets associated with antislavery poetry, he insulated his practice of the poetic image from the effects of other systems of communication by turning to what we can describe as the logic of the parasite. What I have in mind by this term are not primarily biological parasites, but rather what systems theorist Michel Serres has described as "parasitic" social relations—that is, social interactions "organized with one-way relations, where one [party metaphorically] eats the other and where the second cannot benefit at all from the first" (Serres 1982: 5). For Serres, parasites denote apparent points of disturbance within a system, sources of "noise" where exchange, reciprocity, and communication break down. Within social systems, these effects are often attributed to specific individuals, such as beggars, royal sycophants, and financial speculators—but also, as my first epigraph suggests, to poets, literary critics, and all those who make their living by the pen.[3] Part of the effort of Serres's systems theory is to insist that parasites are in fact irradicable, for "[t]here is no system without parasites" (Serres 1982: 12). Yet more provocatively, he also contends that it is precisely from parasitic relations that new systems can emerge

(Serres 1982: 14), and it is this latter claim that forms the guiding thread of this chapter.

My argument, in brief, is that Wordsworth initiated his system of poetry—a system that was to become, for both Wordsworth's contemporaries and subsequent literary critics, emblematic of the "system" of British Romantic poetry itself—by parasiting tropes of speculation and wealth from British financial discourse of the late 1790s. Rather than developing his poetics from a stable point within a system, as had Yearsely (at least in the case of her antislavery poetry), Wordsworth developed a poetics that was intrinsically parasitical upon other systems. My point is not that Wordsworth was "influenced" by other systems in the sense that he took up a logic, set of ideas, or tropes that originated elsewhere (for example, the system of political discourse). Such arguments for influence tend to treat homologies between systems as identities, and inevitably focus on the "master" system that drives the others (as when, for example, the sudden efflorescence of financial logic and terminology in Wordsworth's poetry of the late 1790s is taken as a symptom of the poet's "capture" by the interests of bourgeois hegemony).[4] In place of this model of influence, I focus on relationships of parasitism, and I suggest that by understanding Wordsworth as a parasite of—rather than influenced by—the discourse of state finance, we can understand the ways in which he could create a new system of poetry that was able to draw on the resources, but at the same time partially seal itself off from the effects, of the system of finance and economy.

My argument has two moments: in the first, I align Wordsworth's personal concerns with more general tensions in his social context, in order to establish a relationship of resonance between the two, while in the second moment, I describe the mechanisms by means of which Wordsworth parasited elements of his social context in order to establish a new system of literary communication. Thus, in the first two sections of the chapter—and drawing on previous literary criticism that has isolated Wordsworth's financial difficulties in the mid- to late 1790s as a powerful factor in the development of his mature poetry and his practice of the poetic "image"—I point toward structural similarities between the young poet's struggles with debt in the late 1790s and a well-publicized collapse of the British gold standard in 1797. This latter event produced a crisis in British monetary value, which itself resulted in both emergency legislation—the Bank Restriction Act—and a lengthy debate in which politicians and pamphleteers sought to decide fundamental questions about money, debt, and finance, in order to resolve the question of how the nation could revive a system of state finance that seemed to have arrived at what MP Charles James Fox called the "gulph of bankruptcy" (*PH*, vol. 32:1537–38). In precisely the same year, in other words, Wordsworth and British legislators found themselves in structurally analogous positions and asking similar questions: in the absence of the money that had purportedly served as foundation for the future, how could belief in continuing prosperity be restored? And could a system of wealth emerge from potentially irremediable debt?

The second moment of my argument turns to those mechanisms that allowed Wordsworth to draw on the terms and logic of this larger debate about finance while at the same time allowing him to establish a *new* system by partially sealing himself off from the influence of other systems. Both Wordsworth and British legislators turned to the parasite as the solution to problems of debt and finance, each locating parasitical social relations—exemplified by acts such as gift-giving and begging—as the foundation for new systems of "credit." What differentiated the two, however, was the self-reflexivity of the poet's turn to the parasite: where British legislators sought primarily to differentiate a "good" mode of British financial parasitism from the "bad" system of parasitical French finance, Wordsworth created a new system of poetry precisely by giving himself over fully to the logic of the parasite. Through readings of several of Wordsworth's early poems—"The Old Cumberland Beggar," *The Ruined Cottage*, and "The Pedlar"—I argue that the young poet isolated and analyzed two central operations of parasitism—what I call "entwining" and "mineralization"—that allow new systems to emerge. Mineralization refers to the image of stability, or tranquility, that makes a new system appear stable and capable of being projected into the future, and it was precisely such an image of tranquility that British legislators sought to establish for their new system of unbacked currency. Yet Wordsworth suggested that mineralization was only possible because of a prior operation of parasitic "entwining." Where mineralization oriented individuals toward the future and new possibilities, entwining required an obsessive relationship to the past, as individuals circled around and around representations of the dead, thereby partaking of—but also protecting themselves from—the powers of the dead. I conclude the chapter with a discussion of Wordsworth's gradual move away, in the first two decades of the nineteenth century, from his earlier interest in the parasite, and I suggest that as his financial situation improved, Wordsworth abandoned his insights into the powers of the parasite, seeking instead to ground the poet's powers in a unique capacity for "identification."

I. WORDSWORTH, DEBT, AND THE PARASITE

For Wordsworth, the events of the 1790s unfolded under the shadow of lost speculative possibilities. John Wordsworth, William's father, died in 1783, leaving Wordsworth (then only 13) and his siblings a sizeable inheritance. However, before his death, John had loaned a significant portion of this money (roughly £5000) to his employer, James Lowther, the first Earl of Lonsdale. Following John's death, Lord Lonsdale refused to repay this debt, and Wordsworth's brother Richard, as well as brother-in-law Christopher Cookson, initiated a legal proceeding against the Earl in 1788. Lonsdale agreed in 1791 to settle out of court, but in fact the matter was not settled until after the first Earl's death in 1802, at which point Lonsdale's heir agreed to return the money his father had received from John Wordsworth, as well as interest on the principal.[5]

William felt the first Earl's refusal to repay his debt primarily as a speculative loss, as he noted in an 1803 letter to his brother Richard, written as the final details of the settlement were being determined. Acknowledging that John Graham, the agent of Lonsdale's heir, was offering roughly £3500 beyond the original £5000, Wordsworth wondered "what principle" was being applied in order to determine that extra amount (though he did not doubt "that he goes upon some rule by which professional men are guided in like cases," *LWDW* 382). While the Wordsworths apparently had asked for more than the £8500 offered (William mentions a figure of £10,380), he also suggested that Mr. Graham was addressing their requests for additional funds with a "spirit of liberality" (*LWDW* 382). "[I]t is evident," William wrote, "that he [Mr. Graham] does not consider the case merely as a man of business; that is, he does not merely look at what we could recover in a court of Law," and he urged his brother to respond to Graham's offer with the same spirit of liberality by himself offering a deduction from the original request. Because Graham is "disposed to deal not unfeelingly but liberally with us," William wrote,

> it becomes us to shew to him and Lord Lowther that we have a proper sense of their handsome conduct, and have a like spirit of liberality in ourselves and therefore are prepared to admit that a considerable deduction [i.e., from the original request] should be made. (*LWDW* 382)

Yet William also suggested that Graham's spirit of liberality might be plumbed a bit further. "[B]efore Mr Graham finally determines what this deduction should be," William wrote to his brother,

> it might be proper to perhaps respectfully remind him that no money can ever make us complete amends for the loss which we have sustained; I do not speak of the hardships & anxieties &c these I leave entirely out of the question, but the mere comparative value of the money to us now when set against the service it might have done us 15 years back. No doubt Mr Graham must have thought of this, and you have hinted it to him; and all I mean is simply that when you finally settle this matter you should remind him of it. (*LWDW* 382)

Significantly, William did not ask Richard to remind Mr. Graham of actual past sufferings ("hardships and anxieties &c"), but rather stressed lost speculative possibilities. Between 1783 (the year in which the debt should have been paid) and 1804 (the year in which the money was actually returned), almost twenty years had passed, and there was no way of knowing how much money had been "lost" because the Wordsworths were unable to invest this money due them. William thus wanted Mr. Graham to sympathize with a virtual event—what would have been the case, had they had the money—rather than with any actual instances of suffering. William's stress on lost speculative opportunities was undoubtedly clever maneuvering, for by stressing virtual sufferings, he was effectively preventing Mr. Graham from any sort of itemization of particular hardships that would allow the two sides to agree on a particular figure for damages. Yet as I will detail in what follows, William's approach to the question of his inheritance was not an opportunistic strategy particular to these financial negotiations, but rather continuous with his earlier efforts in the mid to late 1790s to generate communities of feeling around speculative imaginative engagements with loss and debt.

For much of the 1790s, Wordsworth was committed to the quasi-revolutionary project of propagating "benevolence" throughout Britain and perhaps beyond its borders. However, the purely speculative status of Wordsworth's inheritance during this decade restricted the possible forms such philanthropy might take, and in one of his earliest endeavors, he sought to create a structure that would allow others to foot the bill. In correspondence with his friend William Mathews, Wordsworth outlined plans for a journal to be entitled *The Philanthropist; A Monthly Miscellany.*[6] The journal was to contain articles on "general politics," "morals and manners," "biographical papers," "taste and criticism," "works of imagination and fiction," reviews, poetry, and summaries of parliamentary debates, and the periodical itself was to be a "vehicle of sound and exalted Morality" which encouraged governmental fiscal responsibility.[7] Such a journal could be published, however, only if it was funded, and Wordsworth proposed to Mathews that they leave this task to others. As Wordsworth noted, he "could not advance any thing [toward the foundation of the journal], and I am afraid that you are equally unable to contribute in that way!" (*LWDW* 118).[8] Wordsworth and Mathews hoped to solicit financial gifts that would fund the journal, with the result that, as Liu notes, "endowment would come philanthropically to the author [i.e., Wordsworth and Mathews] with no more obligation than that of friendship, and would allow [them] in turn to endow the world with the very spirit of philanthropy" (Liu 1989: 334).[9] Wordsworth and Mathews, in short, would receive material sustenance, in the form of money, which they would translate into beneficial information. However, Wordsworth insisted that even should *The Philanthropist* turn a profit, it was fundamentally a system that translated financial endowments into moral influence.[10]

Wordsworth seemed to have imagined the efficient cause of the journal's influence in Godwinian terms. In *Enquiry Concerning Political Justice* (1793), William Godwin had distinguished between the contagious diffusion of sympathy, on the one hand, and the exponential spread of reason, on the other, and had warned against the "sympathy of opinion [which] catches from man to man, especially in numerous meetings" (Godwin 1992, vol. 1: 208). At the same time, though, he argued for a "contagious" aesthetic of proper political discourse, arguing that the beauty of a few examples "of the advantages of political discussion undebauched by political enmity and vehemence" would present such a beautiful "spectacle" that the example would soon be rendered "contagious," and the light of reason propagated geometrically (Godwin 1992, vol. 1: 214). Wordsworth, following Godwin, imagined that *The Philanthropist* would appeal to "dispassionate advocates of liberty and discussion" (*LWDW* 126) and thereby expand its influence exponentially by "diffus[ing] by every method a knowledge of those rules of political justice, from which the farther any government deviates the more effectually must it defeat the object for which the government was ordained" (*LWDW* 124). The spirit of philanthropy that supported *The Philanthropist* financially was thus to be multiplied by the journal itself, as it transformed each of its readers into a new center of rationalized love of humanity.

Yet *The Philanthropist* never came into being, in part because Wordsworth began to lose faith in the Godwinian principles upon which its conception was grounded, but probably also as a consequence of a large grant of money that Wordsworth received.[11] In 1794, William's dying friend Raisley Calvert left him a legacy of £600 (later raised to £900).[12] While Calvert's largess did not make Wordsworth financially independent, it was certainly adequate capital for generating a respectable source of income, provided it was invested wisely. However, from the perspective of the project of *The Philanthropist*, the problem with Calvert's bequest was not that it was not enough, but rather that it was too much: such a sum could fund the journal itself, thus negating the need for the more distributed source of income that was the raison d'être of the periodical. As a consequence of both of these reasons, Wordsworth and Mathews abandoned their literary endeavor even before it began, and Wordsworth turned to other modes of speculative philanthropy.

Paradoxically, Wordsworth's receipt of the Calvert legacy had the effect of initiating severe financial problems, for during the middle years of the 1790s, Wordsworth found himself perpetually short on cash as the result of his tendency to make loans to people willing to receive but not give back. Upon receiving the first sums of the Calvert legacy, for example, Wordsworth immediately searched around for profitable investments, and after considering different possibilities, lent out £500 to his friends Basil Montagu and Charles Douglas at rather hefty rates of interest (rates that William later acknowledged a court of law might deem "usurious").[13] Unfortunately, these turned out to be rather bad investments, for Wordsworth had not insisted on any security for the loans, apparently depending instead on the bonds of friendship. "Friendship loans" proved to be far more speculative than Wordsworth had anticipated, for by 1797 Montagu was consistently failing to make good on his payments (and on at least one occasion, appropriated a £100 payment that Douglas had asked him to pass on to Wordsworth; see Douglas 1948: 629). As Liu notes, Calvert's benevolent endowment had the paradoxical effect of allowing Wordsworth to discover personal debt, for by lending money from the legacy, Wordsworth found himself in need of taking out loans.

Yet if the Calvert legacy enabled Wordsworth's discovery of debt, it also enabled the would-be poet's discovery of the constitutive relationship between speculation, systems, and what Serres calls the parasite. For Serres, the parasite refers not to biological entities, but to relationships within systems in which communication and reciprocity break down; that is, relationships in which one element takes but never gives back. Serres illustrates his point with La Fontaine's fable of a tax farmer who is woken in the middle of the night by the noise of mice eating his food: this is thus an example of one parasite (the tax farmer) being parasited by another parasite (the mouse). However, Serres also describes as parasitic relationships in which an individual gives in one register (for example, information) but receives in another, more primary, register (for example, energy or food). While parasites are often understood as contingent elements that latch upon already constituted systems, Serres argues that systems in fact emerge from relationships of parasitism, for "the parasitic relation precedes exchange in general," and "exchanged things travel in a channel that is already parasited" (Serres 1982: 80).

Serres's model helps us to understand both of Wordsworth's early attempts to create systems of philanthropic speculation—that is, the system of *The Philanthropist* and the system of "friendship loans"—for it illuminates Wordsworth's consistent tendency to isolate the position of parasite as the one most capable of producing large effects. In the case of *The Philanthropist*, Wordsworth and Mathews sought to play the role of beneficial parasites, always taking in at one register (cash) and giving back only another (information). Wordsworth's second system—the loans to Montagu and Douglas—also began with Wordsworth in the position of parasite, receiving from the dying Calvert money that could not be returned.[14] While Wordsworth's receipt of this legacy would have allowed *The Philanthropist* to become self-subsistent, such a step would have distanced Wordsworth from the position of the parasite, and thus he used the legacy instead as the basis for a series of "usurious"—that is, parasitical—loans to his friends. The usurious nature of these loans seemed, at least initially, to position Wordsworth as *both* powerful parasite and master of a system of speculation. However, as Wordsworth quickly learned, one could not move to the center of the system without necessarily making the position of the parasite available to others (in this case, both Montagu and Douglas). In short, Wordsworth did not simply discover personal debt in 1797; he also discovered the parasite as the most liberating position in systems of speculation. Wordsworth found himself in debt not *because* he had sought to parasite others; rather, his debt was the result of a failure to hew consistently to the position of parasite, as he instead attempted to become both parasite and master of a system of financing.

II. GIFTS AND BEGGARS: WORDSWORTH AND THE ORIGINS OF PUBLIC CREDIT

Locating the parasite as Wordsworth's central discovery of 1797 allows us to reread the relationship between his financial projects and the changing content and form of his poetry during this period. Earlier readings that positioned debt as the key to understanding the development ofWordsworth's mature verse have interpreted the budding poet's unsuccessful financial adventures as impetus for his desire to establish poetry as a "vocation." Yet this emphasis on debt, while not precisely incorrect, implies a psychological trajectory—Wordsworth feared debt, and as a consequence capitulated to "the System" of bourgeois interests—that does not fully explain his poetic project between 1797 and the time that he received his inheritance. If profession had been Wordsworth's only goal, poetry was certainly a strange choice. While it was respectable for gentlemen to write poetry, less financially secure individuals who made verse their sole source of income risked being seen as simply flatterers and parasites of their patrons, an understanding of the poet that stretched from Horace's description of Fannius as a "parasite" (entry for "Fannius" in Vosgien 1799–1801), to the description in the radical *Pigs Meat* of "orators and poets" as "the constant parasites of princes" (Anon. 1795: vol. 1: 53), to Thomas Love Peacock's later description of poets as "beggars" and "thieves" (Peacock 1924–34, vol. 8: 3, 22). Rather than seeking out an already respectable profession, Wordsworth's project involved a wholesale transformation of the image of the poet as parasite, a project he initiated by demonstrating the *necessity* of one-way social relations in genre of his poems. Reading Wordsworth's problems with debt as a consequence of his more primary interest in parasitical social relations also helps account for the change in genre of Wordsworth's verse in the late 1790s. Where Wordsworth's earlier poetry was written in a locodescriptive mode (e.g., *Descriptive Sketches*, *An Evening Walk*), or aimed at political protest (*Salisbury Plain*, *The Borderers*), his so-called mature verse—that is, the poetry he began writing in 1797—focused almost obsessively on the speculative power of parasitical figures such as beggars and pedlars.

"The Old Cumberland Beggar" offers a striking example of Wordsworth's shift from "descriptive" poetry to verse that focused on the speculative potential of the parasite. The chronology of this poem is contested, with critics offering either 1797 or 1798 as the probable year of composition.[15] In either case, however, it is clear that the poem first began as simply a description of an aged beggar. However, that description was later integrated into a poem that explicitly argued for the social virtue of beggars as a class, and a defense of forms of communal bonding that the beggar's existence made possible. The version that became "The Old Cumberland Beggar," in fact, devotes relatively little space to description of the beggar himself: the first stanza describes the beggar's "look of/idle computation" as he "scans" a gift of food from villagers ("the dole of village dames"), and a few lines are devoted to an account of his physical decrepitude (ll. 11–12, 9). The poem's narrator, however, is much more interested in arguing against centralized forms of state poverty relief than in describing the beggar. The narrator contends that the beggar should not be deemed "useless," for his abjection allows the villagers to

> Behold [in him] a record which together binds
> Past deeds and offices of charity,
> Else unremembered, and so keeps alive
> The kindly mood in hearts which lapse of years. (ll. 88–92)

The beggar's existence allows even the poor to make donations, and thus "know and feel that they have been,/Themselves, the fathers and the dealers-out/Of some small blessings" (ll. 149–51). The true subject of "The Old Cumberland Beggar" is thus not the beggar himself, but his *function* as an agent of virtuous social bonding.

Recent literary criticism has tended to read "The Old Cumberland Beggar" in the context of the Poor Laws legislation of the 1790s. While the proper role of government in providing relief for the indigent was a topic of legislative concern throughout the eighteenth century, bad harvests in 1794 and 1795 brought this issue to the fore. Many plans for poor relief were proposed, and Prime Minister Pitt gave his support to the "Speenhamland system," which provided monetary supplements to the indigent, designed to offset the rise of food staple prices. Wordsworth's poem is clearly addressed to such legislative solutions, chastising "Statesmen" as "ye/Who are so restless in your wisdom, ye/Who have a broom still ready in your hands/To rid the world of nuisances" (ll. 68–70).[16]

Yet if mid-1790s Poor Relief legislation is an important referent for understanding the politics of "The Old Cumberland Beggar," the poem's recommendations for the poor also point to a link between questions of poor relief and questions of speculation and state finance. The connection between systems of public credit and poor relief was stressed in 1793 in the anonymously published *An Inquiry into the Causes of the Present Derangement of Public Credit*, a pamphlet that attributed the sufferings of the poor to failed public credit and contained, as its subtitle noted, "Some Hints to the Legislature for the Formation of a Plan for the immediate Employment of the numerous destitute Poor" (Anon. 1793). By 1797, however, some commentators saw an even more direct link between Pitt's speculative policy of state finance and his proposed reform of domestic poor relief. In order to encourage its allies in the fight against France, Pitt's government had sponsored large loans to nations such as Austria and Prussia, and some commentators saw an analogy between Pitt's strategy for bringing in war allies and his proposals for alleviating the sufferings of the poor. In a letter to the editor published in the February 1797 edition of the *Monthly Magazine, and British Register*, "A. B." suggested that Pitt's

> intention of allowing a shilling per week to a poor family, for each child, is not made the first clause of the act without a meaning. It is of a piece with that little policy by which the minister has attempted to regulate the affairs of great nations. It is a bait to catch the *straggling benevolence*, as it has been most aptly termed, of many well-meaning people. (no. 14: 115)

For commentators such as "A. B.," Pitt's remittances to the poor were of a piece with his loans to European nations; in both cases, they were essentially bribes to encourage support of the Pitt government.[17]

In addition to this perceived connection between Pitt's policy of poor relief and his system of state finance, Edmund Burke had linked beggars and state finance in his *Letters on a Regicide Peace* (1795–97). In *Reflections on the Revolution in France* (1790), Burke had argued that the new French state had sacrificed "everything human and divine...to the idol of public credit" by basing their new republic on "paper circulation and a stock-jobbing constitution" (*WEB,* vol. 3: 282, 300), and in his *Letters*, he stepped up his criticism of French state finance. He described the French Republic as "a vast, tremendous, unformed spectre" that thrived on bankruptcy just as other states took their subsistence from land and gold (*WEB,* vol. 5: 237). Yet even as Burke criticized the speculative and parasitical finance policies of the French republic, he felt compelled to distinguish its system from the apparently similar British system, for the British, too, used paper money and the government had added to its national debt with every war.[18] Moreover, just as France's current system of paper money was founded on the bankruptcy of the state, Great Britain's public credit, founded in the late seventeenth century, also "had its origin, and was cradled...in bankruptcy and beggary" (*WEB*, vol. 5: 294), and Burke attributed England's commercial success after the Restoration to the "talents of the English financiers" (*WEB*, vol. 5: 374).

Burke distinguished between the bad French, and good British, systems of finance through the figure of the beggar. In his account of the origins of British public credit following the Restoration, Burke painted a picture of "the Chancellor of the Exchequer of that day, Montagu, the father of publick credit" "begging from door to door" in a desperate attempt to find enough capital to establish public credit (*WEB*, vol. 5: 294, 296). While the figure of Montagu as beggar was designed to highlight the contrast between the weak state of British credit at the end of the seventeenth and its strength at end of the eighteenth centuries, it also emphasized the *consensual* nature of British public credit. Burke contended that France, while it had originally allowed its "gifts" and "contributions" to depend on the choice of individuals, soon made such donations "compulsory" (*WEB,* vol. 5: 460). In Britain, by contrast,

> the public contribution is in its name and substance a grant. In its origin it is truly voluntary; not voluntary according to the irregular, unsteady, capricious will of individuals, but according to the will and wisdom of the whole popular mass, in the only way in which will and wisdom can go together. (*WEB,* vol. 5: 461)

In Burke's model, the British state begged, and "the public" collectively decided whether or not to respond to that appeal; the state's entreaties thus provided occasions for the nation's collective imagination to express itself, while at the same time maintaining a separation between the systems of commerce and politics. Public credit in both Britain and France was founded on bankruptcy, but the former overcame deficit through a system of voluntary contributions that linked (but kept separate) the systems of commerce and politics, while the French relied on a single system of enforced "gifts." To return to Serres's schema, in Burke's reading, both British and French systems of state finance depended upon the power of the parasite, but where the British system fully committed itself to the position of beggar, the French system tried to have it both ways, both begging and commanding at the same time.

Wordsworth probably read at least the first two of Burke's *Letters on a Regicide Peace* sometime in 1797, and the correspondences between the function of begging in Burke's account of the rise of British public credit and in Wordsworth's account of social virtue in "The Old Cumberland Beggar" are striking.[19] For both Burke and Wordsworth, "begging" named an appeal (whether actually articulated or merely implicit) that solicited the "will and wisdom of the whole popular mass" while allowing different social systems to maintain their autonomy. Moreover, for both authors, begging produced a mysterious synthesis of self-interest and sympathy. Burke insisted that the possibility of profit ensured that capital was in fact freely given to the state (otherwise it would simply be a tax), while Wordsworth focused on the moral "returns" that acts of benevolence entailed (for example, the beggar's existence allowed the "abject poor" to be the "dealers-out" of "small blessings": ll.142, 150–51). To stress these similarities is not to deny the differences between Wordsworth's beggar and Burke's Montagu: Wordsworth's beggar is located in the countryside and Burke's in the City; Wordsworth's beggar does not actually appear to beg, while Burke's makes explicit entreaties; Wordsworth's beggar receives material assistance (crumbs of bread), while Burke's receives pledges of money. Yet begging has the same *function* for Wordsworth and Burke; for both, it denotes a parasitic social relation that is able to gather together decentralized "donations," and thereby instantiate and extend the "will and wisdom of the whole popular mass."

However, where Burke simply assumed the virtues of entreaty, Wordsworth's poem analyzed more extensively the parasitical social relation of begging. All of the relationships that occur in the village described in the poem are one-way relationships: the "small mountain birds" that cluster around the beggar take crumbs and give nothing in return; the beggar takes food from the villagers but gives them nothing material in return; the villagers unify their community around the beggar's exclusion; and the poet takes his story from the villagers and gives them nothing in return. Yet the poem reveals this chain of parasites not as a proof of man's invidious nature, but rather as evidence of the utility and necessity of one-way social relations; the parasite is not simply a "nuisanc[e]" or "burthen of the earth," but rather the originating principle of social systems (ll. 70, 73). The birds, at one end of the chain, naturalize the parasitic relation; the poet, at the other, humanizes and moralizes the form of the parasite in the context of human relations.

Understanding Wordsworth's beggar as a figure for the parasite, rather than as a semirealistic representative of the poor, allows us to resolve a problem that has plagued attempts to read this poem as exclusively interested in questions of poor relief. Interpretations of the poem are often vexed by the lack of correspondence between the beggar of Wordsworth's poem and representations of the poor presented by Poor Laws reformers, for the latter generally sought to differentiate the poor from social parasites by stressing the potential vigor and capacity for work of the indigent. John Rieder, for example, suggests that Wordsworth's poem had much in common with the paternalist reforms suggested by Sir William Young and Reverend J. Howlett, but Young and Howlett attribute capacities to the poor—namely, the capacity for "industry" and "vigorous exertions," if the poor are given the chance to work (Rieder 1997: 67)—that are explicitly denied in the case of Wordsworth's beggar. Wordsworth's beggar is incapable of "vigorous exertions," and if he instantiates "independence," it is of an inhuman form and stands unallied with domestic affections, for the beggar "appears/To breathe and live but for himself alone" (ll. 164–65). Where Young and Howlett believed that parasites were destructive, but sought to show that, with help, the poor could move from the position of parasite to a position of utility, Wordsworth sought to reveal the power and virtue of the parasite *as* parasite. Wordsworth's beggar is not a potential worker, but a liminal figure, between life and death, incapable of exchange or reciprocity.

Wordsworth's beggar, in fact, has more in common with the dead described in Adam Smith's *The Theory of Moral Sentiments* than he does with descriptions of the poor by Poor Laws reformers. As I noted in chapter 2, Smith contended that we sympathize with the dead, and such fellow-feeling serves as the foundation for our sympathy with living others. Yet we do not, according to Smith, enter into any sort of sympathetic *exchange* with the dead: the dead demand our sympathy but are incapable of reciprocating. Like Smith's dead, Wordsworth's beggar is a figure of death in life, a body already returning to dust—"scarcely do his feet/Disturb the summer dust; he is so still/In look and motion" (ll. 59-61)—and he serves the same function as Smith's dead. While it is tempting to read the relationship between beggar and villagers as one of exchange—doesn't the beggar receive food, in exchange for which he provides the villagers with a record of their past good deeds?—this is a one-way "exchange," in part because the two transfers occur in different registers (food, on the one hand; information, on the other) but also because the beggar is simply the occasion that allows the villagers to feel virtuous, rather than a figure with whom they enter into reciprocal relations.

The beggar, in other words, provides a figure for the principle of the parasite. This figuration should be understood as "somapoiea," rather than prosopopoiea: a giving-body, rather than giving-face, to the principle of the parasite. The beggar is separate from others, a "solitary Man," yet the narrator does not stress this point in order to encourage sympathy. The beggar's "isolation" cannot be understood in a psychological sense—as emotional deprivation, for example—for the beggar has no psychology: he is aware of nothing but "the one little span of earth" before him, and even in the act of seeing, he "seldom know[s] that he sees" (ll. 53–54). The beggar in this poem does not give face to the horrors of psychological isolation; rather, he allows Wordsworth the opportunity to isolate, and give body to, the relationship of the parasite. Where many of Wordsworth's previous poems, such as *Descriptive Sketches*, *An Evening Walk*, and "Old Man Travelling: Animal Tranquillity and Decay" (which served as the nucleus for "The Old Cumberland Beggar"), *described* vagrants and beggars, "The Old Cumberland Beggar" does not describe a beggar but rather the social relation of begging. The "solitary" status of the beggar is not a matter of representational reference ("were beggars really solitary in the 1790s?"); rather, it denotes an operation of isolation that Wordsworth performs, in order to better reveal for readers the essence of the parasitic relation. This essence is exemplified by the involuntary tremor that passes through the beggar, which allows the birds a free meal as crumbs scatter from his "palsied hand," and thus makes visible the parasitical relations that connect all of the living entities in the poem. The birds parasite the beggar, the beggar parasites the villagers, the villagers parasite the beggar—and that entire collective is then parasited by the poet. The beggar is the center of the poem, but rather than being understood as a representative of the "abject poor," he should be seen as the coming-to-body of the mechanism of social relations. Where Burke sought to give begging a face through the character of Montagu, Wordsworth embodied the relationship of the parasite in the body of the beggar.

III. GIFT, COMPULSION, AND THE IMAGE OF TRANQUILLITY: THE BANK RESTRICTION ACT

If the connections established in the early 1790s between the figure of begging and the dynamics of state finance provided Wordsworth with a point of departure for his analysis of the powers of the parasite, a crisis in public credit provided further encouragement for the poet's project. On Sunday, February 26, 1797—a month after Burke began writing his third *Letter*, in which he extolled the strength of British credit—the Directors of the Bank of England requested an emergency meeting with Prime Minister Pitt, at which they revealed that the Bank could not in fact meet the demand for specie.[20] Pitt and Parliament issued an Order of Council that "restricted" the Bank of England from dispensing any gold in payment, arguing that

> it is indispensably necessary for the public service, that the directors of the Bank of England should forebear issuing any cash in payment, until the sense of parliament can be taken on the subject, and the proper measures adopted thereupon, for maintaining the means of circulation, and supporting the public and commercial credit of the kingdom, at this important conjuncture. (*PH,* vol. 32: 1518)

The House of Lords and the House of Commons complied by passing the Bank Restriction Act, but both Houses also initiated investigations into, and debates about, the Bank's finances and holdings and the causes of its specie failure, debates that spilled over into journalistic and pamphlet literature.[21] This section explores some of the key topoi of this discourse, focusing especially on the image of "scenes of instruction" developed by Pitt and his supporters and the competing "images of tranquility" proposed by the Opposition, for—as I argue in the subsequent section—Wordsworth parasited precisely these elements in a long verse project that he began a few months after passage of the Bank Restriction Act.

In the weeks following the Bank Restriction Act, legislators, journalists, and pamphlet writers sought to explain the causes of the specie shortage. The directors of the Bank, pro-Pitt MPs, and pro-government newspapers such as *The Times* attributed the cash shortage to widespread, though misplaced, fears of an imminent invasion by the French. Pitt argued that specie had "retreated" to the countryside, hoarded by fearful Britons. He urged legislators to pass measures capable of "drawing forth that cash, which persons from their fears, or other local habits, might withhold from the public" (*PH,* vol. 33: 70), and he returned repeatedly to the need to "draw into circulation the specie hoarded up at home" (*PH,* vol. 33: 342). Pitt's opponents were not convinced by either his analysis of the causes of specie shortage or his solution, and argued instead that Pitt's loans to Britain's military "friends"—for example, a £5,570,000 loan to the Austrian emperor and an "advance" to Prussia—were the real drain on specie.[22] Benjamin Hobhouse countered Pitt's suggestion that people "had buried their money in the earth" with the satirical contention that "more money had been buried in Germany than in the ground" (*PH*, vol. 32: 1539); for Hobhouse, specie could not be exhumed from its country graves, for it had never been interred there in the first place.[23]

What particularly vexed the Opposition was the apparent ability of the Bank of England to *create* money. A spectacular British commercial and financial crash in 1793 had revealed that private country banks could create money in the short term by making "unsecured" loans with banknotes they themselves issued. However, the consequences of that earlier event—a massive number of bankruptcies and country bank failures—had seemed to prove that the paper money thus created was not real, could not last for long, and bore no relation to the notes issued by the Bank of England (especially since the latter *had* been able to meet all demands for specie in 1793).[24] Yet the events of 1797 did not allow for this distinction between the "bad" paper money of the private banks and the "secured" notes of the Bank of England. As Fox pointed out, if a private banker "issues beyond that due proportion of cash, and without a corresponding security in effects, then the transaction is stigmatized as fraudulent" (*PH*, vol. 33: 336), and he wondered why the same should not hold true of the Bank of England.

Pitt and his supporters suggested that Fox's question betrayed an ignorance of the principles of banking. The Bank of England, Pitt contended, could "never answer in cash the whole of the demands that might be made on them in one day," and the Attorney General concurred, claiming that "every person who took a Bank note knew that the Bank was not in a situation to give cash for every bank note, supposing every one be presented for payment in cash at one time" (*PH*, vol. 33: 335, 339).[25] The problem was that banks issued banknotes that could be exchanged for specie on demand, but at the same time entered into legal agreements with their customers that allowed the latter to pay back loans at specified points in the future.[26] Banking, in other words, depended upon the ability to issue paper money in the present—that is, to create bank debt in the present—even though the bank assets that purportedly "secured" these loans would not be available until the future. As more recent economists such as Joseph Schumpeter and Geoffrey Ingham have noted, "the production of credit-money in a banking *system* is a self-generating, relatively autonomous process, in so far as the 'banks can always grant further loans, since the larger amounts going out are then matched by larger amounts coming in'" (Ingham 2004: 108; embedded quote from Schumpeter 1917: 207).

For Opposition MPs such as Fox and Sheridan, the fact that the Bank of England created money and debt on the basis of minimal specie highlighted the extent to which Pitt had transformed Britain into the double of its opponent, France. Drawing on Burke's comparison of British and French modes of speculation, Fox contended that it was now impossible to distinguish between the speculative foundations of the French constitution and the purportedly solid foundations of the British system:

> Year after year the minister [i.e., Pitt] has been amusing us with his ideas of the finances of France—now on the verge, now in the gulph of bankruptcy! What computations upon their assignats and their mandates! They could not possibly continue. All perfectly true. But the misfortune is, that while he was thus amusing us, he has led us to the very same verge, aye, into the very same gulph! (*PH,* vol. 32:1537–38)

"The minister," Fox concluded, "has conducted the war upon the hope, that we should be able to defeat the French by a contest of finance; and you now see the expedients to which we are driven" (*PH,* vol. 32: 1538).[27] Sheridan echoed Fox's concern, arguing that "a forced circulation would infallibly lead to bankruptcy," for he could see no difference between such a system and French *assignats*:

> [i]t might be answered, that the paper money of this country rested upon a different security from that of the French assignats or mandates; but to this, he [i.e., Sheridan] would reply, that if they both contained the idea of compulsion, this ingredient alone would produce a depretiation [sic], and though not in the same rapid progress, the paper of this country would ultimately experience the fate of the French. (*PH,* vol. 33: 64)

Opposition MPs such as Fox and Sheridan drew on Burke's vocabulary of speculation to argue that Pitt was displacing the British system of speculative "gifts" with a "compulsory" (i.e., French) system of finance. Fox contended that the Bank's refusal to pay in specie amounted to a "tax" on the "income of the stock-holder," and MP Nicholls ominously warned that Pitt was seeking to produce a "revolution in property," which in turn "might produce a revolution in government, and all those scenes of blood which had disgraced France" (*PH,* vol. 32; 1529; *PH,* vol. 33: 326).

This debate about the nature of state finance served both sides as an opportunity for articulating their visions of the origins of public credit. Pitt argued that the integrity of public credit was secured by a relatively small number of "public creditors" upon whose opinion the faith of the economy as a whole rested (*PH,* vol. 33: 342–43). These creditors, Pitt argued, were interested solely in the probability of "future prosperity" (that is, the probability of future commercial opportunities), and for such investors, specie convertibility was a nonissue. Anticipating the psychoanalytic analysis of panic that I outlined at the end of chapter 2, Pitt's camp suggested that financial panic was brought on by a temporary loss of faith in the economic leadership, leaving each member "solicitous on his own account," because "the emotional ties, which have hitherto made the danger seem small to him, have ceased to exist" (Freud 1953–74, vol. 18: 96).[28] However, if financial panic resulted from the temporary waning of faith in leadership, it could be countered by steps that publicized the confidence and faith of the leaders in themselves.

Opposition critics, by contrast, argued that public credit had its roots in a much more widespread "confidence." The Opposition believed that the run on the banks in the early months of 1797 demonstrated widespread suspicion of Pitt's leadership, but they argued that such panic, far from demonstrating the destruction of affective ties, instead revealed a resurgence of "horizontal" affective ties between citizens. In the face of the ever-increasing domestic power of Pitt's government, Opposition critics figured public credit as a mysterious principle of systemic affective connection, resistant to all governmental attempts to control it, and repository of the traditional British value of "independence." The Marquis of Lansdown contended that the "precise seat" of public credit "could not be discovered," for

> it at once pervaded over and proceeded out of the whole. It both gave and received its animation and its existence.... It was that thing which sprung from the happy concoction of all the vital juices of the national frame, which proceeded from the nice distribution of our parts, and their mutual co-operation; which gave to the system a sympathetic connexion.... (*PH*, vol. 32: 1565)

In the first of his *Letters on a Regicide Peace*, Burke had attributed national unity to the fact that "[m]en are not tied to one another by papers and seals," as the French seemed to assume, but were rather "led to associate by resemblances, by conformities, by sympathies," for a "secret, unseen, but irrefragable bond of habitual intercourse, holds them together" (*WEB*, vol. 5: 317–18). Lansdown's description suggested that public credit was the medium of that unseen bond. For Opposition critics, public credit, while perhaps not precisely synonymous with sympathy, had become its principle of articulation in the British "national frame." For an Opposition movement that seemed increasingly incapable of stemming what it saw as Pitt's unconstitutional overthrow of the principles of the British constitution, public credit was presented as a redemptive, organic collective force, capable of escaping Pitt's control while at the same time unifying and redeeming the British nation.

The difference of opinion between Pitt and the Opposition critics concerning the origin of public credit led them to different understandings about how to produce public images that facilitated the stability of public credit. For Pitt, since the ultimate source of public credit's stability was the confidence of wealthy investors, more widespread public confidence was produced simply by representing the faith of financiers. The pro-government *Times* provided precisely such a "scene of instruction" for worried Britons: noting that a day after the specie suspension "most of the opulent

Merchants and Bankers in the City of London" had met at the "Mansion-House," *The Times* reported that these influential individuals had agreed to "promote the universal Circulation of Bank of England Notes instead of specie," and in six long columns (and four more the next day), it listed the names of these would-be opinion-makers.[29] While the February 28, 1797 issue of *The Times* acknowledged that one member of this club of influence apparently had proposed that a "more public Meeting" be held in order to gather "the sense of the country," the newspaper noted that "[t]his suggestion was generally and very properly scouted [i.e., mocked]." Public faith could be saved, *The Times* suggested, by *making visible* the faith of the key nodes in the system of opinion; one created faith in others, in short, by representing the influence-makers being convinced. Pitt supporter and wealthy banker Sir Francis Baring provided another scene of instruction in a pamphlet, arguing that he was personally convinced that both the "internal tranquility" and the ever-increasing "prosperity of the country" depended upon the stability of the Bank of England (Baring 1797: 64). For Pitt and his supporters, public credit originated in the influence of a small number of knowledgeable creditors, and there thus was simply no reason to take "the sense of the country."

For the Opposition, by contrast, public credit relied on a much more extensive and distributed network that included everyone who used money in any form, and thus public images of stability could not rely on representations of the wealthy enjoying the prospect of future wealth. Instead, public credit was supported to the extent that its past stability could be projected through the present into a continuous future. The Bank of England, for example, only operated to the extent that it seemed to be "a sort of pillar, which nothing could shake," while Hobhouse declared that public credit depended on perceptions of Bank as "the great wheel which gives uniform and steady motion to our extensive circulation" (*PH,* vol. 33: 373, 325).[30] For the Opposition, what Baring had called "the internal tranquility" of the country depended less upon the assurances of the wealthy than on a collective perception that state finance was proceeding with the uniform, steady motion of the wheel (a movement not unlike the slow, almost imperceptible circuit of the old Cumberland beggar). Only by means of such images of tranquility, Opposition critics argued, could the stability of the past to be projected into the future. Thus, for the Opposition, the importance of specie was its status as a sign of the past; it was, as Adam Smith had described it, the "dead stock" of the past upon which the present and future necessarily depended.

The disagreement between Pitt's supporters and the Opposition was less a debate over the need for images of tranquility per se—both sides agreed that public credit must appear to be stable and tranquil—than a debate over the way that such images were produced. Pitt located the stability of public credit in the future, in the promise of future prosperity as attested to by knowledgeable opinion-makers. Opposition critics, by contrast, located the past as the origin of public credit, arguing that the public maintained its faith in finance only to the extent that the present manifested its links with the dead. As we will see in the next section, Wordsworth parasited both of these claims by creating a scene of instruction in which sympathy with the dead was "refined" into poetic currency by a gifted individual.

IV. DRAWING FROM THE DEAD: *THE RUINED COTTAGE* AND "THE PEDLAR"

In precisely the same months that the Bank Restriction Act provoked wide-ranging reflections on the system of British public credit, Wordsworth was analyzing relationships among wealth, scenes of instruction, and images of tranquility in *The Ruined Cottage* and "The Pedlar," two parts of a longer poem that occupied the poet's attention from spring 1797 through spring 1798.[31] In a sense, these linked works presented a more "poetic" interrogation of the logic of the parasite that he had earlier outlined in "The Old Cumberland Beggar." The latter poem engaged the reader primarily at the level of statement, rather than image. If the reader found him- or herself in agreement with the poem's message, it was because it had been explicitly argued within the verse, rather than because the reader had been made to feel the moral appeal of this position; the poem was, as Charles Lamb noted, "too like a lecture" (Lamb, cited in Johnston 2000: 546). In *The Ruined Cottage* and "The Pedlar," by contrast, Wordsworth outlined the function of the *poet* in the production of the differentiated social system he had outlined in "The Old Cumberland Beggar." This section explores Wordsworth's deployment of two key images from the Bank Restriction debate—the scene of instruction and the image of tranquility—within *The Ruined Cottage* and its companion texts. The mouthpiece of wisdom in *The Ruined Cottage* is a character within the poem, the pedlar, and the poem stages a scene of instruction grounded in the ability of this itinerant salesman to convert perceptions of the sufferings of others into redemptive images. Yet this scene of instruction in turn depends upon the pedlar's power to communicate images, first by drawing the power of the dead away from the clutches of the past through an operation of "entwining," and then by "mineralizing" this power into an image that has social currency. The poem suggests that both of these operations (entwining and mineralizing) are fundamentally parasitical, and thus behind the key image of the poem—"silvered o'er" speargrass—lies an image of parasitical bindweed twining around a rose.

Gold, wages, and army finance

The Ruined Cottage describes—in several different registers—the emergence of meaning from noise. At the start of the poem, the narrator finds himself surrounded by meaningless natural "murmurs" and "tedious noise," but he concludes the verse with a capacity to hear "melodies" (ll. 25, 532). This latter capacity is a function of the narrator's—and by extension, the reader's—capacity to understand the meaning of the pedlar's story about a weaver (Robert), his wife (Margaret), and their children. In the pedlar's account, general economic hardship, illness, and crop failures forced Robert out of work, and the unemployed weaver lingered in a state of lassitude and depression for months, until one day he simply disappeared, leaving Margaret a bag of gold in his place. Later that day a stranger visited Margaret and told her that Robert had "joined a troop/Of soldiers, going to a distant land," suggesting that the gold was the bounty given civilians willing to volunteer for service in the army. The pedlar returned to the cottage periodically, only to find Margaret wasting away as she waited for Robert's return, and eventually she and most of her children die. At the start of the poem, the pedlar tells the narrator (and by extension, the reader) that he can "see around me...things which you cannot see," and the task of the poem, critics have agreed, is to teach both narrator and reader to "read/ The form of things" with a worthy eye (ll. 67–68; 510–11).

As I noted in the introduction to this chapter, recent criticism has emphasized the importance of economic and financial metaphors to *The Ruined Cottage* and its companion text "The Pedlar," and Alan Liu's discussion of the speculative logic of the poem remains the most thorough and impressive of these interpretations. Liu argues that Robert's plight registers the increasing "capitalization" of weaving practices in England. The process of capitalization transformed the means of production such that formerly independent weavers were conscripted into a "putting-out" system of production, in which workers accepted material and wages from a central distributor. The putting-out system also forced weavers to abandon what Liu argues was a premodern credit system in favor of a "modern" credit system that forced employed workers into debt (Liu 1989: 328).[32] Thus, concludes Liu, the purse of gold that Robert finally accepts is "the poem's imagination of a wage," and, as a consequence, marks Robert's fall from independent artisan to the putting-out system of wage labor: "[t]he ultimate marker of ...dependence on capitalists, perhaps, is the 'purse of gold' Robert at last accepts. In the economy of debt, the self mortgages itself for a wage and then disappears, in total indebtedness, into the armies of the other" (Liu 1989: 330).

While Liu's interpretation is compelling, the details of Robert's disappearance suggest that he not only symbolizes the temporally extended process of capitalization, but also indexes Wordsworth's more specific response to British speculative troubles in the late 1790s. While Robert's disappearance may serve as an allegory of the telos of wage slavery, it is striking that Wordsworth picks the army—rather than a more clearly capitalist institution, such as a workhouse—as the medium of his fate. Nor is it entirely clear why *gold* should stand in for "wages," since the international mobility of specie makes it far less appropriate for a medium of capitalistic indebtedness than monetary instruments such as scrip or paper.

Yet both of these details would have been significant to the poem's readers in 1797 and 1798, for the form of sailors' and soldiers' payments was a hotly debated topic in Parliament in the months following the Bank Restriction Act. Both pro-government and Opposition legislators recognized that an unpaid army was a potentially disruptive force, and each side sought to take advantage of this fact. Pitt advocated for an exemption to the specie suspension for the armed forces, making the argument that soldiers should be paid in gold by reminding his listeners of the dangers of a "disbanded army, with arms and without pay" (*PH,* vol. 33: 347). Paying soldiers in gold, Pitt suggested, was equivalent to removing any threat of insurrection. Opposition MPs, for their part, interpreted such a claim as Pitt's "direct confession of the establishment of a military government" (*PH,* vol. 33: 348), and argued against such an exemption.[33]

In addition to reminding *The Ruined Cottage*'s readers of these debates about the form of army wages, the "purse of gold" that appears in place of Robert also would have recalled another aspect of Pitt's war policy. While bounties had been paid to enlisting soldiers for much of the eighteenth century, this practice became especially pronounced in the 1790s, with the army using bounties to lure away men from the (homeland) militia (though it is not clear whether bounties were paid in specie following the Bank Restriction Act of 1797). In addition, the purse of gold that draws the British weaver Robert into the army registered the much broader changes British military and financial policy had undergone since the beginning of hostilities in 1793. In the early 1790s, Britain had fought its war with France in large part through German and Sardinian mercenaries. Paying these mercenaries depended upon a complicated system of international credit. In the first step of this system, the British quartermaster in a foreign country was issued Bank of England bills of exchange by the government. The quartermaster then located merchants in the host country willing to exchange the bills of exchange for specie, with which he paid the soldiers. These foreign merchants could then use the Bills of Exchange to purchase British goods—for example, British woolens—or, alternatively, return them to the Bank of England for specie. As Larry Neal notes, the result of this system was that "British woolens were thus transformed into Hessian mercenaries fighting the French," a fact that—as later British commentators noted—linked Britain's war effort to the spread of its commerce, provided that Britain was successful in the conflict (that is, the more areas within which Britain deployed mercenaries, the greater the territory that it could enclose within its commercial network: Neal 1990a: 202). However, as the war dragged on, Pitt increasingly had to turn from an army of foreign mercenaries to an army of domestic soldiers, such that by 1798, foreign troops made up a miniscule portion of the British land forces.[34] Where in 1794, Pitt's foreign secretary Lord Grenville defended the use of mercenaries by arguing that "it was certainly cheaper and more politic to pay foreign troops, than to take our own youth from the plough, and the loom" (*PH*, vol. 31: 452), by 1797, the "British loom" had to be raided for soldiers. Even worse, in the wake of the Bank Restriction Act, Britain had to raid its meager supplies of specie both to lure soldiers into the army through the payment of bounties, and to pay wages in order to keep armed forces from staging domestic insurrection.

Robert's new occupation, as well as his form of payment, is thus significant not only of a changing system of labor, as Liu suggests, but also of the much more immediate failure of Britain's war efforts and its system of finance. By 1797, the Pitt ministry found that it had to send its weavers, rather than their woolens, to war, and it had to pay them directly from British stores of gold, rather than obtaining specie via an international credit system. Robert's disappearance is thus less symptomatic of the moral depravity of "capitalism" in general, than of the particular failure of the British system of wartime finance in the 1790s. By 1797, Wordsworth himself had learned the hard way that a system of benevolent loans to friends undercut its own foundation, and it seemed—at least to Pitt's critics—that Britain as a whole was learning the same lesson. Britain's loans to its "friends" had not only ceased to pay dividends in trade, but were threatening to transform the foundation of British commerce—the loom—into fodder for French cannons. Robert and Margaret served as symbol and allegory, respectively, of Britain's all-or-nothing speculative stance toward the future. Robert's entrance into the army symbolized Britain's move away from a mediated war (in which foreign mercenaries would pay the price of defeat) and toward a war that would either result in absolute victory and the return of the weavers or absolute defeat. Margaret functioned as an allegory of the speculative stance that underwrote this strategy, for she (like Britain) bet everything on the return of the weavers.

Sympathy, death, and the image of tranquillity

If Robert symbolized the failure of Pitt's system of war finance, what force did the poem position as the locus of a successful opposition to British foreign policy in the 1790s? Wordsworth's solution adopted elements of both the pro-Pitt and Opposition positions articulated in the Bank Restriction Act debate. Pitt and his supporters had argued for the efficacy of "scenes of instruction," which represented economically astute individuals being convinced of the possibilities of future prosperity, and Wordsworth's poem suggested, in similar fashion, the utility of such gifted individuals. As Rieder notes, the pedlar serves as the narrator's and reader's investment broker (Rieder 1997: 76), able to see things that others cannot ("I see around me here/Things which you cannot see," ll. 67–68). The pedlar is especially sensitive to those "[s]ympathies.../That steal upon the meditative mind/ And grow with thought" (ll. 79–81), and as a consequence, he is able to lead both narrator and reader away from problematic emotional investments with the tale of Robert's departure and Margaret's decline—those emotional investments from which one can "draw" only "momentary pleasure"—seeking instead to develop our ability to "read" such a story with a "worthy" eye (ll. 225, 511).

Yet even as Wordsworth drew on the *form* of Pitt's scene of instruction, the poet's choice of a pedlar as investment banker emphasized the importance of parasitism to the British economy. Wordsworth's use of a pedlar as his "gifted" interpreter has struck many commentators as puzzling or problematic. Such a decision was not entirely without precedent: in 1796, for example, Charles Dibdin published a rather limpid collection of poems and stories entitled *The Pedlar*, which contained a number of attacks on governmental corruption and economic monopolizing (Dibdin 1796). Nevertheless, many of Wordsworth's contemporaries found the choice of peddlar questionable. Immediately following the 1814 publication of *The Excursion*, which contained versions of both *The Ruined Cottage* and "The Pedlar," Francis Jeffery wondered in the November 1814 *Edinburgh Review* whether Wordsworth could really have imagined "that his favourite doctrines were likely to gain anything in point of effect of authority by being put into the mouth of a person accustomed to higgle about tape, or brass sleeve-buttons?" (vol. 24: 30). More recent criticism has been less judgmental about Wordsworth's choice of profession for his mouthpiece, but as Liu notes, for most contemporary critics, the pedlar's occupation is significant only to the extent that "it is peripatetic" (Liu 1989: 341), an interpretation in part encouraged by Wordsworth's redescription of the pedlar as the "Wanderer" in the later *The Excursion*.

Yet Wordsworth's choice of peddling was motivated by far more than its pedestrian mobility, for the figure of the pedlar played an important part in the discourse of finance in the 1790s. Liu has already pointed us in this direction, arguing that Wordsworth's pedlar functions as the virtuous double of a black marketeer: just as the latter creates untaxable profit by illegally engaging in hoarding or speculating, so too did the Pedlar store up mental wealth which he converted into "rich imagery" in ways that defied logical calculation or explanation. However, where Liu reads peddling as a *regressive* economic form—a "holdover" from a past "system of production and distribution" (Liu 1989: 345)—late eighteenth-century pedlars were in fact *both* holdovers from a declining system of production and distribution *and* part of the "avant garde" of capitalism. As Jeffrey's quote suggests—and as historians such as Neil McKendrick, Margaret Spufford, and Laurence Fontaine have confirmed—pedlars were vital vectors for the expansion of eighteenth-century consumerism, serving to extend consumer markets into rural areas. As a result, pedlars and peddling did not disappear in the nineteenth century, but became, if anything, even more central to processes of production, providing producers with raw materials for industrial production of products such as paper.[35] The importance of pedlars for the future of commerce was explicitly recognized by manufacturing interests in the late 1780s. When Pitt proposed his so-called "Hawkers and Pedlars Act" in 1785—a component of the "Shop Tax" by which Pitt tried to buy the support of shop owners with a promise to outlaw their rivals, the pedlars—linen, wool, and cotton manufacturers petitioned against the Act. Supporters of the Act described pedlars as parasites: "pest[s] to the community" and "nuisance[s]" who partook of the benefits of taxes without paying their fair share (*PH,* vol. 25: 554, 566). Manufacturers, by contrast, argued that pedlars were vital for the commercial process, both because they extended existing markets and because they developed new markets among the working class (McKendrick 1982: 87, and—for legislative debate on the bill—*PH,* vol. 25: 553–67, 790–97, 885–88, 1164–86; vol. 26: 5–16, 1021–32). For these manufacturing interests, while "Hawkers and Pedlars" might well operate by what Liu calls "undisclosed deals and transactions pushed through secretly with unaccounted sources of funds" (Liu 1989: 345), they were also an absolutely necessary parasite, functioning, as Burke had described hawkers and pedlars in his third *Letter on a Regicide Peace*, as the "capillary vessels of the system" which circulated the "life-blood of the State" (*WEB*, vol. 5: 498–99). Wordsworth's decision to locate the pedlar at the center of his scene of instruction thus should be read not primarily as a function of his nostalgia for a waning mode of production, but rather as the symbol for the inevitability of parasitism in all economic relations.

Even as Wordsworth drew on the pro-government topos of the scene of instruction, he also drew on the Opposition's claims concerning the need for images of tranquility, though the poet also transformed this latter notion by emphasizing parasitism. In "The Old Cumberland Beggar," Wordsworth had instantiated his principle of social bonding in the image of the tranquil beggar, but the corporeal materiality of that figure—the fact that the beggar was still living and could be fed—unnecessarily obscured the nature of this principle of sociality. More specifically, the quasi-vitality of the beggar allowed for the (incorrect) interpretation that social relations depended upon "exchange," when in fact the poem stressed the fundamental importance of parasitism. In *The Ruined Cottage* and "The Pedlar," Wordsworth depicted a moral economy that could not be grounded in exchange, for the subject of sympathy, Margaret, is quite dead in the narrative present of the poem. As a result, the sympathy generated by the reader's encounter with Margaret is grounded in one-way social relations, rather than reciprocity.

Rather, Wordsworth followed Smith, for whom, as Esther Schor notes, our relationship to the dead begins as one of irremediable debt (see Figure 4.1). Smith suggested that this unpayable debt to the dead served as the condition for our sympathy with the living: just as "paper money converts the dead stock [of silver and gold] into active and productive stock" (*WN* 1.341), so too does sympathy with those who have passed away "transmute

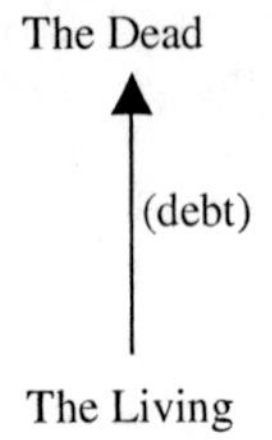

Figure 4.1 The irremediable debt with the dead.

the dead into a vital moral resource" (Schor 1994: 37). Where Smith was a bit hazy on the specific mechanism by means of which an unpayable debt to one party (the dead) enables a surplus with respect to another (the living), *The Ruined Cottage* dramatizes the encounter with death in order to probe more deeply the economy between the dead and the living.

As both Schor and Liu have noted, *The Ruined Cottage* suggests that the path to virtuous power lies through the image, and more specifically, the "image of tranquillity."[36] As the pedlar explains at the end of the poem, the weeds and speargrass that now grow where Margaret used to dwell "convey" to his mind "So still an image of tranquillity,/So calm and still" that all the "uneasy thoughts" that result from "what we feel of sorrow and despair/From ruin and from change" disappear (ll. 516–25). It is this image—the image of weeds and speargrass "silvered o'er" by mist and rain (l. 515)—that the pedlar passes on to the narrator (and by extension, to the reader). However important the narrative of Margaret's sufferings might be to the poem, the efficacy of the verse hinges on the image, for it is the ability of the narrator (and reader) to "read" the redeeming image that in turn enables each to trace "with milder interest/That secret spirit of humanity" that still survives in the weeds that have taken Margaret's place (l. 502–3). It is the poetic image, in other words, that transforms our unpayable debts to the dead into sympathetic bonds with the living. Yet, we might ask, how is the pedlar able to locate the image of tranquility? And how should such an image release us from the pull of the dead, who otherwise demand our sympathy but never give anything back in return?

"The Pedlar" provides an answer to the first question—that of how the pedlar can locate images of tranquility—that is reminiscent of Wordsworth's relationship to the Calvert legacy. At the origin, "The Pedlar" suggests, was the parasitic relation, in the form of "[a] precious gift" from nature to the boy who would become the pedlar. This gift ensured both that the pedlar was "by Nature tuned/.../To sympathy with man," and that he would be able to develop "[a]n *active* power to fasten images/ Upon his brain" (ll. 34–35, 275–77, 40–41). Together, these two capacities allow the pedlar to convert all that he sees into pacific and redemptive images; even in the case of "show[s] of vice," for example, the pedlar was able to "produc[e]/That tender interest which the virtuous feel/Among the wicked" (ll. 253, 255–57). And because the pedlar is able to draw images from every encounter, he can even "afford to suffer/With those he saw suffer" (ll. 253–57; 283–84). "Hence it was," the narrator writes, "[t]hat in our best experience he was rich" (ll. 284–85); though "poor in outward show," the narrator stresses again, the would-be pedlar "was most rich" (ll. 338).

The poem suggests, however, that in order for the pedlar to impart his riches to others—that is, for him to enable others to earn those dividends of "milder interest" that the narrator experiences in *The Ruined Cottage*—he must create not just images, but images of tranquility. The pedlar's internal images, in other words, do not become communicable—they cannot become the foundation for a community—unless they are characterized by "tranquility." The speculative power of the pedlar (his ability to turn anything into an image) becomes a socializing power only through a rigorous transformation of internal images into externalized images of tranquility. While previous criticism has explained Wordsworth's theory of the image by positioning it against historically extended discourses such as eighteenth-century dramatic theory (Averill 1980: 116–46) or the emerging language of political conservatism (Chandler 1984: 120–43), I focus again on the much more topical debate on "internal tranquility" and public credit that I have described above.

Mineralization and entwining

In its effort to restore public confidence in British finance while still opposing Pitt, the Opposition had described public credit as a human construction that functioned only so far as it replicated those architectural structures that themselves draw on stable principles of nature: public credit, for example, had to mimic the pillar that draws its strength from the immobility of rock, or the steadily moving wheel that depends upon the invariability of friction and gravity. There was, of course, a significant difference between the causes of solidity and stability in the case of pillars and mill wheels, on the one hand, and public credit, on the other. The phenomenological reality of pillars, mill wheels, and agriculture—that is, their appearance as regular and stable—depended upon an actual capacity to harness heterogeneous series of nonhuman forces (the tensile strength of stone, for example, in the case of the pillar, or the constant flow of water, in the case of the wheel). Public credit, by contrast, could not draw its phenomenological solidity and stability from forces that operated outside of perception (for example, gravity or mineral strength); rather, solidity and stability somehow had to emerge from perception itself. Opposition commentators recognized this fact, and suggested that the perception of public credit could become its own support if it could "mineralize" itself, that is, lend itself the patina of the money that purportedly served as its foundation. Adam Smith had outlined the operation of mineralization in the *Wealth of Nations* when he argued that paper money in particular (and public credit more generally) converted "the dead stock [of silver and gold coins] into active and productive stock," but this functioned only to the extent that this dead stock remained virtually present in paper money. For Smith, this meant that one had to see actual coins on a periodic basis, but Opposition commentators recognized that simply the faith that such conversion was possible was sufficient. As an anonymous pamphlet writer noted, "[f]aith is the evidence of things unseen, the substance of things hoped for. This faith must, however, receive it as a thing not to be questioned, that there is a substance, although it is not this moment visible" (Anon. 1797: 10). The Opposition implied that while no one ever actually had to convert paper money into specie, everyone had to believe that it was possible. Public credit could not literally draw on the tensile strength of minerals, as an actual pillar might, but it could nevertheless establish solidity and stability if it remained phenomenologically linked with the minerality of gold and silver: that is, the image of paper money had to retain the patina of gold and silver. Paper money retained this patina—it appeared "silvered o'er"—to the extent that its conversion into minerals seemed possible. The problem with the Bank Restriction Act, however, was that it had dissolved the appearance of this linkage.

In *The Ruined Cottage*, Wordsworth also explored the processes by which images become "silvered o'er," but he recognized that mineralization itself depended upon a prior operation, that of continual bending, or folding—an entwining—which rechannelled the powers of the dead, turning them in a different direction. On their own, the dead of *The Ruined Cottage* press too close, overwhelming the narrator with the "impotence of grief" (l. 500); the dead are like the "unprofitable bindweed" that "drag[s] the rose from its sustaining wall/And ben[ds] it down to earth" (ll. 316–17). However, *images* of vegetation, such as that of the "weeds and speargrass," enabled the narrator to attenuate these attachments to the dead, and they accomplished this by bending the destructive powers of nature in another direction. At the start of *The Ruined Cottage*, the pedlar described nature as a power of ruin that erases all traces of human activity:

> We die, my friend,
> Nor we alone, but that which each man loved
> And prized in his peculiar nook of earth
> Dies with him, or is changed, and very soon
> Even of the good is no memorial left. (ll. 68–72)

Both the dead and the vegetation of the poem—bursting gorse, matted weeds, unprofitable bindweed, and rank speargrass—trope nature's colonizing negativity, its tendency to draw parasitically on human remnants until it has erased all traces of human activity.[37] Yet the poem suggests that humans can appropriate this power of parasitism for themselves by following the path of nature itself. At a first level, for example, one can harness nature's power simply by imitating the path of the vegetation: just as the weeds have crossed over the garden wall, so too have passersby "o'erleap[ed]/The broken wall" of the garden to eat the wild currants that now grow inside it. However, this is a rather simple form of imitation: in following the weeds over the wall, the passersby have followed the product, rather than the process of nature. As a result, while the passersby may seem to parasite nature (taking but not giving in return), this is illusory, since these same passersby have to leap back over the wall, thus allowing the vegetation to spread its seeds more widely.

The Ruined Cottage suggests that the negative power of nature can only be truly parasited if one follows the *process* of the parasitical vegetation. The narrator's image of the bindweed twining about the rose instantiates this parasitical process. As Erasmus Darwin noted in *The Botanic Garden*, "[a] contest for light obtains throughout the whole vegetable kingdom," and different plants had developed different strategies for engaging this agonistic field:

> shrubs rise above herbs; and, by precluding the air and light from them, injure or destroy them; trees suffocate or incommode shrubs; the parasite climbing plants, as Ivy, Clematis, incommode the taller trees; and other parasites, which exist without having roots on the ground, as Mistletoe, Tillandsia, Epidendrum, and the mosses and funguses, incommode them all. (Darwin 1789, vol. 2: 108)[38]

The rose and the bindweed each seek material energy in the form of light, but for both, this heliotropism is linked to parasitism. The rose employs a limited form of parasitism, growing thorns that allow its relatively solid stem to hook onto, and parasite, the upward growth of other vegetation, while the bindweed develops a much more extensive form of parasitism—it parasites the parasite—for rather than using thorns to link itself to the structure and upward growth of other plants, it twines continuously around the stem of the rose. By bending with the rose, rather attempting to overleap it with a rigid stem structure, the bindweed moves upward with minimal outlay of energy direction (see Figure 4.2).

Twining, unlike heliotropism, is an endogenous form of plant growth; that is, it results from stimuli that are internal to the plant responding to signals from the outside.[39] We might say, then, that the bindwind treats the rose as an informational field by means of which it orients its own movement. To say

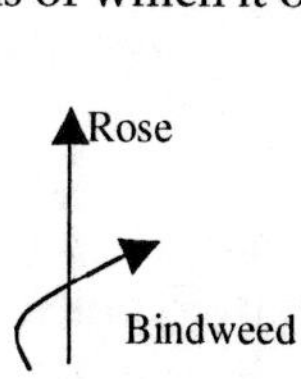

Figure 4.2 Bindweed entwining itself around the rose.

that the bindweed parasites by entwining means that it treats the contours of the rose stem surface as signs, or signals, that determine its movement.

For the pedlar to imitate this process, then—that is, for him to parasite by twining—means to treat nature as information rather than energy; to treat it as image rather than actual object. The passersby who physically leaps over the wall mimic the rose, practicing a partial form of parasitism, for they directly follow the vegetation into the ruin to a source of energy (the berries) and then depart. The pedlar, by contrast, acts like the bindweed by treating the weeds as informational field, rather than a direct source of energy; the pedlar creates an image by asking the narrator (and the readers) to return again and again to this sign. This points to the difference between a metaphor and an image in the context of these poems: a metaphor is a (helio)tropism that directs the reader in one direction; the image allows the reader to change direction continuously. The image allows more freedom of movement: it is by means of the image, for example, that the pedlar and the narrator are able to "leave the shade" at the end of the poem, as both depart from the cottage and distance themselves from the demands of the dead (l. 536).[40] The old Cumberland Beggar's narrow vision had provided a figural approximation for this power of bending—the beggar is "Bowbent, his eyes for ever on the ground" and "one little span of earth/Is all his prospect" (ll. 52, 50–51)—but *The Ruined Cottage* isolates the operation of entwining by separating it from the human body and revealing it to be a symbolic power.

Once the pull of the dead has been attenuated by means of entwining, *then* the image of weeds and speargrass can be mineralized ("silvered o'er") and communicated. To mineralize is to capitalize by securing a hard border around this process of twining; that is to keep it continually bending in the same way, so as to continue to treat nature as an informational field. To mineralize is thus to stop (or at least stall) time, for as Serres notes, whatever form "capital" takes, it is always "a pocket of time": it "is the reservoir above the dam, an iron mine...a stock of energy and of primary material; it is an island of negative entropy" (Serres 1982: 171).[41] The mineralized image is capital, and thus communicable: it passes from the pedlar to the narrator, and then on to the reader.

Yet how is this hard border around the image—this mineralization—produced? How, in other words, are images able to *move* from the pedlar to narrator (and the reader)? Anticipating recent monetary theory, *The Ruined Cottage* suggests that images become "currency" only to the extent that debt is created; that is, images only become mineralized (i.e., communicable) to the extent that they produce a debt between the pedlar/poet and the narrator/reader. Just as the bindweed overcomes gravity by treating the rose as informational field (thereby appropriating its structure at minimal energy cost), the image overcomes the pull of the unpayable debt to the dead by treating the dead as information, appropriating from them a

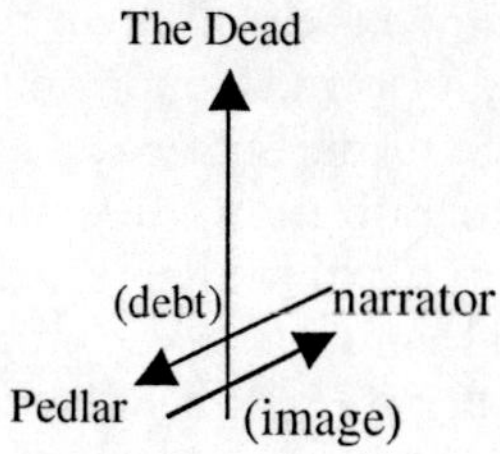

Figure 4.3 The silvered o'er speargrass: Entwining and mineralization.

structure (debt). To receive the image, in short, is to become indebted to a new authority (see Figure 4.3).

Yet the pedlar's creation of debt is not as insidious as it sounds, for two reasons. First, this new debt between the pedlar and the narrator allows the latter to discharge his otherwise unpayable debt to the dead (the pedlar tells the narrator that "enough to sorrow have you given" [l. 508]). Even more important, the fact that the image has been mineralized means that it provides a form by means of which new debt can be discharged; what the pedlar provides, in other words, is the *form* of debt-creation. Thus, the narrator is able to pass this story, its image, and its debt, on to the reader. As I note in the next section, there is no necessary limit on this process, for each reader could, in principle, locate images and pass on debt to others.

Wordsworth's analysis of images of tranquility as dependent upon a *double* operation—both entwining and mineralization—highlighted the shortcomings of both the pro-Pitt and Opposition positions on public credit. Pitt's supporters understood public credit as a sort of automatic tropism: public credit, they believed, would automatically orient itself toward the sun of future prosperity, and thus the Bank and the government could continue to create credit and debt relationships without reference to the dead stock of the Bank of England's specie reserves. The Opposition, by contrast, was more attentive to the ways in which public credit—far from constituting an automatic movement—depended instead upon "endogenous" forces within perception. However, Wordsworth's analysis of debt and "currency" suggests that the Opposition was overly obsessed with the secondary operation of mineralization at the expense of the more primary operation of bending. The Opposition recognized that public credit depended upon treating paper like coin (the operation of mineralization), but was unwilling to acknowledge that it also depended upon creating new debts that could not be directly tied back to "real" money (the operation of bending). Fox may have feigned his shock at the discovery that banks did not hold specie equivalent to the loans they made, but whether sincere or not, his reaction illuminated the problem: to demand that each paper note be tied to "dead stock" in a vault was to eliminate public credit itself.

The tendency of both Pittites and Opposition commentators to gloss over the complicated operations necessary for mineralizing paper money and public credit also determined their different responses to the question of the powers of negativity and ruin. Opposition commentators were as obsessed with ruins as Wordsworth, but because the former glossed over the productive powers of mineralization, they understood ruin only as a sign of irredeemable negativity. Rather than seeking to harness the powers of negativity, they limited themselves to debating the different forms of ruin to which they believed Britain was heading. The Earl of Lauderdale contended that "nothing appears to a common understanding so likely to ruin the country...as Mr. Pitt's operations in Finance" and a year later he emphasized the "ruin and misery" to which the system had brought "our most industrious artisans" (Maitland 1797: 33; 1798: 1). Francis Burroughs despaired of the "system of concealed ruin" that Pitt's finances entailed (Burroughs 1797: 40), and William Morgan "shudder[ed]" at the thought of the "utter ruin" to which Pitt's new proposed tax must lead Britain (Morgan 1797: 47). Pitt's supporters were equally uninterested in explicitly harnessing negativity, for they claimed to see nothing but prosperity in the future, and thus simply dismissed the ruin as an illusory construct, a position exemplified by the pro-Pitt pamphlet *Prosperity of England Midst the Clamors of Ruin, by a Merchant of London* (Winsor 1799). Yet where the Opposition feared ruin, and Pitt's camp simply dismissed it, the ruin signified for Wordsworth the possibility of something radically new: something beyond the projection of past tranquility into the future, on the one hand, or the prediction of future from past prosperity, on the other. Instead, *The Ruined Cottage* suggested that the power of ruin could be harnessed by bending along its path, and then mineralizing images that attenuated the power of the dead over the present.

V. PROFITABLE SYMPATHIES: PARASITES AND INDENTIFICATION IN *LYRICAL BALLADS*, 1798–1802

While Wordsworth's vocational yearnings may have been sparked by his discovery of debt in 1797–98, the more primary structure of the parasite nevertheless dominated the content and form of the poetry produced during that year. The structure of the parasite extended even to the initial distribution of his verse, for after "finishing" long sections of *The Ruined Cottage* and "The Pedlar" in 1797 and 1798, Wordsworth's sister Dorothy copied parts of the poems and sent them to a correspondent, potentially preempting Wordsworth's capacity to exchange the verse for money within what Liu has called the "bookseller system" (Liu 1989: 339).[42] This distribution system enabled the parasite to become a floating position: just as Calvert's dying gift to Wordsworth positioned the latter as parasite—and just as Nature's gift to the Pedlar positioned the latter as parasite—so did Wordsworth's gift of the verse to friends enable the latter to receive something for nothing. Moreover, because such correspondence could be easily (and legally) copied and sent on to other acquaintances, this form of distribution enabled a perpetual transfer of the position of parasite.

Yet Wordsworth eventually did opt for the bookseller system, publishing versions of these poems in 1814 as part of the opening book of his epic, *The Excursion*. By 1814, Wordsworth's fortunes had improved drastically: not only had he received his inheritance in 1803, but a few years later, William Lowther—the same Earl of Lonsdale with whom the Wordsworths successfully negotiated for a return of their inheritance—obtained for the poet a lucrative position as Distributor of Stamps for the county of Westmoreland, a position which, as Mary Trevelyan Moorman notes, involved collecting duties on "[a]ll legal documents, wills, licenses of all kinds, as well as pamphlets, books, papers, and insurance policies" (Moorman 1957–65, vol. 2: 244). This change in Wordsworth's personal fortunes was reflected in the image of the poet in his verse: where the 1798 *Ruined Cottage* and "The Pedlar" had described a practicing pedlar, the pedlar of *The Excursion* had achieved material success and retired from his former occupation (and thus is referred to as the Wanderer, rather than the Pedlar).[43] Moreover, where the 1798 drafts of *The Ruined Cottage* and "The Pedlar" had positioned the poet as productive parasite, *The Excursion* was much more committed to validating its claims with an appeal to system. In the Preface to his vast poem, Wordsworth contended that it was "not the Author's intention formally to announce a system," but nevertheless noted that if "he shall succeed in conveying to the mind clear thoughts, lively images, and strong feelings, the Reader will have no difficulty in extracting the system for himself" (Wordsworth 1814: x). No longer content with parasiting the terms of the existing system of financial discourse, Wordsworth sought to outline in *The Excursion* the contours of his own authoritative system. The Wordsworthian poet of *The Excursion* was the fully professionalized poet, whose "expertise" necessarily distinguished him from his readers.[44]

Yet the transformation of Wordsworth's image of the poet cannot be explained solely as the result of Wordsworth's financial stability after 1803, for suggestions of this drift toward a model of professional expertise is already evident in the years between 1798 and 1803—the result, I propose, of a tension between the position of authority and the relation of transmission outlined in the theory of the image in *The Ruined Cottage*. In that poem, the communicability of the image depended upon the creation of a debt relationship between pedlar and narrator (and by extension, poet and reader). Yet the nature of this debt was not entirely clear: did it indebt the narrator/reader to the pedlar/poet in perpetuity, or could this debt—like the apparently unpayable debt to the dead—be parasited and overcome by the reader? Did the theory of the image, in other words, depend upon a central authority at the center (something along Pitt's "centers of influence" model), or did it instead signal a return to a neo-Godwinian model in which each point of reception became its own center by creating its own images and relationships of credit and debt?

Between 1798 and 1803, Wordsworth moved further away from the neo-Godwinian model and toward an authority-centered approach. In his other, more well-known, project of 1798—the *Lyrical Ballads* collection, anonymously published with Samuel Taylor Coleridge—Wordsworth still seemed to lean toward a Godwinian solution, for the volume implied that readers could learn from the poems of *Lyrical Ballads* how to dispense with the need for the poet's expertise. The Advertisement to *Lyrical Ballads* described the volume as one that was designed to increase readerly flexibility of judgment by undercutting "that most dreadful enemy to our pleasures, our own preestablished codes of decision" (Wordsworth and Coleridge 1798: ii). As Coleridge noted years later in *Biographia Literaria*, Wordsworth had hoped to enable such readerly flexibility by directing the

> mind's attention...to the loveliness and the wonders of the world before us; an inexhaustible treasure, but for which in consequence of the film of familiarity and selfish solicitude we have eyes, yet see not, ears that hear not, and hearts that neither feel nor understand. (Coleridge 1969–2002, vol. 7: 7)

In their effort to "bend" around natural objects, the poems of the 1798 volume of *Lyrical Ballads* picked up where *The Ruined Cottage* and *The Pedlar* had left off. Also like those latter two poems, the poems in *Lyrical Ballads* focused heavily on experiences of death, both real or imagined: of the twenty-three poems included in the London edition, roughly half focus directly on an experience of death (and many of the remainder are linked to death in some significant sense: in "Simon Lee, the Old Huntsman," for example, Simon Lee casts such a pitiful character that his gratitude leaves the narrator "mourning" (l. 104), while "Expostulation and Reply" contrasts books, which allow one to "drink the spirit breathed/From dead men to their kind" with the "wise passiveness" that feeds on other powers (ll. 7–8, 22, 24)). The point of the collection as a whole, however, was not to privilege one experiential attitude toward death over another, but to teach a mobile and speculative relationship to death; that is, to force the reader to continually qualify any particular understanding of death in favor of treating mortality as a point in an informational field around which one must navigate. The volume, in other words, teaches navigation, rather than content, and its images, as Thomas Pfau notes, are designed less to "secure some determinate knowledge than to 'invigorate and sharpen and refine' the process of judgment" (Pfau 1997: 119). By multiplying the objects upon which such invigoration operated, the poems in this edition aimed to create an expanding ring of quasi-poets (a potential already emphasized by the anonymous authorship of the volume).

Yet if the 1798 edition of *Lyrical Ballads* encouraged a model of contagious imaginative mobility, the two versions that followed in 1800 and 1802 highlighted Wordsworth's increasing dissatisfaction with this model. The title page announced an element of this shift already: rather than maintaining the authorial anonymity of the 1798 edition, both the 1800 and 1802 versions attributed the poems to "W. Wordsworth." The collection also became more systematic, with a Preface in the 1800 version that outlined Wordsworth's theory of poetry (and in the expanded Preface of 1802, his theory of the poet). Finally, *Lyrical Ballads* became a two-volume work, with Coleridge's poems either squeezed out or pushed to the end of the first or middle of the second volumes. Instead of twenty-three, the 1800 edition consisted of sixty-one poems, and Wordsworth stressed, via explanatory notes at the end of the second volume, two of the volume's new "pastoral" poems, *Michael* and "The Brothers."

With the addition of his pastoral poems to the collection, Wordsworth turned toward what David Simpson has called "agrarian idealism," which located Britain's salvation less in widespread readerly imaginative mobility than in readers' acceptance of values maintained by small rural landowners (Simpson 1987). Wordsworth outlined this position in a letter he sent Charles James Fox in the early winter of 1801. While Fox had retired from Parliament in 1797 as a sign of protest against Pitt's war policy, Wordsworth apparently felt that the former Whig leader retained enough political influence to justify correspondence. Enclosing a copy of the 1800 edition of *Lyrical Ballads* along with his letter, Wordsworth acknowledged that Fox did not know him, but the poet explained that he "had feelings within me which I hope will so far shew themselves in this letter, as to excise the trespass which I am afraid I shall make" (*LWDW* 313). Wordsworth contended that he had reason to suspect that Fox would prove to be a sympathetic listener for, the poet wrote, "[i]n common with the whole of the English people I have observed in your public character a constant predominance of sensibility of heart" (*LWDW* 313). Wordsworth drew especial attention to "The Brothers" and *Michael*, and suggested that both addressed the causes of the "rapid decay of the domestic affections along the lower orders of society." While Wordsworth believed that "the spirit of independence" was still "deeply...rooted in some parts of the country," he was worried that such liberty was in danger of disappearing. He claimed that in these two poems, he had represented "small independent *proprietors* of land," whose little "tract[s] of land serves as a kind of permanent rallying point for their domestic feelings," but bemoaned the fact that "[t]his class of men is rapidly disappearing." Like *The Ruined Cottage*, both "The Brothers" and *Michael* represented virtuous inhabitants of the countryside who were destroyed by systems of inequality, and both also employed images of tranquility to convert the contingency represented within these poems into virtuous sentiments. Since, Wordsworth suggested, Fox had always been friendly to the claims of the poor, he hoped that, "whatever effect they [the poems] may have on you, you will at least be able to perceive that they may excite profitable sympathies in many kind and good hearts" (*LWDW* 313–14). Wordsworth's stress on the content of his pastoral poems thus signaled a shift in his sense of what a poem should do. Moreover, the fact that he chose to send the volumes to a perceived political leader implied a changed conception of agency, suggesting that Wordsworth now believed one ought to convince influential authorities rather than aiming at the much broader readership toward which the 1798 edition was oriented.

Less than a year later, Wordsworth published a prose defense of this authority-centered position in the Preface to the 1802 *Lyrical Ballads*, supplementing his account of the origin of the poet that he had provided in *The Ruined Cottage* and "The Pedlar." In the biographical sketch of the pedlar-poet in the latter poem, Wordsworth had suggested that imagination served as the ground of the ontological distinction between the poet and his auditors, for the pedlar's imagination was able to generate "ideal stores" which provided the schemata for images of tranquility. These ideal stores were the sources of the "riches" which allowed him to make "a world around him" (ll. 37; 338–40). Yet in "The Pedlar," it was still not clear how, precisely, the poet's imagination differed from that of his auditors. If the poet opened his imaginative accounts by means of sympathy—he is "by Nature tuned/… to constant sympathy with man" (ll. 275–77)—and the auditor engaged the image of tranquility through sympathy, what prevented the audience from making its own images, thereby parasiting the poet?

In the 1802 Preface to *Lyrical Ballads*, Wordsworth established the grounds for the author's authority as his capacity for identification. The term "identification" had played an important role in Wordsworth's earlier, Godwinian-based understanding of collective affect outlined in his unpublished *Letter to the Bishop Llandaff* (1793), but it meant something quite different in the 1802 Preface. In the *Letter*, identification had been tied to Rousseau's notion of the general will, denoting the process by means of which legislators with temporary terms of office could imagine their own place among the populace at the end of their term. Wordsworth had argued that inequity of property created separate interests between the governors and the governed, thus hindering what he called "the grand principle of identification" (*PrW*, vol. I: 46, 37). In the 1802 Preface, however, an implicit contrast between sympathy and identification served as a means for distinguishing between the imaginations of poet and audience.

While the 1798 Advertisement for, and 1800 Preface to, *Lyrical Ballads* had been relatively silent on the nature of the poets who had composed its verse, Wordsworth devoted a significant portion of the 1802 Preface to this topic, arguing that the poet is a man "endowed with more lively sensibility, more enthusiasm and tenderness" than other men, and he also has "a greater knowledge of human nature, and a more comprehensive soul, than are supposed to be common among mankind" (*WSPP* 453). The poet also has a fundamentally different relationship to sympathy than do other men. It is true, of course, that the poet exists within social systems dominated by sympathy, and he must produce his verse in accordance with its laws. The most primary of these laws is that sympathy occurs only through pleasure.

"We have no sympathy," writes Wordsworth, "but what is propagated by pleasure: I would not be misunderstood; but wherever we sympathize with pain, it will be found that the sympathy is produced and carried on by subtle combinations with pain" (*WSPP* 455). The poet's job was to enable sympathy by allowing his listeners to take pleasure in images without having to labor. However, since not all affecting situations were in themselves agreeable, if the poet is to make these tableaux pleasurable, he must retain an ability to engage these situations outside the bounds of sympathy and pleasure. "Identification" is the term Wordsworth selected to denote this capacity of the poet. The poet, he contended, will

> wish...to bring his feelings near to those of the persons whose feelings he describes,—nay, for short spaces of time, perhaps, to let himself slip into an entire delusion, and even confound and identify his own feelings with theirs; modifying only the language which is thus suggested to him by a consideration that he describes for a particular purpose, that of giving pleasure. (*WSPP* 453)

The poet's identification of his feelings with those of his subject is a capacity that is like sympathy, in that it allows him to appropriate the feelings of others, but it does not require pleasure as its precondition. Rather, it is on the basis of the poet's identification with his subject that the reader's sympathy can be produced. Identification involves an almost impossible union of passivity and activity (the poet actively "lets himself slip" into delusion, to the point that the distinction between self and other is "confounded"), with the result that this state can be maintained only for "short spaces of time."

While experiencing the pleasures of the poem through sympathy cost the auditors nothing and provided them with pleasure, identification required labor on the part of the poet. Identification did not allow the poet to simply "channel" the sentiments of others into language; rather, he had to "industriously... appl[y]" the "principle of selection" such that his words would not impede sympathy in others (*WSPP* 454). Nor should the poet consider himself as a sort of "translator, who does not scruple to substitute excellencies of another kind for those that are unattainable by him" (*WSPP* 454). To take this view, Wordsworth contended, "would be to encourage idleness and unmanly despair" (*WSPP* 454), for it would mean the poet's abdication from his role as origin of imaginative value. Like the pedlar, the poet must make "a world about him," and this is impossible if he seeks to obtain approval from others by including extraneous "excellencies."

Wordsworth's introduction of the term "identification" in the Preface to the 1802 *Lyrical Ballads* represented a significant transformation of his understanding of the relationship between poet and social systems. In "The Old Cumberland Beggar," *The Ruined Cottage*, and "The Pedlar," Wordsworth had linked the power of the poetry to its capacity to function *as* parasite: it was precisely because the poet could parasite existing systems that poetry had the power to create new systems. In the Preface to the 1802 edition of *Lyrical Ballads*, however, Wordsworth introduced the term "identification" in order to prove that the poet was not a parasite, but rather a laborer: that is, a respectable part of the existing system. This representation facilitated the professionalization of Wordsworth's understanding of poetry, allowing him to explain why only the poet was able to create images of tranquility. While the 1802 Preface thus retained the category of sympathy as the medium through which the poet shared his imaginative gifts with others, the category of "identification" rejected the possibility of a homogeneous social field in which everyone contributed to the emergence of images of tranquility. The category of "identification," in other words, allowed Wordsworth to maintain sympathy as medium of communication while at the same time controlling the direction of transmission. Sympathy came naturally to everyone, but identification was a skill, or gift, that only a few could master. As a result, everyone could be auditors, but only a few the authors, of poetry.

CONCLUSION: THE PARASITE AND LITERARY CRITICISM

As economic historian Frank Whitson Fetter notes, the 1797 Bank Restriction Act "touched off one of world's historic monetary controversies," a debate that continued for most of the nineteenth century, and which determined "most of the principles of monetary and banking orthodoxy, not only of England but of virtually the entire Western world in the forty years before 1914" (Fetter 1965: vii, 1). Prior to 1797, most Britons were able casually to assume that paper money simply "represented" banked specie, but after the Bank Restriction Act, it became increasingly clear that money could be *created* by the government and maintained by "public confidence" even in the absence of gold and silver. As Francis Horner noted in the October 1802 *Edinburgh Review*, the actual "system" of money was far more complex than previous descriptions had assumed, for the premise "[t]hat the immediate convertibility of paper into gold is an indispensable condition of its credit, as we are taught by the language of system, has been disproved by the recent history of the Bank of England." All that was necessary, Horner suggested, was "a full persuasion on the part of the public, that the paper is secured by ample funds" (vol. 1: 177). The Bank Restriction Act revealed that "the capital of banks is not gold but confidence" (Christensen 2000: 122), and for the next quarter century—that is, until the reassumption of the gold standard in 1821—critics of the new British system of state finance devoted their energies to understanding and demystifying this confidence, guided by the belief, as Thomas Paine put in 1796, that public credit is "*suspicion asleep*" (Paine 1796: 15).

Romantic era poets such as Wordsworth occupied an ambiguous position in this context. Jerome Christensen, one of the few critics to stress the importance of the Bank Restriction Act for an understanding of British Romanticism, has outlined a formal similarity between the "small bands" of poets that make up the geography of literary Romanticism and the small bands of bankers that seemed to regulate the economy and British finance. Christensen notes that emerging prophets of political economy such as Henry Thornton and Francis Horner ascribed the operation of paper credit and banking in general to the efforts of small coteries of bankers who "self-regulated" transfers of money between the "system of banks" not by slavishly hewing to theory, but rather by "an improvisation impenetrably dark to the empirical eye and ungraspable by [what Wordsworth called] 'pre-established codes of decision'" (Christensen 2000: 125). Christensen suggests that we see homologies between "the mysterious formalities"

> by which poets group to write poems with indubitable if elusive social consequences, by which clerks efficiently concoct a banking culture, and by which an editorial board would put its stamp on the yammering of contemporary discourses. (Christensen 2000: 127–28)

Christensen also argues that political economists such as Thornton and Horner prefigured the activities of literary criticism itself, for they attempted to account theoretically for these "mysterious formalities" that transcended the past, at the same as they established new, preestablished codes of decision.

While Christensen's account provides a powerful description of the structural similarities between the social systems of finance and that of Romantic literature, it is equally important not to lose track of the differences. Both state finance and Wordsworth's poetry of the late 1790s began by embracing the position of the parasite, generating silvered o'er images by creating relationships of debt, and both systems manifested a colonizing impulse (here we can recognize Burke's description of France as an exporter of bankruptcy as a misplaced image of capital). Yet precisely because Wordsworth's system began from the position of the parasite, one cannot conclude from these similarities that his poetry internalized a specifically bourgeois logic of finance. As I have noted throughout this chapter, to parasite is not to replicate, but rather to bend and mineralize in such a way that a *new* system is created. From this perspective, the version of *The Ruined Cottage* that contains the oft-reviled "consolation" of the Revised Addendum is in fact far more radical than the earlier version, which ended on a note of political protest. To conclude with protest was to remain in the field of traditional politics; to bend and mineralize was to create the possibility of a new system.

Focusing on the role of the parasite in the emergence of Wordsworth's poetry of the late 1790s also allows us to understand better our own practice—or, at any rate, the goals of practice—as literary critics. On the one hand, to emphasize the relationship of parasitism from which Wordsworth's system emerged is not to deny that his system in turn could subsequently be parasited by the system of bourgeois interests; as Serres notes "[w]hen the one who was excluded has produced, the enclosure sheltering the parasites opens, sending out pseudopodia to include this new work, new blood that helps perpetuate the enclosure" (Serres 1982: 171). New Historicist work on Wordsworth's poetry has described the many ways in which Wordsworth's poetry could be, and often was, conscripted by the class interests of the rising bourgeoisie (for example, readings that privilege "nature" as a way of obscuring real relationships of labor, or interpretations of the image of the speargrass as a "reconciliation" that ignores the historical reality of the displacement of weavers). Yet such a historicist critique is possible—and, more to the point, effective—only because the critic also takes on the role of parasite; that is, bends and mineralizes the poetry to serve aims other than those it seems to have given itself. Liu is close to recognizing this when he suggests that

> [c]riticism, perhaps, should be an act of boat stealing, in which truly to give restitution to the other we must first commandeer the artifact of the other and row away toward as sharply defined a spur of difference as possible. (Liu 1989: 36)

Liu recognizes that criticism begins in the position of parasite, but at the same time he seems uncomfortable with this role, and describes it as a temporary detour that leads back to fair exchange: from the parasite to restitution, and from differential back to equilibrium. Liu positions the critic's "theft" as an unfortunate expedient that responds to the original bad faith of the work: that is, one isn't really parasiting, but simply acting "in kind." Liu's commitment to reciprocity between critic and poet is also consonant with his criticism of the New Critical belief in the "humanizing" potential of poems such as *The Ruined Cottage*. Liu urges us to be suspicious of New Critical claims that poems can provide "cultural value"—a "music of humanity"—that is distinct from economic value, for, as Liu notes, "any legitimate commerce between culture and poetry requires *some* medium of exchange, some pricing mechanism based on a demonstrable, earnable, and commonly held 'cash' of human value allowing cultural and poetic premiums to be weighed alike." In the absence of such belief, we must take the value of such verse on faith—that is, on the basis of "some blind trust fund"—that is always, in the end, determined by authority figures (Liu 1989: 323).

While I agree that such an aporia vexes any attempt to understand *The Ruined Cottage* as a humanist gift, my emphasis on the parasite steers us away from the specific content of the poem's purported "music of humanity," and focuses instead on the poem's account of the *emergence* of "melody" from "noise," the genesis of system from parasite. The parasite *can* denote relationships of pure dependence that simply perpetuate existing systems—it is this sense of the term, for example, that Marx intends when he claims that usury "does not alter the mode of production, but attaches itself to it as a parasite and makes it miserable" (Marx 1976–78, vol. 3: 700), yet both Wordsworth and Serres suggest that the parasite is also the condition of possibility of new systems. More specifically, the parasite is the position that is able to link unconnected potentials within or between systems—as when, for example, Wordsworth deploys the logic of finance within verse. Because "the parasitic relation precedes exchange in general," the emergence of new systems and possibilities cannot be understood on the basis of exchange, reciprocity, and restitution, and from this perspective, Liu's desire for reciprocal exchange with Wordsworth—to steal but then give back—is misplaced. One "follows" Wordsworth not by giving back to him, but by parasiting him. The parasite does not "return" a potential already contained within "the artifact of the other"; rather, it produces that noise that is the condition of possibility for any system of "soothing melod[ies]" (l. 15).

5 The ghost of gold

National debt, imagery, and the politics of sympathy in P. B. Shelley

Like a Poet hidden
In the light of thought,
Singing hymns unbidden,
Till the world is wrought
To sympathy with hopes and fears it heeded not (*SPP* ll. 36–40)

When the Bank Restriction Act was passed in the early months of 1797, it was intended to be a temporary measure, lasting a few weeks at most. Instead, it became one of the most enduring institutions of the Romantic era, remaining in effect until 1822, and thus outlasting both Pitt's ministry and the French Republic. The ability of paper money to substitute, seemingly indefinitely, for specie, provoked a variety of reactions. In the October 1802 volume of the *Edinburgh Review*, political economist Francis Horner suggested that the suspension of gold payments had enabled the public to better understand the inner workings of finance, a system that had "remained in a great measure unknown to all but the bankers and traders of London, until the suspension of cash payments at the Bank of England produced the copious information, which, in various forms, has been communicated to the public" (vol. 1: 176). More radical commentators, such as William Cobbett, agreed with Horner that the Act allowed insight to the inner workings of state finance, but contended that what was illuminated was the rot of a system that employed paper money and the national debt to shuttle money from the poor and middling classes to rich merchants, and encouraged the poor to counterfeit money and then executed them for their troubles (Cobbett 1817; see also Anon. 1818?).

The chapter explores Percy Bysshe Shelley's engagement with this debate, and especially the relationship between his reflections on state finance and the poetics of his late literary works. Shelley had been a vocal critic of the British government since 1812, when he published his first political pamphlet ("An Address to the Irish People"), and reflections on the nature of money and public credit appear sporadically throughout his early political writings.[1] However, the nature of British state finance and currency began to interest him in earnest in late 1817, perhaps spurred by his friendship with Leigh Hunt, who had published a number of articles critical of the Bank Restriction Act and the growing national debt in his periodical *The Examiner.* Shelley's writings from this period positioned the system of the national debt and paper money as one of the key causes of Britain's current political troubles, and references to the problems of "paper money" marked many of Shelley's poems from this period, including *The Mask of Anarchy* (1819), "Sonnet: England in 1819" (1819) and the satirical drama *Oedipus Tyrannus, or, Swellfoot the Tyrant* (1820). Even more significant, Shelley began a long treatise entitled *A Philosophical View of Reform*, in which he traced political unrest in contemporary England to structures of state finance established in the late seventeenth century.

The question of the relative importance of Shelley's reflections on state finance to his late poetry and prose has divided literary critics working on Shelley's philosophy and poetics. For commentators interested in the politically radical aspects of Shelley's work, his discussions of paper money and the national debt are important evidence of the specificity of the poet's knowledge of, and resistance to, repressive state institutions.[2] By contrast, critics interested in promoting more "philosophical" interpretations of Shelley have generally ignored his writings on state finance, implying that such reflections have little to do with the poet's late interest in Platonic and Lucretian philosophies and philosophical skepticism, or his efforts to develop a new philosophy of "love."[3] My interpretation in this chapter stresses the compatibility of these two approaches: to emphasize the importance of state finance for Shelley's late work is not to privilege a political over a philosophical reading, but rather highlights the extent to which Shelley engaged state finance as a fundamentally philosophical topic.[4] I argue in this chapter that Shelley's interest in institutions of state finance was not simply topical, but rather provided him with a topos within which to rethink the relationships among sympathy, causality, and aesthetics that had informed his political philosophy and poetic practice since the start of his career. In his early political writings, Shelley had struggled to articulate what he understood as the fundamentally *temporal* dimension of sympathy, its power to expand "time consciousness" in such a way as to make the present (rather than the past) appear as the active source of future events. This focus on time consciousness and perceptions of causality, I suggest, encouraged Shelley's interest in state finance, for he recognized that the conservative temporal structure of institutions such as paper money and the national debt—their tendency to locate the active source of events in past debts—directly opposed the expansion of time consciousness that his poetry sought to encourage.

My argument is divided into five parts. I begin by discussing Shelley's early efforts to understand the role of sympathy in a philosophy of social change, noting that while he sometimes positioned fellow-feeling as an intrinsically liberatory force, at other times he acknowledged the state's capacity to appropriate what should be "fertilizing streams of sympathy" for its own purposes (*SP* 164). The second section explores Shelley's attempt to resolve this apparent contradiction by focusing on the role of "time consciousness" in acts of sympathy. Where earlier commentators such as Hume and Smith had described sympathy as a neutral medium of affective communication between individuals, Shelley suggested that true sympathy—that is, sympathy that could not be appropriated by the state—was intrinsically linked to an expansion of the consciousness of time. Shelley was convinced that the inhabitants of early nineteenth-century Britain perceived the world on the basis of a "savage" and "illiterate" time consciousness, which perpetuated the belief that both the present and the future were causally determined by the past. True sympathy, by contrast, expanded time consciousness by illuminating the present, rather than the past, as the active source of future events, and it did so by allowing "shadows of futurity" to exert their weight on the present. It was this understanding of time consciousness as the key to sympathy, I argue in the third section, which encouraged Shelley's intense interest in the system of state finance in *A Philosophical View of Reform*. He recognized that institutions such as the national debt and paper money provided the state with technical means for perpetuating the savage mode of time consciousness, since the promissory structures of these financial institutions encouraged the belief that the present and future were continually indebted to the past. Shelley suggested that these institutions of debt could only be countered by developing images that enabled a truly speculative mode of time consciousness, and in sections four and five, I explore Shelley's efforts to create liberatory images of time in poems such as *The Mask of Anarchy* and the verse included in the *Prometheus Unbound* volume. While *The Mask of Anarchy* explicitly connected the liberatory image to the topic of state finance and its "ghosts of gold," the poems of the *Prometheus Unbound* volume focused less on the system that Shelley opposed, and more exclusively on the expansion of time consciousness itself, providing readers with speculative images designed to enable intuitions of time beyond a linear series of causal relations. Yet Shelley remained invested in distinguishing between the speculative dynamics of state finance, on the one hand, and poetry, on the other, and the publication of Thomas Love Peacock's *The Four Ages of Poetry* (1821) provided the poet with an opportunity to further refine his understanding of the links between sympathy, causality, and speculation. In his essay, Peacock positioned poets as "mountebanks" and speculators responsible for the first economies of credit, but in *A Defence of Poetry*, Shelley argued that the poetic image allowed readers access to the shadows of futurity by enabling what he called an "identification" with the beautiful.

I. SYMPATHY AND REFORM IN SHELLEY'S EARLY PROSE

Like Wordsworth roughly two decades earlier, Shelley's early engagement with politics took place under the banner of "philanthropy." It was clear from the start, however, that Shelley's version of philanthropic politics was to be more visible and public than that of the early Wordsworth. In 1811, Shelley and his friend Thomas Jefferson Hogg were expelled from Oxford University for publishing a pamphlet entitled *The Necessity of Atheism*, and Shelley wasted little time in finding futher, and more explicitly political, topics to which he could devote his energies. By the next year, he had taken up the cause of Catholics in Ireland, who were legally prevented from voting. Shelley wrote a lengthy pamphlet on the topic—"An Address to the Irish People" (1812)—and traveled to Ireland to give a talk at a public meeting. A series of related political essays and pamphlets followed, and Shelley also included a number of political and philosophical "Notes" in his long poem *Queen Mab* (1813).

In all of these writings, but especially in his pamphlets, Shelley sought to maintain a tenuous balance between emotional agitation, on the one hand, and rationally guided and gradual reform, on the other. Shelley's early political writing was grounded in the political philosophy outlined by William Godwin in *Of Political Justice* (1793, 1796, 1797), and, following Godwin, Shelley was committed to a gradual process of nonviolent political reform, rather than revolution. Godwin had underscored his commitment to placid and reasoned change in the form of his text, a long philosophical treatise that slowly developed its arguments. Shelley, however, developed many of his early political writings in occasional pamphlets, a form more suited to engaging readers emotionally with respect to specific issues (a point emphasized by Shelley in "An Address to the Irish People" through his constant references to his ability to "feel for" the sufferings of the Irish). On the one hand, Shelley wanted his writings to engage his readers emotionally to the extent that they would commit themselves to political action in the present. On the other hand, he did not want to stoke passions to such an extent that his writings would encourage violence and immediate political revolution. This dilemma became an explicit, though unresolved, theme within Shelley's early political writings, and "sympathy" functioned as a nexus for his efforts to understand the role of affect in promoting political reform.

Shelley's dilemma was essentially a repetition of the tension between reason and affect that had troubled Godwin's *Political Justice*. Though the first edition of *Political Justice* (1793) had positioned "benevolence" as one of primary motivating forces of human behavior, the text nevertheless seemed to oppose reason and sentiment, suggesting that reason operated through calm and nonsectarian discussion, while emotional attachments functioned as impediments to the exercise of reason. The two subsequent editions of 1796 and 1798 allowed emotion and sympathy a greater role in the progressive improvement of society, but Godwin nevertheless insisted in all three editions that justice was "that *impartial* treatment of every man in matters that relate to his happiness," and as a result, our actions ought to be guided by a sense of the "general good," a sense that bore little relation to our particular emotional attachments (Godwin 1985: 169).[5] He exemplified the unimportance of "local attachments" with the example of choosing between lives: if for example, one could save the life of the author Fénelon just at the moment that he conceived the plan for his work *Telemachus*, or save the life of one's own brother or father, one must choose Fénelon, Godwin argued, for his writings "promot[ed] the benefit of thousands who have been cured by the perusal of that work of some error, vice and consequent unhappiness" (170). As I noted in the last chapter, in the first edition of *Political Justice*, Godwin also warned against the contagious spread of "sympathy of opinion [which] catches from man to man, especially in numerous meetings" (Godwin 1992, vol. 1: 208). While Godwin moderated his distrust of "local" emotional attachments in the second and third editions of *Political Justice* (1796, 1798), allowing sympathy to play a more extensive role, he never fully resolved the question of the proper role of sympathy and affect in his political philosophy.

Shelley's early writings were marked by this same ambivalence toward both the passions and sympathy. Like Godwin, Shelley presented rational discussion as the only appropriate means for effecting political reform, and he positioned the institutions of the state as impediments to reform. He urged the readers of "An Address to the Irish People" to understand that violence and rebellion "will bind you more closely to the block of the oppressor," while discussion of truth and calm resistance would lead to the "increase of virtue and wisdom," which in turn "will lead people to find out that force and oppression are wrong and false; and this opinion, when it gains ground, will prevent government from severity" (*SP* 47, 48). Shelley, like Godwin, also presented sympathy as a problematic force, and suggested—as Adam Smith had noted in *The Theory of Moral Sentiments*—that it encouraged both socially progressive *and* divisive forms of fellow-feeling. In his "Essay on the Punishment of Death" (unpublished during his lifetime but probably written between 1813 and 1815), Shelley argued against capital punishment in part because it encouraged, through sympathy, behavior precisely the opposite of what legislators intended.[6] When a condemned individual went bravely to his death, then the

> multitude, instead of departing with a panic-stricken approbation of the laws which exhibited such a spectacle, are inspired with pity, admiration, and sympathy, and the most generous among them feel an emulation to be the authors of such flattering emotions as they experience stirring in their bosoms. (*SP* 156)

The sympathy sparked by executions thus "extenuates crime and discredits the law which restrains it" (*SP* 157). However, if in the case of state punishment sympathy hindered the goals of the legislator, Shelley also acknowledged that the state was in other instances able to exploit sympathy for its own limited ends. In "An Address to the People on the Death of Princess Charlotte" (1817), Shelley noted that sympathy could easily be appropriated by the state to create emotional dependence on the government. He contended that public mourning for Princess Charlotte's death tended "to waste on inadequate objects those fertilizing streams of sympathy which a public mourning should be the occasion of pouring forth," and he bemoaned the fact that "*man* has murdered Liberty" with the result that "there descended on the heads and on the hearts of every human thing the sympathy of an universal blast and curse" (*SP* 164, 169).

Yet even as Shelley sometimes presented sympathy as a potential obstacle to the progress of truth and virtue, at other times he presented it as a necessary support of political improvement. He suggested, for example, that his support of particular political projects was a consequence of his own sympathy with the sufferings of other people. "I am not an Irishman," Shelley wrote in "An Address to the Irish People," "yet I can feel for you" (*SP* 40). Moreover, the literary form in which Shelley cast many of his early political philosophy—the occasional pamphlet—was designed precisely to produce such corresponding "vivid impressions" upon the minds of his readers (*SP* 57).

The distinction between "good" and "bad" forms of sympathy, Shelley suggested, was that the former *generalized* affect by spreading it beyond the local context that served as its initiating occasion. In "An Address to the Irish People," he wrote that

> I am interested in your cause [enfranchisement of Catholics and a repeal of the Act of Union]; and it is not because you are Irishmen or Roman Catholics that I feel with you and I feel for you; but because you are men and sufferers. (*SP* 45)

While sufferers were always located within specific contexts—they suffered on account of some particular set of ills—Shelley suggested it should be only their status as *sufferers* that encouraged sympathy. In his "Proposals for an Association of Philanthropists" (1812), Shelley argued that the capacity of sympathy to generalize in this fashion suggested that philanthropic reformers should focus their attention and efforts on those particular events and occasions which lent themselves most readily to such generalization; that is, those

> which excite the benevolent passions, that generalize and expand private into public feelings, and make the hearts of individuals vibrate not merely for themselves, their families, and their friends, but for posterity, *for a people*, till their country becomes the world and their family the sensitive creation. (*SP* 60)

Shelley suggested in this pamphlet that philanthropists could channel the streams of sympathy away from government control by carefully choosing objects of reform, selecting only those that were most "generalizable."

While Shelley's willingness to position sympathy as both an ally of and hindrance to progressive reform might seem to suggest that he subscribed to a Scottish Enlightenment understanding of sympathy as an intrinsically neutral medium of emotional communication between individuals, his emphasis on the function of the *future* in "good sympathy" suggests an alternative understanding that differed radically from earlier theories of sympathy outlined by Hume and Smith. Shelley's focus on instances of "generalizable" sympathy suggested that sympathy had an intrinsically historical dimension, functioning as a form of communication between the inequitable present and a utopian future. Sympathy, that is, did not denote an indiscriminate engagement with suffering, but rather focused attention on behalf of those *particular* instances of suffering that, if ameliorated, promised a more equitable collective future. In "Proposals for an Association of Philanthropists," Shelley contended that if he was "happy…at the near approach of [Irish] emancipation," it was

> not for the good which it will bring with it, but because it is a sign of benefits approaching, a prophet of good to come; and therefore, do I sympathize with the inhabitants in this great cause…it is the foreground of a picture in the dimness of whose distance I behold the lion lay down with the lamb and the infant play with the basilisk. (*SP* 61)

Shelley presented sympathy with the Irish as *a function of* the way that their struggle served as a sign "from" the future; that is, the capacity of their struggle to point toward a more equitable condition for all. Shelley's metaphor of the picture suggests the conventions of classical landscape painting: that is, the "prospect" of suffering Irish agitating for emancipation in the near future/foreground, and more general amelioration in the distant future/background (one can perhaps even imagine a foreground Irish figure pointing with his right hand to the typological redemption of universal suffering in the Biblical image of the lamb and the lion lying down together). Yet Shelley's metaphor of a "picture" must be interpreted carefully, for in fact he is not suggesting that his pleasure is a function of a subjective act of imaginatively creating such a "prospect." Rather, his point is that both this imaginative prospect and sympathy *result from* the prophetic nature of the Irish cause; it is the connection of that cause with the future that enables both this quasi-pictorial image and any fellow-feeling. The subject-that-sympathizes does not preexist this "sign" from the future; rather, the sign calls this subject into being.[7]

This second understanding of sympathy—that is, as a force of communication with the future—depended upon a form of historicity that was completely alien to the theories of emotional communication developed by Hume and Smith. For both these Scottish philosophers, sympathy was a universal truth of human nature and psychology, and it thus operated at all times in the same way. Of course, neither Hume nor Smith believed it operated indifferently or uniformly with respect to particular sufferings, and both stressed that the effects of sympathy were dependent upon geographic, cultural, national, and familial forms of distance. Both also implied that sympathy had some relationship to "historical progress," in the sense that sympathy had a wider and more nuanced field of action in "civilized" than in "savage" nations. Yet Shelley's version suggested that the *particular* objects of "good" sympathy were historically specific, for good sympathy employed particular events and individuals as a means of signifying the potential of an utopian future. In these instances, sympathy could not be understood as a medium of communication between already constituted and self-representing subjects, but rather as a force that *constituted* individuals as historical subjects.

II. DETERMINATIONS OF THE WILL: SYMPATHY AND TIME-CONSCIOUSNESS

Shelley's innovative understanding of sympathy depended in part on his progressive historicism, derived from Godwin, but it also relied upon what we might call his analysis of "internal time consciousness." While some of Shelley's early writings seemed to rely on a materialist "Necessitarianism," which positioned future events as simply the culmination of linear chains of causality rooted in the past, he had also begun to develop a much less deterministic understanding of the relationship between past and future, one that stressed *perceptions* of causality, rather than making ontological claims.[8] In a note to "An Essay on the Punishment of Death," for example, Shelley argued that "philosophic necessity" did not mean that the future should be understood as the causal unfolding of the past. Rather, it meant that the future should be understood as radically *free from* the past and present:

> The savage and the illiterate are but faintly aware of the distinction between the future and the past; they make actions belonging to periods so distinct, the subjects of similar feelings; they live only in the present, or in the past, as it is present. It is in this that the philosopher excels one of the many; it is this which distinguishes the doctrine of philosophic necessity from fatalism; and that determination of will, by which it is the active source of future events, from that liberty or indifference, to which the abstract liability of irremediable actions is attached, according to the notions of the vulgar. (*SP* 157)

Shelley's attempt to distinguish between the "savage" sense of necessity, on the one hand, and "philosophic necessity," on the other, was indebted to Hume's analysis of causality in *A Treatise in Human Nature*. Hume had famously argued that the belief in a *causal* relation between two phenomena—for example, the belief that every rock released from my hand will fall—is in fact an extrapolation from our perceptions of "constant conjunctions" between these two phenomena. Belief in causality thus went beyond what we were given in experience by transforming "conjunctions" into "causal relations." Hume suggested that his skeptical critique of causality had few practical implications, since we could not help but act as though causality were a real force in both the physical and moral worlds. Shelley, however, was more interested in probing the conditions of possibility for such perceptions of causality. How was it possible, in other words, that we could conjoin two impressions at all? And might such an analysis reveal *two* kinds of necessity, one of which tended to perpetuate existing institutions (Hume's conclusion), while the other enabled a more open relationship to the future?

Shelley recognized, in other words, that "perceptions" of causality were in fact modes of time consciousness. Hume had hinted at this, noting that our capacity to conjoin impressions ("releasing a rock" + "rock falling") by means of the idea of causality ("releasing a rock causes it to fall") depended upon the plasticity of the imagination: that is, its ability to contract into an impression two phenomena (releasing; falling), and to ground these in an internal feeling of expectation (when I drop the rock, I expect it will fall). As Gilles Deleuze notes, the "contraction" that Hume attributes to the imagination should not be misunderstood as "memory, nor indeed an operation of the understanding: contraction is not a matter of reflection"; "[i]t is not carried out by the mind, but occurs *in* the mind which contemplates, prior to all memory and reflection" (Deleuze 1994: 70, 71). Hume's "contraction" of the imagination, Deleuze writes, enables the consciousness of time itself:

> Time is constituted only in the originary synthesis which operates on the repetition of instants. This synthesis contracts the successive independent instants into one another, thereby constituting the lived, or living, present. It is in this present that time is deployed. To it belong both the past and the future: the past in so far as the preceding instants are retained in the contraction; the future because its expectation is anticipated in this same contraction. (Deleuze 1994: 70–71)

What Hume described as the contraction effected by the imagination is thus another way of describing what more recent phenomenologists have called "retention" (holding the past in the present, or what Shelley called "the past, as it is present") and "protention" (the anticipation of the future within the present).[9] While retention and protention happen under or before self-consciousness, these operations serve as the necessary support for operations of self-consciousness, such as conscious "memory" and "prediction" (Deleuze 1994: 71). As Deleuze notes, in the case of conscious memory, "the past" is "no longer the immediate past of retention but the reflexive past of representation," which allows me to recall and represent to myself specific instances in which I released a rock and it fell. In similar fashion, consciousness of "the future" is no longer "the immediate future of anticipation" but "the reflexive future of prediction, the reflected generality of the understanding (the understanding weights the expectation in the imagination in proportion to the number of distinct similar cases observed and recalled)" (Deleuze 1994: 71). Prediction allows one to collate numerous experiences of similar objects, whether they are the trajectories of stones or financial stocks, and assert that *this* stone (or stock) will also fall. The "active synthesis of memory and the understanding" is thus "superimposed upon and supported by the passive synthesis of the imagination" (Deleuze 1994: 71).

While conscious memory and prediction were necessary capacities for human life, Shelley argued that the problem with "normal" memory and prediction was their tendency to locate the agency of change in the distant (and inaccessible) past. He suggested that normal time consciousness was in fact "savage," for it positioned the past as the source and origin of the present and future; the savage "live[s]...in the past, as it is present." The "passion of revenge," he suggested, provided an example of the limited sense of potential inherent in savage time consciousness. An individual sought revenge, Shelley argued, as a result of his or her "habitual perception of the ideas of the sufferings of the person who inflicts an injury...with security that that injury will not be repeated in the future" (*SP* 157). Acts of revenge, in other words, were actually attempts to secure peace in the future by following a "law" purportedly proved by past experience (namely, that harming the guilty=security in the future). Yet such habitual perceptions were flawed insofar as they located all agency in past experiences; rather than determining a new future, those who sought revenge simply repeated the past.[10] For the savage and illiterate, the past thus manifested itself not only as the origin of the present, but also appeared to be the origin of the future; time appeared homogenous, with all creative and motive powers of causal connection firmly locked in the past.

Yet, Shelley insisted, protention—that is, the unconscious "anticipations" that serve as the foundation for temporal awareness in the first place—could enable more than simply conscious "prediction," for the link between the future and the present could also manifest itself as *philosophic* necessity. Prediction tied anticipation to the form of causal necessity, and from the perspective of someone who makes a prediction, the past appears as the origin of present and future. However, when anticipation took the form of philosophic necessity, *the present* appeared as the origin of the future (that is, the present is "the active source of future events"). It was precisely this latter form of necessity that allowed individuals to initiate, or attach themselves to, new systems. Savages and illiterates, since they literally perceived the past "taking care of" the future, believed themselves to be free from responsibility for the coming-into-being of the future. The civilized and literate individual, by contrast, perceived the future as dependent upon determinations of the will in the present, and thus had to *search* for the right choices and actions. In this context, then, to become "civilized" and "literate" meant the development of new capacities of time consciousness, and more specifically, the development of a mode of open protention.[11]

It is precisely this latter mode of protention that grounded the form of sympathy that Shelley outlined in "Proposals for an Association of Philanthropists"; that is, the form of "good sympathy" that served to draw attention to the potential for a new collective future. Shelley suggested that it was only because he could perceive the emancipation of the Catholics as "a sign of benefits approaching, a prophet of good to come" that the poet was then able to "sympathize with the inhabitants in this great cause." This redemptive mode of sympathy depended upon the capacity to read the present as the origin of the future, which in turn relied upon the "philosophical" sense of necessity outlined in "An Essay on the Punishment of Death"—or, more precisely, a "philosophical" sense of necessity was equivalent to a time consciousness capable of open protention.

III. STATE FINANCE, TIME CONSCIOUSNESS, AND THE SENTIMENT OF NECESSITY IN *A PHILOSOPHICAL VIEW OF REFORM*

These two theories of sympathy—a Scottish Enlightenment understanding of sympathy that stressed emotional communication between individuals, and a more idiosyncratic theory of sympathy as force of communication with the future—coexisted uneasily in Shelley's early political prose. The state played an important, but vexed, role in Shelley's speculations on sympathy, as he sometimes positioned sympathy as a force that intrinsically opposed state repression, while at other times he acknowledged that the state was able to appropriate the semiotic potential of sympathy, as in the case of public mourning for Princess Charlotte.[12] Shelley's difficulties in accounting for the relationships between sympathy and the state was in part a consequence of his choice of literary form, for while occasional pamphlets and short essays allowed Shelley to hint at links between the state, sympathy, and reform of time consciousness, these were not textual venues within which these connections could be analyzed in any comprehensive fashion. In 1819, however, he turned to a different form—the philosophical treatise—in an attempt to articulate more precisely the relationship between these various terms, and it was in this context that he first began to articulate an important link between state finance and the time consciousness of sympathy.

The four years between the end of the Napoleonic wars and the start of Shelley's work on *A Philosophical View of Reform* had certainly given both Shelley and Great Britain as a whole many reasons to reflect on the relationship between the state, reform, and finance. While war with France had provided at least the semblance of justification for British domestic hardships for most of the period between 1793 and 1815, the conclusive end of hostilities in the latter year seemed to bring little, if any, relief. Thousands of workers found themselves jobless as wartime production ceased, staple food prices increased, and taxes remained at their wartime levels, and England was wracked with numerous rallies, protests, and occasionally even violent confrontations between workers and the government during the waning years of the second decade of the nineteenth century.[13] For many critics of the government, the "distresses" of the country could not be attributed solely to the "sudden transition from protracted warfare to a state of peace," for the problems had "assumed a character of universality which, while it brings them home to the conviction and feelings of every class, evidently refers their existence to some very general cause" (Comber 1817: 1). Numerous pamphlets and books, such as *The Extraordinary Red Book*, appeared which purported to reveal the true causes of the distresses in which the country found itself, and radical authors took the occasion to publish tables of government graft and inequity (Anon. 1816).

For those authors who saw the various distresses of Britain as systemically connected to one another, the national debt and its corollary, "paper money," served as a privileged site of analysis. "The time is now come," William Cobbett wrote in 1817, "[w]hen every man in this kingdom ought to make himself, if possible, well acquainted with all matters belonging to the *Paper-Money System*. It is that System, which has mainly contributed towards our present miseries" (Cobbett 1817: ii).[14] The "Paper-Money System" received so much attention after 1815 in largest part because its original justification apparently had disappeared. As I noted in the last chapter, the 1797 Bank Restriction Act had been presented as a wartime necessity, and subsequent extensions of the Act had been premised on the claim that the Bank would resume gold payments shortly after the cessation of hostilities.[15] Yet the end of war with France did not bring a return to currency convertibility, for the Bank Directors and their Parliamentary supporters argued that any rapid move to make paper money redeemable would prove too disruptive to justify the measure. For commentators such as Cobbett, this was evidence that the war had never been more than a pretext for the suspension of specie payments, and that the real goal of the Act was to give corrupt government and bank officials the ability to add as much as they liked to the national debt.[16]

Such an understanding of paper money and the national debt was central to *A Philosophical View of Reform*, begun by Shelley in the fall of 1819. Though Shelley was in Italy in 1819, he kept abreast of developments in Britain, and, judging by his correspondence, he became increasingly interested in state finance in the spring and summer of 1819. In letters to friends, he applauded Cobbett's proposal to destroy the system of paper money by flooding the streets of London with counterfeit money; he immediately connected the often violent unrest of the fall of 1819 with questions of finance; and in early November, he urged his friends the Gisbornes to take their money "out of the funds."[17] In November 1819, Shelley began organizing his thoughts on state finance within a long prose essay. While this work was left unpublished during Shelley's lifetime (it did not appear in print until 1920), commentators have generally agreed that it provides important evidence of Shelley's late theories of history and political philosophy, and is vital in helping elucidate elements of his published prose, such as the prefaces to *Prometheus Unbound*, *The Cenci*, and *Hellas*. *A Philosophical View of Reform* is an ambitious document, providing, among other elements, a reading of the history of Europe since the dissolution of the Roman Empire to 1819, an analysis of the causes of contemporary political unrest in Britain, a theory of the relationship between money and labor, and several concrete proposals for political reform. At the center of Shelley's analysis, however, was his claim that the roots of contemporary political unrest in Britain could be traced back to the institution of a "second aristocracy" that emerged at the end of the seventeenth century with the creation of the Bank of England.

Shelley's discussion of the Bank of England appears in the second chapter of the text, entitled "On the Sentiment of the Necessity of Change." Following the first chapter's rather schematic history of Europe since the fall of the Roman Empire, Shelley argued in the second chapter that Britain's political problems in 1819 had their source in institutions developed shortly after William III's assumption of power in 1688. According to Shelley, the most significant development of William III's early reign was the formal institution of "the device of public credit" as an "instrument of government." Echoing early eighteenth-century descriptions of state finance, Shelley argued that public credit was developed less to "mee[t] the financial exigencies of the state" than for its ability to bind together two dominant social groups: those who held political power and those who had money. Public credit was "a bond to connect those in the possession of property with those who had, by taking advantage of an accident of party, acceded to power" (*SP* 243). Through the institution of the Bank of England and public credit, the wealthy loaned money to the government, which the government promised to pay back by creating a *national* debt for which the entire country was responsible.

Shelley's account of the consequences of the development of the system of state finance in the late seventeenth century also echoed more contemporary pamphleteers and journalists. Shelley followed Cobbett, for example, in stressing the extent to which the system of state-mandated paper money created a closed system that forced more and more labor out of those who lacked access to credit. Shelley acknowledged that governments had always controlled the creation and, to a lesser extent, the distribution, of money. However, he argued that in a monetary system dominated by coins created out of precious metals, money still bore a direct relationship to labor. "The precious metals," Shelley wrote, "have been from the earliest records of civilization employed as the signs of labor and the titles to an unequal distribution of its produce" (*SP* 243), and coins functioned as signs of labor precisely because considerable effort was required to find and mint the metals necessary for currency (to obtain ore, for example, ships had to be created and outfitted and mines opened up and worked, and artisans had to be employed to create the coins themselves). The advantage of a coin-dominated monetary system, Shelley suggested, was that it instituted a single, unified, and quasi-global field of economic "communication." Any attempt to increase the total amount of money—by, for example, private counterfeiting or government coinage—had the effect of decreasing the buying power of each particular coin, thereby producing "public confusion and misery" (*SP* 244). While such confusion and misery was no doubt unpleasant for those involved, it nevertheless meant that governments had to maintain a stable connection between labor and money, or, through steps such as revaluations or recoinage, make clear to the populace their attempts to alter these connections.

The institution of public credit, by contrast, enabled the emergence of a new social system that excluded a sizeable portion of the population—namely, all those who lacked access to significant amounts of cash or credit—from the self-communication of the monetary system. Modern financial transactions, rather than being tied solely to precious metals that had value only as a function of the total amount of coin in circulation, were instead negotiated by attaching names and numbers to pieces of paper. "All great transactions of personal property in England," Shelley wrote, "are managed by signs and that is by the authority of the possessor expressed upon paper, thus representing in a compendious form his right to so much gold, which represents his right to so much labor" (*SP* 244). The amount of gold (and therefore, labor) at an individual's command depended only upon his ability to engender belief in others:

> A man may write on a piece of paper what he pleases; he may say he is worth a thousand when he is not worth a hundred pounds. If he can make others believe this, he has credit for the sum to which his name is attached. (*SP* 244)

Just as in the case of counterfeited coin, this had the effect of devaluing the existing stock of monetary instruments in circulation. Such devaluation in turn forced the poor—who possessed no instruments of credit—to labor for an ever-increasing number of hours in order to earn the "same" amount of money. Unlike measures such as counterfeiting of coin and government recoinage, however, the connection between paper money and depreciation was not immediately obvious to the populace, for the expansion of money took place in "private" spaces, such as Bank and merchant offices.[18] By drawing attention to the different ways in which money was "uttered"—that is, introduced into the system of economic transactions—Shelley isolated the link between governmental creation of money, on the one hand, and the production of debt for the poor, on the other.[19]

Yet for Shelley, the most worrisome aspect of the system of paper money and the national debt was its tendency to encourage the "savage" mode of time consciousness that he had outlined in "An Essay on the Punishment of Death." Like many critics of the government, Shelley believed that the ever-increasing national debt enslaved future generations by deferring ever more interest and principal repayment to the future in order to meet the purportedly more pressing financial needs of the present.[20] From Shelley's perspective, the real issue was not whether such deferrals made financial sense, but rather the fact that the act of deferral itself perpetuated and strengthened the seeming "necessity" of debt. Tax money, Shelley argued, represented a claim by the present on the labor of the future, and there were, in principle, no limits to the different projects that the present might undertake. "The labor which this money [i.e., that of the national debt]" represented, Shelley argued, could be used for numerous projects, ranging from the outlandish step of "cove[ring] our land with monuments of architecture exceeding the sumptuousness and the beauty of Egypt and Athens," to the much more equitable step of making "every peasant's cottage, surrounded with its garden, a little paradise of comfort" (*SP* 249). The existence of the national debt, however, limited future possibilities by enslaving both the present and the future to the past. Thus, no matter how liberating it might seem to defer payment of parts of national debt to the future, the act of deferral perpetuated the form of causal necessity that Shelley argued was characteristic of savage time consciousness. The state, moreover, sought to negate the possibility of more open forms of protention with appeals to "national emergencies":

> The usual vindication of national debts is that, [since] they are contracted in an overwhelming measure for the purpose of defence against a common danger, for the vindication of the rights and liberties and posterity, it is just that posterity should bear the burthen of the payment. (*SP* 252)

The future, according to this argument, owed its very existence to decisions made in the present, and as a result, future generations could not object to being indebted literally to the past. The problem with this argument, Shelley argued, was that it assumed that "states of exception" were in fact exceptional, and thus implied that such forms of indebtedness occurred infrequently. Yet the history of Europe proved the opposite: "This reasoning is most fallacious. The history of nations presents us with a succession of extraordinary emergencies, and through their present imperfect organization their existence is perpetually threatened by new and unexpected combinations of foreign or internal force" (*SP* 252).

Not only did national debt encourage savage time consciousness by perpetuating the idea of never-ending debt, but it also perpetuated this restricted mode of temporal perception by technical means, namely, paper money. The constant—and, after 1797, extensive—use of paper currency in daily transactions reinforced, at the level of time consciousness, the hegemony of causal necessity, for the form of money (a promissory note) grounded future payment of bills in past actions taken by bank managers (and, moreover, past actions that had occurred outside the experience of most bill users; paper money thus represented a microform of "tertiary memory," or tradition). While a sense of "the future" played an absolutely essential part of the phenomenology of paper money, insofar as bills oriented their possessors toward future possibilities (even the hoarding of paper money was a future-oriented action), paper money also constrained this sense of the future within what Shelley called "Expectation": that is, the future as extrapolated from—and thus contained within—past events.[21] Paper money was tied to the state, in the sense that it formed a working system of "communication" only if the state persisted, and thus its use encouraged possessors to limit their sense of the future to structures of "likelihood" and "probability" that took the continued existence of the state for granted.

If the national debt and paper money provided technical means for perpetuating the hegemony of "savage" time consciousness, how could the more liberatory "philosophic" perception of necessity—that is, a form of protention open to an undetermined future—be developed? *A Philosophical View of Reform* did not provide a clear answer to this question. The form in which Shelley cast his reflections (a systematic historico-philosophic treatise) implied that knowledge of a social system enabled one to transform or destroy the system, but how, precisely, systematic knowledge led to change remained an open question in this text. In his critique of the national debt, Cobbett had suggested one link between system-knowledge and system-destruction, arguing that to reveal the hypocrisy of the "Paper-Money System" in a "plain and practical way" would deprive the system of its affective support, resulting in the downfall of that system (Cobbett 1817: 22). Yet such an explanation would have had relatively little appeal to Shelley, for Cobbett's method relied upon precisely the same understanding of causal necessity that Shelley opposed. Cobbett, in other words, located the necessity of system breakdown in a "corruption" or "flaw" that contaminated its origins, and he implied that exposing the fact of systemic corruption would lead inexorably to the system's downfall. Since precisely this sense of causal inevitability was the object of Shelley's critique, such an understanding of the effects of literary form was not an option for Shelley.

Within the treatise itself, Shelley hinted at two other means by which more libratory forms of perception might be encouraged. His first alternative drew upon his earlier analyses of sympathy. In the section of *A Philosophical View of Reform* entitled "Probable Means" (i.e., of reform), Shelley suggested that one ought to promote mechanisms that enabled the contagious sympathy of public opinion. Arguing against secret ballots as a system that was "too mechanical" to allow public opinion to manifest itself, Shelley suggested that

> [t]he elector and the elected ought to meet one another face to face and interchange the meanings of actual presence and share some common impulses and, in a degree, understand each other. There ought to be the common sympathy of the excitements of popular assembly among the electors themselves. (*SP* 254–55)

Should such common sympathy prevail, political conflicts could be resolved by means of contagious enthusiasm, Shelley contended, for

> [i]f the majority are enlightened, united, impelled by a uniform enthusiasm and animated by a distinct and powerful apprehension of their object—and full confidence in their undoubted power—the struggle [between classes] is merely nominal. The minority perceive the approaches of an irresistible force.... [and they] divest themselves of their usurped distinctions; the public tranquillity is not disturbed by the revolution. (*SP* 256)

Yet even as Shelley positioned sympathy as capable of preventing violent conflict and transforming public opinion in ways that strengthened and unified the social body, he remained ambivalent about this term. He suggested, for example, that sympathy was also responsible for current Britain's credit economy, for it facilitated the affective bonds between the political and financial elites. Shelley, like Hume and Smith, suggested that "disinterested affection" is generally "confined within the narrow circle of our friends," and as a result, one could always expect to find a "class of men considerable from talent, influence, and station who of necessity are enemies to Reform," since they sympathize with their fellow elites, rather than the wider populace (*SP* 241). Moreover, sympathy often hindered actual reform, for in periods of rapid political change, sympathy might encourage violence and revenge. In a fragment on political reform written at the same time as, and probably intended as part of, *The Philosophical View of Reform*, Shelley contended that in cases of violent revolution,

> [t]he people sympathize with the passions of their liberators without reflecting that these in turn may become their tyrants, and without perceiving that the same motives and excitements to act or to feel can never, except by a perverse imitation, belong to both. (*SP* 261)

The imitation that occurred during periods of flux was "perverse" because it limited, rather than enabled, the expansion of sympathy, and because it depended on the same restricted understanding of temporality that Shelley had earlier analyzed in his "Essay on the Punishment of

Death." Sympathy on its own, in short, would not create the conditions for new and more equitable social systems.

Shelley's second solution, at which he only hinted in the final pages of *A Philosophical View of Reform*, centered on the role of publicly circulated images. He began on a dour note, suggesting that the state employed martial images to perpetuate the hegemony of savage time consciousness. "War," Shelley wrote, "is a kind of superstition; the pageantry of arms and badges corrupts the imagination of men" (*SP* 260). War corrupted the imagination by producing physical misery, for the latter encouraged "superstition": "misery on earth begets a diseased expectation and panic-stricken faith in miseries beyond the grave" (*SP* 246). The result was the domination of time consciousness by savage forms of time consciousness, as

> the gleams of hope which speak of Paradise seem [to those in physical misery] like the flames in Milton's hell only to make darkness visible, and all things take [their] color from what surrounds them. They [the people] become revengeful. (*SP* 246)

In the context of such misery, the government's saturation of public space with martial images ("pageantry") served to dampen alternative modes of time consciousness that might otherwise be sensitive to "gleams of hope" in political events. Yet however much government pageantry obscured gleams of hope, Shelley held out the possibility that other modes of imagery might encourage more expansive modes of time consciousness. He suggested, for example, that in place of the state's use of the "pageantry of arms and badges," it would be "far more appropriate" to employ "symbols of an inconsolable grief" and to

> [v]isit in imagination the scene of a field of battle or a city taken by assault, collect into one group the groans and distortions of the innumerable dying, the inconsolable grief and horror of their surviving friends...the burning of the harvests and the obliteration of the traces of civilization. (*SP* 260)

While such an image was clearly designed to produce sympathy, it did so by altering time consciousness. Against the consciousness of causal necessity and inevitability that the state's "pageantry of arms and badges" perpetuated, Shelley suggested an image of temporal totality and caesura. In place of the repetition of the same implied by rituals of state pageantry, Shelley's image of a suffering unity—all of a battle's sufferers, or all of a city, gathered into an image, and all of the traces of civilization erased—introduced a break in time by distinguishing between an "after" that was cut off from its "before" (the city is fundamentally altered by the battle and the traces of civilization destroyed). While the content of such an image might be depressing, Shelley suggested that its form—the form of nonlinear, "broken" time—was revitalizing, for it brought to the fore a capacity of time consciousness that generally went unrecognized in daily existence.[22]

IV. TIME AND THE IMAGE I: *THE MASK OF ANARCHY*

A Philosophical View of Reform had helped Shelley consolidate important features of his political philosophy. The form of the treatise allowed Shelley to isolate the national debt and credit economy as the source of Britain's contemporary political problems in ways that were hinted at, but not fully developed, in earlier essays and pamphlets. In *A Philosophical View of Reform*, Shelley suggested that the real danger of institutions of state finance was their ability to perpetuate the impoverished mode of savage time consciousness that he had outlined in "An Essay on the Punishment of Death," thus hindering the ability of people to intuit the present as the active source of future events. The treatise also allowed Shelley to consider the extent to which the struggle over time consciousness was a fight over "images," though his closing suggestion that the state's pageantry of arms and badges might be countered by temporal images of suffering was schematic at best.

Shelley took up the task of refining his theory and practice of the liberating image in a series of poems and dramas composed in 1819. Shelley's interest in poetry, rather than prose, as the proper venue for an articulation of the distinction between good and bad political imagery was no doubt encouraged by his engagement with the circle around Leigh Hunt and his periodical *The Examiner*.[23] Shelley had published several poems in *The Examiner*, and the periodical itself reminded its readers in the February 18, 1816 issue not only that "[p]oetry has often been made the direct vehicle of politics," but that, moreover, such employment was proper to poetry as poetry (98). In the October 12, 1817 issue, readers of *The Examiner* learned that the editors'

> have long been accustomed...to look at politics with a broader and more comprehensive eye than the readers of most newspapers; they know, that every thing which regards the community in it's [sic] social character ought to be one of the very first objects with statesmen, though the latter would generally have us believe that politics are grave, exclusive, and difficult things, for only to be discussed by a few flourishing gentlemen.... (641)

Shakespeare, Chaucer, and Milton were positioned as poets who had contributed to political freedom, while the "apostasies" of formerly "Jacobin" poets such as Robert Southey, S.T. Coleridge, and William Wordsworth were mocked repeatedly in the post-Napoleonic period.[24] As Jeffrey N. Cox notes, none of the circle around Hunt "doubted the importance of politics to poetry," nor, conversely, did they doubt the importance of poetry to politics (Cox 1998: 31). For Shelley, Hunt's *Examiner* seemed to offer a technical means—the daily periodical—with which to counter the stultifying effects of state finance.

The slaughter by government troops of a number of demonstrators at the "Peterloo" Massacre on August 16, 1819 provided Shelley with an opportunity to articulate his understanding of the link between poetry and politics. Despite a local ban, a public gathering of somewhere between 80,000 and 100,000 people met in St. Peter's Fields in Manchester, protesting for parliamentary reform. The local magistrates, apparently convinced that insurrectionary elements were among those gathered, attempted to arrest Henry "Orator" Hunt and other purported ringleaders, but as the Yeomanry (and later Hussars) moved in, the troops were either attacked and defended themselves, or they preemptively attacked the crowd. In any case, numerous deaths and injuries resulted, with a death toll of hundreds reported immediately after the event (though subsequent reports have since placed it much closer to fifteen: see Scrivener 1982: 196–97; Walmsley 1969). The slaughter at "Peterloo" was fertile ground for poets in Britain, and a number of poems appeared in radical periodicals immediately after the event.[25] Shelley, in Italy at the time, first learned of this event on September 5, and composed a poem entitled *The Mask of Anarchy, Written on the Occasion of the Massacre at Manchester*, sometime shortly after that date. He intended his Peterloo poem to be published in the September 23, 1819 issue of Hunt's *Examiner*, though Hunt, fearful of government reprisals, did not in fact print it until 1832.

As Michael Scrivener notes, Shelley's *Mask of Anarchy* was "radical" insofar as it sought to promote widespread, yet nonviolent collective action, whereas other poetic responses urged either revenge or indefinite waiting. Many poems written after the massacre either advocated immediate violence or threatened violence should legal means fail. The anonymous "An Address to 'The Rabble,'" for example, urged its readers "T'avenge the infernal deed" (Scrivener 1992: 245, ll. 21–22), while the narrator of "On a Bloody Massacre" suggested its readers initially "wait the law," but proclaimed that if justice were not rendered, "we will sacrifice/The murderers! And eager snatch Revenge!" (Scrivener 1992: 244, ll.16, 21–22). Shelley was not interested in "solutions" based on a desire for vengeance, for, as he had outlined in both the "Essay on the Punishment of Death" and *A Philosophical View of Reform*, revenge depended upon an impoverished mode of time consciousness that was incapable of breaking free from the past. More moderate reformers, for their part, seemed less certain how to respond to Peterloo, and often limited themselves to demanding that Parliament "investigate" the affair (though supporters of Thomas Spence called for a general strike).[26] Shelley, in contrast to both groups, suggested that the path to a progressive future lay in collective nonviolent action, which he initially figured in his poem through the allegorical image of Hope lay-ing "down in the street,/Right before the horses' feet" (*SPP* 304, ll. 98–99), and then represented more realistically near the end of the poem, urging his readers to stand "calm and resolute" in the face of charging artillery and fixed bayonets, contending that even if troops did "Slash, and stab, and maim, and hew," the nonviolent response of protesters would "steam up like inspiration"—like "A volcano heard afar"—and inspire the Nation "in unvanquishable number" (*SPP* 309–10, ll. 319, 307, 311, 342, 361, 363, 369).

As Cox has noted, Shelley's choice of poetic form was probably motivated in part by Hunt's published writings on the masque, which had positioned this mode as a particularly good way to oppose the state's "pageantry of arms and badges" (Cox 1998: 125–30). Hunt had prefaced his drama *The Descent of Liberty: A Mask* (1814) with a long historical essay on the form of the masque, arguing that this form was especially suited to topical political allusions; Hunt's play, for example, took up the fight between France and Britain, describing the dissipation of the "Enchanter" Napoleon's forces and their replacement by peace and the triumph of the arts.[27] Moreover, the allegorical nature of the characters in a masque allowed the author to create an image of social totality while at the same time the "unmasking" implicit in the form encouraged auditors to decode the concrete social institutions that stood behind these allegories. Shelley employed all of these elements in his masque, linking a specific event, the "Peterloo" massacre, to a Pageant of allegorical forces. The latter part of the poem then unmasked this allegory, revealing behind them the social institutions that were also the focus of *A Philosophical View of Reform*. As in his essay, *The Mask of Anarchy* emphasized the extent to which social relations had become dominated by the logic of credit, as Hope described slavery as equivalent to a situation in which people

> ...let the Ghost of Gold
> Take from Toil a thousand fold
> More than e'er its substance could
> In the tyrannies of old.
>
> Paper coin—that forgery
> Of the title deeds which ye
> Hold to something of the worth
> Of the inheritance of Earth. (*SPP* 306, ll. 176–83)

Yet even as Shelley's poem depended upon the unveiling characteristic of the form of the masque, it also interrogated the phenomenological conditions that made "unmasking" possible. There is a temptation to read unmasking in Shelley's poem as "simply" the movement from illusion to reality, from mask to actual face. "Murder" is masked "like [Lord] Castlereagh," "Hypocrisy" is "[c]lothed with the Bible," paper money is a "ghost" of gold (*SPP* 301–2, ll. 5–6, 22–25), which seems to suggest that unmasking is a sort of tropism, that is, a movement away from the realm of the virtual (masks, disguises, ghosts) and toward reality and materiality. Yet such a reading is complicated by the fact that Freedom also pursues its goals by means of virtual devices such as masks and echoes. Though freedom depends upon material objects—"clothes, and fire, and food," rather than simply simulations, or promises, of those forms of materiality (*SPP* 307, l. 221)—this truth can be recognized only through the mediation of an immaterial "Shape." Thus, when "Hope," seeking to prevent the progress of anarchy, lays herself "down in the street,/Right before the horses' feet" (*SPP* 304, ll. 98–99),

> ...between her and her foes
> A mist, a light, an image rose,
> Small at first, and weak, and frail
> Like the vapour of a vale: (*SPP* 304, ll. 102–5)

The indeterminate image grows until it achieves the form of "a Shape arrayed in mail," though even in this form it remains imperceptible, moving so swiftly that the populace "knew the presence there/And looked,—but all was empty air" (*SPP* 304, ll. 110, 120–21). Yet if the image-become-Shape remains unseen, it nevertheless encourages thought: "Thoughts sprung where'er that step did fall" (*SPP* 304, l. 125). This unseen shape resuscitates Hope and allows for the emergence of another protean apparition of "rushing light of clouds and splendour" that reveals to the English people the fact of their oppression. Rather than simply opposing virtuality to reality, then, *The Mask of Anarchy* distinguishes between different modes of virtuality, contrasting ghosts, echoes, shadows, on the one hand, with the imageless image and invisible Shape, on the other. These two classes of virtual entities cannot be distinguished along an axis of presence/absence—the imageless image and the libratory shape are no more "present" than echoes or ghosts—but instead must be differentiated in their relationship to time consciousness. Echoes and ghosts appear as copies of past presences, while the imageless image and the shape intimate a presence-to-come. Unmasking in Shelley's poem is thus not simply a matter of revealing the true face behind the mask—the reality behind the illusion—but rather first a matter of opening oneself to another form of virtuality (the imageless image).

The complicated temporal structure of unmasking in Shelley's poem meant that topical allusion in *The Mask of Anarchy* operated in a manner fundamentally different from the case of Hunt's masque. Hunt's drama, written and published in the immediate wake of Napoleon's capture, allegorically narrated the fall of Napoleon and the possible future that could develop from this event (peaceful unity of the nations and rise of the arts). Shelley's poem, rather than tracing the seeds of a possible future to the structure of past events, provided an alternative history—a rewriting of the events of Peterloo—that sought to isolate the transformative potential of that event itself. In Shelley's version of Peterloo, the protestors did not fall down in fear of being trampled, but sat to await their fate, and the charging troops did not massacre anyone, but were shamed into retreating. The poem suggests that both of these stories (the actual massacre; the fantasized successful protest) are equally real, even if only one of them actually took place. Shelley's masque, in other words, did not seek to replicate, or represent, the events of Peterloo, and then plot out possible futures, but rather sought to repeat the events in such a way as to make legible their potential. Thus, while the specific points of reference in the poem—the "vast assembly," the "tramp of horses' heels," the flashing of "horseman's scimitars" (*SPP* 309, ll. 295, 310, 315)—led back to an actual event, the poem did not allow the reader to link those references to create a coherent representation of the past as it had happened. Rather, *The Mask of Anarchy* sought to represent the actual event and its virtual potentialities.

The imageless image and the unseen Shape of *The Mask of Anarchy* allowed Shelley to develop his suggestions in *A Philosophical View of Reform* concerning the liberatory power of the image, while at the same time distinguishing his theory of the image from that outlined by the "apostate" Wordsworth in *The Excursion*. Following the appearance of Wordsworth's long poem in 1814, members of the Hunt circle, including Shelley, read it immediately. Most were disappointed (though it received a less critical review in *The Examiner* than in the *Edinburgh Review*), and Shelley was unhappy with its obvious didacticism. *The Excursion* staged numerous scenes of education, but as I noted in the last chapter, two particularly important didactic moments were developed in the story of Margaret and Robert. Standing beside a well, the pedlar informed the narrator (and reader) that "I see around me here/Things which you cannot see" and then interpreted the image of the well for the narrator; in similar fashion, following the story of Margaret's decline, the pedlar reminded the narrator and reader of the redemptive powers of the image of speargrass. Shelley already had developed a poetic critique of the Wordsworthian theory of the image in *Alastor; or, the Spirit of Solitude* (written 1815; published 1816), outlining there the asocial decay and death of a poet who sought superhuman "wild images" (Shelley 1816: 9; *SPP* 73, l. 117). The poet of Shelley's earlier poem also came to "a well," but saw within it only himself:

> His eyes beheld
> Their own wan light through the reflected lines
> Of his thin hair, distinct in the dark depth
> Of that still fountain; as the human heart,
> Gazing in dreams over the gloomy grave,
> Sees its own treacherous likeness there.
> (Shelley 1816: 32–33; *SPP* 81, ll. 457, 469–74).

Alastor suggested that while the poet was correct to look for "gleams of hope" from natural phenomena, such a strategy ran the risk of subverting the solvent powers of the image if the poet (and reader) sought recognition in the image, rather than using it to break the ties that bound one to the past and death. Shelley had hinted at an alternative understanding of the relationship between nature and image in "Mt. Blanc; Lines written in the Vale of Chamouni" (written 1816; published 1817). In that poem, the narrator connected the power of the "unsculptured image" that lay hidden behind the "ethereal waterfall" to poetry's attempt to locate "some faint image" of the ravine within which the waterfall was located, suggesting that by locating such images, the poet was able to channel the power of Mont Blanc to "repeal/Large codes of fraud and woe" (Shelley 1991: 176, 177, 179; *SPP* 90, 91, ll. 26–7, 47, 80–81). Where Wordsworth's image provided the reader with the coordinates of a specific natural object (the "silvered oe'r" speargrass), Shelley's "unsculptured" image gave the reader little to "see" or think. The Shelleyian image was little more than a gleam—the play of light and water—rather than the mineralized patina around a natural object at which Wordsworth had aimed.

The "unsculptured" nature of the Shelleyian image meant that its relationship to temporality was different than that of the Wordsworthian image. Wordsworth's image functioned as a compressed narrative—to reflect on the image of speargrass was to recall from it the story of Margaret—and it was intended to produce a feeling of tranquility. Shelley's image, by contrast, was opposed to narrative, and sought instead to expand the reader's consciousness of time by encouraging a state of "active passivity." Neither the image nor the Shape of *The Mask of Anarchy* functioned as compressed narratives. Rather, their appearance signaled an end to temporal continuity, for the future that the image enabled was not contained by, and did not develop from, the past, but was rather autonomously "grounded" in the future. In keeping with Shelley's reflections on time in "An Essay on the Punishment of Death," Hope emphasizes in *The Mask of Anarchy* that true change cannot result from an understanding of time as a continuous process that develops elements of the past into the present and the future. The figure of Father Time suggests the futility of such an approach:

> My father Time is weak and gray
> With waiting for a better day;
> See how idiot-like he stands,
> Fumbling with his palsied hands! (*SPP* 304, ll. 90–93)

Echoing Wordsworth's description of the old Cumberland beggar, the past ("father Time") is presented as impotent, for it provides the present and future with nothing but seeds of decay. True change, the poem suggests, does not originate in a past origin that "develops" into the present, but rather results from the shadows cast by futurity on the present.

These shadows are intuited not by means of Wordsworthian tranquility, but rather by means of active passivity, as when Hope lays herself down before the horses' feet. Hope's immobility before the horses is not the result of despair or exhaustion—she watches "with a patient eye" as the horses advance upon her—but is rather an example of what Deleuze calls "immobility beyond movement." Rather than seeking immediate outlets for sensation in movement, Hope suspends movement in order to become hypersensitive to sensation itself (Deleuze 2003: 36).[28]

Fearing government reprisals, Hunt eventually decided not to publish Shelley's *Mask of Anarchy* in the *Examiner*, and the poem only appeared posthumously in 1832.[29] Yet even had the *Mask of Anarchy* appeared in Hunt's periodical, the poem itself was vexed by a potential confusion between form and content. If Shelley's doctrine of the image was to have any meaning, a poem such as *The Mask of Anarchy* could not simply *represent* people being affected by imageless images and opening themselves to the future; in addition, the poem had to provide its actual readers with such images. From this perspective, *The Mask of Anarchy* was not entirely successful, for it focused primarily upon describing the effects of imageless images upon a populace. While the poem implicitly positioned the poet as the source of liberatory images—the sudden appearances of the imageless image and unseen Shape within the poem were presumably figures for the (desired) publication of the *Mask of Anarchy* itself—this primarily thematic approach did not ensure that the poem would provide the actual readers of Hunt's periodical with any "imageless images" of the sort described in the content of the poem.

V. TIME AND THE IMAGE II: THE *PROMETHEUS UNBOUND* VOLUME

If *The Mask of Anarchy* was caught between two different tasks—on the one hand, representing *for* readers the practical effects of expanded time consciousness, and, on the other, facilitating *in* readers the expansion of time consciousness by means of "unsculptured" images—the latter task took center stage in Shelley's *Prometheus Unbound* volume, published a year after *The Mask of Anarchy* was written. While *The Mask of Anarchy* had emphasized the explicit links between state finance, time consciousness, and the image that Shelley had articulated in *A Philosophical View of Reform*, the poems included in *Prometheus Unbound* focused more purely on the development of imageless images; in addition, Shelley abandoned the publication venue of the periodical in favor of the book, a form over which Shelley would have greater control. As Shelley noted in his Preface to the long "lyrical drama" from which the collection took its name, his imagery was unusual, in that it was often "drawn from the operations of the human mind, or from those external actions by which they [the operations of the mind] are expressed." However, he stressed that his aims were not didactic in the usual sense, for Shelley sought to

> familiarize the highly refined imagination of the more select class of poetical readers with beautiful idealisms of moral excellence; aware that until the mind can love, and admire, and trust, and hope, and endure, reasoned principles of moral conduct are seeds cast upon the highway of life which the unconscious passenger tramples into dust.... (Shelley 1820: ix–x, xiv; *SPP* 133, 135)[30]

In both the four-act drama *Prometheus Unbound* as well as the nine "Miscellaneous Poems" that followed, Shelley's efforts at imaginative refinement took the form of expanding time consciousness by focusing on images that distorted commonsense conceptions of linear time and space.

The peculiarities of the images in Shelley's late poetry, especially those of the poems included in the *Prometheus Unbound* volume, have been the source of significant critical commentary. Critics have noted that Shelley's images emphasize phenomena that are particularly difficult to "image" (in the sense of "representing to oneself"): Frederick Pottle, for example, suggested that Shelley was attacked by the New Critics precisely because he "seldom takes a gross, palpable, near-at-hand object from the world of ordinary perception...[rather], he starts with objects that are just on the verge of becoming invisible or inaudible or intangible and he strains away even from those," while David Perkins suggests that Shelley's "frequent resort to an imagery lacking in individuation" was the result of an attempt to guide readers to "the One" that stood behind all phenomena (Pottle 1952: 601; Perkins 1965: 168). The unstable nature of Shelley's images have been defended from a variety of critical perspectives, ranging from William Keach's suggestion that these images were the result of Shelley's rigorous application of his philosophy of language to poetry, to Jerrold Hogle's contention that the tendency of the images in Shelley's late poetry to "dissolve" are the result of Shelley's "sense of being incomplete and unbounded" while at the same time he sought "possibilities for extending himself in space, time, and writing" (Keach 1984; Hogle 1988: 3, viii). My reading of images from the *Prometheus Unbound* volume shares much with these latter interpretations, but I focus specifically on the ways in which these poems challenged readers' powers of representation in order to expand the consciousness of time, thereby soliciting the powers of futurity.

"Ode to Heaven"

"Ode to Heaven," the third of the volume's "miscellaneous poems," provides a useful introduction to the method of the Shelleyian imageless image. The Pindaric strope-antistrophe-epode structure of Shelley's ode guides readers through three increasingly complex images of heaven, each of which seeks to articulate the relationship between eternity, on the one hand, and "normal" time and space, on the other. The first voice in the poem—the "First Spirit"—represents heaven as a container, within which the events of time and space unfold: it is a "Presence chamber, Temple, Home,/Ever-canopying Dome" of "the present and the past," as well as of "acts and ages yet to come!" (Shelley 1820: 182; *SPP* 219, ll.7–9). Yet the poem suggests that such an image, while perhaps comforting, is problematic insofar as it attempts to understand the relationship between time and eternity by means of spatial categories, as though temporal events could be contained "within" an eternal chamber or dome. Thus, the second voice ("Second Spirit") criticizes this confusion of space and time by suggesting that such an image, rather than providing an accurate representation of reality, is instead a misrecognition of the mind's own limitations. If heaven is a "chamber," it is

> but the mind's first chamber,
> Round which its young fancies clamber,
> Like weak insects in a cave,
> Lighted up by stalactites; (Shelley 1820: 183–84; *SPP* 220, ll. 28–31)

This second voice suggests that to understand heaven as a "chamber" is to confuse a mental structure for an external reality. Yet even as the second voice refuses to spatialize heaven, it relies on an understanding of time as a linear series, dividing temporality into a "before" and "after." The second voice suggests that after the moment of death, the Mind will discover "new delights," beside which the "best glories" of heaven will seem like dimmed reflections: "a dim and noonday gleam/From the shadow of a dream" (Shelley 1820: 184; *SPP* 220, ll. 33–36). Time is approached through the mode of "expectation," that is, extrapolating a certain (or at least probable) future from the past. The second voice thus avoids spatializing time as a volume only to then spatialize it as a continuous line.

In response to this second image, a third spirit provides an image that seeks to image time *as* time. It suggests that heaven is:

> a globe of dew,
> Filling in the morning new
> Some eyed flower whose young leaves waken
> On an unimagined world;
> Constellated suns unshaken,
> Orbits measureless, are furled
> In that frail and fading sphere,
> With ten millions gathered there,
> To tremble, gleam, and disappear.
> (Shelley 1820: 184–85; *SPP* 220, ll. 46–54)

On the one hand, this third voice seems to provide the most literal image of heaven, representing it as a dew drop on a plant (even if, of course, this "literal" image had a thick literary pedigree, recalling Andrew Marvell's "On a Drop of Dew," as well as descriptions of the "worlds" inside drops of water that populated the prose and poems of authors such as Joseph Addison and James Thomson).[31] Yet, on the other hand, if by "image" we mean a set of either spatiotemporal or logical relations that a subject can represent to itself, the vision of the third voice troubles this understanding of image, for the more that one attempts to coordinate with one another the internal relations depicted in the final stanza, the more the subject is deprived of stable coordinates with which it could represent them. As Hugh Roberts notes, Shelley's image echoes Andrew Marvell's "On a Drop of Dew," which compares a drop of dew on a plant to the heaven-oriented nature of the human soul, but the identity (rather than analogy) that Shelley establishes between the dew drop and heaven does not allow for the analogical mapping that is possible in the case of Marvell's poem.[32] From what perspective, in Shelley's poem, does heaven appear as a "globe of dew"? From within the globe? From a position outside the globe? These questions are difficult, if not impossible to answer, for Shelley's image links the various objects of this stanza (plant, dew drop, constellated suns, the ten million) into a single continuous "thick surface." The role of the surface is one of the most striking differences between Marvell's and Shelley's images of the drop of dew: since Marvell wanted to emphasize the *spiritual* essence of the soul, his dew drop is "[s]carce touching" the flower (Marvell 1972: 102; l. 10); for Shelley, by contrast, the globe of dew is the medium of a dynamic surface that links light, water, and the surface of the plant. Shelley's spatial prepositions ("on," "in," "there"), which in principle should allow the reader to establish spatial relations (the difference between surface and depth, or figure and ground, for example), are instead employed to embed objects in this thick surface: the awakening of the young leaves "[o]n an unimagined world," for example, can be understood as a figure for sight (the eyed flower "sees" an unimagined world), but must also be understood literally (the surface of the "young leaves" touch the dew drop, thus hastening the disappearance of the latter). In similar fashion, Shelley's use of "in" (rather than "on") to describe the relationship between the "constellated suns" and the "frail and fading sphere" of the dew drop suspends questions of reference—we cannot tell whether this light is a reflection from a source outside the drop, or emanations from minute particles in the dew drop itself—in order to locate the constellated suns as *part of* the drop.

If we are nevertheless able to "make sense of" this image, the poem suggests that we do so not by *conceiving* it (that is, representing a set of relations to ourselves), but rather by grasping it on the basis of an understanding of time that is dynamic rather than spatial. What creates the thick surface is fundamentally time, and only incidentally spatial contiguity. This is true both in the superficial sense that we can represent to ourselves all of the image elements touching only if we "add" the linear passage of time, but it is also true in the more significant sense that this thick surface is itself composed of temporal objects. The constellated suns and their measureless orbits, for example, stand as figures for both the past-as-it-was-present (the finite speed of light ensured that the illumination reflected in the drop originated in the distant past) and the future (the stars will continue to exist in the future).[33] Yet this image that joins past and future is located in a dynamic present (the collapsing or evaporating dew drop), which "furls" both the past-as-it-was-present and the future along its own dynamic lines of pressure. Such an image provides the reader with no more "realistic" a representation of heaven than do images of chambers or expectations of future glories; rather, it manifests the structure of "open" time by bending space into time—"on," in," and "there" are furled into temporal, rather than spatial, relations—which in turn allows the reader to grasp the present as a temporal complex. The reader's ability to grasp this image even without being able to form a representation of it thus highlights capacities for temporal awareness that neither of the preceding two images acknowledged; that is, it enables an intuition of philosophic necessity by breaking familiar associations of heaven with linear time and space.[34]

"Ode to Liberty"

While the connection between temporal consciousness and the politico-economic concerns of *A Philosophical View of Reform* and *The Mask of Anarchy* is muted in "Ode to Heaven," this relationship is more explicitly emphasized in "Ode to Liberty," the final poem of the *Prometheus Unbound* volume. Shelley's "Ode to Liberty" should be read as a temporally expansive version of *The Mask of Anarchy*, for both poems purported to be transcription of "voices" that came to the poet upon news of political insurrection—unrest in Manchester, in the case of *The Mask of Anarchy*; rebellion in Spain, in the case of the "Ode to Liberty"—and both poems recounted past moments of tyranny and liberty to solicit from them their revolutionary potential. However, while *The Mask of Anarchy* limited itself to a single political event, the "Ode to Liberty" outlined the history of liberty from the origin of the universe to the present. The poem begins by suggesting that at the birth of the universe, and even some way into the early history of humans, liberty did not yet exist. The "gleam" of liberty made its first appearance in Athens, the poem contends (Shelley 1820: 211; *SPP* 231, l. 70), and the rest of the verse recounts its various points of emergence and disappearance in European history (Rome; the reign of Alfred; the English Revolution; the French Revolution and its aftermath).

However committed the poem is to documenting the history of Liberty, the effects of the *Ode to Liberty* on readerly time consciousness depend not on its capacity to accumulate examples from the past, but rather on its ability to manifest the "vibration" (Shelley 1820: 207; *SPP* 229, l. 1) that runs through all those instances. "Proof" of liberty by historical example would depend on precisely the savage mode of time consciousness that Shelley opposed, for such a method would seek to convince by revealing an inner tendency of history, established in the past, which necessitates a particular future. Simply to accumulate examples, in other words, would be essentially proof by tradition, in Edmund Burke's sense, for it would ask a reader to be convinced by tertiary memory (what others have experienced and handed on). Thus, while the "Ode to Liberty" presents a series, rather than subordinating the series under an accumulative strategy, the poem seeks to make legible the productive power that runs through all of these events. In order for this productive power to become legible, each instance of the series—Athens, Rome, etc.—must function as a sign that points beyond itself to something that cannot be seen but which nevertheless instantiates itself in these examples. Shelley uses the term "gleam" to denote this signifying function: Athens gleamed at liberty's origin and, in the present, liberty gleams in Spain (Shelley 1820: 211, 207; *SPP* 231, 229, ll. 70, 5). The gleam is something that borders on the limits of representation itself, as Shelley's opening description attests:

> A glorious people vibrated again
> The lightning of the nations: Liberty
> From heart to heart, from tower to tower, o'er Spain,
> Scattering contagious fire into the sky,
> Gleamed. (Shelley 1820: 207; *SSP* 229, ll. 1–5)

It is difficult to form a representation of the gleam of liberty because its two aspects—scattering and contagion—cannot be understood within a stable space-time geography. These two aspects represent opposed spatializing operations: on the one hand, the extensive distribution of scattering; on the other, the intensive assimilation of contagion. As a result, the gleam can be referred to neither pure sensation nor pure conception: it is neither a set of optical sparkles of light, each of which could be mapped back to an originating location in space, nor does it denote a conceptual operation, such as mapping paths of transmission.

The "Ode of Liberty" suggests that the double operation of the gleam—scattering and contagion—can be grasped only on the basis of an expanded mode of time consciousness. Immediately following his description of the birth of liberty in Athens, the narrator provides an image of the relationship between time and liberty:

> Within the surface of Time's fleeting river
> Its wrinkled image lies, as then it lay
> Immovably unquiet, and for ever
> It trembles, but it cannot pass away!
> (Shelley 1820: 211; *SSP* 231, ll. 76–79)

One can intuit liberty only by considering temporal phenomena, but the image perceived by means of the events lies beyond the limits of representation as one normally understands that latter term. The image of liberty appears as an internal deformation and distortion of time; the image appears wrinkled precisely because it makes visible temporal folds, cusps, and eddies ("Time's fleeting River"). If such an image "makes sense," it does not do so because we can represent it to ourselves as analogous to a physical situation (for example, a stable object reflected in rushing water). We do not make sense of the image by "unfolding" from time into space, for liberty appears *within* (rather than on or under) the surface of time's fleeting river; it is thus not a reflection of an object present elsewhere, but rather, an image that appears only as the result of temporal folding. Our ability to make sense of this image (even if we cannot provide a representation of it) testifies to the ability of time consciousness to break the form of causal necessity, and bring past, present, and future together.[35] Thus, the poem, and the volume as a whole, can end on a note of loss—"the Spirit of that might singing/To its abyss was suddenly withdrawn," and the poet's "song, its pinions disarrayed of might/ Drooped"—and yet still "liberate" the reader by making legible that "echo" which sustained the poetic voice in the first place (Shelley 1820: 222; *SPP* 236, ll. 271–72, 281–82).

Prometheus Unbound

Just as the "miscellaneous poems" of the *Prometheus Unbound* volume embedded liberatory images within larger dramatic or narrative structures, the titular poem of the collection also sought to provide both a representation of, as well as images that would enable, an expansion of time consciousness. As I noted above, Shelley's four-act lyrical drama did not seek to dramatize relationships between humans, but rather sought to create images of "the operations of the human mind" (Shelley 1820: ix–x; *SPP* 133). While twentieth-century critics have pointed to this representation of the poem as a "psychodrama" to justify psychoanalytically oriented interpretations of the poem that emphasize sexual desire, paternal rivalry, and sublimation, I am more interested in the role of Shelley's depiction of the *temporality* that attends the "operations of the human mind."[36] While quite a few things happen in the play, there are few "actions": Prometheus's "betrayal" of Jupiter happened long before the play begins, and the only "event" of the drama is Prometheus's decision to "repent" an earlier curse made against Jupiter in the prehistory of the play. Prometheus repents his curse because he recognizes that he "wish[es] no living thing to suffer pain" (Shelley 1820: 34; *SPP* 144, 1.305), and this psychological action then "causes" the events of the following three acts, which outline the fall of Jupiter at the hands of his son Demogorgon, and the subsequent reformation of human relations and the transformation of earth into an utopia.

When read against Shelley's earlier reflections on the distinction between savage and philosophic necessity, *Prometheus Unbound* emerges as a play focused on the connection between time consciousness and perceptions of causal necessity. While Prometheus is represented as physically bound and tortured, his real antagonist is a limited conception of causality. When Furies are sent to torture Prometheus, for example, they only begin to achieve their effect when they half-convince the Titan that his gift of knowledge to humans in the past was causally responsible for the human "thirst" that has resulted in "[m]any a million-peopled city/Vomit[ing] smoke in the bright air" (Shelley 1820: 46–47; *SPP* 152, 1.543, 551–52). In this moment, when "Past ages crowd" on Prometheus, and "the future is dark," he begins to despair ("Drops of bloody agony flow/From his white and quivering brow"), for he unconsciously locates the ability to change the future in the inaccessible past (Shelley 1820: 47; *SPP* 152, ll. 561–62, 564–65). What the play dramatizes, then, is Prometheus's movement from this limited conception of causality, in which the determinants of the present are contained in the past, to one that locates the future as capable of exerting effects on the present.

The transformation of Prometheus's time consciousness centers on his repenting of his earlier curse against Jupiter. The curse is important to the play less for its content—Prometheus's imperative that time "[h]eap on [Jupiter's] soul.../Ill deeds," so that the latter would be "damned, beholding good" (Shelley 1820: 33; *SPP* 144, 1. 292–93)—than for its form. The form of the curse bears a paradoxical relationship to time consciousness, for while it is fully dependent upon savage time consciousness, at the same time it cleaves close to the structure of what Shelley called philosophic necessity. Thus, on the one hand, the perceived efficacy of the curse depends upon the capacity of the present to serve as "the active source of future events." This sense of the curse's efficacy goes to the fundament of time consciousness: in cursing, the speaker does not "predict" what will happen on the basis of past experience; rather, for a speaker to believe in his curse, the anticipation of protention must be loosened from retention. The curse is like the promise, which also seeks to bind the future to an event that will become past. However, where promises can be broken, the curse positions itself as the continually *active* source of future events; that is, the curse seeks to bind or "clasp" the future (Shelley 1820: 33; *SPP* 144, 1. 287). From the perspective of the one who curses, the power of the curse to bind the future is in no way dependent upon human memory or psychology; once it has been spoken, the curse is inscribed in the nature of things. The curse employs the passage of time to force its way into the nature of things: even as it is spoken, it becomes immediately encased in the past, sealed up so that neither the present nor the future can undo it. To curse, in other words, is to release protention from retention for a moment—to allow a sense of the future as open and not bound by the past—before immediately returning protention to the constraints of savage time consciousness, which then binds all future events to the past curse.

Yet if the initial act of cursing binds anticipation to retention, the *repetition* of the curse in the play frees anticipation in a way that does not allow it to be bound again. We are witness to an admittedly peculiar form of repetition in the play: it is not the repetition of memory (Prometheus has forgotten the words of his curse), but rather a virtual repetition, spoken by the "Phantasm" of Jupiter. The character of "Earth" reveals to Prometheus that underneath the world of conscious perception there is another world, in which past "[d]reams and the light imaginings of men/And all that faith creates, or love desires" remain virtually present (Shelley 1820: 29; *SPP* 144, 11. 200–1). Prometheus makes the past curse virtually present again by calling up the "Phantasm" of Jupiter, who speaks the curse Prometheus had spoken in the past. In hearing the curse repeated, Prometheus finds "[i]t doth repent me," and he is freed from the constraints which the form of the curse had imposed upon him when he originally uttered it (Shelley 1820: 34; *SPP* 144, 1.303). It may seem strange that repetition of the curse should produce an effect different from its original enunciation. Yet in fact it is repetition itself that frees Prometheus. The fact that the curse can be "cited"—that is, an instance can be recognized *as* a curse without *being* a curse—requires, and reveals, a mode of engagement with temporality which conserves the past yet does *not* bind the future (as the curse does). The phantasm of Jupiter allows Prometheus to encounter pure, or unbound, anticipation; it isolates the curse's affirmation of itself as active source of future events, and separates that potentiality from savage time consciousness. As a result, Prometheus can react to the curse in multiple ways (he can affirm it, renounce it, etc.).

The image of Prometheus recanting his curse—like the image of the dewdrop in the "Ode to Heaven" and the image of the gleam in the "Ode to Liberty"—aimed to liberate readers from the savage understanding of Necessity that Shelley had located as the key to institutions such as state finance (and the forces of Murder, Fraud, Hypocrisy, Destruction, and Anarchy that such institutions made possible). Each of these imageless images operated by introducing a fault into the notion of linear time and space: the image of the dew drop by furling the modalities of time (past, present, future) into a single tenuous surface; the image of Liberty's gleam by forcing the reader to imagine simultaneously two opposed operations (extensive distribution and intensive assimilation); the image of Prometheus's recantation of his curse by positioning the present as the active source of future events, thereby disrupting the schema of causality. Images of time furled, dispersed, or gathered up into a moment enabled open modes of protention, which in turn facilitated the liberatory form of sympathy that Shelley had analyzed in earlier essays such as his "Proposals for an Association of Philanthropists." Thus, though the volume did not explicitly link the imageless image with the institutions of state finance, as had been the case in *The Mask of Anarchy*, the poems included in *Prometheus Unbound* were arguably more successful in providing readers with the sort of images that Shelley's poem on the Peterloo Massacre had simply described.

VI. FROM SYMPATHY TO IDENTIFICATION: *A DEFENCE OF POETRY*

While the poetry that Shelley wrote after his *Prometheus Unbound* volume also eschewed explicit mention of institutions such as the national debt and paper money, the publication in 1821 of Thomas Love Peacock's *The Four Ages of Poetry* provided Shelley with an opportunity to revisit the connections between time consciousness, speculation, and the "shadows of futurity." In his essay, published in the short-lived periodical *Ollier's Literary Miscellany*, Peacock presented the poet as the original of the financial speculator, arguing that poetry began as a technical mechanism that allowed kings to extend their prestige and "credit." Contemporary poets were even more parasitical, for while poetry might have served a (dubious) function in the ancient world, it had been since outstripped by "the progress of reason," and as a result "a writer of poetry in the present state of society is…a waster of his own time, and a robber of that of others" (Peacock 1924–32, vol. 8: 21–22). Shelley's response, *A Defence of Poetry*, written immediately after the publication of *The Four Ages of Poetry*, defended the figure of poet against Peacock's charges, employing the concept of "identification" to articulate the connection between poetic images, expansion of time consciousness, and the liberatory form of sympathy that Shelley had described in his earlier work.

Peacock's attack on contemporary poetry has generally been understood as satiric, but Phillip Connell observes that the doctrines outlined in *The Four Ages of Poetry* were seriously espoused by a number of different groups in early nineteenth-century Britain (Connell 2001: 210–33). The group of political economists grouped around the *Edinburgh Review*, for example, frequently attacked Lake School poetry, and Francis Jeffery suggested that poetry itself was problematic in a civilized society. Poetry, Jeffery argued in the February 1813 volume of the *Edinburgh Review*, tends to "habituate the mind to transitory and passive impressions," and he preferred that educated readers study instead "philosophy, eloquence, history, and those other departments of learning which refer chiefly to the heart and understanding, and depend upon a knowledge of human nature, and an attentive study of all that contributes to its actual enjoyments" (vol. 21: 8, 7). While Shelley would have placed Jeffrey among his opponents, even individuals and groups far more friendly to the Hunt circle had adopted similar views. In the 1818 first issue of the *Yellow Dwarf*, for example, William Hazlitt favored Jeremy Bentham's philosophical radicalism over the political mutability of the Lake Poets, and wondered whether "the progress of knowledge and refinement has a tendency to circumscribe the limits of the imagination, and to clip the wings of poetry" (Hazlitt, cited in Connell 2001: 224). The "philosophical radicals" centered around Bentham also viewed imaginative literature with extreme suspicion, and Peacock's friendship with this other group suggests that his satire is best understood "as an attempt to force these issues into the open by representing some of the implications of the utilitarian distrust of imaginative 'fiction' in the most extreme terms" (Connell 2001: 225).

Shelley took seriously the attack on poetry developed in *The Four Ages of Poetry*, responding point by point to Peacock's claims.[37] Where Peacock represented the poet as an atavism, Shelley argued that modern poetry was not a regressive form, but rather a technology that solicited the powers of the future: the poet "beholds the future in the present, and his thoughts are the germs of the flower and the fruit of latest time" (*SP* 279). Where Peacock presented reason as holding precedence over imagination, Shelley presented imagination as the "agent," "spirit," and "substance" of the soul (*SP* 277). And where Peacock described the history of poetry as broken into two epochs (each of which was broken into four ages), Shelley suggested a timeless view of poetic function.

Peacock's critique represented a rather uncanny application to poetry of Shelley's critique of the credit economy as outlined in *A Philosophical View of Reform. The Four Ages of Poetry* characterized modern poetry as crass capitalization, portraying poets as irresponsible "mountebanks" who provided "gewgaws and rattles for the grown babies of the age" (Peacock 1924–32, vol. 8: 25, 19). Even more damning, Peacock argued that poetry was itself the original form of "public credit"—that is, the original technology by means of which the political leaders parasited "Opinion" in order to extend their power. Yet in employing poetry in this way, kings were simply following the poets' lead, for poets and poetry was always dependent upon a credit economy, as "[a] skillful display of the little knowledge [poets] have gains them credit or the possession of much more which they have not" (Peacock 1924–32, vol. 8: 6). Just as Shelley had presented the modern credit economy as the result of an alliance between two self-interested groups (those with political power and those with money), Peacock presented poetry as the product of an alliance between those with political power and those with the means to advertise this power, and just as Shelley had presented credit as inimical to real production or labor, Peacock contended that poetry itself "cannot claim the slightest share in any one of the comforts and utilities of life" (Peacock 1924–32, vol. 8: 21). Peacock's use of monetary metals to label the ages of poetry (iron, gold, silver, brass) simply highlighted what he saw as the stock-jobbing logic of the history of verse.

In order to distinguish between financial and poetic speculation in *A Defence of Poetry*, Shelley enlarged on his understanding of the connections between the imagination and sympathy. Shelley positioned the imagination as the central agent of human activity; it was the "agent," "spirit," and "substance" of action, while reason was demoted to "instrument," "body," and "shadow." The corruption of social systems began, but was also cured, in the imagination (*SP* 286), for it was "the faculty which contains within itself the seeds at once of its own and of social renovation" (*SP* 287). Sympathy was the force that actuated these positive potentialities of imagination. In a general sense, poetry produced its social effects insofar as it "awakens and enlarges the mind itself by rendering it the receptacle of a thousand unapprehended combinations of thought" (*SP* 282), but more specifically, poetry enlarged the imagination through a special modality of sympathy. Shelley suggested that the imagination was akin to a flexible surface, like a muscle, that possessed a plasticity and capacity for growth that allowed it to expand continually beyond its own internal limits, and sympathy was the means by which it "grew," for "[t]he imagination is enlarged by a sympathy with pains and passions so mighty, that they distend in their conception the capacity of that by which they are conceived" (*SP* 285). Poetry provided occasions for sympathetic acts, and thus "poetry strengthens that faculty which is the organ of the moral nature of man, in the same manner as exercise strengthens a limb" (*SP* 283). Moreover, Shelley suggested, this process of enlargement was always a social process, for the poet's conception "communicates itself to others, and gathers a sort of reduplication from that community" (*SP* 278).

"Identification" served as the term that allowed Shelley to distinguish this good form of sympathy from the "bad" form of sympathy that, as he had outlined in his earlier writings, could be appropriated by the state. Identification appeared in the essay in the context of a discussion of poetry's power to position an individual vis-à-vis "role models." Shelley praised the poetry of Homer, suggesting that "those who read his verses were awakened to an ambition of becoming like to Achilles, Hector and Ulysses" (*SP* 282), and he suggested that Homer's audience was so inspired because their

> sentiments...must have been refined and enlarged by a sympathy with such great and lovely impersonations, until from admiring they imitated, and from imitation they identified themselves with the objects of their admiration. (*SP* 282)

Shelley acknowledged that the violence and passion of Homeric heroes might seem to make them unlikely candidates for identification, but he argued that any such objection was based on a misunderstanding of the "manner in which poetry acts to produce the moral improvement of man" (*SP* 282). The characters of poetry, Shelley argued,

> clothed in [poetry's] Elysian light stand thenceforward in the minds of those who have contemplated them, as memorials of that gentle and exalted content which extends itself over all thoughts and actions with which it coexists. The great secret of morals is Love; or a going out of our nature, and an identification of ourselves with the beautiful which exists in thought, action, or person, not our own. (*SP* 282–83)

"Identification" was thus the result of a process that began with sympathy: sympathy allowed audience members to admire a character; the audience then imitated that character; and only then could audience members identify with "the beautiful which exists in thought, action, or person, not our own." From a post-Freudian perspective, Shelley's series (sympathy→admiration→identification) is surprising, for psychoanalytic theory suggests that identification *precedes* admiration and imitation. Shelley insisted, however, that identification *follows* admiration and imitation—and that, moreover, one identifies not with a person per se, but rather with "the beautiful." One can *sympathize* with people and social groups, but one can only *identify* with the beautiful. As a result, identification requires a self-alienation in a way that sympathy does not. "The people [can] sympathize with the passions of their liberators" for essentially selfish reasons (*SP* 261), but identification requires "a going out of our own nature" which cannot be appropriated for regressive political purposes in this way.[38] Sympathy creates unities out of existing identities; identification destroys existing identities in favor of future, more comprehensive, identities. These are not disjunctive, either–or possibilities; as the quote about Greek drama suggests, sympathy often leads to identification. Yet if the movement from sympathy to identification is forestalled, the result is slavish admiration and imitation based on misinterpretations of the gleams of the good and beautiful.

If poetry enables identification with "the beautiful which exists in thought, action, or person, not our own," how is this related to the capacity of the poetic image to expand time consciousness? Shelley addressed this question by first distinguishing the powers of the poetic image from "stories." Shelley defined a "story" as "a catalogue of detached facts, which have no other bond of connexion than time, place, and circumstance, cause and effect," and which, because of its linkage to a particular time and place, "applies only to a definite period of time, and a certain combination of events which can never again recur" (*SPP* 485). A poem, by contrast, is defined as "the creation of actions according to the unchangeable forms of human nature," and is as a result "universal, and contains within itself the germ of a relation to whatever motives or actions have place in the possible varieties of human nature" (*SPP* 485). Since Shelley's term "story" clearly encompasses what we would call "history," it may seem that his distinction revolves around the question of reference: does the work refer to true or created events? Yet this is not in fact a distinction of reference, for he notes that individual parts of an historical account—a "single sentence" or a "single word"; a "trait in the representation of a scene or a passion"—can contain "living images" (*SPP* 485, 486, 505). Instead, the distinction between stories and poems is grounded in time: that is, it is a question of whether the content of the work binds itself to a particular matrix of space-time causality (in which case it does not matter whether that matrix is "true" or "imaginary"), or, on the other hand, brings itself under the power of "eternal truth" (*SPP* 485). To bring a single sentence, word, trait, or a series of events under the power of the eternal does not mean to represent it *as* eternal; rather, it means to infuse the textual element with a "germinal" eternity that inseminates the present with the productive powers of the future (from this perspective, to represent something *as* eternal is decidedly unpoetic, equivalent to locating causal power in an inaccessible past or a "beyond").

For Shelley, "identification" named precisely this intuited awareness of the productive powers of time as they were manifested in the poetic image. In creating poetry, the poet "beholds the future in the present, and his thoughts are the germs of the flower and the fruit of latest time," and identification refers to the auditor's analogous capacity for grasping the future as germinal inseminator of the present (*SPP* 483). Identifications are thus relations of sensation, rather than representation. While the "epitome," or moral, of a narrative can be grasped conceptually, and the sympathies that narratives encourage can be translated into subjective feelings, identifications can be grasped only dimly by representational thought: when people encounter poetic images, they "are as men entranced by the melody of an unseen magician, who feel that they are moved and softened, yet know not whence or why" (*SPP* 486). Identification with the beautiful through the poetic image thus involves a mode of repetition in the auditor, but not in the terms that one associates with the Freudian sense of the term. Identification motivates neither submission (that is, admiration) nor bare repetition (imitation); rather, it names a form of repetition that produces something new. Shelley's version of identification is similar to "apprenticeship" as Deleuze describes it: just as "learning to swim" occurs when "a body combines some of its own distinctive points with those of a wave" (Deleuze 1994: 23), identification occurs when the subject, sensing in its thought what Shelley called in his *Essay on Love* "the chasm of an insufficient void," links its own points of distinction to the ideal (*SPP* 170). In identifying, the subject does not "copy," "imitate," or "map" the ideal within itself; rather, by combining itself with the ideal, it creates new relations within itself.

Peacock and Shelley agreed that poetry linked the present and future, but where *The Four Ages of Poetry* represented the poet as a speculator who constrained the limits of the possible by cheating people of their time and utility, Shelley argued that poets brought the productive powers of the future into the present. In *A Defence of Poetry*, Shelley distinguished the effects of poetry from the effects encouraged by "the principle of Self, of which money is the visible incarnation," describing the latter as the "God and Mammon of the world" (*SPP* 293). Poetry achieves what Shelley believes paper money aims at but in fact limits, for poetry

> transmutes all that it touches, and every form moving within the radiance of its presence is changed by wondrous sympathy to an incarnation of the spirit which it breathes; its secret alchemy turns to potable gold the poisonous waters which flow from death through life...(*SPP* 295)

Shelley's alchemical terminology ("transmutation," "potable gold") allowed him to preserve the connection between material wealth and poetry, while at the same time distinguishing between the effects of sympathy (which could support repressive systems, such as that of the national debt) and identification (which enabled new systems of social relations). Poetic images facilitated identification by allowing the intuition of otherwise unseen forces; as a result, poetry could touch "every form moving within the radiance of its presence," turning those forms into an "incarnation of the spirit which it [poetry] breathes." Poetry did not provide an *escape* from the world of images and forms with which a given culture perceived itself, but it rather animated those forms in new ways by soliciting the powers of the future.

CONCLUSION: SHELLEY, TIME CONSCIOUSNESS, AND LITERARY CRITICISM

Shelley died shortly after composing *A Defence of Poetry*, but even as he was working on that text, the British government had begun to make good on its oft-repeated promise to require the Bank of England to return to "bullion." The Bank Restriction Act of 1797 had been renewed multiple times, but finally, in 1821, a schedule for the return to specie payments was established, and by 1823, British paper money could be once again redeemed for cash (Jenks 1927: 25–64; Hilton 1977: 31–170). Yet the return to a bullion standard did not immediately provide the financial stability for which government officials and investors had hoped, and it was gold itself that lay at the heart of a massive investment bubble that rocked England in 1824–25. In 1824, following several reductions of interest on government securities—which had the effect of increasing the amount of available capital in the domestic market—scores of newly formed joint-stock companies gathered up millions of pounds from hopeful investors (Jenks 1927: 53; Hilton 1977: 202–31). Yet as investors began to realize that many of these companies would never produce any return on investment, share prices fell quickly and drastically. The result was a crash that was arguably even more dramatic than the South Sea Company Bubble of a hundred years earlier, for the collapse of 1825 caused a series of country bank failures (Jenks 1927: 57; Hilton 1977: 202–31). Rather than stabilizing the speculative tendencies of an increasingly internationalized British system of finance, the return to gold highlighted the extent to which the unstable dynamics of state finance had become an intrinsic part of British economic and social systems. The bubble of 1825 may have marked the end of the Romantic era of state finance, but it did so by signaling what was to become a national intensification and global expansion of finance more generally (Arrighi 1994).

Precisely because Shelley developed his analysis of state finance within this period of transition between the Napoleanic war years and the emergence of Victorian finance, his approach contains numerous resources for contemporary literary and cultural critics interested in analyzing the dynamics of state finance and speculation from the eighteenth century to the present. Most significant among these resources is Shelley's analysis of time consciousness as the key to the system of state finance. As both Hume and later phenomenologists have pointed out, consciousness of the present must be grounded in retention and protention, and Shelley reminds us that these three aspects of time consciousness can be linked by two different modes of "necessity." In his analysis of the national debt and paper money, Shelley suggested that state finance depended upon, and also perpetuated through technical means, "savage" time consciousness, which determined the link between past and future as one of causal necessity. Financial speculation depended upon precisely the capacity of savage time consciousness to plot out multiple possible and probable futures, demanding that each investor base decisions in the present upon predictions about the possible futures of British companies, currency flows, and government stability. Shelley's critique of savage time consciousness was that it treated the present and future as simply modalities of the past: that is, the present and future were limited to the development of causes located in the past. What Shelley called a "philosophic" sense of necessity, by contrast, located the origin of the future in the present, rather than the past, and sought to enable potentials, rather than plotting probabilities.

Shelley's approach to time consciousness reveals some of the limits of contemporary literary critical analyses of the emergence and development of state finance in the eighteenth and nineteenth centuries. In his influential analysis of the early eighteenth-century British "Financial Revolution," intellectual historian J.G.A. Pocock argued that state finance secured the stability of the state by locating this stability in an ever-retreating future. Insofar as "[g]overnment stock is a promise to repay at a future date... [which] will in reality never be reached," then postfinancial revolution governments were "maintained by the investor's imagination concerning a moment which will never exist in reality," and the investing citizen of the new economy "does not even live in the present, except as constituted by his fantasies concerning a future" (Pocock 1985: 112). Shelley's analysis of the national debt and paper money demonstrates that Pocock's claim about the role of the future in an investing society, while accurate in a limited sense, risks missing the far more significant transformations of time consciousness encouraged by state finance. We could just as easily say, Shelley suggests, that the stability of a government supported by state finance is located not in the future, but in the *past*, for the "promissory" structures of national debts and paper money subordinate the future to an irrevocable event in the past (the promise of legislators to repay financiers). This apparently paradoxical capacity of state finance to locate stability in *both* the future *and* the past can be understood only on the basis of a more thorough understanding of time consciousness than either Pocock or the literary critics who have followed his lead have provided.

Shelley's approach also suggests a different way of understanding relationships between finance and literature. As I noted in the introduction to this book, literary critics have struggled to theorize the relationships between the system of state finance and the systems of literature, and have sometimes risked mistaking system resonance for system identity. The desire to interpret eighteenth-century and Romantic era systems of literature and systems of state finance as virtual parts of one another results, I suggest, from a tendency to see *narrative* and *representation* as the primary media and means of the effects of literature. Such a tendency is by no means unwarranted, of course, and eighteenth-century readers no doubt engaged literature in large part by representing narratives to themselves. Such representations, as critics such as Sandra Sherman, James Thompson, and Ian Baucom have noted, require a series of operations—"modeling"; location of "the average"; plotting of probabilities—that demand a consciousness of time analogous to that which dominates the realm of finance. Yet Shelley's work on images suggests that narrative and representation are only one of the ways in which readers engage with literature, and if we hope to understand the *potential* of literary works—the points at which they bring the constrained futures of finance under the sway of a more powerful and open future—we should look not to narratives and representation, but to images. This is by no means advocacy for a return to the New Critical understanding of the image—that "rich" image that, though closed from history, somehow managed to reveal (and limit us to) "our humanity"—but rather a suggestion that we attend to those aspects of literary texts that demanded the emergence of a new (and possibly even a-human) consciousness of time.

Conclusion
State finance, systems, and literary criticism

The restructuring of British state finance during the Napoleonic Wars and in the post-Waterloo period significantly altered both British society and international relations. The wars themselves established the centrality of finance to modern conflict: as Burke had predicted in 1790, the war against France was in part a contest of systems of finance, and the British system—despite the massive debt and suffering to which it led in the post-Waterloo period—won out. The war allowed British financiers to establish London as the financial clearing house of Europe, and the great financial families and firms of the nineteenth century, such as the Rothschilds and Barings, came to prominence as war debt brokers (Hilton 1977; Arrighi 1994: 166–71). In the immediate post-Waterloo period, these firms also helped establish British finance as one of the key mechanisms of global relations, as British financiers (with the implicit approval of the British government) loaned money to the new revolutionary governments in Spain, Chile, Peru, Buenos Aires, Mexico, Guatemala, and Greece.[1] In addition, the Napoleonic Wars propelled the so-called Industrial Revolution and the division of labor upon which industrialism came to depend. Cheap credit and strong government demand for iron products during the wars with France had encouraged the creation of factories, but as these latter were idled following the war, industrialists sought out new markets (Arrighi 1994: 159–61). Finally, by the 1820s, the press—especially in the form of the *Edinburgh Review*, but also by means of dailies such as the *Morning Chronicle* and *The Times*—had come to play an increasingly central role in the dissemination of the idea that "economics were inseparable from the problems of the day" (Poovey 2003: 27; see also Parsons 1989: 20).

Yet if the basic structures of Victorian finance were in place by the end of the 1820s, so too were the conditions for the eventual "flight" of capital away from Britain and toward the United States. While the increased credit available to British merchants and manufacturers during the Napoleonic Wars initiated an expansion of capital goods markets, domestic demand for such products leveled off by the 1840s, and British manufacturers had to search abroad for new markets (Arrighi 1994: 161). While this had the effect of further "globalizing" the world economy in a way that strengthened the financial position of London, it also eventually led to the

"Great Depression" of 1873–96. As Arrighi notes, "the great expansion of world trade of the middle of the nineteenth century, like all the phases of material expansion of previous systemic cycles of accumulation [i.e., the phases of material expansion in sixteenth-century Genoa and seventeenth-century Netherlands]...led to a system-wide intensification of competitive pressures" (Arrighi 1994: 164). As worldwide competition in goods production increased, profits decreased, which produced a late nineteenth- and early twentieth-century "'precautionary' or 'speculative' withdrawal of cash flows from trade" and into purely financial instruments (Arrighi 1994: 171, 221). London financial houses such as the Rothschilds and Barings remained central during this period of high finance, but both the armaments race that led up to the First World War—and the war itself—signaled the shift of the center of finance from the City to Wall Street.

In the twentieth- and twenty-first centuries, finance, both in the form of state securities and private speculative instruments, has played an ever-more important role in the global economy. While a few tens of thousands of Britons invested in securities in the eighteenth century, closer to a hundred thousand Britons were investors in the late nineteenth, and by the end of the twentieth century, millions of Britons and Americans are directly tied into financial markets (Dickson 1967: 250; Michie 1999: 72). Extremely sensitive and speculative finance instruments, such as hedge funds and futures, have become an increasingly common and important part of global trade, and the expansion of credit instruments such as house mortgages, pension plans, credit cards, and payday loans means that even individuals who do not directly invest in state or private securities are nevertheless linked to the movements of high finance.[2] Speculative capital also increasingly determines the care of human bodies, as many medical protocols, as well as biotech start-up funding, become tied to speculative investment structures (Cooper 2006; Waldy and Mitchell 2006).

The contemporary importance of finance highlights the need for concepts and approaches adequate for understanding the social implications and logic of speculation. For the last part of the nineteenth, and almost all of the twentieth century, finance and speculation were generally understood as falling within the domain of "economics," and thus as topics inaccessible to nonspecialists.[3] At the same time, the implicit promise of mastery that would result from such specialization has not been borne out, for while sophisticated information technologies now allow "finance organisations [to] marshall mountains of data" in order to "rationally" predict whether fiduciary promises will be kept, an increase in information has not led to any greater control over speculation. As Jocelyn Pixley notes, "the major problem with data is that it can only describe the past; it cannot predict the future; promises may be broken, wealth creation may not eventuate" (Pixley 2004: 16).

This book is part of a larger project of "new economic literary criticism" that implicitly contests the purported disciplinary specificity of topics such as finance and speculation. If such a project is necessarily inter- or multidisciplinary, this methodological flexibility is assisted in part by the disciplinarily vexed nature of many Romantic era texts.[4] While the process of disciplinarity had already begun in the eighteenth century, discussion about the causes and effects of state finance was not rigidly parsed into any one discourse, and eighteenth- and early nineteenth-century authors debated the causes and effects of finance and credit in a wide array of genres, discourse, and modes, inventing many ways of understanding the logics of speculation. To recall again André Orléan's observation, finance "transform[s] our manner of conceiving of life in common" (Orléan 1999: 14; my translation), and eighteenth- and early nineteenth-century British commentators contested with one another the terms by—and genres and discourses within—which this new speculative "life in common" should be described. Should one begin with the premise of the self-interested, rational individual willing to place "faith" in his fellows, as the Edinburgh political economists (following the Adam Smith of the *Wealth of Nations*) suggested? Or should one begin with the premise—common to both Hume and Shelley—that the epistemological condition of possibility of state finance was an affective openness that was prior—and by no means limited—to the "subject" upon which state finance depended? Did state finance encourage the formation of autonomous subsystems that extended the powers of rational control over social life, or did it instead encourage the formation of social systems that bound us every more firmly to the past?

As I noted in the introduction, my readings of texts by Hume, Wordsworth, Shelley, and others are indebted to earlier accounts of linkages between eighteenth-century poetry and novels and institutions of credit and state finance, but my methodological focus on the relationship between social systems and theories of sympathy points toward different avenues of future research. Earlier literary critical approaches often focused on ways that eighteenth- and nineteenth-century novels, poems, and sentimental moral philosophy perpetuated subjective illusions of continuity and stability even as they also transformed social systems (by, for example, providing psychological "balance" in the face of anxiety over social change, or by forging new modes of subjectivity and social practices suited to a world of credit). While I also see "system stabilization" as an important function of literature, I have tended to emphasize the often unrealized potentials of such literature; that is, those elements that did not perform "ideological work," but rather pointed—and continue to point—toward modes of speculation that operate beyond, or before, financial investment (for example, Hume's distinction between the founding convention and the promise, Rousseau's attempt to develop a haptopraxology able to account for an "energetic" mode of identification, and Ann Yearsley's interest in inspiring sympathy by means of *non*-"typical" images). Such an emphasis points not so much to the ways that literature maintains social systems, but rather to its speculative moment, when it parasites existing social systems in order to bend the elements of the latter toward a system yet to come.

Notes

Introduction

1. "Irrational exuberance and "millennial dreams" are the titles of two recent books (Shiller 2005; Smith 1997), while the phrase "collective folly" appears in Henwood 2003: 1.
2. The anonymous author of the broadsheet *A Curious Calculation on the National Debt* argued that the imaginatively excessive nature of the national debt could be highlighted by translating the sums owed into physical terms: if the debt were "counted in shillings," it would take a man "269 years, 219 days, and 20 hours!" to count the whole, and it would take 1,258,064 men to carry the entire sum from London to York (Anon. 1817?).
3. I am thus employing the notion of a "long Romanticism" proposed by Clifford Siskin in Siskin 1998a: 10.
4. I also draw on a series of both old and newer articles that focus on links between eighteenth-century finance and literature, including Hentzi 1993, Markley 1995, Mulcaire 1999, and Moore 2002.
5. For other wide-ranging, and important, discussions of literature and finance, see Poovey 1998 and Baucom 2005. For discussions of Victorian finance and literature, see Poovey 2003: 1–37; Knezevic 2003; Houston 2005; and the "Victorian Investments" Special Issue of *Victorian Studies: An Interdisciplinary Journal of Social, Political, and Cultural Studies* 45:1 (2002).
6. Many of these studies focus on the importance of finance for P. B. Shelley's prose writings (e.g., Cameron 1943: 197–209 and 1974: 137–40; Hogle 1988: 234–59; Cox 1998: 187–225; Chandler 1999: 82–86). I have particularly benefited from Alan Liu's treatment of debt and speculation in Wordsworth's poetry (Liu 1989: 311–58), Peter de Bolla's discussion of the national debt and the sublime (de Bolla 1989), Esther H. Schor's reading of the "paper money economics" of Adam Smith's theory of sympathy in (Schor 1994: 24–40), Jerome Christensen's analysis of the "Dark Romanticism" that emerged in the *Edinburgh Review* (Christensen 2000: 107–28), Gillian Russell's discussion of the link between "Faro banks" and the Bank of England during the currency crisis of 1797 (Russell 2000), and Phillip Connell's reading of the relationship between "political economy" and "Romanticism" (Connell 2001).
7. My discussion of this challenge faced by new historicist critics interested in finance draws on Jameson 1993: 181–259.
8. As I note in the coda to chapter 2, Slavoj Žižek's Lacanian Marxism, especially as articulated in *The Sublime Object of Ideology* (1989) and *Tarrying with the Negative* (1993) has been particularly important for literary critics

interested in relationships between finance and literature; see, e.g., Thompson 1996, Brantlinger 1996, Mulcaire 1999, and Baucom 2005.

9. My point is not that psychoanalytic theories of the subject *cannot* provide such a metatheory, but rather that advocates of this approach bear the burden of proof of explaining why theories that position subjectivity as fundamentally imaginative are exempt from the class interests that determine other social theories, such as those of political economy. For a related critique of identification—"the modern term for what we do with characters"—as a category that "obscures the historical specificity, the relative novelty, of our codes of reading," see Lynch 1998: 10. I am also indebted to Forest Pyle's reading of the social functions Romantic era theories of the imagination performed for their readers—most fundamentally, the function of "making a linkage, an articulation" (Pyle 1995: 2)—but my account proposes a different methodological framework for understanding these functions (and suggests as well that many of the functions that Pyle attributes to late eighteenth- and early nineteenth-century authors were already present in the early eighteenth-century texts).
10. Classic Marxist work on financial capitalism includes Marx 1977: 914–26 and Hilferding 1981; see also the survey of the roles of finance capital in Marxist theory in Ingham 1984: 17–39, and the entries for "Finance Capital," "finance capital," and "financial capital and interest" in Bottomore 1991. For Marxist literary criticism that is explicitly critical of interest in finance, see Jameson 1993: 181–259, but see also Jameson's more recent reassessment of the importance of finance capitalism, Jameson 1997.
11. For other critical accounts of (primarily contemporary) finance and economics that draw on Luhmann, see Lash and Urry 1994: 42, 253; Leyshon and Thrift 1997: 304–5; Jessop 2002: 192–222; Daly 2004. Accounts of eighteenth-century and British Romantic literature that draw on Luhmann include Kaufmann 1995, Poovey 1998, and Burgess 2000: 10–16.
12. For an alternative account of the rise of disciplines, see Siskin 1998a.
13. In "The Year of the System," Siskin outlines a threefold typology that corresponds roughly to my first, third, and fourth meanings above. However, insofar as Siskin is primarily interested in the development of the fourth meaning—"The System"—he devotes less attention to the use of this term to describe institutions designed to achieve practical results (Siskin 1998b).
14. For discussion of the system by means of which loan rates were determined, publicized, collected, and interest returned, see Dickson 1967: 79, 83 and Neal 1990a: 15. For figures on number of investors, see Dickson 1967: 249–303. To take a representative example, Dickson notes that in 1737, an eighteenth-century commentator estimated about 25,000 investors in state finance in a population of 10 million (Dickson 1967: 250).
15. Luhmann notes that the concept of "closed" systems functioned as a "limit case" for an older school of systems theory, which understood these as "systems for which the environment has no significance," or is significant only through extremely constrained channels (Luhmann 1995: 7; see also 204). While I follow Luhmann in using the concept of autonomy rather than closure to describe the reality of social systems, I occasionally employ the term "closed" when it helps to articulate eighteenth-century and nineteenth-century *perceptions* of systems. So, for example, even if the system of early eighteenth-century public credit was in fact an autonomous system, it often appeared to early eighteenth-century observers as though it were "closed."
16. The system of economy, for example, "is continually concerned with gaining time and forming capital so that it can have time available at all times.

Thus the system develops its own future/past perspectives, its own temporal horizons and temporal urgency. One cannot simply assume that this system-time accords with the temporality of the processes in the ecological or even the social environment of the system" (Luhmann 1989: 57). For Luhmann's reflections on the temporality of systems, see Luhmann 1982: 202–48 and 1995: 41–52, 278–357.

17. For Luhmann's discussion of figures of autonomy as signifiers of new systems, see Luhmann 1986: 64.
18. This concept of crisis connects the financial sense of speculation with G.W.F. Hegel's philosophical conception of the term. In the *Logic*, Hegel suggested that both "matrimonial" and "commercial speculation" were simply special cases of the speculative tendencies of *Geist* itself; all forms of speculation depend upon a "dialectical" moment, in which "what is immediately at hand has to be passed and left behind," but the properly speculative moment goes beyond negation to instantiate a new positive content within reality. So, for example, in the case of commercial speculation, speculators do not limit themselves to imagining new systems, but seek actually to bring them into existence: "the subject-matter of such speculations, though in the first place only subjective, must not remain so, but be realized or translated into objectivity" (Hegel 1975: 120).
19. For Simondon's account of affect, see Simondon 1964: 11–14, 148–52. For Deleuze's account of affect (which draws on Simondon's), see Deleuze 1991: 103, Deleuze and Guattari 1987: 258–62 and 1994: 163–99. Other useful accounts of affect include Massumi 2002: 23–45 and Hansen 2004a and 2004b.
20. Anderson tied the emergence of the nation as "imagined community" specifically to the spread of print media (Anderson 1991), but subsequent critics have tended to see the connection between nations and imaginary communities in more generic terms. Patrick Brantlinger notes that most contemporary theories of nationalism and imperialism, "no matter what the perspective or methodology...are agreed in understanding these phenomena as ideologies, hence as versions of belief or imagination" (Brantlinger 1996: 11).
21. See, for example, David Marshall's suggestion that when eighteenth-century "moral philosophers, aestheticians, novelists, and protopsychologists" used the term "sympathy," what they really meant was "an act of identification in which one left one's own place, part, and person and took the place and part of someone else" (Marshall 1988: 146).

Chapter 1

1. For representative examples of these positions, see Anderson 1991; Boltanski 1999; Butler 1993: 93–120. Boltanski in fact explicitly positions Smith as a theoretical precursor of his project of understanding "distant suffering" in the context of mass media.
2. The emergent nature of this understanding of the imagination has been explicitly recognized in the case of Rousseau; as Trousson and Eigeldiner note, Rousseau was not only "one of the first French authors to analyze the different facets of the imagination in an exhaustive manner," but one of the first to extend its reach to all forms of sociality ("Imagination" in Trousson and Eigeldinger 1996: 436).
3. For discussions of pre-seventeenth-century theories of the imagination, see Bundy 1927; Anderson 1927; Starobinski 1970: 177–189; and Huet 1993: 1–63. For discussions of the transition from scholastic to seventeenth-century

conceptions of the imagination, see Rousseau 1969; Eigeldinger 1962: 21–46; Todd 1995: 52–63 and 96–101; and Bond 1935. For eighteenth-century theories of the imagination, see Starobinski, Eigeldinger, and Todd (cited above), as well as Engell 1981 and Wasserman 1947.

4. On the physiology of the imagination in the seventeenth and eighteenth centuries, see Todd 1995: 52–63.
5. For discussion of the role of the imagination in the natural magic tradition to which Bacon referred, see Couliano 1987: 87–106.
6. On the role of "enthusiasm" in the seventeenth and eighteenth centuries, see Manuel 1983: 34–51; Heyd 1995; Klein and La Vopa 1998; Morillo 2001; Todd 1995: 64–105; Mee 2003; and Frank 2005.
7. Though Hobbes's philosophy presented a remarkably far-reaching and developed conception of the role of the imagination in social relationships, the form in which these reflections were cast—systematic treatises that sought to employ a "geometrical" method of reasoning—discouraged significant uptake of these claims about the imagination. As Steven Shapin and Simon Schaffer have stressed in their discussion of the debate between Hobbes and Robert Boyle over "experimental" natural philosophy, texts such as *Human Nature* and *Leviathan* (1651) were explicitly designed to counter the differentiation of society into autonomous social systems—whether these were the social systems of "priests" or those of "experimentalists"—for Hobbes believed that "civil war and confusion" were the inevitable results of "allow[ing] authority and power in the state to be fragmented and dispersed among professional groups each claiming its share" (Shapin and Schaffer 1985: 97). Recalling Luhmann's distinction between stratified and functionally differentiated societies, we can say that Hobbes set himself the difficult, if not impossible, task of developing a philosophy that would transform a society increasingly characterized by functional differentiation into a stratified society, unified under a single sovereign. The "absolutist" nature of Hobbes's writings thus presented his reader with an all-or-nothing choice: either accept, or reject, the "proofs" of the text in their entirety. While few historians now subscribe to the view that the only real impact of Hobbes's absolutist political philosophy was "the widespread re-assertion of accepted principles," it was nevertheless the case that his various claims were more frequently rejected than adopted, and this was true of Hobbes's theory of imagination as well (Bowle 1951: 43, cited in Skinner 1966: 286). For assessments of seventeenth- and eighteenth-century reactions to Hobbes's philosophy, see Skinner 1966 and 1993, and Lamprecht 1993.
8. We might see Bernard Mandeville's combination of satirical verse and philosophical notes as an attempt to present the Hobbesian system in a form more amenable to widespread reception. We can thus see in Hobbes's interest in the imagination the paradigm for what Mandeville called the "imaginary general equivalent" that was able to transmute self-love into the love of others, thereby creating polities ("An Enquiry into the Origin of Moral Virtue" [1714] in Mandeville 1988, vol. 1: 42).
9. In *An Essay upon Reason, and the Nature of Spirits* (1694), Richard Burthogge provided the schema for this sort of claim, arguing that the group phenomena that characterized enthusiasm "must be reckon'd an effect of Sympathy, and not of *intellectual Apprehension*; I mean, they [the enthusiasts] understand one another not *judiciously*, by conceiving; that is, by framing clear and consistent Notions of what is said, but only *sympathetically*, by having, upon such Expressions some Notions, and consequent Thoughts, excited in them, that are conformable to theirs that use the Expressions: it

being with *Enthusiasts*, who possess the same Frame and texture of mind, as with *unison Lutes*, or other *Instruments* fitly tuned; in which to touch one, is to affect and stir all within a convenient distance" (Burthogge 1694: 44). As in the case of More, Burthogge wavered between a materialist explanation of influence (highlighted by his metaphor of the tuned string) and an explanation that focused on the role of representations.

10. In France, Blaise Pascal also had hinted that the imagination might be central to political life. In fragments nos. 303 and 304 of the posthumously organized *Pensées*, for example, Pascal suggested that communities originally emerged through acts of force and violence, but later the imagination served as the "binding" force of social ties, such that "these ropes that attach respect to such and such a person in particular, are thus imaginary cords, cords of the imagination" (Pascal 1897: 472; translation from Keohane 1980: 269). However, as Keohane notes, the extent of Pascal's influence in the eighteenth century is difficult to determine, in part because of the very abridged versions of the *Pensées* that circulated in that century (Keohane 1980: 265, 294). For a study of the versions of the *Pensées* extant in the eighteenth century, see Vamos 1974.
11. Even into the first two decades of the eighteenth century, the British government continued to overcome "its [financial] difficulties by offering its creditors exclusive rights to some region of finance or trade, in return for a reduction in the rate of interest and the advance of further moneys" (Ashton 1959: 118); this was the origin, for example, not only of the Bank of England, but also of the New East India Company (1698) and the South Sea Company (1711).
12. As Larry Neal notes, stock listings were not consistent, with John Freke's *Price of All Stocks* suggesting a high point of £1050 per share on June 24, 1720, while John Castaing, Jr.'s *Course of the Exchange* indicates a peak of £950 per share on July 1, 1720 (Neal 1990a: 101).
13. For more extended discussions of the premises and goals of these "capital satires" of the early eighteenth century, see Nicholson 1994 and Moore 2002.
14. For more complete explications of this sense of information as a field of choices, see Rasch 2000: 52–69 and Mitchell and Thurtle 2003: 6–10.
15. Seventeenth-century economic theory is described by Vicker 1959; Letwin 1963; Appelby 1978; and Finkelstein 2000. Terence Hutchison notes that the 1690s "might well be regarded as the *major* concentrated burst of development in the history of the subject [of economics]" (Hutchison 1988: 56). For the distinction between late seventeenth-century "political arithmetic" and eighteenth-century "political economy," see Poovey 1998: 93–143, 214–63.
16. While most recent commentators are in agreement that the development of political economy depended upon the production of abstractions that would serve as objects of analysis, there is less agreement about the precise nature of those abstractions. I am convinced by Schabas's claim that the abstraction of "the economy"—understood as a "distinct entity...subject, not to natural processes, but to the operation of human laws and agency" (Schabas 2005: 2)—did not emerge until the mid-nineteenth century, but I also agree with Poovey's suggestion that "the market" functioned for political economists as a "system" that could be analyzed without extensive analysis of human psychology (Poovey 1998).
17. In the context of finance, the distinction between early eighteenth-century "moral" readings of investment and midcentury "objective" readings is exemplified by the contrast between Daniel Defoe's *The Anatomy of Exchange Alley* (1719), which sought to expose stock-jobbing as "a compleat System

of Knavery" and an "Original System of Cheat and Delusion" that depended upon "imaginary Terrors" (Defoe 1719: 3, 7, 3–4) and Thomas Mortimer's *Every Man His Own Broker* (1761), which actually described in great detail the system by means of which stocks and government securities could be bought and sold.

18. For accounts of the emergence of political economy as a system of communication that reflects on "the economy," see Luhmann 1982: 190–225; 1995: 453–55, 461–62; 1999; Brantlinger 1996: 7, 33–34; Siskin 1998a: 44–53. William Letwin's more traditional account of the rise of economics also describes it in terms of the emergence of a "system," though he uses that latter term to describe a collection of "a small number of principles" that possess explanatory power, rather than in Luhmann's sense of a linkage of communications (Letwin 1963: viii).
19. For accounts of the rise of "conservative" political philosophy, see Quinton 1978 and O'Gorman 1986. My thanks to Katey Kuhns Castellano for her help on the question of eighteenth-century conservativism.
20. For examples of Bolingbroke's reading of the South Sea Company as a conspiracy, see, for example, *The Craftsman* for December 19, 1726, January 16, 1727, January 23, 1727, September 7, 1728, January 24, 1730, and April 8, 1732. For discussion of the authorship of the articles in *The Craftsman*, see Kramnick 1968: 273–74 note 43.
21. While I agree with Brantlinger's suggestion that eighteenth-century "counterdiscourses that attacked public credit... and the national debt"—that is, the "counterdiscourses" of Bolingbroke, Swift, and Pope—"were politically reactionary or 'residual' rather than 'emergent'" (Brantlinger 1996: 6), it is vital not to confuse interests with discourses. While Bolingbroke, Swift, and Pope were clearly defending what they understood as a traditional order, their defenses of this order established a new form of discourse, that of political "conservatism."
22. For discussion of Hutcheson's political allegiances, see Robbins 1959: 7–10, 185–96 and Winch 1978: 46.
23. For discussion of both the 1734 Act against stock-jobbing and the financial dimensions of the War of Jenkin's Ear (1739–42), see Dickson 1967: 518–19, 67.
24. For discussion of Hume's obsession with factions (and the ways they might be avoided) see Phillipson 1989: 17–34.
25. For discussions of Hume's notion of the imagination, see Wilbanks 1968 and Deleuze 1991: 55–72.
26. Hume contended that even the "generosity" to which sympathy can lead is not in itself a good thing: while "generosity must be acknowledg'd to the honour of human nature, we may at the same time remark, that so noble an affection, instead of fitting me for large societies, is almost contrary to them, as the most narrow selfishness" (*T* 487).
27. In *Leviathan*, Hobbes contended that "in the nature of man, we find three principal causes of quarrel. First, competition; secondly, diffidence; thirdly, glory." The latter cause of quarrel encouraged individuals to resort to violence "for reputation," and "for trifles, as a word, a smile, a different opinion, and any other sign of undervalue, either direct in their persons, or by reflection in their kindred, their friends, their nation, their profession, or their name" (Hobbes 1966, vol. 3: 112).
28. Hume did not claim that the sense of self can occur *only* in reference to others; as is evident from his analyses in book 1 of the *Treatise*, a sense of self can occur in isolation as well. However, Hume suggests that the sense of self only

becomes "practical"—that is, bound to actions—when it emerges in tandem with the sense of the other.

29. Forbes also cites C. W. Hendel's claim that, for Hume, sympathy "brings the thoughts and feelings and activities of different persons into unison, before they ever understand the grounds of their community with each other" (Hendel 1983: 264; cited in Forbes 1975: 105–6). While I agree with the tenor of Hendel's claim, it is important to note that "unison" does not necessarily mean, nor does it necessarily result in, "pacific harmony."
30. Jerome Christensen has argued that Hume's account of sympathy depends upon the metaphor of theater to "legitimate" this transfer of sentiments from one person to another; that is, for Hume, "[s]ympathy is theft. Or would be theft were it not that every feeling occurs in a 'kind of theatre'.... The theater, like sympathy at large, works as an implicit guarantor of property rights because appropriation conventionalized is not the theft of property but its transfer" (Christensen 1987: 72). I am persuaded by Pinch that Christensen's reading overemphasizes the importance of the trope of theater to the *Treatise* in general and to Hume's account of sympathy in particular. Hume compares the mind to a theater only once, in Book 1, which makes it difficult to justify the link Christensen proposes between the conventions of theater and the conventions of property exchange (Pinch 1996: 198 note 17).
31. Other discussions of the gift include Bataille 1991; Bourdieu 1977; Derrida 1992; Weiner 1992; and Frow 1997: 102–217.
32. For Mauss, the circulation of gifts could escalate into competitive displays of "generosity" that ended in violence (Mauss 1990: 37ff.).
33. While "phase shift" is of course an anachronistic term, developed by twentieth-century physicists to describe the transformation of quantitative into qualitative differences in matter (e.g., the transformation of liquid water into ice), it nevertheless captures well Hume's emphasis on the importance of qualitative shifts to an understanding of the emergence of social systems. As I will note below, the shift from the individual to the family, or the family to small groups, is not primarily a function of the addition of individuals, but instead depends upon structural changes in the systems that bind these individuals together. For an application of the concept of phase shifts to human groups, see Simondon 1964 and 1989.
34. Annette Baier reads the "new tye" that enables the family as a specific species of passion, which she describes as "family feeling," and which she understands as distinct from sympathy (Baier 1982: 648). Hume does not himself mention family feeling, but in any case, it is sympathy that underwrites the affective relations of the parents and children toward one another. For other readings of the role of the family in Hume's *Treatise*, see Forbes 1975: 70–71, 79; Baier 1980 and 1982; and Deleuze 1991: 39–40.
35. Hume distinguished between "three different species of goods": (1) "internal satisfaction of our mind," (2) "the external advantages of our body," and (3) "the enjoyment of such possessions as we have acquir'd by our industry and good fortune" (*T* 487). The first type of good cannot become a source of conflict, for it cannot be stolen from us, while the second, though it can be "ravish'd" from us, cannot be used by the ravisher. Social conflict thus revolves around the third species of property.
36. As Christensen notes, Hume questioned the zero-sum logic of critics such as Bolingbroke. Against a mercantilist understanding of commerce, in which a gain for one party entailed a loss for another, Hume contended that every gain was beneficial for the system of economy (and thereby society) as a whole. This held true even if systemic gain was not "immediately perceptible

to both members in the exchange," that is, even if both parties felt that one had lost and the other won. The belief in the possibility of one party losing "is not so much false as insufficiently true: the error lies in a narrowness or partiality that distorts perception and thereby thwarts the smooth operations of the greater economy" (Christensen 1987: 149). The form and content of Hume's *Treatise* was designed to produce precisely that sense of society *as* a system, for by means of this "systemic" perception, one could recognize individual losses as collective gains.

37. What I am calling open anticipation is structurally similar to what Hume describes as the "obligation" that arises out of love for others. In the case of "such persons as I love," I perform services as *gifts*; that is, without any expressed requirement that these others reciprocate (though they very well may) (*T* 521). In this case as well, the future actions of the minicommunity made of myself and those I love are not *bound* by my present actions, for these others can choose whether or not to reciprocate without any repercussions.
38. For discussion of the differences between Hume's conceptions of sympathy in the *Treatise* and *Enquiry*; see Kemp-Smith 1960: 150–52; Stewart 1963: 329; Whelan 1985: 160, 169; Abramson 2000).
39. For readings of Hume as a "liberal," see Stewart 1992 and (arguably) Forbes 1975; for interpretations of Hume as a conservative, see Miller 1981, Livingston 1984, and Whelan 1985. Other ideological readings in this vein include Winch 1978; Livingston 1984; and Pocock 1985.
40. See also Kramnick 1968, as well as Dumont 1977 (though Hume is mentioned only in passing) and Christensen 1987: 34ff. (which is more poststructuralist than Marxist).

Chapter 2

1. For discussion of Rousseau's theory of pity, see Wolker 1974; Catherine Kintzler's Introduction in Rousseau 1993: 12–24; Marshall 1988: 135–77; Starobinski 1988: 281–322; Derrida 1976: 97–100 and 165–268. Force 1997 is one of the few readings to focus explicitly on Rousseau's theory of identification. However, where Force emphasizes "the relationship between self-love, identification, and commerce" (Force 1997: 49), I focus more narrowly on the link between Rousseau's theories of imagination and identification and the speculative logic that motivates the economic subsystem of state finance.
2. Readings of Smith that focus on the politics of the Scottish Enlightenment include Winch 1978 and Lawrence 1979. For discussion of Smith in the context of theatricality, see Marshall 1986: 167–92. For the impact of French sentimental literature on the successive editions of *The Theory of Moral Sentiments*, see Dawson 1991. On Smith and bourgeois ideology, see Eagleton 1990: 37–39 and Ellison 1999: 1–12, 69–72.
3. Only eight copies of Dupin's initial *Réflexions sur quelques parties d'un livre intitulé 'De l'esprit des loix'* were printed, apparently because Dupin stopped the production process so that he could revise these *Réflexions* into his *Observations* (Cranston 1983: 213). For the question of Rousseau's collaboration on the *Réflexions* and *Observations*, see François 1943–45; Shackleton 1980; Cranston 1983: 213–14.
4. "Tax farming" refers to the state practice of subcontracting the collection of taxes to private individuals who guaranteed the state a fixed sum, the tax "farmer" retaining as profit whatever was collected over that amount. For an account of eighteenth-century tax farming in France, see Matthews 1958.

5. Dickson notes that this equation between France's ability to pay off its debts and to "give the Law" to Europe was a constantly reiterated topos in Britain since at least 1711 (Dickson 1967: 22–23).
6. For other early comments on finance and commerce, see the heading "Économie et Finances" in *OCR*, vol. 3: 525–26.
7. Discussions of Rousseau's theory of the imagination include Derrida 1976: 171–92; Robinson 1984: 133–65; and "Imagination" in Trousson and Eigeldinger 1996: 436–38.
8. Rousseau did not publish his *Essay*. For dating of this text, see Kintzler's Introduction to Rousseau 1993: 5–12; Starobinski in *OCR*, vol. 5: cxcvii–cciv; Wolker 1974: 222–23 note 182; and Derrida 1976: 171ff.
9. In *Emile,* Rousseau translated his species-historical thesis into individual-biographical terms, arguing that the imagination of children is not "lit" until they are teenagers; as a result, children do not begin to identify with anyone until that late age (*Emile* 222–23; *OCR*, vol. 4: 505–6).
10. As Force has demonstrated, "identification" and "pity" are completely distinct terms in Rousseau's vocabulary (Force 1997), but unfortunately this distinction has been obscured in otherwise reliable reference guides, such as Trousson and Eigeldinger *Dictionnaire de Jean-Jacques Rousseau* (Trousson and Eigeldinger 1996), Fauconnier's *Le vocabulaire pédagogique de J.-J. Rousseau* (Fauconnier 1993), and Bourez *et al.*'s *Le Vocabulaire du sentiment dans l'oeuvre de J.-J. Rousseau* (Bourez *et al.* 1980). The distinction between pity and identification in Rousseau's thought is noted in Robinson 1984: 133–34, and generally observed, if not specifically marked, in Derrida 1976: 171–92 and Markovits 1986: 57–95. Starobinski also briefly refers to Rousseau's "Théorie de l'identification" in a note to Rousseau's *Letter to M. D'Alembert on the Theater* (*OCR*, vol. 5: 1333).
11. Rousseau distinguished self-preservation (*amour de soi*) from egoistic self-love (*amour propre*), arguing that the former, natural mode of self-love does not require any *consciousness* of self, but is simply that feeling for self that impels natural man to eat, find shelter, and have sex. Egoistic self-love (*amour propre*), by contrast, occurs only within society, and involves a representation of oneself to oneself. The passion of self-preservation explains our natural relationship to ourselves, and pity explains our natural relationship to others, for pity can "mitigate, in certain circumstances, the ferocity of one's egocentrism [i.e., *amour propre*] or the desire for self-preservation [*amour de soi*] before this egocentrism came into being" (*BPW* 53; *OCR*, vol. 3: 154).
12. With the exception of Derrida's and Force's analyses, which I describe at more length below, most previous criticism that compares the *Essay* and the *Discourse* has focused on the concept of pity, rather than identification; see Espinas 1895; Masson 1913; Derathé 1950: 146 note 3; Starobinski in *OCR*, vol. 5: clxv–cxcvii; Wolker 1974: 223 note 182; and Marshall 1988: 150–51.
13. David Marshall develops a useful reading of Rousseau's discussion of recognition in the *Essay*, connecting this term to the categories of monstrosity and figural language that appear in Rousseau's account (Marshall 1988: 205–8).
14. Even in the *Essay*, Rousseau distinguished between perception and recognition, arguing that natural man first perceived other humans without recognizing them *as* others: "Upon encountering others, a natural man will at first be afraid. His fright will make him see those men as taller and stronger than himself. He will give them the name *Giants.* After many experiences he will recognize that…these supposed Giants are neither taller nor stronger than himself…. He will therefore invent another name common to them and to

him" (*Essay* 294–95; *OCR*, vol. 5: 381). Within Rousseau's system, natural man's initial misperception of others as giants is *not* an imaginatively generated error, for in his account, fear impinges on self-preservation (*amour de soi)* rather than egoistic self-love (*amour propre*) and desire, and only the latter mode of love is subject to imaginative distortions.

15. For Derrida's discussion of the distinctions between the voice and cry in Rousseau, see Derrida 1976: 195–200. See also Rousseau's discussion in *Emile* of the child's first language, which "is not articulate, but it is accented, sonorous, intelligible" (*Emile* 65; *OCR*, vol. 4: 285).
16. One must thus distinguish Rousseau's "natural instinct" from Francis Hutcheson's "natural, kind Instinct" which "hurries" people, without reflection, "to see Objects of Compassion, and expose themselves to this Pain when they can give no reason for it; as in the Instance of publick Executions" (Hutcheson 1729: 241). Rousseau's model of energetic identification is not fundamentally about *seeing*, but rather about *doing*.
17. For discussions of the medical concept of the *vis mediatrix naturae*, see Canguilhem 1994: 287–319 and Coulter 1973–77.
18. For a similar description of pity as the foundation of society, see Addison's and Steele's *Spectator* for June 5, 1712, in which Addison describes pity as "a kind of pleasing Anguish, as well as generous Sympathy, that knits Mankind together, and blends them in the same common Lot" (Addison and Steele 1965, vol. 3: 486), as well as the issue for September 1, 1714, in which Henry Grove claims that pity "arises on sight of Persons in Distress" (Addison and Steele 1965, vol. 5: 12).
19. For deconstructive readings of this conflict between the *Essay* and the *Discourse*, see Derrida 1976 and Force 1997.
20. For other accounts of the development of concepts of the republic of letters in France and Britain, see Eisenstein 1983: 99–102 and Christensen 1987: 120–200.
21. For discussion of the social and cultural dimensions of the Scottish Enlightenment, see Lawrence 1979; Phillipson 1981 and 1989; Hont and Ignatieff 1983; Sakamoto and Tanaka 2003.
22. In 1759, Smith wrote to Lord Shelburne of the "nobility" of the latter's method of introducing "arts, industry and independency" to Ireland, and complained that this method was not being pursued more assiduously in Scotland (*CAS* 32).
23. As a result of the central role played by sympathy in *The Theory of Moral Sentiments*, almost every discussion of Smith's text engages this term at length, which makes unfeasible a complete list of secondary sources. However, in addition to the sources cited in note 2 of this chapter, I have found particularly useful Lindgren 1973: 2–59 and Dwyer 1998.
24. Such claims had been made about banks and public credit earlier in the century: in the July 11, 1730 issue of *The London Journal*, for example, an anonymous author argued that it allowed "dead money to be gathered into stocks and [then be] made to circulate in the form of Bonds or notes" (cited in Kramnick 1968: 53).
25. While Smith left implicit the link between sympathy and economy in *The Theory of Moral Sentiments*, he explicitly articulated this connection in his *Lectures on Jurisprudence*, which he delivered in the early 1760s immediately following the publication of *The Theory of Moral Sentiments*. In a discussion of the origins of "testamentary property"—that is, goods passed from a dead parent to a living heir—Smith noted the peculiarity of this kind of property: "there is no extension of property so great as this...it was very

natural to give a man a right to dispose of his property while he lived, but a testament supposed him to dispose of a right when properly speaking he can have none himself [i.e., because he is dead]" (*LJ(B)* 165).Yet the willingness of the community to allow such transfers depends upon our ability to sympathize with the wishes of the dead parent. We "enter as it were into his dead body," Smith wrote, "and conceive what our living souls would feel if they were joined with his body, and how much we would be distressed to see our last injunctions not performed" (*LJ(B)* 165). What this limit case reveals, in short, is that both sympathy and property have their origins in precisely the same relationship to the dead.

26. Despite its important place in *The Theory of Moral Sentiments*, Smith's discussion of resentment has received less examination than one might expect. Useful studies of the role of this concept in Smith's work include Campbell 1971: 190–93, 211; Raphael 1972–73: 73–92; Haakonssen 1989: 63–65, 114–17; Berry 1997: 131–34; Dwyer 1998: 30 note 51; Salter 1999; Rosen 2000.
27. Smith called the "proper" object of gratitude *beneficence.* Unlike justice, beneficence is not vital for the maintenance of society. Thus, while we will always reward beneficence, we do not force people to be beneficent: beneficence is "always free, it cannot be extorted by force, [and] the mere want of it exposes to no punishment" (*TMS* 2.ii.1.3). "Society may subsist," Smith wrote, "though not in the most comfortable state, without beneficence; but the prevalence of injustice must utterly destroy it" (*TMS* 2.ii.3.3). Beneficence is the "ornament which embellishes, not the foundation which supports the building"; justice, on the other hand, "is the main pillar that upholds the whole edifice" (*TMS* 2.ii.3.4).
28. For a more extended discussion of the importance, and political background, of Smith's account of executions in the *Treatise*, see Mitchell 2003a.
29. For a concise overview of the pragmatics of executions in the eighteenth century, see McLynn 1992: 257–76; Linebaugh 1991; and McGowen 1987. Gatrell 1994 is an indispensable source for tracking the connections between theories of sympathy and executions, and Gatrell acknowledges the importance of Smith's theory of sympathy for subsequent British moral theory. Curiously, though, Gatrell cites Smith in connection with executions only once (Gatrell 1994: 37), which seems to be a function of the fact that Gatrell himself understands sympathy as a force that by its nature works *against* executions.
30. In his 1790 additions to *The Theory of Moral Sentiments*, Smith proposed another, less Hobbesian solution to the problems of violence engendered by sympathy, encouraging a practice of self-control in which each person habituated himself to sympathy with the impartial spectator. He described this practice of moral ascesis in terms of "identification," suggesting that the "man of real constancy and firmness" will develop the "habit" of regarding "whatever relates to him" through the eyes of the impartial spectator"; as a result, this constant and firm individual "almost identifies himself with, he almost becomes that impartial spectator" (*TMS* 2.iii.25). This unreciprocated process of "identifying" with the impartial spectator is strikingly similar to Smith's description of our relationship with the dead, suggesting that while the state initially served as the counterweight to the violence of sympathy for Smith, by 1790 he had glimpsed another solution, in which the subject (and its capacity for violence) could be suspended between two (forever unpayable) debts. My thanks to Alex Ruch for his comments on the differences between Smith's and Rousseau's theories of identification.
31. Borch-Jacobsen 1988 presents the most extended and rigorous account of identification as the aporetic center of Freudian psychoanalysis; see also

Lacoue-Labarthe 1989: 43–138 and Lacoue-Labarthe and Nancy 1979. Less critical accounts of the history and importance of identification for Freudian psychoanalysis are presented in Meissner 1970 and 1971; Wollheim 1974; Florence 1978; and Fuss 1995.

32. Freud first used the term "identification" (*sich identifizieren mit*) in the late 1890s, employing it as simply a diagnostic category that allowed him to determine the source of particular hysterical symptoms. In a letter dated December 6, 1896 and written to his friend Wilhelm Fliess, Freud explained the headaches of one of his female patients as the result of her identification with her brother, who also suffered from headaches; as a result of a connection she saw between herself and her brother, Freud wrote, "durfte sie sich mit ihm identifizieren, seinen Kopfschmerz übernehmen" ("she allowed herself to identify with him and assume his headaches") (Freud 1985a: 224; translation from Freud 1985b: 213). However, the term eventually shifted to the center of psychoanalysis, allowing Freud to explain even features of "normal" subjectivity, such as the development and resolution of the Oedipal complex, and the emergence of "group psychology."
33. *Group Psychology* was intended to prove that most social relations were in fact "group" phenomena, to distinguish the psychoanalytic category of "identification" from purportedly less theoretical alternatives such as "suggestion" and "sympathy," and to make manifest the utility of the concept of identification for the analysis of group phenomena. Thus, where an early twentieth-century theorist such as William McDougall focused on the "group mind" that purportedly emerged in extreme cases of group phenomena such as panic, and sought to explain such a group as the result of forces of "sympathy" (McDougall 1920: 36–43), Freud focused on "normal groups"—the church or army, for example—and argued that panic was not in fact a group phenomenon, but rather the result of the *loss* of bonds of identification. In Freud's account, the loss of a group leader meant the end of the group and the end of identification; if "an individual in panic fear begins to be solicitous on his own account," this was because "the emotional ties, which have hitherto made the danger seem small to him, have ceased to exist" (Freud 1953–1974, vol. 18: 96).
34. For examples of critics who rely on Žižek—especially *The Sublime of Object of Ideology* (1989)—see Markley 1995; Brantlinger 1996; Thompson 1996; and Mulcaire 1999.

Chapter 3

1. Following a number of recent critics, I generally use the term "antislavery," rather than "abolition." As David Brian Davis notes, "antislavery" is better able than "abolition" to capture the wide variety of goals of antislavery advocates. "Antislavery," Davis writes, can describe "an organized social force; political activity aimed at eradicating the slave trade or slavery itself; a set of moral and philosophic convictions that might be held with varying intensities; or simply the theoretical belief that Negro slavery is a wasteful, expensive, and dangerous system of labor which tends to corrupt the morals of white Christians" (Davis 1975: 164). See also the discussion of the term "antislavery" in Kaul 2000: 311–12 note 1.
2. Elsewhere, I have outlined the ways in which Helen Maria Williams's *A Poem on the Bill Lately Passed for Regulating the Slave-Trade* (1788) also exemplifies this latter strategy (Mitchell 2003b).

3. In *The Problem of Slavery*, Davis argues that "[t]he antislavery movement, like Smith's political economy, reflected the needs and values of the emerging capitalist order" (Davis 1975: 350). The "Williams thesis" is questioned in Anstey 1975 and Drescher 1977, who both argue that in fact slavery *was* profitable during the period that antislavery efforts began in earnest (1770s and '80s). For a concise overview of the debate among historians concerning the relationships between capitalism and slavery, see Drescher 1987.
4. Sypher cites Defoe's *Reformation of Manners* (1702) as the "earliest unmistakably antislavery verse in the eighteenth-century" (Sypher 1969: 157). Sypher also provides a useful chronology of the stages of the broader literary abolition campaign (Sypher 1969: 10).
5. For a firsthand account of the Society's activities in the 1780s and '90s, see Clarkson 1808, vol. 1; for more recent accounts, see Davis 1975, Anstey 1975; Drescher 1977; and Midgley 1992.
6. For the archive of antislavery poems consulted in this chapter, see the titles listed under the category "Imaginative Literature" for the years 1780 to 1800 in Hogg 1973: 324–331.
7. My discussion of rhetorical and aesthetic theory is indebted to De Bolla 1989. De Bolla notes that early eighteenth-century translations of Longinus's *Peri Hupsous* set the basic terms for many eighteenth-century understandings of the ways in which political speech and poetry "transported" the reader (De Bolla 1989: 53, 58, 61–71). For discussion of the linkages established between political rhetoric and poetry in the eighteenth century, see Golden 1990: 8.
8. As Samuel Wilbur Howell notes, while Smith "may confidently be called the earliest and most independent of the new British rhetoricians of the eighteenth century," Smith's failure to publish *Lectures on Rhetoric and Belles Lettres* before his death limited his influence to his students, though some number of these went on to publish their own theories of rhetoric and oratory (Howell 1971: 576).
9. In the *Monthly Review*'s October 1787 discussion of Edward Rushton's *West-Indian Ecologues* (1787), for example, the anonymous reviewer contended that "[m]uch has been written on the subject of plantation slavery:—but that writers have greatly exaggerated in their account of the *cruelties* exercised towards the Negroes, we have every reason to believe" (vol. 78: 283). In debates in the House of Commons, Lord Penrhyn contended that a bill for regulating the slave trade was founded on "idle stories of cruelties" and "groundless calumnies" (*PH*, 27: 578), while in the House of Lords, Lord Rodney declared that he had spent four years in Jamaica, and "had never heard of a negro being treated cruelly in all the time he had been in the West Indies, but had often spoken of their happiness in terms of rapture" (*PH*, 27: 648).
10. In the body of the text, the second quoted line reads "Those woes, which Hist'ry sanctions what she sings," but the errata corrects the "which" to a "for."
11. See also the anonymous review in the March 1788 *Monthly Review* of Thomas George Street's *Aura; or the Slave: A Poem in Two Cantos* (1788), in which the author awards a back-handed compliment to Street's verse, noting that "[i]n a work directed to this object [the slave trade], a small portion of [the Muses'] influence is sufficient to render it interesting. Though the stream be not altogether pure from the Heliconian spring, we can drink of it with pleasure if it flows combined with the *milk of human kindness*" (vol. 78: 247).

12. For representations of the Middle Passage, see Roscoe 1787 and Jamieson 1789. For descriptions of plantation slavery, see Jamieson 1789 and Marjoribanks 1792. For representations of "Quashi," see More 1788 and Pratt 1788. For couples separated by slavery, see, for example, Yearsley 1788, which tells the story of "Luco and Incilanda"; Ingall 1792, which tells the tale of "Oran and Orra"; and Cobbold's "Atomboka and Omaza: An African Story" in Cobbold 1787.
13. Pratt's imperative mode drew from eighteenth-century sermonizing; see, for example, Dore 1788 and especially Winchester 1788, in which the latter commands his female readers to "THINK, O ye tender mothers, how would you feel, if, when you should send your little boys or girls to fetch a pitcher, or calabash of water from the spring, you should never seem them return again!" (Winchester 1788: 18) He also commanded his readers to "transport yourselves in imagination to Africa, and see two armies assembled to battle; how they meet with fury! they rush like lions and tigers to the prey; both parties fight with great obstinancy, knowing what will be the fate of the conquered [i.e., they will be made slaves] .... Oh, the dying groans! The cries of the wounded! The shrieks of the women and children who have lost their friends in battle, and are now being seized and sold! —But the scene is too shocking to describe to this assembly—let imagination conceive of the rest if possible!!!" (Winchester 1788: 19–20).
14. As the subtitle of *Humanity* reminded readers, Pratt had written a long poem on "sympathy" the year before; both poems were supposed to be part of a larger project entitled *Society, or a Prospect of Mankind* (Pratt 1788: 1).
15. In his 1808 history of the abolition of the slave trade, Thomas Clarkson suggested a relatively seamless fit between Scottish moral theory and the abolitionist cause, positioning moral philosophers such as Hutcheson, Hume, and Smith as "forerunners" of antislavery advocacy (Clarkson 1808, vol. 1: 85–86). Contemporary historians and literary critics have tended to follow Clarkson's lead. Davis argues that the growth of an "ethic of benevolence" (equivalent to an "insistence on man's inner goodness, identified with his power of sympathy") was one of four major "source[s] of the antislavery impulse." He argues that "this liberal spirit led in two directions, each described by the titles of Adam Smith's two books: *The Theory of Moral Sentiments* and the *Wealth of Nations*. If there were unresolved tensions between sympathetic benevolence and individual enterprise, both theories condemned slavery as an intolerable obstacle to human progress" (Davis 1975: 46). Anstey makes a similar argument in Anstey 1975: 91–125. Following critics such as Julie Ellison, I argue that claims for such apparently seamless linkages between Scottish moral theory and antislavery efforts underestimate the amount of friction between these two discourses (Ellison 1999: 10–12).
16. It is also important to stress that Hume's example is much more focused on the *temporal*, rather than emotional, distance of the stranger's pain; that is, the stranger is not currently suffering, since he is asleep and unaware of his danger, but because we are awake, and able to "anticipate by the force of imagination" his danger, it is in fact more present to us than to him.
17. For extended discussions of the connections eighteenth- and early nineteenth-century poets made between gender and slavery, see Ferguson 1992 and Mellor 1995.
18. Through readings of several unpublished abolitionist texts, Brown also makes the fruitful suggestion that there were important "ties between the first aspirations for slavery reform and attempts at imperial organization," which in turn suggests that "[i]n the[se] schemes for slavery reform lie not

only the germs of an abolitionist ethos but also the seeds of the nineteenth-century imperial mission that lauded Christianity, civilization, and commerce" (Brown 1999: 301, 305).

19. For discussions of the role of empire in both Cowper and More (as well as a number of other authors), see Kaul 2000: 230–68 and Gould 2003: 43–85,
20. As Charlotte Sussman notes, "[m]ost supporters of abolition ...generally advocated free trade. They saw proponents of slavery as mercantilists whose economic philosophy put up barriers to a more competitive and efficient market economy" (Sussman 2000: 113).
21. Baucom notes that Africans who arrived in North American were often not "bought" by agents in North America in the usual sense of that term, but instead became a form of investment, as agents remitted to British merchants not specie or even paper notes, but rather interest bearing bills of exchange (with the principal due in two to three years). Thus, as Baucom notes, slaves "functioned in this system, simultaneously as commodities for sale and as the reserve deposits of a loosely organized, decentered, but vast trans-Atlantic banking system: deposits made at the moment of sale and instantly reconverted into short-term bonds" (Baucom 2005: 61).
22. Other proslavery authors sought to provide alterative visions of the family. In *A Treatise on Sugar* (1800), for example, Benjamin Mosely suggested that whatever harm slavery might inflict on particular families, it created a much more inclusive global family, for "the merchant, from the transatlantic operation...makes the industrious world one great family" (Mosley, cited in Sussman 2000: 39).
23. "The Negro's Complaint" was first published in *Stuart's Star, and Evening Advertiser* (2 April 1789), and reprinted frequently (for example, in the April 1792 *Lady's Magazine*, though it is there signed by "B. R."). For a discussion of the ballad "Hosier's Ghost," see the Editors' note in *LPWC*, 3: 127 note 2. "The Morning Dream" was first published in the November 1788 issue of *Gentleman's Magazine* and Cowper recommended it be sung to the tune of "Tweedside." "Sweet Meat" was first published posthumously in 1836 in Robert Southey's edition of Cowper's work.
24. James Montgomery echoed this claim several decades later, when he suggested in *The West Indes, and Other Poems* (1810) that "the African slave trade" was "a subject which had become antiquated, by frequent, minute and disgusting exposure; ...public feeling has been wearied into insensibility, by the agony of interest which the question excited, during twenty-three years of almost incessant discussion" (Mongomery, cited in Gould 2003: 84).
25. Cowper described Burke's speeches as a "species of eloquence," and suggested to Lady Hesketh that "perhaps there is not so much difference as one would at first imagine, between being pilloried and pelted with addled eggs, and placed at the Bar of such a court .... The main difference seems to be, that in the former case the Mob are the Agents and the Spectators, and in the latter, persons of consideration, quality and fashion" (*LPWC*, 3: 112–13).
26. Kaul seems to concur with Cowper's judgment, arguing that "[t]he ironic distance between the form of the enunciation (as also the attitude being enunciated) and the moral aims of the poem is so large that it destabilizes the ethical polarities that were the foundation of antislavery discourse" (Kaul 2000: 248). However, as I suggest in my section on Yearsley's verse, Cowper's poem "destabilizes the ethical polarities" of a particularly limited self-understanding of the practice of antislavery literary production, but in fact anticipates the ethical foundation of later antislavery verse.

27. Midgley notes that the Abolition Society had Cowper's "Pity for Poor Africans" printed "on fine quality paper" and had it "distributed in thousands with the superscription, 'A Subject for Conversation at the Tea-Table,' suggesting its suitability for polite discussion among women in the home" (Midgley 1992: 32), while Hannah More's *Slavery: A Poem* was explicitly written for a more "elevated" audience than Cowper's verse, for she worried that if it did "not come out at the particular moment when the discussion comes on in parliament, it will not be worth a straw" (More in Roberts 1834, vol. 2: 97).
28. While most modern commentators have described Yearsley's origins as "lower class," Mary Waldron provides a more nuanced reading of Yearsley's status, noting that milkwomen "appear to have been self-employed, with a respectable traditional position in their home villages," and thus in status they were "far removed from that of wage-dependent farm laborer" (Waldron 1996: 14).
29. For additional discussions of Yearsley's poem, see Ferguson 1995: 55–58 and Gould 2003: 50–52.
30. As Winchester noted in his sermon *The Reigning Abominations*, "[m]any men, even those who have wives, keep negro wenches, and have children by them, which children they not only keep as slaves, but sometimes will sell them to strangers for ever; and such slaves will frequently bring twice or thrice as much as common negroes.... Thus the temptation to sin in that awful manner, is increased by the profit attending it" (Winchester 1788: 22 note 1). For a poetic representation of this phenomenon (purportedly based on an eyewitness account), see Marjoribanks's *Slavery*, in which the narrator notes that "I knew a foetus, in mere wanton play,/Sold from the mother in whose womb it lay" (Marjoribanks 1792: 21). For accounts of the purported African practice of selling family members see William Snelgrave's *New Account of Guinea* (1734, cited in Sypher 1969: 32).
31. Yearsley's depiction of imagination as a speculative faculty that produced real sympathy by means of a passage through absolute negativity is consistent with, though it complicates, her reflections on fancy and imagination in earlier poems. In the volumes *Poems on Several Occasions* (1785) and *Poems on Various Subjects* (1787), Yearsley consistently portrayed "fancy" as a faculty capable of revealing truth. As Cole and Swartz note, Yearsley's poem "Night; To Stella" (Yearsley 1785: 1–16) suggests a "sublime" understanding of the imagination, for in that verse, the narrator's claim to be inarticulate dramatizes a linguistic blockage that serves as the basis for an imaginative triumph. "What rises from the ashes of this failure," Cole and Swartz write, "is the recognition that consciousness or imagination is not determined by the sensuous world but is a law unto itself" (Cole and Swartz 1994: 151). At the same time, however, Yearsley did not seem to favor the complete emancipation of imagination from worldly concerns, and in "A Fragment" (Yearsley 1785: 37–42), she criticized the use of imagination to attempt to provide knowledge about our postearthly existence. In *A Poem on the Inhumanity of the Slave Trade*, Yearsley combined these two aspects of the imagination, suggesting—as in "Night; To Stella"—that its power was manifested through a negation of the actually existing world, but only insofar as it worked in the service of explicitly political goals. For Yearsley's depictions of fancy and imagination as a faculty capable of ascertaining truth, see "To Stella" and "TO HER GRACE The Duchess Dowager of PORTLAND" (Yearsley 1785: 65–70; 97–100).
32. I am thus using the term "virtual" differently from the way it was sometimes employed by antislavery advocates, who used it to describe mediated causal

relationships. William Bell Crafton, for example, argued that the consumer of West Indian produce was the "virtual" cause of slavery: "let us not think, that the crime rests alone with those who conduct the traffic, or the legislature by which it is protected. If we purchase the commodity, we participate in the crime. The slave-dealer, the slave-holder, and the slave-driver, are virtually the agents of the consumer, and may be considered as employed and hired by him to procure the commodity. For, by holding out the temptation, he is the original cause, the first mover in the horrid process" (Crafton 1792: 21).

33. Waldron identifies Andrew Fletcher as the author of the review (Waldron 1996: 171).
34. For a discussion of "the typical," see Baucom 2005: 35–79. For a perceptive discussion of the role of consumer choice and free market ideology in antislavery verse, see Sussman 2000: 110–29. While some antislavery poems were apparently distributed for free, many others were sold (Helen Maria Williams's 1788 poem on the slave trade, for example, lists a price of "one shilling six pence" on the title page, and there is no evidence the proceeds went into the coffers of the Abolition Society). Josiah Wedgwood's "Am I not a man and a brother?" cameo provides an illuminating example of the link between antislavery commodities and fashion. As Drescher notes, Wedgwood facilitated his sales of medallions "with a generous seeding of free samples" (Drescher 1987: 202), and when they became widely available, contemporary commentators suggested that fashion had been "moralized." In the April 3, 1788 issue of *The Morning Post and Daily Advertiser*, a commentator suggested that "*fashion* has extended her influence to the *cause of humanity*, and figures, similar to what we have described, are making in *cameo* as bracelets for the ladies," a sentiment echoed by Thomas Clarkson in 1808, when he contended that "[a]t length, the taste for wearing them became general; and thus fashion, which usually confines itself to worthless things, was seen for once in the honourable office of promoting the cause of justice, humanity, and freedom" (Clarkson 1808, vol. 2: 132).
35. Haskell suggests that "[h]istorically speaking, capitalism requires conscience and can even be said to be identical with the ascendancy of conscience" (Haskell 1998: 265). For an incisive discussion of the ambiguity of Haskell's notion of "the market," see Bender 1992: 11.

Chapter 4

1. If we take the poems included in Peter C. Hogg's *The African Slave Trade and its Suppression: A Classified and Annotated Bibliography of Books, Pamphlets and Periodical Articles* as either a comprehensive or at least representative list of eighteenth- and early-nineteenth century antislavery poetry, the period 1786–90 is clearly the high watermark of this genre, with at least twenty-five unambiguously antislavery poems or poetry collections published during that period (see Hogg 1973: 324–41). Only a few antislavery poems or collections were published in each of the three preceding half-decades (1770–75, 1776–80, 1781–85), and while somewhere on the order of twenty antislavery poems or collections were published between 1791–95, fewer than fifteen antislavery poems or collections were published between 1796–1800 and fewer than ten between 1801–5. (These numbers do not include plays or reprints of previously published poem or collections.)
2. Readings that highlight the differences between Wordsworth's representations of suffering in his early poems and in *The Ruined Cottage* include Averill 1980: 38, 116 ff.; Wordsworth 1969: 50–67; and Jacobus 1976: 133–83.

3. As Lawrence R. Schehr notes, Serres draws on the fact that the French term "parasite" has "three meanings: a biological parasite, a social parasite, and static" (Scher in Serres 1982: vii).
4. New Historical as well as more recent historically inflected criticism has emphasized ways in which Wordsworth internalized the logic and language of speculation in poems such as *The Ruined Cottage* and "The Pedlar." Liu, for example, argues that the capacity of the Wordsworthian poet to appreciate "rich imagery" is akin to "speculation in wheat futures," and has suggested that *The Ruined Cottage* is "not a poem about humanity... [but rather] a capitalization upon humanity" (Liu 1989: 346, 325), while Rieder contends that Wordsworth denied his reader "the place of a co[-]laborer," instead positioning him as "something more like...a stockholder sharing the poet's metaphysical dividends" (Rieder 1997: 76).
5. For a summary of these monetary issues, see the Editor's note to letter 1 in *LWDW* (4, note 1).
6. See letters 40 and 42, *LWDW* 118–120, 123–29.
7. Wordsworth wrote to Mathews that "a writer who has the welfare of mankind at heart should call forth his best exertions to convince the people that they can only be preserved from a convulsion by oeconomy in the administration of the public purse and a gradual and constant reform of those abuses which, if left to themselves, may grow to such a height as to render, even a revolution desirable" (*LWDW* 124). For the topics to be covered by the periodical, see letter 42 in *LWDW* 125–26. Critical discussions of Wordsworth's hopes for *The Philanthropist* include Liu 1989: 332–35; Roe 1988: 175–86; Schoenfield 1996: 88–93.
8. As Wallace W. Douglas noted, Wordsworth's complaints of poverty should be taken with a grain of salt, for both he and his sister seem to have had a relatively comfortable living during this decade (Douglas 1948).
9. For reasons not clear to me, Liu describes these linked forms of philanthropic endowment as a "perfectly circular conservatorship of endowment." Liu's choice of figure seems inaccurate, for the effects of *The Philanthropist* were not to remain within the static form of the circle, but rather were to multiply exponentially, as each converted reader converted others.
10. In letter 40, Wordsworth wrote to Mathews that if the journal was to gain any "pecuniary advantage (from the public at least)," they should avoid writing on topics that "maintain[ed] the existence of prejudice...and error" (*LWDW* 119), for many existing periodicals accomplished that task.
11. Mark L. Reed notes that winter to spring of 1795 "may be counted as that of W[ordsworth's] firmest adherence to the doctrines of William Godwin" (Reed 1982: 163), but by 1797 and 1798, Wordsworth was actively writing against the "philosopher of necessity"; see Reed 1982: 163–66, 182–83, 211 and Moorman 1957–65, vol. 1: 262–65, 297.
12. Accounts of Wordsworth and the Calvert legacy include Liu 1989: 335–36; Reed 1982: 178–93; Moorman 1957–65, vol. 1: 252–97.
13. In September 1795, for example, Wordsworth queried his brother about the difference between annuities and a "rent charge on landed estates." See letters 51 and 66 in *LWDW* 152, 182–85.
14. While it is more common to think of the Calvert legacy as a gift, it can be understood as such only in the anomalous sense of a "final gift" (the gift that prevents a return-gift), since the gift-giver's death is its condition of possibility. The parasite is thus a more useful term with which to capture Wordsworth's relationship to this money, since Wordsworth received something from Calvert, but did not have to—in fact, could not—return anything.

15. E. de Selincourt dated its composition to 1797 (Wordsworth 1952–63, vol. 4: 234), while Reed dates its composition to spring or winter of 1798, arguing that while Wordsworth had been writing poems on the poor since the early 1790s, he does not seem to have begun a poem that was analogous in form to "The Old Cumberland Beggar" until that later date (Reed 1982: 342).
16. While the poem clearly positions itself against the Poor Laws legislation of the 1790s, the politics of the particular position it outlines has been a contested point. Chandler reads the poem as symptomatic of Wordsworth's turn toward a conservative "Burkean" politics, arguing that the poem's proposals for poor relief are structurally identical to those outlined by Burke in "Thoughts and Details on Scarcity" (Chandler 1984: 84–95). Rieder, by contrast, argues against aligning Burke's and Wordsworth's recommendations concerning poor relief (Rieder 1997: 60–72).
17. Some of the proposals made for poor relief in the mid-1790s were designed to unfold on the basis of speculative financial structures, such as "Friendly Society" insurance schemes. In a letter to the editor published in the August 1797 *Monthly Magazine, and British Register*, for example, J. Housman proposed that "[e]very parish, hundred, county, or such other political district as should be found most convenient" could establish a "friendly society" for poor relief. He also outlined a series of criteria that would allow friendly societies to remain solvent, and thus "be rendered extremely conducive towards the public weal," while also enabling "a great reduction of the poor rates" (no. 21: 88).
18. Paine provided a chart of the increase of the national debt after British wars in 1697, 1703, 1739, 1756, 1775, and 1793, and he argued that the debt had multiplied by 150 percent following every war (Paine 1796: 5–8).
19. While our knowledge of Wordsworth's reading in the late 1790s is notoriously imprecise, on March 20, 1797, James Losh sent Wordsworth (at the poet's request) a package of books and periodicals that included the first two of Burke's *Letters on a Regicide Peace*. Selincourt suggests that this package also may have contained Burke's third *Letter on a Regicide Peace* (*LWDW* 186 note 2), but this seems unlikely, for that letter was not published until after Burke's death in July 1797.
20. It is not clear whether Burke knew about the Bank Restriction Act. He began writing the third *Letter on a Regicide Peace* in January 1797, and died six months later in July. For much of the period between January and July, Burke was sick and in seclusion, and therefore perhaps ill-informed about current events. However, given the numerous topical references in the third *Letter* (for example, to the Loyalty Loan), it seems unlikely that he was unaware of the Restriction Act, and it is thus striking that no mention of this act appears in his text.
21. Both Houses also initiated a series of supplementary measures, such as making paper money legal tender for all personal debts (without this measure, an individual could be jailed for refusing to pay private debts in specie even though it was not possible to get specie from the Bank; *PH* vol. 33: 324). However, as Fetter notes, banknotes were still not considered legal tender (Fetter 1965: 30).
22. The Austrian loan was private, but guaranteed by the British government (Fetter 1965:18–19).
23. The precise form of loans to foreign governments was disputed by legislators. Sheridan and Fox contended that a sizeable amount of the loans to the Emperor of Germany was in the form of gold, while Pitt contended that this was not the case (*PH* vol. 32: 1520–24).

24. According to Matthew Carey, there were seventy-one bank failures in 1793, which pushed business bankruptcies from an average of 650 per year for the previous ninety-three years to 1304 bankruptcies in 1793 (Carey 1795?: 13; see also Fetter 1965: 12–16).
25. The two sides also disagreed about how to list £11 million owed the Bank by the British government: did it constitute a Bank asset, or, as Sheridan argued, was it improper to list it in this way, since the government could not be compelled to return it on demand of the Bank? (*PH* vol. 33: 34).
26. As Carey noted, given the ratio of paper money to gold reserves in 1793 (by his calculation, at least 2 to 1), and given that "all the paper circulation must be out for a certain time, or payable on demand, or shortly after sight; and as the longest term is three months, if any real alarm should take place, which might prevent the renewal of paper, ONE MILLION PER DAY would nearly be necessary to pay the bills punctually, as they became due" (Carey 1795?: 18).
27. Accounts of Fox's role as Opposition spokesperson against Pitt include Powell 1989: 183–260 and Mitchell 1992: 108–93.
28. A similar reading of financial panic was outlined in the anonymous *An Inquiry into the Causes of the Present Derangement of Public Credit*, in which the author suggested that "once the public confidence has been disturbed.... Every man naturally looks first to his own interest" (Anon. 1793: 36–37).
29. Precedent for such scenes of instruction existed: in September 1745, following a run on British banks (initiated by the arrival of Charles Stuart on Scottish shores), "a meeting was held at which 1,600 pledged themselves to support Bank notes" (Ashton 1959: 123)
30. Pulteney acknowledged that recent events had, unfortunately, "dispelled this charm," and he argued in favor of a multibank system (*PH* vol. 33: 373).
31. Though *The Ruined Cottage* was not published as such in Wordsworth's lifetime, a version appeared in *The Excursion* (1814). An account of the textual history of the poem, as well as complete copies of extent versions, appear in Wordsworth 1979; see also Rieder 1997: 146–84, 230. I am privileging the version of spring 1798 that contains the so-called "Addendum," and for ease of reference, I cite line numbers from the version of *The Ruined Cottage* (MS D) that appears in Wu 1994 (citations from variant versions are referenced in endnotes). My analysis of "The Pedlar" is also based on the version in Wu 1994, which is a combination of MS. E of "The Pedlar" and sections from "Transcriptions" in Wordsworth 1979: 64–66.
32. Liu describes the premodern credit system as one in which early eighteenth-century weavers purchased bills, bonds, and mortgages, but then hoarded these as "treasure," rather than treating them as "investments" (Liu 1989: 328).
33. The alternative to paying soldiers in specie would have been either payment in paper or no payment at all. At the start of hostilities with France, paper payment to soldiers would have been difficult, as the smallest note denomination was £10. However, Pitt introduced £5 notes in 1795, and £1 and £2 notes were created in 1797 (Smith 1990: 17).
34. In 1793, the Duke of York commanded 17,000 German troops and 6,500 British troops; by 1795, the number of British troops had risen to 119,380, and in 1798, following France's invasion of Germany, only 5,000 mercenaries were serving under British command (Sherwig 1969: 18–19).
35. Neil McKendrick calls pedlars the "lesser agents of the commercializing process" (McKendrick 1982: 86). Accounts of eighteenth-century pedlars as part

of the "consumer revolution" include Spufford 1984; Fontaine 1996; and Brown 2000. In the 1814 edition of *The Excursion*, Wordsworth included a note that referred readers to Robert Heron's *Observations Made in a Journey through the Western Counties of Scotland* (1793), which, he claimed, described pedlars as a progressive force, from which "Society" received "benefits" (Wordsworth 1814: 425). In a later edition of *The Excursion*, Wordsworth expanded his note to include a citation from Heron's text that suggested that pedlars had been, since Roman times, a force that "civilized" by introducing rural people to city wares and habits (Wordsworth 1952–63, vol. 5: 411–12).

36. The pedlar acknowledges that it is possible to "draw" from the dead without the mediation of the image—that is, it is possible to "hold vain dalliance with the misery/Even of the dead, contented thence to draw/A momentary pleasure, never marked/By reason, barren of all future good" (ll. 222–26)—but this produces a morally suspect form of pleasure, since such momentary pleasures do not fundamentally change the structure of indebtedness. The pedlar instead aims to maintain the structure of unpayable debt and the "mournful thoughts" that it produces, but to bend this debt to another purpose, so that it leads to a "power to virtue friendly" (ll. 228–29).
37. Bewell contextualizes this process of natural colonization, suggesting that Wordsworth's descriptions of plant life and insects in *The Ruined Cottage* depict "the emergence of a pathogenic space"—the sort of space more typically associated with the colonies—"in what was believed to be the ideological heart of Englishness—the life of rural cottagers" (Bewell 1999: 51).
38. While neither bindweed nor roses would be categorized as "parasites" within twenty-first-century botanical systems, Darwin's description indicates the greater flexibility of this category in late eighteenth-century botany, for the term was often used to describe any plant that "supports itself like a parasite, on other plants, and mounts to their tops" (entry for "Climbing Plants" in Abercrombie 1778). So, for example, ivy, bindweed, moss, begonias, nightshade, maiden-hair, and hart's tongue were all described as parasites (see, e.g., Saint Pierre 1798, vol. 1: 68 and vol. 2: 180; entry for "Moss" in Middleton et al. 1778; entry for "Parasiticus" in Berkenhout 1789).
39. As J. W. Hart notes "[e]ndogenously regulated movements are initiated or controlled by some factor within the plant, although factors in the external environment may have some indirect effect on the movement" (Hart 1990: 2). While Erasmus Darwin of course did not employ this contemporary botanical terminology, he nevertheless described the endogenous movement of bindweed in *The Botanic Garden* (Darwin 1789, vol. 2: 108 note).
40. I find myself in disagreement with Schor, who argues that the pedlar and narrator are able to look through the image in order to "penetrat[e] nature" and "reveal the immanence of the buried Margaret" (Schor 1994: 122). Margaret may remain as a virtual presence, but she is not there in any ontological (i.e., immanent) sense.
41. Serres's discussion of capital also helps us to understand the "heliotropics" of *The Ruined Cottage* (a poem that, as Liu and others have noted, is obsessively focused on the relationship of growth to light). In *The Parasite*, Serres suggests that "reservoirs" of capital—whether material (oil, coins, etc.) or informational (paper)—are always parasitically related to the ultimate capital, the sun: "[t]hese reservoirs are only subsuns. Their source, far upstream, is the sun. The real, ultimate capital is the sun" (Serres 1982: 173). The capital of Wordsworth's image of tranquility is also generated by parasiting the

sun, for the "silver" that surrounds the weeds and speargrass is created by the refraction of light on water.

42. For the letter from Dorothy Wordsworth to Mary Hutchison that contains parts of the two poems, see *LWDW* 199–210.
43. In *The Excursion*, Wordsworth's narrator noted that "[t]his active course/Chosen in youth, through manhood he pursued,/Till due provision for his modest wants/Had been obtained;— and, thereupon, resolved/To pass the remnant of his days—untasked/With needless services,—from hardship free./His Calling laid aside, he lived at ease," and the volume was dedicated to the Earl of Lonsdale as a "token (may it prove a monument!)/Of high respect and gratitude sincere" (Wordsworth 1814: 22; unnumbered page).
44. Accounts of Wordsworth's "professionalism" include Liu 1989: 311–58; Pfau 1997; and Schoenfield 1996.

Chapter 5

1. See, for example, Shelley's definition of money as sign in "An Address to the Irish People" (1812; *SP* 53) and his note on natural diet in his long poem *Queen Mab* (1813; *SP* 113).
2. See Cameron 1943 and 1974: 137–40; Dawson 1980: 49–51; Scrivener 1982: 215–16; Cox 1998: 187–225; Chandler 1999.
3. Representative examples of this approach include classic interpretations such as Baker 1948; Wassermann 1971; and Curran 1975.
4. My approach, though not methodology, is thus consonant with Jerrold E. Hogle's illuminating "philosophical" discussion of Shelley's writings on money and finance in Hogle 1988: 234–59.
5. Unless otherwise indicated, all further references to Godwin's *An Enquiry Concerning Political Justice* are to this third edition.
6. I follow Clark's attribution of 1813/14 for the composition of the essay (*SP* 154).
7. As a number of commentators have noted, Shelley was perhaps more directly influenced by William Hazlitt's theory of sympathy, as developed in the latter's *Essay on the Principle of the Human Action* (1805), than by Hume's or Smith's theories, though Hazlitt was himself drawing on Smith and Hume. I have found especially useful Deborah Elise White's discussion of both Hazlitt and Shelley, as well as her discussion of the role of the future in Shelley's thought (White 2000: 61–128).
8. The importance of the philosophy of Necessity to Shelley's thought has been a point of critical contention for commentators. Shelley clearly subscribed to a materialist conception of Necessity in *Queen Mab*, contending there that Necessity meant that "[e]very human being is irresistibly impelled to act precisely as he does: in the eternity which preceded his birth a chain of causes was generated, which, operating under the name of motives, make it impossible that any thought of his mind, or any action of his life, should be otherwise than it is" (Shelley 1990: 157). Some commentators have followed Desmond King-Hele's suggestion that "[s]oon after finishing *Queen Mab* Shelley seemed to realize that Necessity was a barren concept, and we hear very little more about it" (King-Hele 1971: 29), but more recent commentary has tended to see Shelley as continuing to grapple with, and refine, the role of necessity in his thought; see, e.g., Sperry 1981; Hogle 1988: 35–49, 194–95; White 2000: 115–18; Roberts 1997: 36–38, 411–20. My analysis follows this latter branch of interpretation by stressing Shelley's later interest in Necessity as a phenomenological, rather than ontological, category; that is, Shelley was

more interested in the conditions of possibility for *perceptions* of Necessity than in making causal claims about the world.

9. The terms "retention" and "protention" originate in Edmund Husserl's *The Phenomenology of Internal Time-Consciousness* (Husserl 1969). In addition to Deleuze's analysis of time consciousness in Deleuze 1994: 70–91, I have also benefited from Stiegler 1998; Mark Hansen's critical discussion of Stiegler's account of technology in mediating time consciousness (Hansen 2004a and 2004b); and Luhmann's very Humean account of psychic and social "expectation" (Luhmann 1995: 267–71).
10. Shelley also suggested that these kinds of habitual perceptions were problematic in large part because they were not, in fact, based on an individual's personal experience, but rather the linkages between ideas were "engrafted" into superstition, and passed along as "tradition" (or tertiary memory, in phenomenological terms).
11. Glossing the section of the "Essay on Punishment of Death" cited above, Deborah Elise White suggests that Shelley positions time as "heterogeneous," in the sense that "the past, the present, and the future are irreducible one to the other. The future can never answer for or answer to the past" (White 2000: 116). I find this helpful and compelling, though I would add that Shelley's claims seem to be phenomenological, rather than metaphysical.
12. The conflict between these two versions of sympathy was also often obscured by the term "benevolence," which implied a distinction between good and bad forms of sympathy without providing any explanation of that difference. See, e.g., "Proposals for an Association of Philanthropists" (*SP* 60–63).
13. For a description of worker unrest during this period, see Thompson 1964: 633–710.
14. Much of Cobbett's *Paper Against Gold* was composed of open letters that Cobbett had earlier published between 1810 and 1811, partly in response to the government's "Bullion Report" on the state of British currency.
15. For a list of the years in which extensions were passed, and the conditions under which the Act would purportedly be recalled, see Anon. 1819?: 5–6.
16. For many critics, the willingness of the state to use force to support this corrupt system was highlighted by the massive increase in executions for paper money forgery since 1797. Between 1783 and 1797, only three people convicted of forging Bank of England banknotes had been executed, while between 1797 and 1817, 308 people had been convicted of this crime (Williams 1818: 24). Many commentators faulted the state for this increase, arguing that paper money could be counterfeited so easily that individuals were almost being dared to do so (Bowdler 1819: 7; see also Anon. 1818?: 5). The "restless, feverish anxiety" that surrounded the topic of bank note forgery was, for many commentators, an index of the public's more general anger about state mismanagement of finances and the harsh measures with which the state supported its policies (Bowdler 1819: 7).
17. On June 20 or 21, 1819, Shelley wrote to Thomas Love Peacock that he found Cobbett's "design to overthrow banknotes by forgery...very comic" (*LPBS* vol. 2: 694). After hearing of the massacre of protestors in Manchester, Shelley immediately connected it to the question of finance, writing to Thomas Love Peacock on September 8, 1819 that: "[t]hese are, as it were, the distant thunders of the terrible storm which is approaching.... [but] I still think there will be no coming to close quarters until financial affairs decidedly bring the oppressors and the oppressed together" (*LPBS* vol. 2: 718). On November 6, 1819, Shelley wrote to John and Maria Gisborne about their status as "public

creditors of the English government," and noted that he "wish[ed] [their] money was out of the funds" (*LPBS* vol. 2: 744, 748).

18. This point was also made by "Solon," who argued in the pamphlet *Aphorisms on Currency* that when Henry VIII "debased the coin 400 per cent, he attempted exactly what modern Government have done with Government Paper, endeavoured artificially to make a new standard of value and *create* at his pleasure, plenty of money of the new denomination to answer his own immediate purposes; but in such cases the public never acquiesce in the imposture. They see distinctly that the money is depreciated and refuse to give value for it, which the caprice of the Government has fixed" ("Solon" 1819: 10).
19. In his discussion of the different ways in which paper money was "uttered," Cobbett contended that no matter how it found its way into the system, banknotes were simply another expression of debt: "is it not as clear as the Sun at noon-day, that they [banknotes] are always the *representatives of* DEBT?" (Cobbett 1817: 85). For a more recent discussion of the necessary connection between all forms of money and state-imposed debt, see Ingham 2004: 1–85.
20. This complaint was heard repeatedly during the 1790s and even more emphatically after the conclusion of hostilities with France in 1814–15. The lead article in the January 26, 1817 *Examiner*, for example, contended that the national debt consumed "the strength and juices not only of the existing generations...but of generations unborn, who are absolutely delivered over to heavy and irredeemable taxation, with as little remorse as a litter of blind puppies to the horse-pond" (50), while the author of an article on the "Progress of Finance" in *The Examiner* of February 16, 1817 argued that "the present generation of Britons... have preyed upon the blood of their children" (99–100).
21. As I describe below, in his "Ode on Liberty" (1820), Shelley contrasted "Expectation" (l. 85) with the much more expansive and unanticipated future potentialities that become perceptible on the basis of Liberty.
22. In correspondence written shortly before he began working on *A Philosophical View of Reform*, Shelley hinted at yet another way in which time consciousness might be expanded, in this case in a context more closely related to the institutions of state finance. As I noted in the Introduction to this book, in the August 22, 1818 issue of *The Political Register*, Cobbett had urged counterfeiters to print millions of pounds worth of Bank of England banknotes, and then "*throw [this] money by night, about the streets*"; the result, Cobbett claimed, would be the collapse of the system of paper money, for "[a]ll money transactions would be at a stand. No buying, no selling." In a June 1819 letter to Thomas Love Peacock, Shelley applauded this plan, writing that "Cobbett still more and more delights me, with all my horror of the sanguinary commonplaces of his creed. His design to overthrow banknotes by forgery is very comic" (*LPBS* vol. 2: 694). What was so delightful about Cobbett's scheme, from the perspective of Shelley's analyses of paper money in *A Philosophical View of Reform*, was its ability to bring into consciousness the temporality of paper money. Flooding the streets with money would provoke in people a two-stage response: at first, an explosion of expectations ("With all this money, I can do this—and then this—and then this!"), followed by a sudden realization that this monetary explosion produces a complete break between the past and the present ("The system has been destroyed: what comes next?"). The epistemological condition for this latter realization was a mode of anticipation that was not limited to the plotting out of causal trajectories from the past,

through the present, and into the future, but rather took the present as cause of the future.

23. For discussions of the group around Hunt and *The Examiner*, see Cox 1998 and Gilmartin 1996: 195–226.
24. For critiques of Coleridge, Southey, and Wordsworth in *The Examiner*, see, for example, December 8, 1816: 769–70; December 15, 1816: 785–87; December 22, 1816: 801–3; February 18, 1816: 97–99; March 9, 1817: 157–59; March 30, 1817: 194–97.
25. For a representative sampling of these poems, see Anon., "An Address to 'The Rabble'"; Anon., "On a Bloody Massacre"; Anon., "The Peterloo Man"; Anon., "Stanzas Occasioned by the Manchester Massacre"; Robert Shorter, "The Bloody Field of Peterloo! A New Song" in Scrivener 1992: 218–19, 224–26, 244–45, 265. See also Scrivener's contexualization of the imagery in Shelley's *The Mask of Anarchy* in Scrivener 1982: 200–10.
26. Scrivener describes the general range of responses in Scrivener 1982: 207; see also Thompson 1964: 603–710.
27. In *The Descent of Liberty*, Hunt defined the mask as "[a] mixed Drama, allowing of natural incidents as of every thing else that is dramatic, but more essentially given up to the fancy, and abounding in machinery and personification, generally with a particular allusion" (Hunt 1816: xxiv). Hunt also reminded his readers that while masks were "generally produced on complimentary occasions," this did not require that the mask itself be "complimentary" (Hunt 1816: xxxv).
28. Recalling Franz Kafka's story of the hunger artist, Deleuze writes that "beyond standing up, there is sitting down, and beyond sitting down, lying down, beyond which one finally dissipates. The true acrobat is one who is consigned to immobility inside the circle" (Deleuze 2003: 36).
29. Hunt's fears seem to have been well-grounded: as Timothy Webb notes, "in 1819 alone there were seventy-five prosecutions for seditious or blasphemous libel" (Webb 1977: 109).
30. In citing prose and poems from this volume, I have first indicated pagination from the 1820 volume, followed by the page number (in the case of prose) or line number (in the case of poems) from *SPP*. I have followed the wording and punctuation of the original 1820 volume.
31. Hugh Roberts notes the resonance of Marvell's "On a Drop of Dew" and Shelley's poem (Roberts 1997: 102). For a discussion of "microscopic views" of water drops and other objects in eighteenth-century literature, see Goodman 2004: 38–66.
32. In Marvell's "On a Drop of Dew," the qualities of the dew drop are mapped onto those of the soul: just as the drop is "shed" from heaven, so too is the soul of divine origin and composed of heavenly material (l. 2); just as the drop gazes at heaven through its "frame" of water (l. 8), so too does the soul long for ascent, though it also "frames" divinity through its own limited means of perception; just as the drop is "restless" on the surface of the plant and worried about material contamination (l. 15), so too the soul, longing for ascent "[s]huns the sweat leaves and blossoms green" (l. 23) (Marvell 1972: 102).
33. For Shelley's discussion of the finite speed of light, see the first of his notes to *Queen Mab* (1813), in which he notes that light takes 8 minutes and 7 seconds "passing from the sun to the earth, a distance of 95,000,000 miles" (Shelley 1990: 125).
34. While different in emphasis, my analysis of the temporal contortions of the Shelleyian image are indebted to Hogle's discussion of the "preconscious

dislocation," "slippage," and "displacement" inherent in both Shelley's theory of thought and in his images themselves (Hogle 1988: 10).

35. This capacity of time consciousness also reconfigures the accumulative series "Athens—Rome—England—France" that forms the narrative content of the poem, revealing it to be what Deleuze describes in *Difference and Repetition* as a "geometric series": that is, "a dynamic symmetry which is pentagonal and appears in a spiral line or in a geometrically progressing pulsation" (Deleuze 1994: 20).
36. Of these interpretations, I have found most helpful Abrams 1971: 299–307; Sperry 1988: 65–126; Hogle 1988: 103–12, 167–205; and Bonca 1999.
37. *A Defence of Poetry* was also to be published in *Ollier's Literary Miscellany*. However, only one issue appeared before the journal went bankrupt, and Shelley's essay was first published in Mary Shelley's 1840 edition of his prose.
38. As Timothy Clark notes, Shelley understands "the self as constituted in the imagination, as opposed to seeing the imagination as a faculty a self might possess" (Clark 1989: 86).

Conclusion

1. Jenks notes that these loans also established a system of global economic dependency, for by 1827, "Spain, Portugal, Greece, and every country in South America to which money had been lent—except Brazil—were in default upon their interest payments" (Jenks 1927: 58).
2. For an account of the expansion of credit instruments in the twentieth century, see Pixley 2004: 9; for an analysis of the increasing importance of finance to pension funds, see Blackburn 2002.
3. For an account of the specialization of writings on finance and the disciplinary emergence of economics, see Parsons 1989 and Poovey 1998: 264–328 and 2003: 25–32.
4. I take the term "new economic criticism" from Woodmansee and Osteen 1999.

Bibliography

Abercrombie, J. (1778) *The Universal Gardener and Botanist; or, A General Dictionary of Gardening and Botany*, London: Printed for G. Robinson and T. Cadell.

Abrams, M.H. (1971) *Natural Supernaturalism: Tradition and Revolution in Romantic Literature*, New York: W.W. Norton.

Abramson, K. (2000) "Sympathy and the Project of Hume's Second Enquiry," *Archiv für Geschichte der Philosophie* 83: 45–80.

Addison, J. and Steele, R. (1965) *The Spectator*, 5 vols, ed. Bond, D.F., Oxford: Clarendon Press.

Anderson, B. (1991) *Imagined Communities: Reflections on the Origin and Spread of Nationalism*, revised ed., New York: Verso.

Anderson, R.L. (1927) *Elizabethan Psychology and Shakespeare's Plays*, Iowa City, Iowa: The University of Iowa Press.

Anon. (1750) *The Necessity of Lowering Interest and Continuing Taxes; demonstrated, in a letter to G. B.*, London: Printed for E. Coxton.

Anon. (1795) *Pigs' meat; or, Lessons for the Swinish Multitude*, 3rd ed., 2 vols, London: Printed for T. Spence.

Anon. (1793) *An Inquiry into the Causes of the Present Derangement of Public Credit; In Great Britain; Occasioned by Mr. Pitt's speech in the House of Commons*, London: Printed for G.G.J. and J. Robinson.

Anon. (1797) *A New Circulating Medium: Being an Examination of the Solidity of Paper Currency, and its Effects on the Country at this Crisis*, London: J. Johnson.

Anon. (1816) *The Extraordinary Red Book: A list of all places, pensions, sinecures, &c. with the various salaries and emoluments arising thereform*, London: J. Blacklock.

Anon. (1817?). *A Curious Calculation on the National Debt*, London: J. Bailey.

Anon. (1818) *Observations on Cobbett's Tremendous and Alarming Scheme for the Annihilation of the Bank of England Paper system by means of Forged Bank Notes: With reflections on its fatal tendency*, London: Printed by and for J. Fairburn.

Anon. (1818?) *Rotten rag manufactory!!! The Threadneedle-Street catechism, or Bank-bubble exposed: appointed by no-directors, to be read in all public and private houses throughout the United Kingdom, for the instruction of John Bull and family in the history and mystery of bank notes*, London: Printed and published by J. Fairburn.

Anon. (1819?) *National Swindling: The Bank-Restriction Catechism, or, The Threadneedle-Street jugglers exposed*, 3rd ed., London: J. Fairburn.

Anstey, R. (1975) *The Atlantic Slave Trade and British Abolition, 1760–1810*, London: Macmillan.

Appelby, J.O. (1978) *Economic Thought and Ideology in Seventeenth-Century England*, Princeton, NJ: Princeton UP.
Arrighi, G. (1994). *The Long Twentieth Century: Money, Power, and the Origins of our Times*, New York: Verso.
Ashton, T.S. (1959) *Economic Fluctuations in England, 1700–1800*, Oxford: Clarendon Press.
Averill, J. H. (1980) *Wordsworth and the Poetry of Human Suffering*, Ithaca, NY: Cornell UP.
Bacon, F. (1825–34) *The Works of Francis Bacon, Lord Chancellor of England*, 16 vols, ed. Montagu, B., London: William Pickering.
Baier, A. (1980) "Helping Hume to 'Compleat the Union'," *Philosophy and Phenomenological Research* 41: 1/2 (September–December): 167–86.
—— (1982) "Hume's Account of our Absurd Passions," *The Journal of Philosophy* 79:11 (November): 643–51.
Baker, C. (1948) *Shelley's Major Poetry: The Fabric of a Vision*, Princeton, NJ: Princeton UP.
Barbauld, A.L. (1791) *Epistle to William Wilberforce, Esq. On the Rejection of the Bill for Abolishing the Slave Trade*, London: J. Johnson.
—— (1812) *Eighteen Hundred and Eleven, A Poem*, London: J. Johnson.
Baring, F. (1797) *Observations on the Establishment of the Bank of England, and on the Paper Circulation of the Country*, 2nd ed., London: Minerva Press.
Barish, J. (1981) *The Antitheatrical Prejudice*, Berkeley: University of California Press.
Bataille, G. (1991) *The Accursed Share: Part I*, trans. Hurley, R., New York: Zone Books.
Baucom, I. (2005) *Specters of the Atlantic: Finance Capital, Slavery, and the Philosophy of History*, Durham, NC: Duke UP.
Bender, T. ed. (1992) *The Antislavery Debate: Capitalism and Abolitionism as a Problem in Historical Interpretation*, Berkeley: University of California Press.
Berkenhout, J.(1789) *Clavis anglica linguæ botanicæ; or, A Botanical Lexicon*, London: Printed for T. Cadell.
Berry, C.J. (1997) *Social Theory of the Scottish Enlightenment*, Edinburgh: Edinburgh UP.
Bewell, A. (1988) "An Issue of Monstrous Desire: Frankenstein and Obstetrics," *The Yale Journal of Criticism: Interpretation in the Humanities* 2:1 (Fall): 105–28.
—— (1999) *Romanticism and Colonial Disease*, Baltimore: The Johns Hopkins UP.
Birkett, M. (1792) *A Poem on the African Slave Trade. Addressed to her Own Sex*, 2nd ed., Dublin: J. Jones.
Black, J. (2001) *The English Press, 1621–1861*, Phoenix Mill, UK: Sutton Publishing.
Blackburn, R. (2002) *Banking on Death, or, Investing in Life: The History and Future of Pensions*, New York: Verso.
Blair, H. (1965) *Lectures on Rhetoric and Belles Lettres*, 2 vols, London: T. Cadell, 1783; reprint ed., ed. Harding, H.F., Carbondale: Southern Illinois UP.
Bloom, E. and Bloom, L. (1971) *Joseph Addison's Sociable Animal: In the Marketplace, on the Hustings, in the Pulpit*, Providence, RI: Brown UP.
Boltanski, L. (1999) *Distant Suffering: Morality, Media and Politics*. Cambridge: Cambridge UP.
Bonca, T.C. (1999) *Shelley's Mirrors of Love: Narcissism, Sacrifice, and Sorority*, Albany: State University of New York Press.
Bond, D.F. (1935)"'Distrust of Imagination' in English Neo-Classicism," *Philological Quarterly* 14: 1 (January): 54–69.

Borch-Jacobsen, M. (1988) *The Freudian Subject*, trans. Porter, C., Stanford, CA: Stanford UP.

Bordo, M.D. and White, E.N. (1990) *British and French Finance during the Napoleonic Wars*, Cambridge, MA: National Bureau of Economic Research.

Bottomore, T., ed. (1991) *A Dictionary of Marxist Thought*, 2nd ed., Oxford: Blackwell.

Bourdieu, P. (1977) *Outline of a Theory of Practice*, trans. Nice, R., New York: Cambridge UP.

Bourez, M.T. *et. al.* (1980) *Le Vocabulaire du sentiment dans l'oeuvre de J.-J. Rousseau*, Geneva: Slatkine.

Bowdler, C. (1819) *On the Punishment of Death in the Case of Forgery: Its Injustice and Impolicy Demonstrated*, 3rd ed., London: T. Hamilton.

Bowle, J. (1951) *Hobbes and His Critics*, London: J. Cape.

Brantlinger, P. (1996) *Fictions of State: Culture and Credit in Britain, 1694–1994*, Ithaca, NY: Cornell UP.

Brennan, T. (1992) *The Interpretation of the Flesh: Freud and Femininity*, New York: Routledge.

Brewer, J. (1989) *The Sinews of Power: War, Money and the English State, 1688–1783*, New York: A. Knopf.

Brown, C.L. (1999) "Empire without Slaves: British Concepts of Emancipation in the Age of the American Revolution," *William and Mary Quarterly* 56:2 (April): 273–306.

Brown, D. (2000) "'Persons of Infamous Character' or 'An Honest Industrious and Useful Description of People'? The Textile Pedlars of Alstonfield and the Role of Peddling in Industrialization," *Textile History* 31:1: 1–26.

Bundy, M.W. (1927) *The Theory of Imagination in Classical and Medieval Thought*, in *University of Illinois Studies in Language and Literature*, vol. 12: 183–472.

Burgess, M.J. (2000) *British Fiction and the Production of Social Order, 1740–1830*, Cambridge: Cambridge UP.

Burroughs, F. (1797) *Strictures, on the Present State of Public Credit and Public Security: Containing a summary review of Mr. Pitt's administration*, Dublin: H. Fitzpatrick.

Burthogge, R. (1694) An *Essay upon Reason, and the Nature of Spirits*, London: Printed for John Dunton.

Burton, R. (2001) *The Anatomy of Melancholy*, 3 vols in one, ed. Jackson, H., New York: New York Review of Books.

Butler, J. (1993) *Bodies that Matter: On the Discursive Limits of 'Sex'*, New York: Routledge.

Byron, Lord (George Gordon) (1986) *Byron: The Oxford Authors*, ed. McGann, J.J., Oxford: Oxford UP.

Cameron, K.N. (1943) "Shelley, Cobbett, and the National Debt," *The Journal of English and Germanic Philology* 42:2 (April): 197–209.

—— (1974) *Shelley: The Golden Years*, Cambridge, MA: Harvard UP.

Campbell, T.D. (1971) *Adam Smith's Science of Morals*, London: George Allen & Unwin.

Canguilhem, G. (1994) *A Vital Rationalist: Selected Writings from Georges Canguilhem*, ed. Delaporte, F., trans. Goldhammer, A., introduction by Rabinow, P., critical bibliography by Limoges, C., New York: Zone Books.

Carey, M. ("Colbert, Jun.") (1795?) *The Age of Paper, or, An Essay on Banks and Banking*, London: Mr. Parsons.

Carswell, J. (1960) *The South Sea Bubble*, Stanford, CA: Stanford UP.

Casaubon, M. (1970) *A Treatise Concerning Enthusiasme*, Gainesville, FL: Scholars' Facsimiles & Reprints.

Chambers, E. (1788) *Cyclopaedia: Or, an Universal Dictionary of Arts and Sciences*, London: Rivington *et al.*

Chandler, J.K. (1984) *Wordsworth's Second Nature: A Study of the Poetry and Politics*, Chicago: University of Chicago Press.

—— (1999) "Ricardo and the Poets: Representing Common-wealth in the Year of Peterloo," *Wordsworth Circle* 24: 2: 82–86.

Chisick, H. (2004) "The Representation of Adam Smith and David Hume in the *Année Littéraire* and the *Journal Encyclopédique*," in *Scotland and France in the Enlightenment*, ed. Dawson, D. and Morère, P., Lewisburg, PA: Bucknell UP: 240–63.

Christensen, J. (1987) *Practicing Enlightenment: Hume and the Formation of a Literary Career*, Madison: University of Wisconsin Press.

—— (2000) *Romanticism at the End of History*, Baltimore: Johns Hopkins UP.

Clark, T. (1989) *Embodying Revolution: The Figure of the Poet in Shelley*, Oxford: Clarendon Press.

Clarkson, T. (1788) *An Essay on the Slavery and Commerce of the Human Species, Particularly the African*, London: J. Phillips.

—— (1808) *The History of the Rise, Progress, and Accomplishment of the Abolition of the African Slave-Trade by the British Parliament, in two volumes*, London: Longman.

Cobbett, W. (1817) *Cobbett's Paper Against Gold: Containing the history and mystery of the Bank of England, the funds, the debt, the sinking fund, the bank stoppage, the lowering and the raising of the value of paper-money*, London: W. Molineux.

Cobbold, E. (1787) *Six Narrative Poems*, London: C. Dilly.

Cole, L. and Swartz, R.G. (1994) "'Why Should I Wish for Words?': Literacy, Articulation, and the Borders of Literary Culture" in *At the Limits of Romanticism: Essays in Cultural, Feminist, and Materialist Criticism*, ed. Favret, M.A. and Watson, N.J., Bloomington: Indiana UP: 143–69.

Coleridge, S.T. (1969–2002) *The Collected Works of Samuel Taylor Coleridge*, 23 vols, Princeton, NJ: Princeton UP.

Comber, W.T. (1817) *A View of the Nature and Operation of Bank Currency: As connected with the distresses of the country*, London: Sherwood, Neely and Jones.

Connell, P. (2001) *Romanticism, Economics and the Question of "Culture,"* Oxford: Oxford UP.

Cooper, A.A. (Third Earl of Shaftesbury) (1999) *Characteristics of Men, Manners, Opinions, Times*, ed. Klein, L.E., Cambridge: Cambridge UP.

Cooper, M. (2006) "Resuscitations: Stem Cells and the Crisis of Old Age" *Body and Society*, 12:1:1–23.

Couliano, I.P. (1987) *Eros and Magic in the Renaissance*, trans. Cook, M., foreword by Eliade, M., Chicago: University of Chicago Press.

Coulter, H.L. (1973–77) *Divided Legacy: A History of the Schism in Medical Thought*, 3 vols, Washington, D.C.: Wehawken Book Co.

Cowper, W. (1980–95) *The Poems of William Cowper*, 3 vols, ed. Baird, J.D. and Ryskamp, C.,Oxford: Clarendon Press.

Cox, J.N. (1998) *Poetry and Politics in the Cockney School: Keats, Shelley, Hunt and their Circle*, Cambridge: Cambridge UP.

Crafton, W.B. (1792) *A Short Sketch of the Evidence Delivered Before a Committee of the House of Commons for the Abolition of the Slave Trade: To which is added, a Recommendation of the Subject to the Serious Attention of People in general*, 3rd ed., London: M. Guerny.

Cranston, M.W. (1983) *Jean-Jacques: The Early Life and Work of Jean-Jacques Rousseau, 1712–1754*, New York: W.W. Norton.

Curran, S. (1975) *Shelley's Annus Mirabilis: The Maturing of an Epic Vision*, San Marino, CA: Huntington Library.

Daly, G. (2004) "Radical(ly) Political Economy: Luhmann, Postmarxism and Globalization," *Review of International Political Economy* 11:1 (February): 1–32.

Darwin, E. (1789) *The Botanic Garden, Containing the Loves of the Plants, a poem, with philosophical notes*, 2 vols, London: J. Johnson.

Davenant, C. (1942) *Two Manuscripts by Charles Davenant*, introduction by Usher, A.P., Baltimore: The Johns Hopkins UP.

Davis, D.B. (1975) *The Problem of Slavery in the Age of Revolution, 1770–1823*, Ithaca, NY: Cornell UP.

Dawson, D. (1991) "Is Sympathy so Surprising? Adam Smith and French Fictions of Sympathy," *Eighteenth-Century Life* 15 (February & May): 147–62.

Dawson, P.M.S. (1980) *The Unacknowledged Legislator: Shelley and Politics*, Oxford: Oxford UP.

Day, T. and Bicknell, J. (1773) *The Dying Negro*, London: W. Flexney.

De Bolla, P. (1989) *The Discourse of the Sublime: Readings in History, Aesthetics, and the Subject*, Oxford: Basil Blackwell.

Defoe, D. (1719) *The Anatomy of Exchange-Alley; Or, A System of Stock-Jobbing*, 2nd ed., London: Printed for E. Smith.

——— (1938) *Defoe's* Review, *reproduced from the original editions*, with an Introduction and Bibliographical Notes by Secord, A.W., 23 vols, New York: Facsimile Text Society/Columbia UP.

Deleuze, G. (1991) *Empiricism and Subjectivity: An Essay on Hume's Theory of Human Nature*, trans. Boundas, C.V. New York: Columbia UP.

——— (1994) *Difference and Repetition*, trans. Patton, P., New York: Columbia UP.

——— (2003) *Francis Bacon: The Logic of Sensation*, trans. and introduction by Smith, D.W., afterword Conley, T., Minneapolis: University of Minnesota Press.

——— and Guattari, F. (1987) *A Thousand Plateaus: Capitalism and Schizophrenia*, trans. Massumi, B., Minneapolis: University of Minnesota Press.

——— (1994) *What is Philosophy?*, trans. Tomlinson, H. and Burchell, G., New York: Columbia UP.

Derathé, R. (1950) *Jean-Jacques Rousseau et la science politique de son temps*, Paris: Presses Universitaires de France.

Derrida, J. (1976) *Of Grammatology*, trans. Spivak, G.C., Baltimore: The Johns Hopkins Press.

——— (1992) *Given Time. I, Counterfeit Money*, Chicago: University of Chicago Press.

Descartes, R. (1984) *The Philosophical Writings of Descartes*, 3 vols, trans. Cottingham, J., Stoothoff, R., and Murdoch, D., Cambridge: Cambridge UP.

Dibdin, C. ("C. I. Pitt") (1796) *The Pedlar; A Miscellany, in Prose and Verse*, London: Printed for Harrison and Co.

Dickson, P.G.M. (1967) *The Financial Revolution in England: A Study in the Development of Public Credit, 1688–1756*, New York: Macmillan.

Diderot, D. and D'Alembert, J.L.R. (1969) *Encyclopédie; ou Dictionnaire raisonné des sciences, des arts et des métiers, par une société de gens de letters*, 28 vols, Paris: Briasson, 1751–65; reprint ed., 5 vols, Elmsford, UK: Pergamon Press.

Dore, J. (1788) *A Sermon on the African Slave Trade*, 3rd ed., London: J. Phillips.

Douglas, W.W. (1948) "Wordsworth as Business Man," *PMLA* 63:2 (June): 625–41.

Drescher, S. (1977) *Econocide: British Slavery in the Era of Abolition*, Pittsburgh: University of Pittsburgh Press.

——— (1987) "Paradigms Tossed: Capitalism and the Political Sources of Abolition," in *British Capitalism and Caribbean Slavery: The Legacy of Eric Williams*, ed. Solow, B.L. and Engerman, S.L., Cambridge: Cambridge UP: 191–208.

Du Bos, L'A. (1740) *Réflexions critiques sur la poésie et sur la peinture*, 4th ed., Paris: Pierre-Jean.

Dumont, L. (1977) *From Mandeville to Marx: The Genesis and Triumph of Economic Ideology*, Chicago: University of Chicago Press.

Dupin, C. (1750–51) *Observations sur un livre intitulé, De l'esprit des loix: divisées en trois parties*, 3 vols, Paris: Guérin.

——— (1913) *Oeconomiques*, 3 vols, privately published, 1745; reprint of first two vols, ed. Aucuy, M., Paris: M. Revière et cie.

Dwyer, J. (1993) "Enlightened Spectators and Classical Moralists: Sympathetic Relations in Eighteenth-Century Scotland," in *Sociability and Society in Eighteenth-Century Scotland*, ed. Dwyer, J. and. Sher, R.B., Edinburgh: Mercat Press: 96–118.

——— (1998) *The Age of Passions: An Interpretation of Adam Smith and Scottish Enlightenment Culture*, East Linton, UK: Tuckwell Press.

Eagleton, T. (1990) *The Ideology of the Aesthetic*, Cambridge, MA: Basil Blackwell.

Eigeldinger, M. (1962) *Jean-Jacques Rousseau et la réalité de l'imaginaire*, Neuchâtel: Editions de la Baconnière.

Eisenstein, E.L. (1983) *The Printing Revolution in Modern Europe*, Cambridge: Cambridge UP.

Ellison, J. (1999) *Cato's Tears and the Making of Anglo-American Emotion*, Chicago: University of Chicago Press.

Engell, J. (1981) *The Creative Imagination: Enlightenment to Romanticism*, Cambridge, MA: Harvard UP.

Espinas, A.V. (1895) "Le 'système' de Jean-Jacques Rousseau," *Revue Internationale de l'enseignement*, 30: 325–56 and 425–62.

Fauconnier, G. (1993) *Le vocabulaire pédagogique de J.-J. Rousseau*, Geneva: Slatkine.

Ferguson, M. (1992) *Subject to Others: British Women Writers and Colonial Slavery, 1760–1834*, New York: Routledge.

——— (1995) *Eighteenth-Century Women Poets: Nation, Class, and Gender*, Albany: State University of New York Press.

Fetter, F.W. (1965) *Development of British Monetary Orthodoxy, 1797–1875*, Cambridge, MA: Harvard UP.

Finkelstein, A. (2000) *Harmony and the Balance: An Intellectual History of Seventeenth-Century English Economic Thought*, Ann Arbor: University of Michigan Press.

Florence, J. (1978) *L'Identification dans la théorie freudienne*, Brussels: Facultés Universitaires Saint-Louis.

Fontaine, L. (1996) *History of Pedlars in Europe*, trans. Whittaker, V., Durham, NC: Duke UP.

Forbes, D. (1975) *Hume's Philosophical Politics*, Cambridge: Cambridge UP.

Force, P. (1997) "Self-Love, Identification, and the Origin of Political Economy," *Yale French Studies* 92: 46–64.

Foucault, M. (1973) *The Order of Things: An Archaeology of the Human Sciences*, New York: Vintage Books.

François, A. (1943–45) "Rousseau, les Dupin, Montesquieu," *Annales de la Société J.-J. Rousseau* 30: 47–64.

Frank, J. (2005) "'Besides Our Selves': An Essay on Enthusiastic Politics and Civil Subjectivity" *Public Culture* 17: 3: 371–92.

Freud, S. (1953–74) *The Standard Edition of the Complete Psychological Works of Sigmund Freud*, 24 vols, ed. Strachey, J., London: The Hogarth Press.

——— (1985a) *Briefe an Wilhelm Fliess, 1887–1904: Ungekürzte Ausgabe*, Frankfurt am Main: S. Fischer.

——— (1985b) *The Complete Letters of Sigmund Freud to Wilhelm Fliess, 1887–1904*, ed. and trans. Masson, J.M., Cambridge, MA: Belknap Press.

Frow, J. (1997) *Time and Commodity Culture: Essays in Cultural Theory and Postmodernity*, Oxford: Clarendon Press.

Fuss, D. (1995) *Identification Papers*, New York: Routledge.

Gallagher, C. (1994) *Nobody's Story: The Vanishing Acts of Women within the Marketplace, 1670–1820*, Berkley: University of California Press.

Gatrell, V.A.C. (1994) *The Hanging Tree: Execution and the English People, 1770–1868*, New York: Oxford UP.

Gilmartin, K. (1996) *Print Politics: The Press and Radical Opposition in Early Nineteenth-Century England*, Cambridge: Cambridge UP.

Godwin, W. (1992) *An Enquiry Concerning Political Justice, and Its Influence on General Virtue and Happiness*, 2 vols, London: G.G.J. and J. Robinson, 1793; reprint ed., ed. Wordsworth, J., New York: Woodstock Books.

——— (1985) *An Enquiry Concerning Political Justice, and Its Influence on Modern Morals and Happiness*, 3rd ed., ed. Kramnick, I., New York: Penguin Books.

Golden, J.L. (1990) *The Rhetoric of Blair, Campbell, and Whately*, Carbondale: Southern Illinois UP.

Goldsmith, O. (1793) *The Traveller; or, a Prospect of Society*, Manchester: G. Nicholson and Co.

Goodman, D. (1994) *The Republic of Letters: A Cultural History of the French Enlightenment*, Ithaca, NY: Cornell UP.

Goodman, K. (2004) *Georgic Modernity and British Romanticism: Poetry and the Mediation of History*, Cambridge: Cambridge UP.

Gould, P. (2003) *Barbaric Traffic: Commerce and Antislavery in the Eighteenth-Century Atlantic World*, Cambridge, MA: Harvard UP.

Haakonssen, K. (1989) *The Science of a Legislator: The Natural Jurisprudence of David Hume and Adam Smith*, Cambridge: Cambridge UP.

Hansen, M.B.N. (2004a) *New Philosophy for New Media*, Boston: The MIT Press.

——— (2004b) "The Time of Affect, or Bearing Witness to Life," *Critical Inquiry* 30: 3 (Spring): 584–626.

Harries, J.M. (1811) *Review of the Controversy Reflecting the High Price of Bullion and the State of our Currency*, London: J. Budd.

Harris, B. (1996) *Politics and the Rise of the Press: Britain and France, 1620–1800*, New York: Routledge.

Hart, J.W. (1990) *Plant Tropisms and Other Growth Movements*, London: Unwin Hyman.

Haskell, T. (1998) *Objectivity is Not Neutrality: Explanatory Schemes in History*, Baltimore: The Johns Hopkins UP.

Hegel, G. W. F. (1975) *Hegel's Logic: Being Part One of the Encyclopaedia of the Philosophical Sciences (1830)*, trans. Wallace, W., foreword by Findlay, J.N., Oxford: Clarendon Press.

Hendel, C.W. (1983) *Studies in the Philosophy of David Hume*, New York: Garland.

Henderson, A.K. (1996) *Romantic Identities: Varieties of Subjectivity, 1774–1830*, Cambridge: Cambridge UP.

Hentzi, G. (1993) "'An Itch of Gaming': The South Sea Bubble and the Novels of Daniel Defoe," *Eighteenth-Century Life* 17 (February): 32–45.

Henwood, D. (2003) *After the New Economy*, New York: New Press.

Heyd, M. (1995) *'Be Sober and Reasonable': The Critique of Enthusiasm in the Seventeenth and Early Eighteenth Centuries*, Leiden: E. J. Brill.

Hilferding, R. (1981) *Finance Capital: A Study of the Latest Phase of Capitalist Development*, trans. Watnick, M., ed. Bottomore, T., London: Routledge & Kegan Paul.

Hilton, B. (1977) *Corn, Cash, Commerce: The Economic Policies of the Tory Governments 1815–1830*, Oxford: Oxford UP.
Hobbes, T. (1966) *The English Works of Thomas Hobbes of Malmesbury*, 11 vols, ed. Molesworth, Sir W., London: John Bohn, 1839–45; 2nd reprint ed., Darmstadt: Scienta Verlag Aalen.
Hogg, P.C. (1973) *The African Slave Trade and Its Suppression: A Classified and Annotated Bibliography*, London: Frank Cass.
Hogle, J.E. (1988) *Shelley's Process: Radical Transference and the Development of His Major Works*, New York: Oxford UP.
Hont, I. and Ignatieff, M. eds. (1983) *Wealth and Virtue: The Shaping of Political Economy in the Scottish Enlightenment*, Cambridge: Cambridge UP.
Houston, G.T. (2005) *From Dickens to Dracula: Gothic, Economics, and Victorian Fiction*, Cambridge: Cambridge UP.
Howell, S.W. (1971) *Eighteenth-Century British Logic and Rhetoric*, Princeton, NJ: Princeton UP.
Huet, M-H. (1993) *Monstrous Imagination*, Cambridge, MA: Harvard UP.
Hume, D. (1741) *Essays, Moral and Political*, Edinburgh: A. Kincaid.
——— (1752) *Political Discourses*, Edinburgh: Kincaid and Donaldson.
——— (1932) *The Letters of David Hume*, 2 vols, ed. Grieg, J.Y.T., Oxford: Clarendon.
——— (1954) *New Letters of David Hume*, ed. Klibansky, R. and Mossner, E.C., Oxford: Clarendon.
——— (1975) *Enquiries Concerning Human Understanding and Concerning the Principles of Morals*, 3rd ed., ed. Selby-Bigge, L.A., Oxford: Clarendon Press.
Hunt, L. (1816) *The Descent of Liberty: A Mask; A New Edition*, London: Printed for Gale and Fenner, by S. Hamilton.
Husserl, E. (1969) *The Phenomenology of Internal Time-Consciousness*, ed. Heidegger, M., trans. Churchill, J.S., Bloomington: Indiana UP.
Hutcheson, F. (1729) *An Inquiry into the Original of Our Ideas of Beauty and Virtue: In Two Treatises*, 3rd ed., London: J. and J. Knapton.
Hutchison, T. (1988) *Before Adam Smith: The Emergence of Political Economy, 1662–1776*, Oxford: Basil Blackwell.
Ingall, T.G. (1792) "The Negroe's Complaint," *Lady's Magazine, or, Entertaining Companion for the FAIR SEX, appropriate solely for their Use and Amusement* (February): 172.
Ingham, G. (1984) *Capitalism Divided? The City and Industry in British Social Development*, New York: Schocken Books.
——— (2004) *The Nature of Money*, Cambridge: Polity.
Ingrassia, C. (1998) *Authorship, Commerce, and Gender in Early Eighteenth-Century England: A Culture of Paper Credit*, Cambridge: Cambridge UP.
Jacobus, M. (1976) *Tradition and Experiment in Wordsworth's Lyrical Ballads (1798)*, Oxford: Clarendon Press.
Jameson, F. (1993) *Postmodernism: Or, The Cultural Logic of Late Capitalism*, Durham, NC: Duke UP.
——— (1997) "Culture and Finance Capital," *Critical Inquiry* 24 (Autumn): 246–65.
Jamieson, J. (1789) *The Sorrows of Slavery, a Poem; Containing a faithful statement of facts respecting the African Slave Trade*, London: J. Murray.
Jenks, L.H. (1927) *The Migration of British Capital to 1875*, London: Nelson.
Jessop, B. (2002) "The Social Embeddedness of the Economy and Its Implications for Economic Governance," in *Economy and Society: Money, Capitalism and Transition*, ed. Adaman, F. and Devine, P., Tonawanda, NY: Black Rose Books: 192–222.
Johnston, K.R. (2000) *The Hidden Wordsworth*, New York: W.W. Norton.

Kames Lord (Henry Home) (1767) *Principles of Equity, Corrected and enlarged in a second edition*, Edinburgh: Printed for A. Millar, A. Kincaid and J. Bell.
Kant, I. (1981) *Grounding for a Metaphysics of Morals*, trans. Ellington, J.W., Indianapolis: Hackett.
Kaufmann, D. (1995) *The Business of Common Life: Novels and Classical Economics Between Revolution and Reform*, Baltimore: Johns Hopkins UP.
Kaul, S. (2000) *Poems of Nation, Anthems of Empire: English Verse in the Long Eighteenth Century*, Charlottesville: UP of Virginia.
Keach, W. (1984) *Shelley's Style*, New York: Methuen.
Kemp-Smith, N. (1960) *The Philosophy of David Hume*, London: Macmillan.
Keohane, N.O. (1980) *Philosophy and the State in France: The Renaissance to the Enlightenment*, Princeton, NJ: Princeton UP.
Ketcham, M.G. (1985) *Transparent Designs: Reading, Performance, and Form in the* Spectator *Papers*, Athens, GA: University of Georgia Press.
King-Hele, D. (1971) *Shelley: His Thought and Work*, 2nd ed., London: Macmillan.
Klein, L.E. (1994) *Shaftesbury and the Culture of Politeness: Moral Discourse and Cultural Politics in Early Eighteenth-Century England*, Cambridge: Cambridge UP.
—— (1995) "Property and Politeness in the Early Eighteenth-Century Whig Moralists: The Case of the *Spectator*," in *Early Modern Conceptions of Property*, ed. Brewer, J. and Staves, S., New York: Routledge: 221–33.
—— and La Vopa, A.J., eds. (1998) *Enthusiasm and Enlightenment in Europe, 1650–1850*, San Marino, CA: Huntington Library Press.
Knezevic, B. (2003) *Figures of Finance Capitalism: Writing, Class, and Capital in the Age of Dickens*, New York: Routledge.
Kramnick, I. (1968) *Bolingbroke and His Circle: The Politics of Nostalgia in the Age of Walpole*, Cambridge, MA: Harvard UP.
Lacan, J. (1966) *Écrits*, Paris: Éditions du Seuil, 1966.
Lacoue-Labarthe, P. (1989) *Typography: Mimesis, Philosophy, Politics*, ed. Fynsk, C., Cambridge, MA: Harvard UP.
—— and Nancy, J-L. (1979) "La panique politique," *Confrontations* 2: 33–57.
Lamprecht, S.P. (1993) "Hobbes and Hobbism," in *Thomas Hobbes: Critical Assessments*, 4 vols, ed. King, P. London: Routledge, vol. 1: 17–36.
Lash, S. and Urry, J. (1994) *Economies of Signs and Space*, London: Sage.
Lawrence, C. (1979) "The Nervous System and Society in the Scottish Enlightenment," in *Natural Order: Historical Studies of Scientific Culture*, ed. Barnes, B. and Shapin, S., Beverly Hills, CA: Sage: 19–40.
Letwin, W. (1963) *The Origins of Scientific Economics: English Economic Thought 1660–1776*, London: Methuen.
Leyshon, A. and Thrift, N. (1997) *Money/Space: Geographies of Monetary Transformation*, New York: Routledge.
Lindgren, J.R. (1973) *The Social Philosophy of Adam Smith*, The Hague: Martinus Nijhoff.
Linebaugh, P. (1991) *The London Hanged: Crime and Civil Society in the Eighteenth Century*, London: Penguin.
Liu, A. (1989) *Wordsworth: The Sense of History*, Stanford, CA: Stanford UP.
Livingston, D.W. (1984) *Hume's Philosophy of Common Life*, Chicago: University of Chicago Press.
Locke, J. (1991) *Locke on Money*, 2 vols, ed. Kelly, P.H., Oxford: Clarendon Press.
Longinus (1987), *Longinus on the Sublime*, trans. Roberts, W.R., New York: Garland Publishing.
Luhmann, N. (1982) *The Differentiation of Society*, trans. Holmes, S. and Larmore, C., New York: Columbia UP.

——— (1986) *Love as Passion: The Codification of Intimacy*, trans. Gaines, J. and Jones, D.L. Cambridge, MA: Harvard UP.
——— (1989) *Ecological Communication*, trans. Bednarz, J., Chicago: University of Chicago Press.
——— (1995) *Social Systems*, trans. Bednarz, J. and Baecker, D., Stanford, CA: Stanford UP.
——— (1999) *Die Wirtschaft der Gesellschaft*, Frankfurt am Main: Suhrkamp.
Lynch, D.S. (1998) *The Economy of Character: Novels, Market Culture, and the Business of Inner Meaning*, Chicago: University of Chicago Press.
Mackie, E., ed. (1998) *The Commerce of Everyday Life: Selections from* The Tatler *and* The Spectator, Boston: Bedford/St. Martin's.
Maitland, J. (Earl of Lauderdale) (1797) *Thoughts on Finance: Suggested by the Measures of the Present Session*, London: G.G. and J. Robinson.
——— (1798) *A Letter on the Present Measures of Finance: In which the Bill now Depending in Parliament is Particularly Considered*, London: Printed for J. Debrett and G.G. and J. Robinson.
Malebranche, N. (1997) *The Search After Truth*, trans. and ed. Lennon, T.M. and Olscamp, P.J., Cambridge: Cambridge UP.
Mandeville, B. (1988) *The Fable of the Bees or Private Vices, Publick Benefits*, 2 vols, ed. F.B. Kaye, Indianapolis: Liberty Fund.
Manuel, F. (1983) *The Changing of the Gods*, London: UP of New England.
Marion, M. (1927–31) *Histoire financière de la France depuis 1715*, 2nd ed., 6 vols, Paris: Rousseau.
Marjoribanks, J. (1792) *Slavery, An Essay in Verse; humbly inscribed to PLANTERS, MERCHANTS and others concerned in the MANAGEMENT of SALE of NEGRO SLAVES*, Edinburgh: J. Robertson, 1792.
Markley, R. (1995) "So Inexhaustible a Treasure of Gold: Defoe, Capitalism, and the Romance of the South Seas," *Eighteenth-Century Life* 18: 3: 148–67.
Markovits, F. (1986) *L'ordre des échanges: Philosophie de l'économie et économie du discours au XVIIIe siècle en France*, Paris: Presses Universitaires de France.
Marshall, D. (1986) *The Figure of Theater: Shaftesbury, Defoe, Adam Smith, and George Eliot*, New York: Columbia UP.
——— (1988) *The Surprising Effects of Sympathy: Marivaux, Diderot, Rousseau and Mary Shelley*, Chicago: University of Chicago Press.
Marvell, A. (1972) *The Complete English Poems*, ed. Dunno, E.S., New York: St. Martin's Press.
Marx, K. (1977) *Capital: Volume One*, introduction Mandel, E., trans. Fowles, B., New York: Vintage Books.
——— (1976–78) *Capital: A Critique of Political Economy*, 3 vols, introduction Mandel, E., trans. Fowkes, B., Harmondsworth, UK: Penguin Books.
Masson, P.M. (1913) "Questions de chronologie rousseauiste," *Annales de la société Jean-Jacques Rousseau*, 9: 37–61.
Massumi, B. (2002) *Parables for the Virtual: Movement, Affect, Sensation*, Durham, NC: Duke UP.
Matthews, G.T. (1958) *The Royal General Farms in Eighteenth-Century France*, New York: Columbia UP.
Mauss, M. (1990) *The Gift: The Form and Reason for Exchange in Archaic Societies*, trans. Halls, W.D., New York: W.W. Norton.
McCusker, J.J. and Gravesteijn, C. (1991) *The Beginnings of Commercial and Financial Journalism: The Commodity Price Currents, Exchange Rate Currents, and Money Currents of Early Modern Europe*, Amsterdam: Nederlandsch Economisch-Historisch Archief.

McDougall, W. (1920) The *Group Mind: A Sketch of the Principles of Collective Psychology, with Some Attempt to Apply them to the Interpretation of National Life and Character*, 2nd ed., New York: G.P. Putnam.

McGowen, R. (1987) "The Body and Punishment in Eighteenth-Century England," *Journal of Modern History* 59 (December): 651–79.

McKendrick, N. (1982) "The Commercialization of Fashion," in *The Birth of a Consumer Society: The Commercialization of Eighteenth-Century England*, ed. McKendrick, N., Brewer, J. and Plumb, J. H., Bloomington: Indiana UP: 34–98.

McLynn, F. (1992) *Crime and Punishment in Eighteenth-Century England*, Oxford: Oxford UP.

Mee, J. (2003) *Romanticism, Enthusiasm, and Regulation: Poetics and the Policing of Culture in the Romantic Period*, Oxford: Oxford UP.

Meissner, W.W. (1970) "Notes on Identification I: Origins in Freud," *Psychoanalytic Quarterly* 39: 563–89.

—— (1971) "Notes on Identification II: Origins in Freud," *Psychoanalytic Quarterly* 40: 277–302.

Mellor, A.K. (1995) "'Am I Not a Woman, and a Sister?': Slavery, Romanticism, and Gender," in *Romanticism, Race, and Imperial Culture, 1780–1834*, ed. Richardson, A. and Hofkosh, S., Bloomington: Indiana UP: 311–29.

Michie, R.C. (1999) *The London Stock Exchange: A History*, Oxford: Oxford UP.

Middleton, E. *et al.* (1778) *The New Complete Dictionary of Arts and Sciences*, London: Printed, by authority, for the authors, and sold by Alexr. Hogg.

Midgley, C. (1992) *Women Against Slavery: The British Campaigns, 1780–1870*, New York: Routledge.

Midriff, Sir. J., Kn[r], M.D. (1721) *Observations on the Spleen and Vapours: Containing Remarkable CASES of Persons of both Sexes, and all Ranks*, London: printed for J. Roberts.

Miller, D. (1981) *Philosophy and Ideology in Hume's Political Thought*, Oxford: Clarendon Press.

Mitchell, L.G. (1992) *Charles James Fox*, Oxford: Oxford UP.

Mitchell, R. (2003a) "The Violence of Sympathy: Adam Smith on Resentment and Executions," Special Issue of *1650–1850: Ideas, Aesthetics and Inquiries in the Early Modern Era* 8: 421–41.

—— (2003b) "'The soul that dreams it shares the power it feels so well': The Politics of Sympathy in the Abolitionist Verse of Williams and Yearsley," *Romanticism on the Net* 29–30 (February–May).

—— (2006) "Beautiful and Orderly Systems: Adam Smith on the Aesthetics of Political Improvement," in *New Voices on Adam Smith*, introduction Haakonssen, K., ed. Schliesser, E. and Leonidas Montes, L., New York: Routledge.

—— and Thurtle, P., eds. (2003) *Data Made Flesh: Embodying Information*, New York: Routledge.

Montesquieu, B. (Charles Secondat) (1873) *Lettres persanes, par Montesquieu*, ed. André Lefèvre, Paris: Alfonse Lemerre.

—— (1949) *The Spirit of the Laws*, trans. Nugent, T., introduction Neumann, F., New York: Hafner.

Moore, S. (2002) "Satiric Norms, Swift's Financial Satires and the Bank of Ireland Controversy of 1720–1," *Eighteenth Century Ireland/ Iris an da Chultur* 17: 26–56.

Moorman, M.T. (1957–65) *William Wordsworth, A Biography*, 2 vols, Oxford: Clarendon Press.

More, H. (1788) *Slavery, A Poem*, London: T. Cadell.

More, H. (1966) *Enthusiasmus Triumphatus*, Los Angeles: The Augustan Reprint Society, no. 118.

Morgan, W. (1797) *An Appeal to the People of Great Britain, on the Present Alarming State of the Public Finances, and of Public Credit*, London: J. Debrett.

Morillo, J. (2001) *Uneasy Feelings: Literature, The Passions and Class from Neoclassicism to Romanticism*, New York: AMS Press.

Morrow, G.R. (1923) "The Significance of the Doctrine of Sympathy in Hume and Adam Smith," *Philosophical Review* 32: 60–78.

Mortimer, T. (1761) *Every Man His Own Broker; Or, a Guide to Exchange Alley*, London: Printed for S. Hooper.

Mossner, E.C. (1980) *The Life of David Hume*, 2nd ed., Oxford: Clarendon Press.

Mulcaire, T. (1999) "Public Credit; or, the Feminization of Virtue in the Marketplace." *PMLA* 114: 5 (October): 1029–42.

Murphy, A.E. (1986) *Richard Cantillon: Entrepreneur and Economist*, Oxford: Clarendon Press.

Neal, L. (1990a) *The Rise of Financial Capitalism: International Capital Markets in the Age of Reason*, Cambridge: Cambridge UP.

—— (1990b)"How the South Sea Bubble was Blown Up and Burst: A New Look at Old Data," in *Crashes and Panics: The Lessons from History*, ed. White, E., Homewood, IL: Dow Jones-Irwin: 33–56.

Nicholson, C. (1994) *Writing and the Rise of Finance: Capital Satires of the Early Eighteenth Century*, Cambridge: Cambridge UP.

Nickolls, R.B. (1788) *Letter to the Treasurer of the Society Instituted for the Purpose of Effecting the Abolition of the Slave Trade, A New Edition with Additions*, London: James Phillips.

O'Gorman, F. (1986) *British Conservatism: Conservative Thought From Burke to Thatcher*, London: Longmans.

O'Neal, J.C. (1985) *Seeing and Observing: Rousseau's Rhetoric of Perception*, Saratoga, CA: Amma Libri.

Orléan, A. (1999) *Le pouvoir de la finance*, Paris: Éditions Odile Jacob.

Paine, T. (1793) *Prospects on the War and Paper Currency of Great Britain*, London: Printed for James Ridgway.

—— (1796). *The Decline and Fall of the English System of Finance*, London: T. Williams.

Parsons, W. (1989) *The Power of the Financial Press: Journalism and Economic Opinion in Britain and America*, Cheltenham, UK: Edward Elgar.

Pascal, B. (1897) *Opuscules et Pensées*, ed. Brunschvicg, L., Paris: Librairie Hachette.

Peacock, T.L. (1924–34) *The Works of Thomas Love Peacock*, 10 vols, ed., introduction and notes Brett-Smith, H.F.B. and Jones, C.E., London: Constable.

Perkins, D. (1965) *The Quest for Permanence*, Cambridge, MA: Harvard UP.

Pfau, T. (1997) *Wordsworth's Profession: Form, Class, and Logic of Early Romantic Cultural Production*, Stanford, CA: Stanford UP.

Phillipson, N. (1981) "The Scottish Enlightenment," in *The Enlightenment in National Contexts*, ed. Porter, R. and Teich, M., Cambridge: Cambridge UP, 19–40.

—— (1989) *Hume*, New York: St. Martin's Press.

Pinch, A. (1996) *Strange Fits of Passion: Epistemologies of Emotion, Hume to Austen*, Stanford, CA: Stanford UP.

Pixley, J. (2004) *Emotions in Finance: Distrust and Uncertainty in Global Markets*, Cambridge: Cambridge UP.

Pocock, J.G.A. (1975) *The Machiavellian Moment: Florentine Political Thought and the Atlantic Republican Tradition*, Princeton, NJ: Princeton UP.

—— (1985) *Virtue, Commerce, and History: Essays on Political Thought and History, Chiefly in the Eighteenth Century*, New York: Cambridge UP.

Pollexfen, J. (1697) *Discourse of trade, coyn, and paper credit, and of ways and means to gain, and retain riches: to which is added the argument of a learned counsel upon an action of a case brought by the East-India-Company against Mr. Sands the interloper*, London: Brabazon Aylmer.

Poovey, M. (1998) *A History of the Modern Fact: Problems of Knowledge in the Sciences of Wealth and Society*, Chicago: University of Chicago Press.

—— ed. (2003) *The Financial System in Nineteenth-Century Britain*, Oxford: Oxford UP.

Pottle, F. (1952) "The Case of Shelley," *PMLA* 67:5: 589–608.

Powell, D. (1989) *Charles James Fox: Man of the People*, London: Hutchinson.

Pratt, S.J. (1788) *Humanity; or, The Rights of Nature: A Poem; in Two Books*, London: T. Cadell.

Pyle, F. (1995) *The Ideology of Imagination: Subject and Society in the Discourse of Romanticism*, Stanford, CA: Stanford University Press.

Quinton, A. (1978) *The Politics of Imperfection: The Religious and Secular Traditions of Conservative Thought from Hooker to Oakeshott*, London: Faber and Faber.

Ramsay, J. (1784) *An Essay on the Treatment & Conversion of African Slaves in the British Sugar Colonies*, London: Phillips.

Raphael, D.D. (1972–73) "Hume and Adam Smith on Justice and Utility," *Proceedings of the Aristotelian Society* 72: 73–92.

Rasch, W. (2000) *Niklas Luhmann's Modernity: The Paradoxes of Differentiation*, Stanford: Stanford UP.

Ray, S.K. (1981) *Economics of the Black Market*, Boulder, CO: Westview Press.

Realey, C.B. (1935) *The London Journal and Its Authors, 1720–1723*, Lawrence: University of Kansas, Department of Journalism Press.

Reed, M.L. (1982) *The Chronology of the Early Years*, Ithaca, NY: The Cornell Wordsworth.

Richardson, A. (1997) "Women Poets and Colonial Discourse: Teaching More and Yearsley on the Slave Trade," in *Approaches to Teaching British Women Poets of the Romantic Period*, ed. Behrendt, S.C., and Link, H.K., New York: The Modern Language Association of America.

Rieder, J. (1997) *Wordsworth's Counterrevolutionary Turn: Community, Virtue, and Vision in the 1790s*, Cranbury, NJ: University of Delaware Press.

Robbins, C. (1959) *The Eighteenth-Century Commonwealthman: Studies in the Transmission, Development, and Circumstance of English Liberal Thought from the Restoration of Charles II until the War with the Thirteen Colonies*, Cambridge, MA: Harvard UP.

Roberts, H. (1997) *Shelley and the Chaos of History: A New Politics of Poetry*, University Park: Pennsylvania State UP.

Roberts, W., ed. (1834) *Memoirs of the Life and Correspondence of Mrs. Hannah More*, 2nd ed., 4 vols, London: R.B. Seeley.

Robinson, P.E.J. (1984) *Jean-Jacques Rousseau's Doctrine of the Arts*, New York: Peter Lang.

Roe, N. (1988) *Wordsworth and Coleridge: The Radical Years*, Oxford: Clarendon Press.

Rorty, A.O. (1982) "From Passions to Emotions and Sentiments," *Philosophy* 57: 159–72.

Roscoe, W. (1787) *The Wrongs of Africa; A Poem, Part the First*, London: Printed for R. Faulder.

Rosen, F. (2000) "The Idea of Utility in Adam Smith's *The Theory of Moral Sentiments*," *History of European Ideas* 26: 79–103.
Ross, I.S. (1995) *The Life of Adam Smith*, New York: Oxford UP.
Rousseau, G.S. (1969) "Science and the Discovery of the Imagination in Enlightened England," *Eighteenth-Century Studies* 3:1: 108–35.
Rousseau, J-J. (1953) *Political Writings*, ed. Watkins, F., New York: Nelson.
——— (1971) *Oeuvres Complètes*, 3 vols, ed. Launay, M., Paris: Éditions du Seuil.
——— (1993) *Essai sur l'origine des langues*, ed. Kintzler, C., Paris: Flammarion.
Russell, G. (2000) "Faro's Daughters': Female Gamesters, Politics, and the Discourse of Finance in 1790s Britain," *Eighteenth-Century Studies* 33:4: 481–504.
Rutherford, T. (1748) *A System of Natural Philosophy being a Course of Lectures in Mechanics, Optics, Hydrostatics, and Astronomy*, Cambridge: J. Bertham.
Saint Pierre, B. de (1798) *Studies of Nature*, 3 vols, London: Printed for Lee and Hurst.
Sakamoto, T. and Tanaka, H. eds. (2003) *The Rise of Political Economy in the Scottish Enlightenment*, New York: Routledge.
Salter, J. (1999) "Sympathy with the Poor: Theories of Punishment in Grotius and Smith," *History of Political Thought*, 20:2 (Summer): 205–24.
Schabas, M. (2005) *The Natural Origins of Economics*, Chicago: University of Chicago Press.
Schoenfield, M. (1996) *The Professional Wordsworth: Law, Labor & the Poet's Contract*, Athens, GA: University of Georgia Press.
Schor, E.H. (1994) *Bearing the Dead: The British Culture of Mourning from the Enlightenment to Victoria*, Princeton, NJ: Princeton UP.
Schrift, A., ed. (1997) *The Logic of the Gift: Toward and Ethic of Generosity*, New York: Routledge.
Schumpeter, J. (1917) "Money and the Social Product," *International Economic Papers* 6: 148–211.
Scrivener, M. (1982) *Radical Shelley: The Philosophical Anarchism and Utopian Thought of Percy Bysshe Shelley*, Princeton, NJ: Princeton UP.
——— (1992), ed., *Poetry and Reform: Periodical Verse from the English Democratic Press, 1792–1824*, Detroit: Wayne State UP.
Serres, M. (1982) *The Parasite*, trans. and notes Schehr, L.R., Baltimore: Johns Hopkins UP.
Shackleton, R. (1980) "Montesquieu, Dupin and the Early Writings of Rousseau," in *Reappraisals of Rousseau: Studies on Honour of R. A. Leigh*, ed. Harvey, S., *et al.*, Totowa: Barnes & Noble Books: 234–49.
Shapin, S. and Schaffer, S. (1985) *Leviathan and the Air-Pump: Hobbes, Boyle, and the Experimental Life*, Princeton, NJ: Princeton UP.
Shelley, P.B. (1816) *Alastor; Or, The Spirit of Solitude, and other poems*, London: Baldwin, Cradock, and Joy.
——— (1820) *Prometheus Unbound, A Lyrical Drama in Four Acts; with other poems*, London: C. and J. Ollier.
——— (1914) *The Letters of Percy Bysshe Shelley*, 2 vols, ed. Ingpen, R., London: G. Bell and Sons.
——— (1990) *Queen Mab* (1813); reprint ed., ed. Wordsworth, J., New York: Woodstock Books.
——— (1991) *History of a Six Weeks' Tour* (1817); reprint ed., ed. Wordsworth, J., New York: Woodstock Books.
Sher, R.B. (1990) "Professors of Virtue: The Social History of the Edinburgh Moral Philosophy Chair in the Eighteenth Century," in *Studies in the Philosophy of the Scottish Enlightenment*, ed. Stewart, M.A., Oxford: Clarendon Press.

Sherman, S. (1995) "Credit, Simulation, and the Ideology of Contract in the Early Eighteenth Century." *Eighteenth-Century Life* 19 (November): 86–102.

——— (1996) *Finance and Fictionality in the Early Eighteenth Century: Accounting for Defoe*, Cambridge: Cambridge UP.

Sherwig, J.M. (1969) *Guineas and Gunpowder: British Foreign Aid in the Wars with France, 1793–1815*, Cambridge, MA: Harvard UP.

Shiller, R.J. (2005) *Irrational Exuberance*, 2nd ed., Princeton: Princeton UP.

Simpson, D. (1987) *Wordsworth's Historical Imagination: The Poetry of Displacement*, New York: Methuen.

——— (1993) *Romanticism, Nationalism, and the Revolt Against Theory*, Chicago: University of Chicago Press.

Simondon, G. (1964) *L'individuation à la lumière des notions de forme et d'information*, Paris: Presses Universitaires de France.

——— (1989) *L'individuation psychique et collective à la lumière des notions de Forme, Information, Potentiel et Métastabilité*, Paris: Aubier Montaigne.

Siskin, C. (1998a) *The Work of Writing: Literature and Social Change in Britain, 1700–1830*, Baltimore: Johns Hopkins UP.

——— (1998b) "1798: The Year of the System," in *1798: The Year of the* Lyrical Ballads, ed. Cronin, R., New York: St. Martin's Press.

——— (2001) "Novels and Systems," *Novel: A Forum on Fiction* 34: 2: 202–15.

Skinner, Q. (1966) "The Ideological Context of Hobbes's Political Thought," *The Historical Journal* 9:3: 286–317.

——— (1993) "Thomas Hobbes and His Disciples in France and England," in *Thomas Hobbes: Critical Assessments*, 4 vols, ed. King, P., London: Routledge, vol.1: 123–38.

Smith, P. (1997) *Millennial Dreams: Contemporary Culture and Capital in the North*, New York: Verso.

Smith, V.C. (1990) *The Rationale of Central Banking and the Free Banking Alternative*, Indianapolis: Liberty Press.

"Solon" (1819) *Aphorisms on Currency, As Connected with the Distresses of the Country*, Glasgow: Young, Gaillie, & Co.

Sperry, S.M. (1981) "Necessity and the Role of the Hero in Shelley's *Prometheus Unbound*," *PMLA* 96: 2 (March): 242–54.

——— (1988), *Shelley's Major Verse: The Narrative and Dramatic Poetry*, Cambridge, MA: Harvard UP.

Spufford, M. (1984) *The Great Reclothing of Rural England: Petty Chapmen and their Wares in the Seventeenth Century*, London: Hambledon Press.

Starobinski, J. (1970) *La Relation Critique: L'œil vivant II*, Paris: Gallimard.

——— (1988) *Jean-Jacques Rousseau: Transparency and Obstruction*, trans. Goldhammer, A., Chicago: University of Chicago Press.

Stewart, J. (1963) *The Moral and Political Philosophy of David Hume*, New York: Columbia UP.

——— (1992) *Opinion and Reform in Hume's Political Philosophy*, Princeton, NJ: Princeton UP.

Stiegler, B. (1998) *Technics and Time 1: The Fault of Epimetheus*, trans. Beardsworth, R. and Collins, G., Stanford, CA: Stanford UP.

Stirling, J. (1733) *A System of Rhetoric in a Method Entirely New*, London: Thomas Astley.

Sussman, C. (2000) *Consuming Anxieties: Consumer Protest, Gender, and British Slavery, 1713–1833*, Stanford, CA: Stanford UP.

Swift, J. (1955–68) *The Prose Writings of Jonathan Swift*, 14 vols, ed. Davis, H. *et al.*, Oxford: Basil Blackwell.

Sypher, W. (1969) *Guinea's Captive Kings: British Anti-Slavery Literature of the XVIIIth Century*, New York: Octagon Books.

Thompson, E.P. (1964) *The Making of the English Working Class*, New York: Pantheon Books.

Thompson, J. (1996) *Models of Value: Eighteenth-Century Political Economy and the Novel*, Durham, NC: Duke UP.

Todd, D. (1995) *Imagining Monsters: Miscreations of the Self in Eighteenth-Century England*, Chicago: University of Chicago Press.

Trousson, R. and Eigeldinger, F.S., eds., (1996) *Dictionnaire de Jean-Jacques Rousseau*, Paris: Honoré Champion.

Usher, J. (1772) *The Philosophy of the Passions; Demonstrating Their Nature, Properties, Effects, Use and Abuse*, London: J. Almon.

Vamos, M. (1974) *Pascal's Pensees and the Enlightenment: The Roots of a Misunderstanding*, Geneva: *Studies on Voltaire and the Eighteenth Century*, vol. 97.

Vermeule, B. (2000) *The Party of Humanity: Writing Moral Psychology in Eighteenth-Century Britain*, Baltimore: Johns Hopkins UP.

Vicker, D. (1959) *Studies in the Theory of Money, 1690–1776*, Philadelphia: Chilton.

Vosgien (1799–1801), *An Historical and Biographical Dictionary, Containing an Account of the Hebrew Patriarchs and Princes, of Emperors, Kings, and Great Captains*, 4 vols, Cambridge: Printed by John Burges.

Waldby, C. and Mitchell, R. (2006) *Tissue Economies: Blood, Organs, and Cell Lines in Late Capitalism*, Durham, NC: Duke UP.

Waldron, M. (1996) *Lactilla, Milkwoman of Clifton: The Life and Writings of Ann Yearsley, 1753–1806*, Athens, GA: University of Georgia Press.

Walmsley, R. (1969) *Peterloo: The Case Reopened*, New York: Augustus M. Kelley.

Walpole, R. (1735) *Some Considerations Concerning the Publick Funds, the Publick Revenues, and the Annual Supplies, granted by Parliament*, 2nd ed., London: Printed for J. Roberts.

Wasserman, E.R. (1947) "The Sympathetic Imagination in Eighteenth-Century Theories of Acting," *The Journal of English and Germanic Philology* 46: 3 (July): 264–72.

—— (1971) *Shelley: A Critical Reading*, Baltimore: Johns Hopkins UP.

Webb, T. (1977) *Shelley: A Voice Not Understood*, Atlantic Highlands, NJ: Humanities Press.

Weiner, A.B. (1992) *Inalienable Possessions: The Paradox of Keeping-While-Giving*, Berkeley: University of California Press.

Whelan, F. (1985) *Order and Artifice in Hume's Political Philosophy*, Princeton, NJ: Princeton UP.

White, D.E. (2000), *Romantic Returns: Superstition, Imagination, History*, Stanford, CA: Stanford UP.

Wilbanks, J. (1968) *Hume's Theory of Imagination*, The Hague: Matinus Nijhoff.

Williams, C.W. (1818) *Considerations on the Alarming Increase of Forgery on the Bank of England, and the Neglect of Remedial Measures; With an Essay on the Remedy for the Detection of Forgeries and an Account of the Measures Adopted by the Bank of Ireland*, London: Longman.

Williams, E. (1994) *Capitalism and Slavery*, Chapel Hill: University of North Carolina Press.

Willis, T. (1971) *Two Discourses Concerning the Soul of Brutes, Which is that of the Vital and Sensitive of Man*, trans. Samuel Pordage (London, 1683); reprint ed., ed. Diamond, S., Gainesville, FL: Scholars' Facsimiles & Reprints.

Willson, G. (1788) "To the generous ASSERTORS of LIBERTY for the oppressed AFRICANS," *New Lady's Magazine*, 3 (May): 267–68.

Winch, D. (1978) *Adam Smith's Politics: An Essay in Historiographic Revision*, Cambridge: Cambridge UP.

Winchester, E. (1788) *The Reigning Abominations, especially the slave trade, considered as causes of lamentation; being the substance of a discourse delivered in Fairfax county, Virginia, December 30, 1774*, London: H. Trapp.

Winsor, F.A. (1799) *Prosperity of England Midst the Clamors of Ruin, by a Merchant of London*. England: Printed for the author.

Wolker, R. (1974) "Rameau, Rousseau and the *Essai sur l'origine des langues*," *Studies on Voltaire and the Eighteenth Century* 117: 179–238.

Wollheim, R. (1974) "Identification and Imagination: The Inner Structure of a Psychic Mechanism," in *Freud: A Collection of Critical Essays*, ed. Wollheim, R., Garden City, NY: Anchor Books: 172–95.

Woodmansee, M. and Osteen, M. (1999) *The New Economic Criticism: Studies at the Intersection of Literature and Economics*, New York: Routledge.

Wordsworth, J. (1969) *The Music of Humanity: A Critical Study of Wordsworth's "Ruined Cottage"; incorporating texts from a manuscript of 1799–1800*, London: Nelson.

Wordsworth, W. (1814) *The Excursion, Being a Portion of* The Recluse, *A Poem*, London: Longman.

—— (1952–63) *Wordsworth's Poetical Works*, 5 vols, ed. de Selincourt, E., Oxford: Clarendon Press.

—— (1979) *The Ruined Cottage and The Pedlar*, ed. Butler, J., Ithaca, NY: Cornell UP.

—— and Coleridge, S.T. (1798) *Lyrical Ballads, with a few other poems*, London: Printed for J. & A. Arch.

Wu, D., ed. (1994) *Romanticism: An Anthology*, 2nd ed., Oxford: Basil Blackwell.

—— ed. (1997) *Romantic Women Poets: An Anthology*, Oxford: Basil Blackwell.

Yearsley, A. (1785) *Poems, On Several Occasions*, London: T. Cadell.

—— (1787) *Poems on Various Subjects*, London: G.G.J. and J. Robinson.

—— (1788) *A Poem on the Inhumanity of the Slave-trade*, London: G.G.J. and J. Robinson.

Žižek, Slavoj (1989) *The Sublime Object of Ideology*, New York: Verso.

—— (1993) *Tarrying with the Negative: Kant, Hegel, and the Critique of Ideology*, Durham, NC: Duke University Press.

Index